MCAT®
Behavioral Sciences Review

2018–2019

Edited by Alexander Stone Macnow, MD

KAPLAN

PUBLISHING

New York

© 2017 by Kaplan, Inc.

Published by Kaplan Publishing, a division of Kaplan, Inc.
750 Third Avenue
New York, NY 10017

ISBN: 978-1-5062-2371-1

10 9 8 7 6 5 4 3 2 1

Kaplan Publishing print books are available at special quantity discounts to use for sales promotions, employee premiums, or educational purposes. For more information or to purchase books, please call the Simon & Schuster special sales department at 866-506-1949.

Preface

And now it starts: your long, yet fruitful journey toward wearing a white coat. Proudly wearing that white coat, though, is hopefully only part of your motivation. You are reading this book because you want to be a healer.

If you're serious about going to medical school, then you are likely already familiar with the importance of the MCAT in medical school admissions. While the holistic review process puts additional weight on your experiences, extracurricular activities, and personal attributes, the fact remains: along with your GPA, your MCAT score remains one of the two most important components of your application portfolio—at least early in the admissions process. Each additional point you score on the MCAT pushes you in front of thousands of other students and makes you an even more attractive applicant. But the MCAT is not simply an obstacle to overcome; it is an opportunity to show schools that you will be a strong student and a future leader in medicine.

We at Kaplan take our jobs very seriously and aim to help students see success not only on the MCAT, but as future physicians. We work with our learning science experts to ensure that we're using the most up-to-date teaching techniques in our resources. Multiple members of our team hold advanced degrees in medicine or associated biomedical sciences, and are committed to the highest level of medical education. Kaplan has been working with the MCAT for over 50 years and our commitment to premed students is unflagging; in fact, Stanley Kaplan created this company when he had difficulty being accepted to medical school due to unfair quota systems that existed at the time.

We stand now at the beginning of a new era in medical education. As citizens of this 21st-century world of healthcare, we are charged with creating a patient-oriented, culturally competent, cost-conscious, universally available, technically advanced, and research-focused healthcare system, run by compassionate providers. Suffice it to say, this is no easy task. Problem-based learning, integrated curricula, and classes in interpersonal skills are some of the responses to this demand for an excellent workforce—a workforce of which you'll soon be a part.

We're thrilled that you've chosen us to help you on this journey. Please reach out to us to share your challenges, concerns, and successes. Together, we will shape the future of medicine in the United States and abroad; we look forward to helping you become the doctor you deserve to be.

Good luck!

Alexander Stone Macnow, MD
Editor-in-Chief
Department of Pathology and Laboratory Medicine
Hospital of the University of Pennsylvania

BA, Musicology—Boston University, 2008
MD—Perelman School of Medicine at the University of Pennsylvania, 2013

Table of Contents

Additional resources available at www.kaptest.com/mcatbookresources

The *Kaplan MCAT Review* Team

Alexander Stone Macnow, MD
Editor-in-Chief
Department of Pathology and Laboratory Medicine, Hospital of the University of Pennsylvania

Áine Lorié, PhD
Editor

Kristen L. Russell, ME
Editor

Derek Rusnak, MA
Editor

Pamela Willingham, MSW
Editor

Mikhail Alexeeff
Kaplan MCAT Faculty

Melinda Contreras, MS
Kaplan MCAT Faculty

Laura L. Ambler
Kaplan MCAT Faculty

Samantha Fallon
Kaplan MCAT Faculty

Krista L. Buckley, MD
Kaplan MCAT Faculty

Jason R. Pfleiger
Kaplan MCAT Faculty

Faculty Reviewers and Editors: Elmar R. Aliyev; James Burns; Jonathan Cornfield; Alisha Maureen Crowley; Nikolai Dorofeev, MD; Benjamin Downer, MS; Colin Doyle; Christopher Durland; M. Dominic Eggert; Marilyn Engle; Eleni M. Eren; Raef Ali Fadel; Elizabeth Flagge; Adam Grey; Tyra Hall-Pogar, PhD; Scott Huff; Samer T. Ismail; Ae-Ri Kim, PhD; Elizabeth A. Kudlaty; Kelly Kyker-Snowman, MS; Ningfei Li; John P. Mahon; Matthew A. Meier; Nainika Nanda; Caroline Nkemdilim Opene; Kaitlyn E. Prenger; Uneeb Qureshi; Bela G. Starkman, PhD; Michael Paul Tomani, MS; Nicholas M. White; Allison Ann Wilkes, MS; Kerranna Williamson, MBA; and Tony Yu

Thanks to Kim Bowers; Eric Chiu; Tim Eich; Tyler Fara; Owen Farcy; Dan Frey; Robin Garmise; Rita Garthaffner; Joanna Graham; Allison Harm; Beth Hoffberg; Aaron Lemon-Strauss; Keith Lubeley; Diane McGarvey; Petros Minasi; John Polstein; Deeangelee Pooran-Kublall, MD, MPH; Rochelle Rothstein, MD; Larry Rudman; Sylvia Tidwell Scheuring; Carly Schnur; Karin Tucker; Lee Weiss; and the countless others who made this project possible..

About *Scientific American*

As the world's premier science and technology magazine, and the oldest continuously published magazine in the United States, *Scientific American* is committed to bringing the most important developments in modern science, medicine, and technology to our worldwide audience in an understandable, credible, and provocative format.

Founded in 1845 and on the "cutting edge" ever since, *Scientific American* boasts over 150 Nobel laureate authors including Albert Einstein, Francis Crick, Stanley Prusiner, and Richard Axel. *Scientific American* is a forum where scientific theories and discoveries are explained to a broader audience.

Scientific American published its first foreign edition in 1890, and in 1979 was the first Western magazine published in the People's Republic of China. Today, *Scientific American* is published in 14 foreign language editions. *Scientific American* is also a leading online destination (**www.ScientificAmerican.com**), providing the latest science news and exclusive features to millions of visitors each month.

The knowledge that fills our pages has the power to spark new ideas, paradigms, and visions for the future. As science races forward, *Scientific American* continues to cover the promising strides, inevitable setbacks and challenges, and new medical discoveries as they unfold.

About the MCAT

ANATOMY OF THE MCAT

Here is a general overview of the structure of Test Day:

Section	Number of Questions	Time Allotted
Examinee Agreement		8 minutes
Tutorial (optional)		10 minutes
Chemical and Physical Foundations of Biological Systems	59	95 minutes
Break (optional)		10 minutes
Critical Analysis and Reasoning Skills (CARS)	53	90 minutes
Lunch Break (optional)		30 minutes
Biological and Biochemical Foundations of Living Systems	59	95 minutes
Break (optional)		10 minutes
Psychological, Social, and Biological Foundations of Behavior	59	95 minutes
Void Question		5 minutes
Satisfaction Survey (optional)		5 minutes

The structure of the four sections of the MCAT is shown below.

Chemical and Physical Foundations of Biological Systems	
Time	95 minutes
Format	• 59 questions • 10 passages • 44 questions are passage-based, and 15 are discrete (stand-alone) questions. • Score between 118 and 132
What It Tests	• Biochemistry: 25% • Biology: 5% • General Chemistry: 30% • Organic Chemistry: 15% • Physics: 25%
Critical Analysis and Reasoning Skills (CARS)	
Time	90 minutes
Format	• 53 questions • 9 passages • All questions are passage-based. There are no discrete (stand-alone) questions. • Score between 118 and 132
What It Tests	Disciplines: • Humanities: 50% • Social Sciences: 50% Skills: • *Foundations of Comprehension*: 30% • *Reasoning Within the Text*: 30% • *Reasoning Beyond the Text*: 40%

Biological and Biochemical Foundations of Living Systems	
Time	95 minutes
Format	• 59 questions • 10 passages • 44 questions are passage-based, and 15 are discrete (stand-alone) questions. • Score between 118 and 132
What It Tests	• Biochemistry: 25% • Biology: 65% • General Chemistry: 5% • Organic Chemistry: 5%
Psychological, Social, and Biological Foundations of Behavior	
Time	95 minutes
Format	• 59 questions • 10 passages • 44 questions are passage-based, and 15 are discrete (stand-alone) questions. • Score between 118 and 132
What It Tests	• Biology: 5% • Psychology: 65% • Sociology: 30%
Total	
Testing Time	375 minutes (6 hours, 15 minutes)
Total Seat Time	453 minutes (7 hours, 33 minutes)
Questions	230
Score	472 to 528

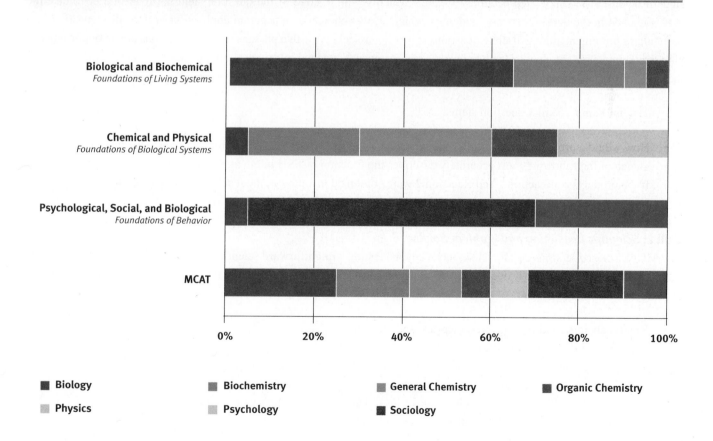

SCIENTIFIC INQUIRY AND REASONING SKILLS (SIRS)

The AAMC has defined four *Scientific Inquiry and Reasoning Skills* (SIRS) that will be tested in the three science sections of the MCAT:

1. *Knowledge of Scientific Concepts and Principles* (35% of questions)
2. *Scientific Reasoning and Problem-Solving* (45% of questions)
3. *Reasoning About the Design and Execution of Research* (10% of questions)
4. *Data-Based and Statistical Reasoning* (10% of questions)

Let's see how each one breaks down into more specific Test Day behaviors. Note that the bullet points of specific objectives for each of the SIRS are taken directly from the *Official Guide to the MCAT Exam*; the descriptions of what these behaviors mean and sample question stems, however, are written by Kaplan.

Skill 1: *Knowledge of Scientific Concepts and Principles*

This is probably the least surprising of the four SIRS; the testing of science knowledge is, after all, one of the signature qualities of the MCAT. Skill 1 questions will require you to do the following:

- Recognize correct scientific principles
- Identify the relationships among closely related concepts
- Identify the relationships between different representations of concepts (verbal, symbolic, graphic)
- Identify examples of observations that illustrate scientific principles
- Use mathematical equations to solve problems

At Kaplan, we simply call these Science Knowledge or Skill 1 questions. Another way to think of Skill 1 questions is as "one-step" problems. The single step is either to realize which scientific concept the question stem is suggesting or to take the concept stated in the question stem and identify which answer choice is an accurate application of it. Skill 1 questions are particularly prominent among discrete questions (those not associated with a passage). These questions are an opportunity to gain quick points on Test Day—if you know the science concept attached to the question, then that's it! On Test Day, 35% of the questions in each science section will be Skill 1 questions.

Here are some sample Skill 1 question stems:

- How would a proponent of the James–Lange theory of emotion interpret the findings of the study cited the passage?
- Which of the following most accurately describes the function of FSH in the human female menstrual cycle?
- If the products of Reaction 1 and Reaction 2 were combined in solution, the resulting reaction would form:
- Ionic bonds are maintained by which of the following forces?

Skill 2: *Scientific Reasoning and Problem-Solving*

The MCAT science sections do, of course, move beyond testing straightforward science knowledge; Skill 2 questions are the most common way in which it does so. At Kaplan, we also call these Critical Thinking questions. Skill 2 questions will require you to do the following:

- Reason about scientific principles, theories, and models
- Analyze and evaluate scientific explanations and predictions
- Evaluate arguments about causes and consequences
- Bring together theory, observations, and evidence to draw conclusions
- Recognize scientific findings that challenge or invalidate a scientific theory or model
- Determine and use scientific formulas to solve problems

Just as Skill 1 questions can be thought of as "one-step" problems, many Skill 2 questions are "two-step" problems, and more difficult Skill 2 questions may require three or more steps. These questions can require a wide spectrum of reasoning skills, including integration of multiple facts from a passage, combination of multiple science content areas, and prediction of an experiment's results. Skill 2 questions also tend to ask about science content without actually mentioning it by name. For example, a question might describe the results of one experiment and ask you to predict the results of a second experiment without actually telling you what underlying scientific principles are at work—part of the question's difficulty will be figuring out which principles to apply in order to get the correct answer. On Test Day, 45% of the questions in each science section will be Skill 2 questions.

Here are some sample Skill 2 question stems:

- Which of the following experimental conditions would most likely yield results similar to those in Figure 2?
- All of the following conclusions are supported by the information in the passage EXCEPT:
- The most likely cause of the anomalous results found by the experimenter is:
- An impact to a man's chest quickly reduces the volume of one of his lungs to 70% of its initial value while not allowing any air to escape from the man's mouth. By what percentage is the force of outward air pressure increased on a 2 cm^2 portion of the inner surface of the compressed lung?

Skill 3: *Reasoning About the Design and Execution of Research*

The MCAT is interested in your ability to critically appraise and analyze research, as this is an important day-to-day task of a physician. We call these questions Skill 3 or Experimental and Research Design questions for short. Skill 3 questions will require you to do the following:

- Identify the role of theory, past findings, and observations in scientific questioning
- Identify testable research questions and hypotheses
- Distinguish between samples and populations and distinguish results that support generalizations about populations
- Identify independent and dependent variables
- Reason about the features of research studies that suggest associations between variables or causal relationships between them (such as temporality and random assignment)
- Identify conclusions that are supported by research results
- Determine the implications of results for real-world situations
- Reason about ethical issues in scientific research

Over the years, the AAMC has received input from medical schools to require more practical research skills of MCAT test-takers, and Skill 3 questions are the response to these demands. This skill is unique in that the outside knowledge you need to answer Skill 3 questions is not taught in any one undergraduate course; instead, the research design principles needed to answer these questions are learned gradually throughout your science classes and especially through any laboratory work you have completed. It should be noted that Skill 3 comprises 10% of the questions in each science section on Test Day.

Here are some sample Skill 3 question stems:

- What is the dependent variable in the study described in the passage?
- The major flaw in the method used to measure disease susceptibility in Experiment 1 is:
- Which of the following procedures is most important for the experimenters to follow in order for their study to maintain a proper, randomized sample of research subjects?
- A researcher would like to test the hypothesis that individuals who move to an urban area during adulthood are more likely to own a car than are those who have lived in an urban area since birth. Which of the following studies would best test this hypothesis?

Skill 4: *Data-Based and Statistical Reasoning*

Lastly, the science sections of the MCAT test your ability to analyze the visual and numerical results of experiments and studies. We call these Data and Statistical Analysis questions. Skill 4 questions will require you to do the following:

- Use, analyze, and interpret data in figures, graphs, and tables
- Evaluate whether representations make sense for particular scientific observations and data
- Use measures of central tendency (mean, median, and mode) and measures of dispersion (range, interquartile range, and standard deviation) to describe data
- Reason about random and systematic error
- Reason about statistical significance and uncertainty (interpreting statistical significance levels and interpreting a confidence interval)
- Use data to explain relationships between variables or make predictions
- Use data to answer research questions and draw conclusions

Skill 4 is included in the MCAT because physicians and researchers spend much of their time examining the results of their own studies and the studies of others, and it's very important for them to make legitimate conclusions and sound judgments based on that data. The MCAT tests Skill 4 on all three science sections with graphical representations of data (charts and bar graphs) as well as numerical ones (tables, lists, and results summarized in sentence or paragraph form). On Test Day, 10% of the questions in each science section will be Skill 4 questions.

Here are some sample Skill 4 question stems:

- According to the information in the passage, there is an inverse correlation between:
- What conclusion is best supported by the findings displayed in Figure 2?
- A medical test for a rare type of heavy metal poisoning returns a positive result for 98% of affected individuals and 13% of unaffected individuals. Which of the following types of error is most prevalent in this test?
- If a fourth trial of Experiment 1 was run and yielded a result of 54% compliance, which of the following would be true?

SIRS Summary

Discussing the SIRS tested on the MCAT is a daunting prospect given that the very nature of the skills tends to make the conversation rather abstract. Nevertheless, with enough practice, you'll be able to identify each of the four skills quickly, and you'll also be able to apply the proper strategies to solve those problems on Test Day. If you need a quick reference to remind you of the four SIRS, these guidelines may help:

Skill 1 (Science Knowledge) questions ask:

- Do you remember this science content?

Skill 2 (Critical Thinking) questions ask:

- Do you remember this science content? And if you do, could you please apply it to this novel situation?
- Could you answer this question that cleverly combines multiple content areas at the same time?

Skill 3 (Experimental and Research Design) questions ask:

- Let's forget about the science content for a while. Could you give some insight into the experimental or research methods involved in this situation?

Skill 4 (Data and Statistical Analysis) questions ask:

- Let's forget about the science content for a while. Could you accurately read some graphs and tables for a moment? Could you make some conclusions or extrapolations based on the information presented?

CRITICAL ANALYSIS AND REASONING SKILLS (CARS)

The *Critical Analysis and Reasoning Skills* (CARS) section of the MCAT tests three discrete families of textual reasoning skills; each of these families requires a higher level of reasoning than the last. Those three skills are as follows:

1. *Foundations of Comprehension* (30% of questions)
2. *Reasoning Within the Text* (30% of questions)
3. *Reasoning Beyond the Text* (40% of questions)

These three skills are tested through nine humanities- and social sciences–themed passages, with approximately 5 to 7 questions per passage. Let's take a more in-depth look into these three skills. Again, the bullet points of specific objectives for each of the CARS are taken directly from the *Official Guide to the MCAT Exam*; the descriptions of what these behaviors mean and sample question stems, however, are written by Kaplan.

Foundations of Comprehension

Questions in this skill will ask for basic facts and simple inferences about the passage; the questions themselves will be similar to those seen on reading comprehension sections of other standardized exams like the SAT® and ACT®. *Foundations of Comprehension* questions will require you to do the following:

- Understand the basic components of the text
- Infer meaning from rhetorical devices, word choice, and text structure

This admittedly covers a wide range of potential question types including Main Idea, Detail, Function, and Definition-in-Context questions, but finding the correct answer to all *Foundations of Comprehension* questions will follow from a basic understanding of the passage and the point of view of its author (and occasionally that of other voices in the passage).

Here are some sample *Foundations of Comprehension* question stems:

- **Main Idea**—The author's primary purpose in this passage is:
- **Detail**—Based on the information in the second paragraph, which of the following is the most accurate summary of the opinion held by Schubert's critics?
- **(Scattered) Detail**—According to the passage, which of the following is FALSE about literary reviews in the 1920s?
- **Function**—The author's discussion of the effect of socioeconomic status on social mobility primarily serves which of the following functions?
- **Definition-in-Context**—The word "obscure" (paragraph 3), when used in reference to the historian's actions, most nearly means:

Reasoning Within the Text

While *Foundations of Comprehension* questions will usually depend on interpreting a single piece of information in the passage or understanding the passage as a whole, *Reasoning Within the Text* questions will typically require you to infer unstated parts of arguments or bring together two disparate pieces of the passage. *Reasoning Within the Text* questions will require you to:

- Integrate different components of the text to increase comprehension

In other words, questions in this skill often ask either *How do these two details relate to one another?* or *What else must be true that the author didn't say?* The CARS section will also ask you to judge certain parts of the passage or even judge the author. These questions, which fall under the *Reasoning Within the Text* skill, can ask you to identify authorial bias, evaluate the credibility of cited sources, determine the logical soundness of an argument, or search for relevant evidence in the passage to support a given conclusion. In all, this category includes Inference and Strengthen–Weaken (Within the Passage) questions, as well as a smattering of related—but rare—question types.

Here are some sample *Reasoning Within the Text* question stems:

- **Inference (Implication)**—Which of the following phrases, as used in the passage, is most suggestive that the author has a personal bias toward narrative records of history?
- **Inference (Assumption)**—In putting together her argument in the passage, the author most likely assumes:
- **Strengthen–Weaken (Within the Passage)**—Which of the following facts is used in the passage as the most prominent piece of evidence in favor of the author's conclusions?
- **Strengthen–Weaken (Within the Passage)**—Based on the role it plays in the author's argument, *The Possessed* can be considered:

Reasoning Beyond the Text

The distinguishing factor of *Reasoning Beyond the Text* questions is in the title of the skill: the word *Beyond*. Questions that test this skill, which make up a larger share of the CARS section than questions from either of the other two skills, will always introduce a completely new situation that was not present in the passage itself; these questions will ask you to determine how one influences the other. *Reasoning Beyond the Text* questions will require you to:

- Apply or extrapolate ideas from the passage to new contexts
- Assess the impact of introducing new factors, information, or conditions to ideas from the passage

The *Reasoning Beyond the Text* skill is further divided into Apply and Strengthen–Weaken (Beyond the Passage) questions, and a few other rarely appearing question types.

Here are some sample *Reasoning Beyond the Text* question stems:

- **Apply**—If a document were located that demonstrated Berlioz intended to include a chorus of at least 700 in his *Grande Messe des Mortes*, how would the author likely respond?
- **Apply**—Which of the following is the best example of a "virtuous rebellion," as it is defined in the passage?
- **Strengthen–Weaken (Beyond the Text)**—Suppose Jane Austen had written in a letter to her sister, "My strongest characters were those forced by circumstance to confront basic questions about the society in which they lived." What relevance would this have to the passage?
- **Strengthen–Weaken (Beyond the Text)**—Which of the following sentences, if added to the end of the passage, would most WEAKEN the author's conclusions in the last paragraph?

CARS Summary

Through the *Foundations of Comprehension* skill, the CARS section tests many of the reading skills you have been building on since grade school, albeit in the context of very challenging doctorate-level passages. But through the two other skills (*Reasoning Within the Text* and *Reasoning Beyond the Text*), the MCAT demands that you understand the deep structure of passages and the arguments within them at a very advanced level. And, of course, all of this is tested under very tight timing restrictions: only 102 seconds per question—and that doesn't even include the time spent reading the passages.

Here's a quick reference guide to the three CARS skills:

Foundations of Comprehension questions ask:

- Did you understand the passage and its main ideas?
- What does the passage have to say about this particular detail?

Reasoning Within the Text questions ask:

- What must be true that the author did not say?
- What's the logical relationship between these two ideas from the passage?
- How well argued is the author's thesis?

Reasoning Beyond the Text questions ask:

- How does this principle from the passage apply to this new situation?
- How does this new piece of information influence the arguments in the passage?

Scoring

Each of the four sections of the MCAT is scored between 118 and 132, with the median at 125. This means the total score ranges from 472 to 528, with the median at 500. Why such peculiar numbers? The AAMC stresses that this scale emphasizes the importance of the central portion of the score distribution, where most students score (around 125 per section, or 500 total), rather than putting undue focus on the high end of the scale.

Note that there is no wrong answer penalty on the MCAT, so you should select an answer for every question—even if it is only a guess.

The AAMC has released a hypothetical correlation between scaled score and percentile, as shown on the next page. It should be noted that the percentile scale is adjusted and renormalized over time and thus should not be overinterpreted.

Total Score	Percentile	Total Score	Percentile
528	>99	499	49
527	>99	498	45
526	>99	497	42
525	>99	496	39
524	>99	495	35
523	>99	494	32
522	99	493	29
521	99	492	26
520	98	491	23
519	98	490	20
518	97	489	18
517	96	488	16
516	95	487	13
515	94	486	12
514	92	485	10
513	90	484	8
512	88	483	7
511	86	482	5
510	84	481	4
509	82	480	3
508	79	479	2
507	76	478	2
506	73	477	1
505	70	476	1
504	67	475	<1
503	63	474	<1
502	60	473	<1
501	56	472	<1
500	53		

Source: AAMC. 2016. *Summary of MCAT Total and Section Scores.* Accessed December 2016. **https://students-residents.aamc.org/advisors/article/percentile-ranks-for-the-mcat-exam/**.

Further information on score reporting is included at the end of the next section (see *After Your Test*).

MCAT POLICIES AND PROCEDURES

We strongly encourage you to download the latest copy of *MCAT® Essentials*, available on the AAMC's website, to ensure that you have the latest information about registration and Test Day policies and procedures; this document is updated annually. A brief summary of some of the most important rules is provided here.

MCAT Registration

The only way to register for the MCAT is online. You can access AAMC's registration system at: **www.aamc.org/mcat**.

You will be able to access the site approximately six months before Test Day. The AAMC designates three registration "Zones"—Gold, Silver, and Bronze. Registering during the Gold Zone (from the opening of registration until approximately one month before Test Day) provides the most flexibility and lowest test fees. The Silver Zone runs until approximately two to three weeks before Test Day and has less flexibility and higher fees; the Bronze Zone runs until approximately one to two weeks before Test Day and has the least flexibility and highest fees.

Fees and the Fee Assistance Program (FAP)

Payment for test registration must be made by MasterCard or VISA. As described earlier, the fees for registering for the MCAT—as well as rescheduling the exam or changing your testing center—increase as one approaches Test Day. In addition, it is not uncommon for test centers to fill up well in advance of the registration deadline. For these reasons, we recommend identifying your preferred Test Day as soon as possible and registering. There are ancillary benefits to having a set Test Day, as well: when you know the date you're working toward, you'll study harder and are less likely to keep pushing back the exam. The AAMC offers a Fee Assistance Program (FAP) for students with financial hardship to help reduce the cost of taking the MCAT, as well as for the American Medical College Application Service (AMCAS®) application. Further information on the FAP can be found at: **www.aamc.org/students/applying/fap**.

Testing Security

On Test Day, you will be required to present a government-issued ID. When registering, take care to spell your name precisely the same as it appears on this ID; failure to provide this ID at the test center or differences in spelling between your registration and ID will be considered a "no-show," and you will not receive a refund for the exam.

You will also be required to provide an electronic thumbprint and electronic signature verification to take the exam. Some testing centers may use a metal detection wand to ensure that no prohibited items are brought into the testing room. Prohibited items include all electronic devices, including watches and timers, calculators, cell phones, and any and all forms of recording equipment; food, drinks (including water), and cigarettes or other smoking paraphernalia; hats and scarves (except for religious purposes); and books, notes, or other study materials. If you require a medical device, such as an insulin pump or pacemaker, you must apply for accommodated testing. During breaks, you are allowed to access food and drink, but not electronic devices, including cell phones.

Testing centers are under video surveillance and the AAMC does not take potential violations of testing security lightly. The bottom line: *know the rules and don't break them.*

Accommodations

Students with disabilities or medical conditions can apply for accommodated testing. Documentation of the disability or condition is required, and requests may take two months—or more—to be approved. For this reason, it is recommended that you begin the process of applying for accommodated testing as early as possible. More information on applying for accommodated testing can be found at: **www.aamc.org/students/applying/mcat/accommodations**.

After Your Test

When your MCAT is all over, no matter how you feel you did, be good to yourself when you leave the test center. Celebrate! Take a nap. Watch a movie. Ride your bike. Plan a trip. Call up all of your neglected friends or stalk them on Facebook. Totally consume a cheesesteak and drink dirty martinis at night (assuming you're over 21). Whatever you do, make sure that it has absolutely nothing to do with thinking too hard—you deserve some rest and relaxation.

Perhaps most importantly, do not discuss specific details about the test with anyone. For one, it is important to let go of the stress of Test Day, and reliving your exam only inhibits you from being able to do so. But more significantly, the Examinee Agreement you sign at the beginning of your exam specifically prohibits you from discussing or disclosing exam content. The AAMC is known to seek out individuals who violate this agreement and retains the right to prosecute these individuals at their discretion.

This means that you should not, under any circumstances, discuss the exam in person or over the phone with other individuals—including us at Kaplan—or post information or questions about exam content to Facebook, Student Doctor Network, or other online social media. You are permitted to comment on your "general exam experience," including how you felt about the exam overall or an individual section, but this is a fine line. In summary: *if you're not certain whether you can discuss an aspect of the test or not, just don't do it!* Do not let a silly Facebook post stop you from becoming the doctor you deserve to be.

Scores are released approximately one month after Test Day. The release is staggered during the afternoon and evening, starting at 5 p.m. Eastern. This means that not all examinees receive their scores at exactly the same time. Your score report will include a scaled score for each section between 118 and 132, as well as your total combined score between 472 and 528. These scores are given as confidence intervals. For each section, the confidence interval is approximately the given score ± 1; for the total score, it is approximately the given score ± 2. You will also be given the corresponding percentile rank for each of these section scores and the total score.

AAMC CONTACT INFORMATION

For further questions, contact the MCAT team at the Association of American Medical Colleges:

MCAT Resource Center
Association of American Medical Colleges
www.aamc.org/mcat
(202) 828-0690
mcat@aamc.org

How This Book Was Created

The *Kaplan MCAT Review* project began shortly after the release of the *Preview Guide for the MCAT 2015 Exam*, 2nd edition. Through thorough analysis by our staff psychometricians, we were able to analyze the relative yield of the different topics on the MCAT, and we began constructing tables of contents for the books of the *Kaplan MCAT Review* series. A dedicated staff of 30 writers, 7 editors, and 32 proofreaders worked over 5,000 combined hours to produce these books. The format of the books was heavily influenced by weekly meetings with Kaplan's learning-science team.

In the years since this book was created, a number of opportunities for expansion and improvement have occurred. The current edition represents the culmination of the wisdom accumulated during that time frame, and it also includes several new features designed to improve the reading and learning experience in these texts.

These books were submitted for publication in April 2017. For any updates after this date, please visit www.kaptest .com/pages/retail-book-corrections-and-updates.

If you have any questions about the content presented here, email KaplanMCATfeedback@kaplan.com. For other questions not related to content, email booksupport@kaplan.com.

Each book has been vetted through at least nine rounds of review. To that end, the information presented in these books is true and accurate to the best of our knowledge. Still, your feedback helps us improve our prep materials. Please notify us of any inaccuracies or errors in the books by sending an email to KaplanMCATfeedback@kaplan.com.

Using This Book

Kaplan MCAT Behavioral Sciences Review, along with the other six books in the *Kaplan MCAT Review* series, brings the Kaplan classroom experience to you—right in your home, at your convenience. This book offers the same Kaplan content review, strategies, and practice that make Kaplan the #1 choice for MCAT prep.

This book is designed to help you review the psychology and sociology topics covered on the MCAT. Please understand that content review—no matter how thorough—is not sufficient preparation for the MCAT! The MCAT tests not only your science knowledge but also your critical reading, reasoning, and problem-solving skills. Do not assume that simply memorizing the contents of this book will earn you high scores on Test Day; to maximize your scores, you must also improve your reading and test-taking skills through MCAT-style questions and practice tests.

LEARNING GOALS

At the beginning of each section, you'll find a short list of objectives describing the skills covered within that section. Learning goals for these texts were developed in conjunction with Kaplan's learning science team, and have been designed specifically to focus your attention on tasks and concepts that are likely to show up on your MCAT. These learning goals will function as a means to guide your study, and indicate what information and relationships you should be focused on within each section. Before starting each section, read these learning goals carefully. They will not only allow you to assess your existing familiarity with the content, but also provide a goal-oriented focus for your studying experience of the section.

MCAT CONCEPT CHECKS

At the end of each section, you'll find a few open-ended questions that you can use to assess your mastery of the material. These MCAT Concept Checks were introduced after multiple conversations with Kaplan's learning science team. Research has demonstrated repeatedly that introspection and self-analysis improve mastery, retention, and recall of material. Complete these MCAT Concept Checks to ensure that you've got the key points from each section before moving on!

PRACTICE QUESTIONS

At the end of each chapter, you'll find 15 MCAT-style practice questions. These are designed to help you assess your understanding of the chapter you just read. Most of these questions focus on the first of the *Scientific Inquiry and Reasoning Skills* (*Knowledge of Scientific Concepts and Principles*), although there are occasional questions that fall into the second or fourth SIRS (*Scientific Reasoning and Problem-Solving*, and *Data-Based and Statistical Reasoning*, respectively).

SIDEBARS

The following is a guide to the five types of sidebars you'll find in *Kaplan MCAT Behavioral Sciences Review*:

- **Bridge:** These sidebars create connections between science topics that appear in multiple chapters throughout the *Kaplan MCAT Review* series.
- **Key Concept:** These sidebars draw attention to the most important takeaways in a given topic, and they sometimes offer synopses or overviews of complex information. If you understand nothing else, make sure you grasp the Key Concepts for any given subject.
- **MCAT Expertise:** These sidebars point out how information may be tested on the MCAT or offer key strategy points and test-taking tips that you should apply on Test Day.
- **Mnemonic:** These sidebars present memory devices to help recall certain facts.
- **Real World:** These sidebars illustrate how a concept in the text relates to the practice of medicine or the world at large. While this is not information you need to know for Test Day, many of the topics in Real World sidebars are excellent examples of how a concept may appear in a passage or discrete (stand-alone) question on the MCAT.

WHAT THIS BOOK COVERS

The information presented in the Kaplan MCAT Review series covers everything listed on the official MCAT content lists. Every topic in these lists is covered in the same level of detail as is common to the undergraduate and postbaccalaureate classes that are considered prerequisites for the MCAT. Note that your premedical classes may include topics not discussed in these books, or they may go into more depth than these books do. Additional exposure to science content is never a bad thing, but all of the content knowledge you are expected to have walking in on Test Day is covered in these books.

New to this edition of the Kaplan MCAT Review series are the Chapter Profiles and the High Yield "badges." The chapter profiles, on the first page of each chapter, represent a holistic look at the content within the chapter, and will include a pie chart as well as text information. The pie chart analysis is based directly on data released by the AAMC, and will give a rough estimate of the importance of the chapter in relation to the book as a whole. Further, the text portion of the Chapter Profiles includes which AAMC content categories are covered within the chapter. These are referenced directly from the AAMC MCAT exam content listing, available on the testmaker's website.

You'll also see new High-Yield badges scattered throughout the sections of this book:

In This Chapter

3.1 Cellular Functions

High-Yield

LEARNING GOALS

After Chapter 3.1, you'll be able to...

These badges represent the top 100 topics most tested by the AAMC. In other words, according to the testmaker and all our experience with their resources, a High-Yield badge means more questions on Test Day.

This book also contains a thorough glossary and index for easy navigation of the text.

In the end, this is your book, so write in the margins, draw diagrams, highlight the key points—do whatever is necessary to help you get that higher score. We look forward to working with you as you achieve your dreams and become the doctor you deserve to be!

STUDYING WITH THIS BOOK

In addition to providing you with the best practice questions and test strategies, Kaplan's team of learning scientists are dedicated to researching and testing the best methods for getting the most out of your study time. Here are their top four tips for improving retention:

Review multiple topics in one study session. This may seem counterintuitive—we're used to practicing one skill at a time in order to improve each skill. But research shows that weaving topics together leads to increased learning. Beyond that consideration, the MCAT often includes more than one topic in a single question. Studying in an integrated manner is the most effective way to prepare for this test.

Customize the content. Drawing attention to difficult or critical content can ensure you don't overlook it as you read and re-read sections. The best way to do this is to make it more visual—highlight, make tabs, use stickies, whatever works. We recommend highlighting only the most important or difficult sections of text. Selective highlighting of up to about 10 percent of text in a given chapter is great for emphasizing parts of the text, but over-highlighting can have the opposite effect.

Repeat topics over time. Many people try to memorize concepts by repeating them over and over again in succession. Our research shows that retention is improved by spacing out the repeats over time and mixing up the order in which you study content. For example, try reading chapters in a different order the second (or third!) time around. Revisit practice questions that you answered incorrectly in a new sequence. Perhaps information you reviewed more recently will help you better understand those questions and solutions you struggled with in the past.

Take a moment to reflect. When you finish reading a section for the first time, stop and think about what you just read. Jot down a few thoughts in the margins or in your notes about why the content is important or what topics came to mind when you read it. Associating learning with a memory is a fantastic way to retain information! This also works when answering questions. After answering a question, take a moment to think through each step you took to arrive at a solution. What led you to the answer you chose? Understanding the steps you took will help you make good decisions when answering future questions.

ONLINE RESOURCES

In addition to the resources located within this text, you also have additional online resources awaiting you at **www.kaptest .com/booksonline**. Make sure to log on and take advantage of free practice and access to online versions of the book!

Please note that access to the online resources is limited to the original owner of this book.

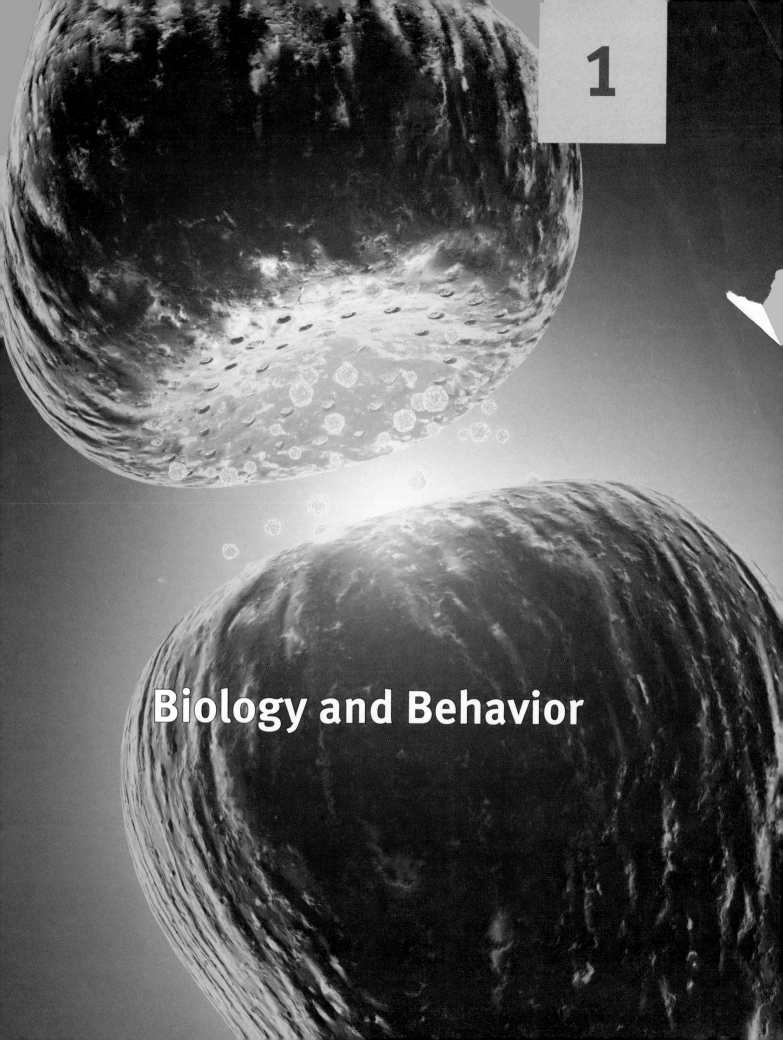

1

Biology and Behavior

In This Chapter

Chapter Profile

The content in this chapter should be relevant to about 9% of all questions about the Behavioral Sciences on the MCAT.

This chapter covers material from the following AAMC content categories:

3A: Structure and functions of the nervous and endocrine systems and ways in which these systems coordinate the organ systems

7A: Individual influences on behavior

Introduction

When you woke up this morning and got ready to start reading *MCAT Behavioral Sciences Review*, you almost certainly had specific feelings about it—perhaps you were excited to crack open the book and start learning some of the material that will get you that top score on the MCAT; perhaps you dreaded the size and rich detail of the information in the book. Either way, your body began to respond to these impulses from your mind: increasing heart rate, increasing breathing rate, dilating the eyes, and slowing down digestion. This link between the mind and the body is still a hot topic in medicine, although we've been exploring the importance of psychology on well-being for almost two centuries now.

In this chapter, we'll begin our exploration of psychology and sociology by looking at the biological side of psychology. After a quick survey of the history of neuropsychology, we'll look at the structure and organization of the human nervous system, communication between the nervous and endocrine systems, the effects of genes and environment on behavior, and some aspects of psychological development.

1.1 A Brief History of Neuropsychology

> **LEARNING GOALS**
>
> After Chapter 1.1, you will be able to:
>
> - Recall the major contributions to early neuropsychology
> - Connect the major contributors of early neuropsychology to their contributions

Researchers in the 19th century began to think about behavior from a physiological perspective. Many of these early thinkers formed the foundation of current knowledge about neuroanatomy, linking the functions of specific areas of the brain with thought and behavior.

Franz Gall (1758–1828) had one of the earliest theories that behavior, intellect, and even personality might be linked to brain anatomy. He developed the doctrine of phrenology. The basic idea was that if a particular trait was well-developed, then the part of the brain responsible for that trait would expand. This expansion, according to Gall, would push the area of the skull that covered that part of the brain outward and therefore cause a bulge on the head. Gall believed that one could thus measure psychological attributes by feeling or measuring the skull. Although phrenology was shown to be false, it did generate serious research on brain functions and was the impetus for the work of other psychologists through the remainder of the 19th century.

Pierre Flourens (1794–1867) was the first person to study the functions of the major sections of the brain. He did this by **extirpation** on rabbits and pigeons, also known as **ablation**. In extirpation, various parts of the brain are surgically removed and the behavioral consequences are observed. Flourens's work led to his assertion that the brain had specific parts for specific functions, and that the removal of one part weakens the whole brain.

William James (1842–1910), known as the father of American psychology, believed that it was important to study how the mind functioned in adapting to the environment. His view was among the first theories that formed **functionalism**, a system of thought in psychology that studied how mental processes help individuals adapt to their environments.

John Dewey (1859–1952) is another important name in functionalism because his 1896 article is seen as its inception. This article criticized the concept of the reflex arc, which breaks the process of reacting to a stimulus into discrete parts. Dewey believed that psychology should focus on the study of the organism as a whole as it functioned to adapt to the environment.

Around 1860, **Paul Broca** (1824–1880) added to the knowledge of physiology by examining the behavioral deficits of people with brain damage. He was the first person to demonstrate that specific functional impairments could be linked with specific brain lesions. Broca found that a man who'd been unable to talk was unable to do so because of a lesion in a specific area on the left side of the brain. This area of the brain is now referred to as Broca's area.

Hermann von Helmholtz (1821–1894) was the first to measure the speed of a nerve impulse. By actually measuring the speed of nerve impulses in terms of reaction time, Helmholtz is often credited with the transition of psychology into a field of the natural sciences.

Around the turn of the century, **Sir Charles Sherrington** (1857–1952) first inferred the existence of synapses. Many of his conclusions have held over time—except for one. He thought that synaptic transmission was an electrical process, but we now know that it is primarily a chemical process.

MCAT Concept Check 1.1:

Before you move on, assess your understanding of the material with this question.

1. Briefly list the main contributions of each of the following scientists to neuropsychology.

   - Franz Gall:

   _____

   - Pierre Flourens:

   _____

   - William James:

   _____

   - John Dewey:

   _____

   - Paul Broca:

   _____

   - Hermann von Helmoltz:

   _____

   - Sir Charles Sherrington:

   _____

1.2 Organization of the Human Nervous System

MCAT Expertise

The "High-Yield" badge on this section indicates that this content represents one of the top 100 topics most commonly tested on the exam.

LEARNING GOALS

After Chapter 1.2, you will be able to:

- Correctly associate regions of the nervous system with the CNS or PNS
- Distinguish between afferent and efferent neurons
- Describe the functions of the somatic and autonomic nervous systems, as well as the sympathetic and parasympathetic nervous systems

The human nervous system is a complex web of over 100 billion cells that communicate, coordinate, and regulate signals for the rest of the body. Mental and physical action occurs when the body can react to external stimuli using the nervous system. In this section, we will look at the nervous system and its basic organization.

Note: Much of the information contained in this section is also discussed in Chapter 4 of MCAT Biology Review.

CENTRAL AND PERIPHERAL NERVOUS SYSTEMS

There are three kinds of nerve cells in the nervous system: sensory neurons, motor neurons, and interneurons. **Sensory neurons** (also known as **afferent neurons**) transmit sensory information from receptors to the spinal cord and brain. **Motor**

neurons (also known as **efferent neurons**) transmit motor information from the brain and spinal cord to muscles and glands. **Interneurons** are found between other neurons and are the most numerous of the three types of neurons. Interneurons are located predominantly in the brain and spinal cord and are often linked to reflexive behavior. Neural circuits called **reflex arcs** control this type of behavior. For example, consider what occurs when someone steps on a nail. Receptors in the foot detect pain and the pain signal is transmitted by sensory neurons up to the spinal cord. At that point, the sensory neurons connect with interneurons, which can then relay pain impulses up to the brain. Rather than waiting for the brain to send out a signal, interneurons in the spinal cord send signals to the muscles of both legs directly, causing the individual to withdraw the foot with pain while supporting with the other foot. The original sensory information still makes its way up to the brain; however, by the time it arrives there, the muscles have already responded to the pain, thanks to the reflex arc.

Let's turn to the overall structure of the human nervous system, which is diagrammed in Figure 1.1. The nervous system can be broadly divided into two primary components: the central and peripheral nervous systems. The **central nervous system** (**CNS**) is composed of the brain and spinal cord. The **peripheral nervous system** (**PNS**), in contrast, is made up of nerve tissue and fibers outside the brain and spinal cord, including all 31 pairs of spinal nerves and the 12 pairs of cranial nerves. The olfactory and optic nerves (cranial nerves I and II) are structurally outgrowths of the central nervous system, but are still considered components of the peripheral nervous system. The PNS thus connects the CNS to the rest of the body and can itself be subdivided into somatic and autonomic nervous systems.

Mnemonic

Afferent neurons **a**scend in the cord toward the brain; **e**fferent neurons **e**xit the cord on their way to the rest of the body.

Figure 1.1. Major Divisions of the Nervous System

The **somatic nervous system** consists of sensory and motor neurons distributed throughout the skin, joints, and muscles. Sensory neurons transmit information through afferent fibers. Motor impulses, in contrast, travel along efferent fibers.

The **autonomic nervous system (ANS)** generally regulates heartbeat, respiration, digestion, and glandular secretions. In other words, the ANS manages the involuntary muscles associated with many internal organs and glands. The ANS also helps regulate body temperature by activating sweating or piloerection, depending on whether we are too hot or too cold. The main thing to understand about these functions is that they are automatic, or independent of conscious control. Note the similarity between the words autonomic and automatic. This association makes it easy to remember that the autonomic nervous system manages automatic functions such as heartbeat, respiration, digestion, and temperature control.

THE AUTONOMIC NERVOUS SYSTEM

The ANS has two subdivisions: the sympathetic nervous system and the parasympathetic nervous system. These two branches often act in opposition to one another, meaning they are antagonistic. For example, the sympathetic nervous system acts to accelerate heart rate and inhibit digestion, while the parasympathetic nervous system decelerates heart rate and increases digestion.

The main role of the **parasympathetic nervous system** is to conserve energy. It is associated with resting and sleeping states, and acts to reduce heart rate and constrict the bronchi. The parasympathetic nervous system is also responsible for managing digestion by increasing peristalsis and exocrine secretions. Acetylcholine is the neurotransmitter responsible for parasympathetic responses in the body. The functions of the parasympathetic nervous system are summarized in Figure 1.2.

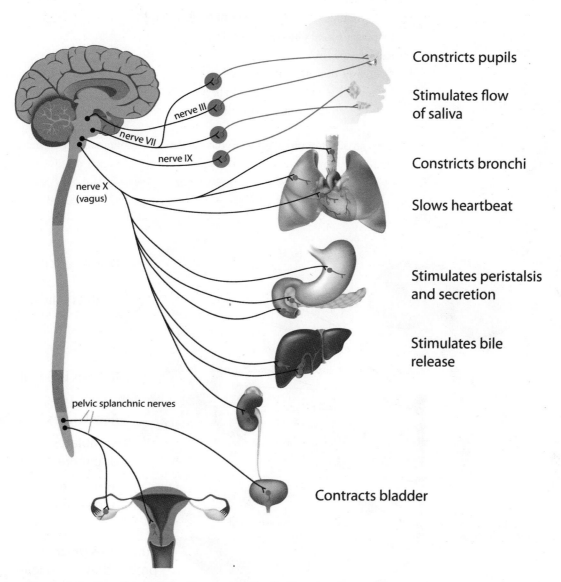

Figure 1.2. Functions of the Parasympathetic Nervous System

In contrast, the **sympathetic nervous system** is activated by stress. This can include everything from a mild stressor, such as keeping up with schoolwork, to emergencies that mean the difference between life and death. The sympathetic nervous system is closely associated with rage and fear reactions, also known as "fight-or-flight" reactions. When activated, the sympathetic nervous system:

Mnemonic

Sympathetic and parasympathetic nervous systems:
- Sympathetic: **"fight**-or-**flight"**
- Parasympathetic: **"rest**-and-**digest"**

- Increases heart rate
- Redistributes blood to muscles of locomotion
- Increases blood glucose concentration
- Relaxes the bronchi
- Decreases digestion and peristalsis
- Dilates the eyes to maximize light intake
- Releases epinephrine into the bloodstream

The functions of the sympathetic nervous system are summarized in Figure 1.3.

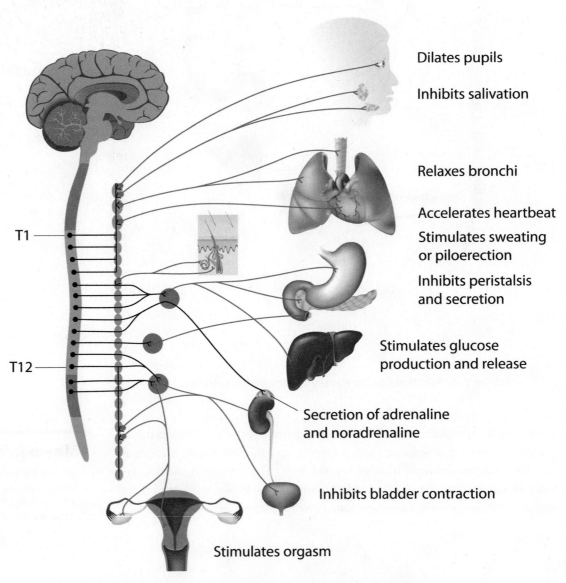

Figure 1.3. Functions of the Sympathetic Nervous System

MCAT Concept Check 1.2:

Before you move on, assess your understanding of the material with these questions.

1. What parts of the nervous system are in the central nervous system (CNS)? Peripheral nervous system (PNS)?

   • CNS:

   _____

   • PNS:

   _____

2. What do afferent neurons do? Efferent neurons?

   • Afferent:

   _____

   • Efferent:

   _____

3. What functions are accomplished by the somatic nervous system? The autonomic nervous system?

   • Somatic:

   _____

   • Autonomic:

   _____

4. What are the effects of the sympathetic nervous system? The parasympathetic nervous system?

   • Sympathetic:

   _____

   • Parasympathetic:

   _____

1.3 Organization of the Brain

> **LEARNING GOALS**
>
> After Chapter 1.3, you will be able to:
>
> - Describe the major functions of the hindbrain, midbrain, and forebrain
> - Recognize the most commonly used methods for mapping the brain
> - Identify the structures protecting and surrounding the brain

Throughout this section, refer to Figure 1.4, which identifies various anatomical structures inside the human brain. As we discuss different parts of the brain, it's important to remember the functions of these brain structures. Different parts of the brain perform remarkably different functions. For instance, one part of the brain processes sensory information while an entirely different part of the brain maintains activities of the internal organs. For complex functions such as playing a musical instrument, several brain regions work together. For the MCAT, you will need to know some of the basics about how the brain integrates input from different regions.

Figure 1.4. Anatomical Structures inside the Human Brain

The brain is covered with a thick sheath of connective tissue called the **meninges**. The meninges help protect the brain, keep it anchored within the skull, and resorb cerebrospinal fluid. They are composed of three layers: the **dura mater**, the **arachnoid mater**, and the **pia mater**, as shown in Figure 1.5. **Cerebrospinal fluid** is the aqueous solution in which the brain and spinal cord rest; it is produced by specialized cells that line the **ventricles** (internal cavities) of the brain.

Figure 1.5. Layers of the Meninges

The human brain can be divided into three basic subdivisions: the hindbrain, the midbrain, and the forebrain. Notice that brain structures associated with basic survival are located at the base of the brain and brain structures with more complex functions are located higher up. The meaningful connection between brain location and functional complexity is no accident. In evolutionary terms, the hindbrain and midbrain were brain structures that developed earlier. Together they form the **brainstem**, which is the most primitive region of the brain. The forebrain developed later, including the **limbic system**, a group of neural structures primarily associated with emotion and memory. Aggression, fear, pleasure, and pain are all related to the limbic system. The most recent evolutionary development of the human brain is the **cerebral cortex**, which is the outer covering of the cerebral hemispheres. In humans, the cerebral cortex is associated with everything from language processing to problem solving, and from impulse control to long-term planning. Most of the key brain regions described in the following sections are summarized in Table 1.1.

Major Divisions and Principal Structures	Functions
Forebrain	
Cerebral cortex	Complex perceptual, cognitive, and behavioral processes
Basal ganglia	Movement
Limbic system	Emotion and memory
Thalamus	Sensory relay station
Hypothalamus	Hunger and thirst; emotion
Midbrain	
Inferior and superior colliculi	Sensorimotor reflexes
Hindbrain	
Cerebellum	Refined motor movements
Medulla oblongata	Vital functioning (breathing, digestion)
Reticular formation	Arousal and alertness

Table 1.1. Anatomical Subdivisions of the Brain

In prenatal life, the brain develops from the neural tube. At first, the tube is composed of three swellings, which correspond to the hindbrain, midbrain, and forebrain. Both the hindbrain and forebrain later divide into two swellings, creating five total swellings in the mature neural tube. The embryonic brain is diagrammed in Figure 1.6, and its subdivisions are described further in the following sections.

Figure 1.6. Subdivisions of the Embryonic Brain

HINDBRAIN

Located where the brain meets the spinal cord, the **hindbrain (rhombencephalon)** controls balance, motor coordination, breathing, digestion, and general arousal processes such as sleeping and waking. In short, the hindbrain manages vital functioning necessary for survival. During embryonic development, the rhombencephalon divides to form the **myelencephalon** (which becomes the medulla oblongata) and the **metencephalon** (which becomes the pons and cerebellum). The **medulla oblongata** is a lower brain structure that is responsible for regulating vital functions such as breathing, heart rate, and blood pressure. The **pons** lies above the medulla and contains sensory and motor pathways between the cortex and the medulla. At the top of the hindbrain, mushrooming out of the back of the pons, is the **cerebellum**, a structure that helps maintain posture and balance and coordinates body movements. Damage to the cerebellum causes clumsiness, slurred speech, and loss of balance. Notably, alcohol impairs the functioning of the cerebellum, and consequently affects speech and balance.

MIDBRAIN

Just above the hindbrain is the **midbrain (mesencephalon)**, which receives sensory and motor information from the rest of the body. The midbrain is associated with involuntary reflex responses triggered by visual or auditory stimuli. There are several prominent nuclei in the midbrain, two of which are collectively called **colliculi**. The **superior colliculus** receives visual sensory input, and the **inferior colliculus** receives sensory information from the auditory system. The inferior colliculus has a role in reflexive reactions to sudden loud noises.

FOREBRAIN

Above the midbrain is the **forebrain (prosencephalon)**, which is associated with complex perceptual, cognitive, and behavioral processes. Among its other functions, the forebrain is associated with emotion and memory; it is the forebrain that has the greatest influence on human behavior. Its functions are not absolutely necessary for survival, but are associated instead with the intellectual and emotional capacities most characteristic of humans. During prenatal development, the prosencephalon divides to form the **telencephalon** (which forms the cerebral cortex, basal ganglia, and limbic system) and the **diencephalon** (which forms the thalamus, hypothalamus, posterior pituitary gland, and pineal gland).

METHODS OF MAPPING THE BRAIN

Neuropsychology refers to the study of functions and behaviors associated with specific regions of the brain. It is most often applied in research settings, where researchers attempt to associate very specific areas in the brain to behavior, and in clinical settings when patients are treated for brain lesions. Neuropsychology has its own experimental methodology and technology.

Studying human patients with brain lesions is one way that researchers have determined the functions of the brain. One problem in studying human brain lesions is that they are rarely isolated to specific brain structures. When several brain structures are damaged, it becomes difficult for researchers to attribute a specific functional impairment to any single brain region; the impairment could just as easily be attributed to any other region that suffered damage.

One method for studying the relationship of brain regions and behaviors is to study brain lesions in lab animals. The advantage of this approach is that precisely defined brain lesions can be created in animals by extirpation. Researchers can also produce lesions by inserting tiny electrodes inside the brain and then selectively applying intense heat, cold, or electricity to specific brain regions. Such electrodes can be placed with great precision by using stereotactic instruments, which provide high-resolution, three-coordinate images of the brain. Notwithstanding the ethical or cruelty concerns such studies have raised, they have greatly increased our understanding of comparable neural structures in humans.

Another method involves electrically stimulating and recording brain activity. Before operating on the brain, one can stimulate a patient's cortex with a small electrode. This causes individual neurons to fire, thereby activating the behavioral or perceptual processes associated with those neurons. For instance, if the electrode stimulates neurons in the motor cortex, it leads to specific muscle movements. If the electrode stimulates the visual cortex, the patient "sees" flashes of light that are not really there. By using electrical stimulation, neurosurgeons can thus create **cortical maps**. This method relies on the assistance of the patient, who is awake and alert. Because there are no pain receptors in the brain, only local anesthesia is required. Electrodes have also been used in lab animals to study deeper regions of the brain. Depending on where they are implanted, the electrodes can elicit sleep, sexual arousal, rage, or terror. Once the electrode is turned off, these behaviors cease.

Electrodes can also be used to record electrical activity produced by the brain itself. In some studies, individual neurons are recorded by inserting ultrasensitive microelectrodes into individual brain cells, recording their electrical activity. Electrical activity generated by larger groups of neurons can be studied using an **electroencephalogram** (**EEG**), which involves placing several electrodes on the scalp. Broad patterns of electrical activity can thus be detected and recorded. Because this procedure is noninvasive (it does not cause any damage), it is commonly used with human subjects. In fact, research on sleep, seizures, and brain lesions relies heavily on EEGs, as shown in Figure 1.7.

Figure 1.7. Electroencephalogram (EEG) during REM sleep

Another noninvasive mapping procedure is **regional cerebral blood flow (rCBF)**, which detects broad patterns of neural activity based on increased blood flow to different parts of the brain. rCBF relies on the assumption that when a specific cognitive function activates certain regions of the brain, the blood flow to those regions increases. For example, listening to music may increase blood flow to the right auditory cortex because that is where music is processed in most individuals' brains. To measure blood flow, the patient inhales a harmless radioactive gas; a special device that can detect radioactivity in the bloodstream can then correlate radioactivity levels with regional cerebral blood flow. This research method uses noninvasive computerized scanning devices.

Some of the other common scanning devices and methods of visualization used for brain imaging include:

- **CT (computed tomography)**, in which multiple X-rays are taken at different angles and processed by a computer to cross-sectional slice images of the tissue.
- **PET (positron emission tomography) scan**, in which a radioactive sugar is injected and absorbed into the body, and its dispersion and uptake throughout the target tissue is imaged.

Bridge

MRI techniques are dependent on the reaction of hydrogen to a magnetic field, and the scientific principles behind MRI scans are also applied in NMR techniques, which can be found in Chapter 11 of *MCAT Organic Chemistry Review*.

- **MRI (magnetic resonance imaging)**, which uses a magnetic field to interact with hydrogen and map out hydrogen dense regions of the body.
- **fMRI (functional magnetic resonance imaging)**, which uses the same base technique as MRI, but specifically measures changes associated with blood flow. This is especially useful for monitoring neural activity, since increased blood flow in regions of the brain is typically coupled with neuronal activation.

MCAT Concept Check 1.3:

Before you move on, assess your understanding of the material with these questions.

1. What are the main functions of the hindbrain? Midbrain? Forebrain?

Subdivision	Functions
Hindbrain	
Midbrain	
Forebrain	

2. What are some of the methods used for mapping the brain?

_____

1.4 Parts of the Forebrain

LEARNING GOALS

After Chapter 1.4, you will be able to:

- Link the regions of the forebrain to their functions
- Describe the laterality of brain–body communication and the role of hemispheric dominance
- Describe the functions of the four lobes of the cerebral cortex

The forebrain is the most "modern" portion of the brain, and—in humans—forms the largest portion of the brain by weight and volume. The forebrain contains regions derived from the diencephalon, such as the thalamus, hypothalamus, posterior pituitary, and pineal gland; it also includes derivatives of the telencephalon, such as the cerebral cortex, basal ganglia, and limbic system.

THALAMUS

The **thalamus** is a structure within the forebrain that serves as an important relay station for incoming sensory information, including all senses except for smell. After receiving incoming sensory impulses, the thalamus sorts and transmits them to the appropriate areas of the cerebral cortex. The thalamus is therefore a sensory "way station."

HYPOTHALAMUS

The **hypothalamus**, subdivided into the lateral hypothalamus, ventromedial hypothalamus, and anterior hypothalamus, serves homeostatic functions, and is a key player in emotional experiences during high arousal states, aggressive behavior, and sexual behavior. The hypothalamus also helps control some endocrine functions, as

Mnemonic

Functions of the Hypothalamus—The Four Fs:
- Feeding
- Fighting
- Flighting
- (Sexual) Functioning

Mnemonic

When the **L**ateral **H**ypothalamus (**LH**) is destroyed, one **L**acks **H**unger.

Mnemonic

When the **V**entro**M**edial **H**ypothalamus (**VMH**) is destroyed, one is **V**ery **M**uch **H**ungry.

Mnemonic

When the **A**nterior hypothalamus is destroyed, one is **A**sexual.

Real World

In the early 1920s, researchers first discovered the hypothalamus's role in rage and fighting through classic experiments conducted with cats. When researchers removed the cat's cerebral cortex but left the hypothalamus in place, the cat displayed a pattern of pseudoaggressive behavior that was called "sham rage"—lashing of the tail, arching of the back, clawing, and biting—except that rage was spontaneous or triggered by the mildest touch. The researchers concluded that the cortex typically inhibits this type of response. When the researchers removed the cat's cortex and hypothalamus together, the outcome was very different. The cat no longer showed any signs of sham rage, and much rougher stimulation was required before the cats showed any defensive behavior at all.

well as the autonomic nervous system. The hypothalamus serves many homeostatic functions, which are self-regulatory processes that maintain a stable balance within the body. Receptors in the hypothalamus regulate metabolism, temperature, and water balance. When any of these functions are out of balance, the hypothalamus detects the problem and signals the body to correct the imbalance; for example, osmoreceptors in the hypothalamus may trigger the release of antidiuretic hormone to increase water reabsorption as part of fluid balance. The hypothalamus is also the primary regulator of the autonomic nervous system and is important in drive behaviors: hunger, thirst, and sexual behavior.

The **lateral hypothalamus** (**LH**) is referred to as the hunger center because it has special receptors thought to detect when the body needs more food or fluids. In other words, the LH triggers eating and drinking. When this part of the hypothalamus is destroyed in lab rats, they refuse to eat and drink and would starve to death if not force-fed through tubes.

The **ventromedial hypothalamus** (**VMH**) is identified as the "satiety center," and provides signals to stop eating. Brain lesions to this area usually lead to obesity.

The **anterior hypothalamus** controls sexual behavior. When the anterior hypothalamus is stimulated, lab animals will mount just about anything (including inanimate objects). In many species, damage to the anterior hypothalamus leads to permanent inhibition of sexual activity. The anterior hypothalamus also regulates sleep and body temperature.

OTHER PARTS OF THE DIENCEPHALON

The diencephalon also differentiates to form the posterior pituitary gland, pineal gland, and connecting pathways to other brain regions. The **posterior pituitary** is comprised of axonal projections from the hypothalamus and is the site of release for the hypothalamic hormones **antidiuretic hormone** (**ADH**, also called **vasopressin**) and **oxytocin**. The functions of these hormones are described in Chapter 5 of *MCAT Biology Review*. The **pineal gland** is the key player in several biological rhythms. Most notably, the pineal gland secretes a hormone called **melatonin**, which regulates circadian rhythms. The pineal gland receives direct signals from the retina for coordination with sunlight.

BASAL GANGLIA

In the middle of the brain are a group of structures known as the basal ganglia. The **basal ganglia** coordinate muscle movement as they receive information from the cortex and relay this information (via the extrapyramidal motor system) to the brain and the spinal cord. The **extrapyramidal system** gathers information about body position and carries this information to the central nervous system, but does not function directly through motor neurons. Essentially, the basal ganglia help make our movements smooth and our posture steady. **Parkinson's disease** is one chronic illness associated with destruction of portions of the basal ganglia. It is characterized by jerky movements and uncontrolled resting tremors. The basal ganglia may also play a role in schizophrenia and obsessive–compulsive disorder.

LIMBIC SYSTEM

The **limbic system**, diagrammed in Figure 1.8, comprises a group of interconnected structures looping around the central portion of the brain and is primarily associated with emotion and memory. Its primary components include the septal nuclei, amygdala, and hippocampus. In Chapter 5 of *MCAT Behavioral Sciences Review*, we will also explore the roles of the thalamus, hypothalamus, and cortex in the limbic system.

corpus callosum

thalamus

fornix

septal nuclei

hippocampus

amygdala

Figure 1.8. The Limbic System

Septal Nuclei

The **septal nuclei** contain one of the primary pleasure centers in the brain. Mild stimulation of the septal nuclei is reported to be intensely pleasurable; there is an association between these nuclei and addictive behavior.

Amygdala

The **amygdala** is a structure that plays an important role in defensive and aggressive behaviors, including fear and rage. Researchers base this observation on studies of animals and humans with brain lesions. When the amygdala is damaged, aggression and fear reactions are markedly reduced. Lesions to the amygdala result in docility and hypersexual states.

Hippocampus

The **hippocampus** plays a vital role in learning and memory processes; specifically, the hippocampus helps consolidate information to form long-term memories, and can redistribute remote memories to the cerebral cortex. The hippocampus communicates with other portions of the limbic system through a long

Real World

James Olds and Peter Milner discovered the association between the septal nuclei and addictive behavior in the 1950s. They demonstrated that when rats could stimulate their septal regions at will by pushing a lever, they found it so pleasurable that they preferred it to eating or any other activities, even after going 24 hours without food or sleep.

Real World

Heinrich Klüver and Paul Bucy performed studies that linked the amygdala with defensive and aggressive behavior in monkeys. When the amygdala of the Rhesus monkey was removed, they noted increased sexual behavior, decreased fear responses, and hyperorality, or the examination of inanimate or animate objects by mouth. These symptoms are now referred to as Klüver–Bucy syndrome.

Bridge

Learning and memory are discussed thoroughly in Chapter 3 of *MCAT Behavioral Sciences Review.*

Mnemonic

Lobes of the brain: **F-POT**
- **F**rontal
- **P**arietal
- **O**ccipital
- **T**emporal

projection called the **fornix**. Researchers originally discovered the connection between memory and the hippocampus through a famous patient named Henry Molaison (known as H.M. in the scientific literature until his death in 2008). Parts of H.M.'s temporal lobes—including the amygdala and hippocampus—were removed in an effort to control epileptic seizures. After surgery, H.M.'s intelligence was largely intact but he suffered a drastic and irreversible loss of memory for any new information. This kind of memory loss is called **anterograde amnesia** and is characterized by not being able to establish new long-term memories, whereas memory for events that occurred before brain injury is usually intact. The opposite kind of memory loss, **retrograde amnesia**, refers to memory loss of events that transpired before brain injury.

CEREBRAL CORTEX

The outer surface of the brain is called the **cerebral cortex**. The cortex is sometimes called the **neocortex**, a reminder that the cortex is the most recent brain region to evolve. Rather than having a smooth surface, the cortex has numerous bumps and folds called **gyri** and **sulci**, respectively. The convoluted structure of the brain provides increased surface area. The cerebrum is divided into two halves, called **cerebral hemispheres**. The surface of the cortex is divided into four lobes—the frontal lobe, parietal lobe, occipital lobe, and temporal lobe. These lobes are identified in Figure 1.9, which shows a side view of the left cerebral hemisphere.

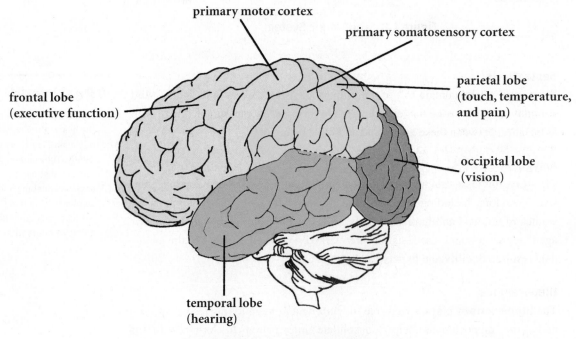

Figure 1.9. Lobes of the Brain

Frontal Lobe

The **frontal lobe** is comprised of two basic regions: the prefrontal cortex and the motor cortex. The **prefrontal cortex** manages executive function by supervising and directing the operations of other brain regions. This region supervises processes associated with perception, memory, emotion, impulse control, and long-term planning. In memory, for instance, the role of the prefrontal cortex is not to store any memory traces, but rather to remind the individual that he or she has something to remember at all. To regulate attention and alertness, the prefrontal cortex communicates with the reticular formation in the brainstem, telling an individual either to wake up or relax, depending on the situation.

Because it integrates information from different cortical regions, the prefrontal cortex is a good example of an **association area**: an area that integrates input from diverse brain regions. For example, multiple inputs may be necessary to solve a complex puzzle, to plan ahead for the future, or to reach a difficult decision. Association areas are generally contrasted with **projection areas**, which perform more rudimentary or simple perceptual and motor tasks. Examples of projection areas include the visual cortex, which receives visual input from the retina, and the motor cortex, which sends out motor commands to the muscles.

Damage to the prefrontal cortex impairs its overall supervisory functions. A person with a prefrontal lesion may be more impulsive and generally less in control of his or her behavior, or depressed. It is not unusual, for instance, for someone with a prefrontal lesion to make vulgar and inappropriate sexual remarks, or to be apathetic.

The **primary motor cortex** is located on the **precentral gyrus** (just in front of the **central sulcus** that divides the frontal and parietal lobes), and initiates voluntary motor movements by sending neural impulses down the spinal cord toward the muscles. As such, it is considered a projection area in the brain. The neurons in the motor cortex are arranged systematically according to the parts of the body to which they are connected. This organizational pattern can be visualized through the **motor homunculus**, as shown in Figure 1.10. Because certain sets of muscles require finer motor control than others, they take up additional space in the cortex relative to their size in the body.

m
e
d
i
a
l

l
a
t
e
r
a
l

Figure 1.10. Motor Homunculus on the Precentral Gyrus of the Frontal Lobe

A third important part of the frontal lobe is **Broca's area**, which is vitally important for speech production. Broca's area is usually found in only one hemisphere, the so-called "dominant" hemisphere; for most people—both right- and left-handed—this is the left hemisphere.

Parietal Lobe

The **parietal lobe** is located to the rear of the frontal lobe. The **somatosensory cortex** is located on the **postcentral gyrus** (just behind the central sulcus) and is involved in somatosensory information processing. This projection area is the destination for all incoming sensory signals for touch, pressure, temperature, and pain. Despite certain differences, the somatosensory cortex and motor cortex are very closely related. In fact, they are so interrelated they sometimes are described as a single unit: the sensorimotor cortex. The somatosensory homunculus is shown in Figure 1.11. The central region of the parietal lobe is associated with spatial processing and manipulation. This region makes it possible to orient oneself and other objects in three-dimensional space, to do spatial manipulation of objects, and to apply spatial orientation skills such as those required for map-reading.

Figure 1.11. Somatosensory Homunculus on the Postcentral Gyrus of the Parietal Lobe

Occipital Lobe

The **occipital lobes**, at the very rear of the brain, contain the **visual cortex**, which is sometimes called the **striate cortex**. *Striate* means furrowed or striped, which is how the visual cortex appears when examined under a microscope. The visual cortex is one of the best-understood brain regions, owing to the large amount of research that has been done on visual processing. Sensation and perception of visual information is discussed thoroughly in Chapter 2 of *MCAT Behavioral Sciences Review*. Areas in the occipital lobe have also been implicated in learning and motor control.

Temporal Lobe

The **temporal lobes** are associated with a number of functions. The auditory cortex and Wernicke's area are located in the temporal lobe. The **auditory cortex** is the primary site of most sound processing, including speech, music, and other sound information. **Wernicke's area** is associated with language reception and comprehension. The temporal lobe also functions in memory processing, emotion, and language. Studies have shown that electrical stimulation of the temporal lobe can evoke memories for past events. This makes sense because the hippocampus is located deep inside the temporal lobe. It is important to note that the lobes, although having seemingly independent functions, are not truly independent of one another. Often, a sensory modality may be represented in more than one area.

Real World

Several techniques have been developed to assess the function of brain regions, especially those associated with language and auditory processing. One such technique is called **speech shadowing**, which is a technique used to research both stuttering and speech perception. Speech shadowing involves participants reciting along with auditory inputs, which can be presented to one or both ears. If different messages are presented to each ear, as in a dichotic listening test, speech shadowing can ensure that the participant is paying attention to the auditory input to the correct ear. This seemingly simple experimental task requires successful functioning of the temporal lobe, parietal lobe, and the frontal cortex!

Real World

The corpus callosum connects and shares information between the two cerebral hemispheres; its function was discovered in epileptic patients whose corpora callosa were severed in a last-ditch effort to limit their convulsive seizures. In these "split-brain" patients, in whom the corpus callosum has been severed, each hemisphere has its own function and specialization that is no longer accessible by the other. Thus, an object felt only by the left hand (which projects to the right hemisphere) could not be named (because language function is usually in the left hemisphere).

Cerebral Hemispheres and Laterality

In most cases, one side of the brain communicates with the opposite side of the body. In such cases, we say a cerebral hemisphere communicates **contralaterally**. For example, the motor neurons on the left side of the brain activate movements on the right side of the body. In other cases (for instance, hearing), cerebral hemispheres communicate with the same side of the body. In such cases, the hemispheres communicate **ipsilaterally**.

We distinguish between dominant and nondominant hemispheres. The dominant hemisphere is typically defined as the one that is more heavily stimulated during language reception and production. In the past, hand dominance was used as a proxy for hemispheric dominance; that is, right-handed individuals were assumed to have left-dominant brains and left-handed individuals were assumed to have right-dominant brains (because the brain communicates contralaterally with the hand). However, this correlation has not held up under scrutiny; 95 percent of right-handed individuals are indeed left brain dominant, but only 18 percent of left-handed individuals are right brain dominant.

The **dominant hemisphere** (usually the left) is primarily analytic in function, making it well-suited for managing details. For instance, language, logic, and math skills are all located in the dominant hemisphere. Again, language production (Broca's area) and language comprehension (Wernicke's area) are primarily driven by the dominant hemisphere.

The **nondominant hemisphere** (usually the right) is associated with intuition, creativity, music cognition, and spatial processing. The nondominant hemisphere simultaneously processes the pieces of a stimulus and assembles them into a holistic image. The nondominant hemisphere serves a less prominent role in language. It is more sensitive to the emotional tone of spoken language, and permits us to recognize others' moods based on visual and auditory cues, which adds to communication. The dominant hemisphere thus screens incoming language to analyze its content, and the nondominant hemisphere interprets it according to its emotional tone. The roles of the dominant and nondominant hemispheres are summarized in Table 1.2; remember that the left hemisphere is the dominant hemisphere in most individuals, regardless of handedness.

Function	Dominant Hemisphere	Nondominant Hemisphere
Visual system	Letters, words	Faces
Auditory system	Language-related sounds	Music
Language	Speech, reading, writing, arithmetic	Emotions
Movement	Complex voluntary movement	–
Spatial processes	–	Geometry, sense of direction

Table 1.2. Comparison of Dominant and Nondominant Hemispheres' Functions

MCAT Concept Check 1.4:

Before you move on, assess your understanding of the material with these questions.

1. Match the parts of the brain below to their functions:

    1. Basal ganglia
    2. Cerebellum
    3. Cerebral cortex
    4. Hypothalamus
    5. Inferior and superior colliculi
    6. Limbic system
    7. Medulla oblongata
    8. Reticular formation
    9. Thalamus

    A. Smooth movement
    B. Sensory relay station
    C. Sensorimotor reflexes
    D. Arousal and alertness
    E. Hunger and thirst; emotion
    F. Complex perceptual, cognitive, and behavioral processes
    G. Vital function (breathing, digestion)
    H. Coordinated movement
    I. Emotion and memory

2. What are the four lobes of the cerebral cortex, and what is the function of each?

Lobe	Function

1.5 Influences on Behavior

> ## LEARNING GOALS
>
> After Chapter 1.5, you will be able to:
>
> - Associate major neurotransmitters with their common functions
> - Detail the links between the endocrine system and the brain
> - Explain the nature *vs.* nurture debate, and the different study types used to explore this question

Merely describing the functions of brain regions does not fully explain the wide variety of human behaviors that are possible. Other influences on behavior include chemical controls (neurotransmitters, hormones in the endocrine system), heredity, and the environment.

NEUROTRANSMITTERS

More than 100 neurotransmitters have been identified. Seven of the most important are described here and are summarized in Table 1.3.

Acetylcholine

Acetylcholine is a neurotransmitter found in both the central and peripheral nervous systems. In the peripheral nervous system, acetylcholine is used to transmit nerve impulses to the muscles. It is the neurotransmitter used by the parasympathetic nervous system and a small portion of the sympathetic nervous system (in ganglia and for innervating sweat glands). In the central nervous system, acetylcholine has been linked to attention and arousal. In fact, loss of cholinergic neurons connecting with the hippocampus is associated with Alzheimer's disease, an illness resulting in progressive and incurable memory loss.

Epinephrine and Norepinephrine

Epinephrine, norepinephrine, and dopamine are three closely related neurotransmitters known as **catecholamines**. Due to similarities in their molecular composition, these three transmitters are also classified as **monoamines** or **biogenic amines**. The most important thing to know about the catecholamines is that they all play important roles in the experience of emotions.

Epinephrine (adrenaline) and **norepinephrine (noradrenaline)** are involved in controlling alertness and wakefulness. As the primary neurotransmitter of the sympathetic nervous system, they promote the fight-or-flight response. Whereas norepinephrine more commonly acts at a local level as a neurotransmitter,

Key Concept

Acetylcholine is the neurotransmitter used by the efferent limb of the somatic nervous system and the parasympathetic nervous system. Acetylcholine can act as an excitatory or inhibitory neurotransmitter in muscle cells, dependent on the type of receptor found on the cell. For example, acetylcholine will transmit an inhibitory response in cardiac muscle cells, but it can also transmit an excitatory response if acting on skeletal muscle cells. Acetylcholine within the central nervous system largely functions as an excitatory neurotransmitter.

epinephrine is more often secreted from the adrenal medulla to act systemically as a hormone. Low levels of norepinephrine are associated with depression; high levels are associated with anxiety and mania.

Dopamine

Dopamine is another catecholamine that plays an important role in movement and posture. High concentrations of dopamine are normally found in the basal ganglia, which help smooth movements and maintain postural stability.

Imbalances in dopamine transmission have been found to play a role in **schizophrenia**. An important theory about the origin of this mental illness is called the **dopamine hypothesis of schizophrenia**. The dopamine hypothesis argues that delusions, hallucinations, and agitation associated with schizophrenia arise from either too much dopamine or from an oversensitivity to dopamine in the brain. Although the dopamine hypothesis of schizophrenia is an important theory, it does not account for all of the findings of the disease.

Parkinson's disease is associated with a loss of dopaminergic neurons in the basal ganglia. These disruptions of dopamine transmission lead to resting tremors and jerky movements, as well as postural instability.

Serotonin

Along with the catecholamines, serotonin is classified as a monoamine or biogenic amine neurotransmitter. **Serotonin** is generally thought to play roles in regulating mood, eating, sleeping, and dreaming. Like norepinephrine, serotonin is thought to play a role in depression and mania. An oversupply of serotonin is thought to produce manic states; an undersupply is thought to produce depression.

GABA, Glycine, and Glutamate

The neurotransmitter **γ-aminobutyric acid (GABA)** produces inhibitory postsynaptic potentials and is thought to play an important role in stabilizing neural activity in the brain. GABA exerts its effects by causing hyperpolarization of the postsynaptic membrane.

Glycine may be better known as one of the twenty proteinogenic amino acids, but it also serves as an inhibitory neurotransmitter in the central nervous system by increasing chloride influx into the neuron. This hyperpolarizes the postsynaptic membrane, similar to the function of GABA.

Finally, **glutamate**, another of the twenty proteinogenic amino acids, also acts as a neurotransmitter in the central nervous system. In contrast to glycine, however, it is an excitatory neurotransmitter.

Peptide Neurotransmitters

Studies suggest that peptides are also involved in neurotransmission. The synaptic action of these **neuromodulators** (also called **neuropeptides**) involves a

Real World

The role of dopamine in both schizophrenia and Parkinson's disease can be seen in their treatment. Antipsychotic medications used in schizophrenia are dopamine blockers, and can cause motor disturbances ("extrapyramidal symptoms") as a side effect. Parkinson's disease can be treated with L-DOPA, which increases dopamine levels in the brain; an overdose of L-DOPA can lead to psychotic symptoms similar to schizophrenia.

more complicated chain of events in the postsynaptic cell than that of regular neurotransmitters. Neuromodulators are therefore relatively slow and have longer effects on the postsynaptic cell than neurotransmitters. The **endorphins**, which are natural painkillers produced in the brain, are the most important peptides to know. Endorphins (and their relatives, **enkephalins**) have actions similar to morphine or other opioids in the body.

Neurotransmitter	Behavior
Acetylcholine	Voluntary muscle control, parasympathetic nervous system, attention, alertness
Epinephrine and Norepinephrine	Fight-or-flight responses, wakefulness, alertness
Dopamine	Smooth movements, postural stability
Serotonin	Mood, sleep, eating, dreaming
GABA and Glycine	Brain "stabilization"
Glutamate	Brain excitation
Endorphins	Natural painkillers

Table 1.3. Neurotransmitters and Their Functions

THE ENDOCRINE SYSTEM

We've already discussed the relatively fast communication network—the nervous system—that uses chemical messages called neurotransmitters. The endocrine system is the other internal communication network in the body, and it uses chemical messengers called **hormones**. The endocrine system is somewhat slower than the nervous system because hormones travel to their target destinations through the bloodstream. The endocrine system is covered extensively in Chapter 5 of *MCAT Biology Review*, so our focus here will be on the role of certain endocrine organs on behavior.

The hypothalamus links the endocrine and nervous systems and, in addition to the roles described earlier, regulates the hormonal function of the pituitary gland. The hypothalamus and pituitary gland are spatially close to each other, and control is maintained through endocrine release of hormones into the **hypophyseal portal system** that directly connects the two organs, as shown in Figure 1.12.

Bridge

The entire endocrine system is covered in Chapter 5 of *MCAT Biology Review*.

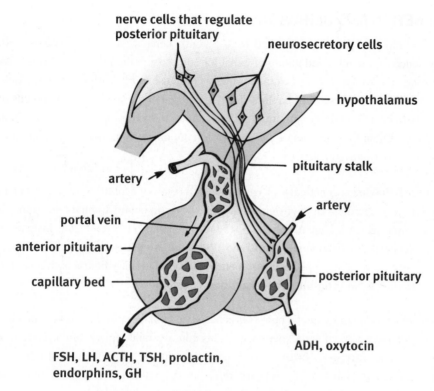

nerve cells that regulate posterior pituitary

neurosecretory cells

hypothalamus

pituitary stalk

artery

artery

portal vein

anterior pituitary

posterior pituitary

capillary bed

ADH, oxytocin

FSH, LH, ACTH, TSH, prolactin, endorphins, GH

Figure 1.12. The Hypophyseal Portal System

The **pituitary gland**, sometimes referred to as the "master" gland, is located at the base of the brain, and is divided into two parts: anterior and posterior. It is the **anterior pituitary** that is the "master" because it releases hormones that regulate activities of endocrine glands; however, the anterior pituitary itself is controlled by the hypothalamus. The pituitary secretes various hormones into the bloodstream that travel to other endocrine glands located elsewhere in the body to activate them. Once activated by the pituitary, a given endocrine gland manufactures and secretes its own characteristic hormone into the bloodstream.

The **adrenal glands** are located on top of the kidneys and are divided into two parts: the adrenal medulla and adrenal cortex. The **adrenal medulla** releases epinephrine and norepinephrine as part of the sympathetic nervous system. The **adrenal cortex** produces many hormones called **corticosteroids**, including the stress hormone **cortisol**. The adrenal cortex also contributes to sexual functioning by producing sex hormones, such as **testosterone** and **estrogen**.

The **gonads** are the sex glands of the body—ovaries in females and testes in males. These glands produce sex hormones in higher concentrations, leading to increased levels of testosterone in males and increased levels of estrogen in females. These sex hormones increase **libido** and contribute to mating behavior and sexual function. Higher levels of testosterone also increase aggressive behavior.

Real World

Bipolar disorder is considered one of the most heritable disorders, including medical illnesses. In one study, having a monozygotic (identical) twin with bipolar disorder was associated with a 43% risk of being diagnosed with the same disorder.

Bridge

Natural selection is discussed in greater detail in Chapter 12 of *MCAT Biology Review*.

GENETICS AND BEHAVIOR

Just as physical traits are inherited from parents, behavioral traits can be as well. Evidence for the inherited nature of behavior comes from the fact that many behaviors are species specific. For example, many animals exhibit mating behaviors only seen within their species. Behaviors can also be bred into a species; many breeds of dog have been bred for certain traits and behaviors. Behaviors are also seen to run in families. Often times, violence and aggression are observed passing along a family line, as are mental illnesses.

Innate behavior is genetically programmed as a result of evolution and is seen in all individuals regardless of environment or experience. In contrast, other behaviors are considered learned. **Learned behaviors** are not based on heredity but instead on experience and environment. **Adaptive value** is the extent to which a trait or behavior positively benefits a species by influencing the evolutionary fitness of the species, thus leading to **adaptation** through **natural selection**.

How much of an individual's behavior is based on genetic makeup and how much is based on environment and experiences? This controversial topic is often referred to as **nature *vs*. nurture**. **Nature** is defined as heredity, or the influence of inherited characteristics on behavior. **Nurture** refers to the influence of environment and physical surroundings on behavior. The answer to this long-debated question is a complicated one, but seems to lie somewhere in the middle. It is possible for particular environmental factors to influence genetic factors in the development of a specific trait. For example, a person can have hereditary components making them more likely to have an addictive personality. Still, the individual would have to have exposure to drugs, alcohol, or gambling to develop an addiction to them.

Research that determines the degree of genetic influence on individual differences between people uses one of three methods: family studies, twin studies, and adoption studies. **Family studies** rely on the assumption that genetically related individuals are more similar genotypically than unrelated individuals. Researchers may compare rates of a given trait among family members to those among unrelated individuals. For example, family studies have determined that the risk of developing schizophrenia for children of schizophrenics is 13 times higher than in the general population. For siblings, the rate is 9 times higher. This has led psychologists to conclude that schizophrenia has a hereditary component. Family studies are limited, however, because families share both genetics and environment. Family studies cannot distinguish shared environmental factors from genetic factors; perhaps the increased rates of schizophrenia in families are a result of experiencing the same emotional climate in the home rather than genetically shared characteristics.

Twin studies, comparing concordance rates for a trait between **monozygotic (MZ**; identical) and **dizygotic (DZ**; fraternal) twins, are better able to distinguish the relative effects of shared environment and genetics. **Concordance rates** refer to the likelihood that both twins exhibit the same trait. MZ twins are genetically identical, sharing 100 percent of their genes, whereas DZ twins share approximately 50 percent of their genes. The assumption (though flawed) is that both MZ and DZ twins share the same environment; thus, differences between MZ and DZ twins are thought to reflect hereditary factors. To better measure genetic effects relative to environmental effects, researchers compare traits in twins raised together to twins raised apart. One study of personality characteristics showed that MZ twins raised in separate families were still more similar than DZ twins raised together. This argues for a strong genetic component to personality.

Finally, **adoption studies** also help us understand environmental influences and genetic influence on behavior. These studies compare the similarities between biological relatives and the adopted child to similarities between adoptive relatives and the adopted child. For example, researchers have found that adopted children's IQ is more similar to their biological parents' IQ than to their adoptive parents' IQ. This research suggests that IQ is heritable. Criminal behavior among teenage boys shows a similar pattern of heritability.

MCAT Concept Check 1.5:

Before you move on, assess your understanding of the material with these questions.

1. Match the neurotransmitters below to their functions:

1. Acetylcholine	A. Wakefulness and alertness, fight-or-flight responses
2. Dopamine	
3. Endorphins	B. Brain "stabilizer"
4. Epinephrine/ norepinephrine	C. Mood, sleep, eating, dreaming
	D. Natural pain killer
5. GABA/glycine	E. Smooth movements and steady posture
6. Glutamate	F. Voluntary muscle control
7. Serotonin	G. Brain excitation

2. Which endocrine organs influence behavior? What hormones do they use, and what do they accomplish?

    _____

3. Briefly discuss the influence of nature *vs.* nurture on behavior.

    _____

4. In each of the study types below, what is the sample group? The control group?

Study	Sample Group	Control Group
Family study		
Twin study		
Adoption study		

1.6 Development

LEARNING GOALS

After Chapter 1.6, you will be able to:

- Describe the process of neurulation
- Link the primitive reflexes with the behaviors to which they correspond
- Identify the main themes that dictate stages of motor development in children

The developmental process begins at the moment of conception. Physiological changes are rapid from embryonic to fetal stages, and well into infancy. Children exhibit surprisingly consistent patterns of motor abilities, as well as physiological changes based on age. Understanding these changes and when they occur is important in the discussion of developmental psychology.

PRENATAL

The development of the nervous system starts with neurulation, at three to four weeks' gestational age. **Neurulation** occurs when the ectoderm overlying the notochord begins to furrow, forming a **neural groove** surrounded by two **neural folds**, as shown in Figure 1.13. Cells at the leading edge of the neural fold are called the **neural crest**, and will migrate throughout the body to form disparate tissues, including dorsal root ganglia, melanocytes (pigment-producing cells), and calcitonin-producing cells of the thyroid. The remainder of the furrow closes to form the **neural tube**, which will ultimately form the central nervous system (CNS). The neural tube has an **alar plate**, which differentiates into sensory neurons, and a **basal plate**, which differentiates into motor neurons. Over time, the neural tube invaginates and folds on itself many times; the embryonic brain begins as three swellings (prosencephalon, mesencephalon, rhombencephalon) that become five swellings (telencephalon, diencephalon, mesencephalon, metencephalon, myelencephalon) as it becomes the mature brain, as demonstrated in Figure 1.6 earlier.

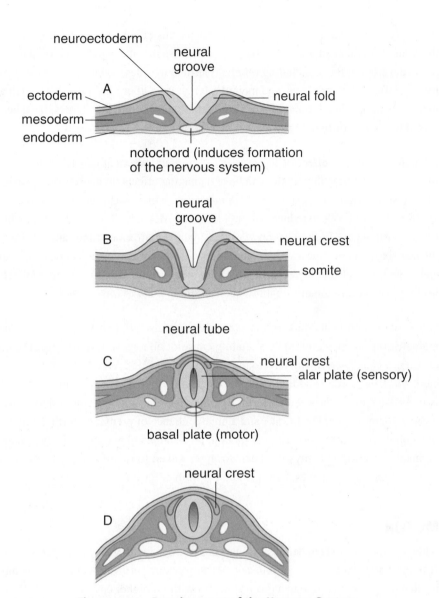

Figure 1.13. Development of the Nervous System

Prenatal development does not occur in a vacuum, of course, but in the mother's uterus. Within this environment, temperature, chemical balance, orientation of the fetus with respect to gravity, and atmospheric pressure are all carefully controlled and remain relatively constant. The fetus is attached to the uterine wall and placenta by the **umbilical cord**. The **placenta** transmits food, oxygen, and water to the fetus while returning water and waste to the mother. Maternal blood supplies many of the proteins and amino acids needed for growth, although the embryo begins to produce them as well.

A variety of external influences can have deleterious effects on the development of the fetus. A number of viruses or bacteria can cross the placenta and cause damage to the developing fetus, including rubella (German measles), which may cause cataracts, deafness, heart defects, and mental retardation. Other viral infections, such as measles, mumps, hepatitis, influenza, varicella (chickenpox), and herpes, have been linked to various birth defects.

An unfortunate side effect of the revolution in pharmaceutical development is that many drugs that help the mother can have damaging effects on the fetus she carries. The most notorious of these drugs is *thalidomide*, which was prescribed in the late 1950s and early 1960s to reduce morning sickness. Mothers who took this drug while pregnant often gave birth to babies with missing and malformed limbs and defects of the heart, eyes, ears, digestive tract, and kidneys. Antiepileptic medications are associated with neural tube defects, in which the neural tube fails to close completely, leading to devastating malformations such as *spina bifida* or *anencephaly*.

A host of environmental factors and exposures may also affect maturation. Maternal malnutrition is considered to be a leading cause of abnormal development. Protein deficiency can slow growth, lead to mental retardation, and reduce immunity to disease. Maternal narcotic addiction produces chemically dependent infants who must undergo severe withdrawal after birth. Regular cigarette smoking can lead to slowed growth, increased fetal heart rate, and a greater chance of premature birth. Daily use of alcohol also leads to slowed growth, both physically and psychologically. Finally, prenatal exposure to X-rays has been strongly linked to retardation; defects of the skull, spinal cord, and eyes; cleft palate; and limb deformities.

MOTOR

Although they may seem helpless, infants are equipped with well-developed somatic structures and a broad array of reflexes that help ensure survival. A **reflex** is a behavior that occurs in response to a given stimulus without higher cognitive input. While motor and startle reflexes exist in adults, infants have a number of **primitive reflexes** that disappear with age. For example, the **rooting reflex** is the automatic turning of the head in the direction of a stimulus that touches the cheek—such as a nipple during feeding. Sucking and swallowing when an object is placed in the mouth are also examples of reflexes related to feeding.

Other primitive reflexes may have served an adaptive purpose in earlier stages of human evolution, but are currently used mainly in assessing infant neurological development. By comparing the point in time at which each of these reflexes disappears relative to the established norms, it is possible to tell whether neurological development is taking place in a normal fashion. One such reflex is the **Moro reflex**, illustrated in Figure 1.14. Infants react to abrupt movements of their heads by flinging out their arms, then slowly retracting their arms and crying. It has been speculated that this reflex may have developed during a time when our prehuman ancestors lived in trees and falling could have been prevented by instinctive clutching. The Moro reflex usually disappears after four months and its continuation at one year is a strong suggestion of developmental difficulties. Asymmetry of the Moro reflex may hint at underlying neuromuscular problems.

Figure 1.14. The Moro Reflex
The infant extends the arms, then slowly withdraws them and cries.

The **Babinski reflex** causes the toes to spread apart automatically when the sole of the foot is stimulated, as seen in Figure 1.15. The **grasping reflex** occurs when the infant closes his or her fingers around an object placed in his or her hand. Adults with neurological diseases may exhibit these primitive reflexes, especially in illnesses that cause demyelination (loss of the myelin sheath).

Figure 1.15. The Babinski Reflex
The big toe extends while the other toes fan outward.

Although reflexive behavior dominates the repertoire of the neonate, other behaviors occur as well. Newborn infants also kick, turn, and wave their arms. These uncoordinated, unconnected behaviors form the basis for later, more coordinated movements.

Infants typically develop motor skills at about the same age, in the same order. Due to this pattern, most psychologists and doctors agree that these are innately programmed abilities for human infants. However, the educational richness of the environment has been observed to affect the rate of learning, with more enriched environments promoting quicker development.

Motor skills are broken down into two classes: gross and fine motor skills. **Gross motor skills** incorporate movement from large muscle groups and whole body motion, such as sitting, crawling, and walking. **Fine motor skills** involve the smaller muscles of the fingers, toes, and eyes, providing more specific and delicate movement. Fine motor abilities include tracking motion, drawing, catching, and waving.

SOCIAL

In addition to motor skills, social development occurs in infancy and through adolescence. At birth, the parental figure becomes the center of the infant's world, and as the infant ages, **stranger anxiety** (a fear and apprehension of unfamiliar individuals) and **separation anxiety** (a fear of being separated from the parental figure) develop at approximately seven months and one year, respectively. During this time, play style progresses from solitary to onlooker, and at two years develops into **parallel play**, in which children will play alongside each other without influencing each other's behavior. At age three, a child has an awareness of his or her gender identity, engages in gender-specific play, and knows his or her full name.

By age five, conformity to peers and romantic feelings for others begin to develop. From ages six through twelve, friend circles tend to be of the same sex without expression of romantic feelings. In the teenage years, children become more self-sufficient, and often express their desire for independence by rebelling against their parents. Cross-gender friendships become more common. Individuals also become more aware of their sexual orientation and sexual relationships begin.

The **developmental milestones** of the first three years of life are listed in Table 1.4. While this is a general timetable based on averages, most children fall within plus or minus two months of the chart. The goal is not to memorize this chart, but to recognize some themes. For example, gross motor skills progress in a head-to-toe order starting with the ability to lift the head, stabilize the trunk, and finally walking. There is also a correlation between the development of motor skills and proximity to the center of the body, with skills being developed at the core prior to extremities. Social skills move from being parent-oriented to self-oriented to other-oriented. Language skills, discussed in Chapter 4 of *MCAT Behavioral Sciences Review*, become more complex and structured.

Age	Physical and Motor Developments	Social Developments	Language Developments
1st year of life	• Puts everything in mouth • Sits with support (4 mo) • Stands with help (8 mo) • Crawls, fear of falling (9 mo) • Pincer grasp (10 mo) • Follows objects to midline (4 wk) • One-handed approach/ grasp of toy • Feet in mouth (5 mo) • Bang and rattle stage • Changes hands with toy (6 mo)	• Parental figure central • Issues of trust are key • Stranger anxiety (7 mo) • Play is solitary and exploratory • Pat-a-cake, peek-a-boo (10 mo)	• Laughs aloud (4 mo) • Repetitive responding (8 mo) • "mama, dada" (10 mo)
Age 1	• Walks alone (13 mo) • Climbs stairs alone (18 mo) • Emergence of hand preference (18 mo) • Kicks ball, throws ball • Pats pictures in book • Stacks three cubes (18 mo)	• Separation anxiety (12 mo) • Dependency on parental figure • Onlooker play	• Great variation in timing of language development • Uses 10 words
Age 2	• High activity level • Walks backwards • Can turn doorknob, unscrew jar lid • Scribbles with crayon • Stacks six cubes (24 mo) • Stands on tiptoes (30 mo) • Able to aim thrown ball	• Selfish and self-centered • Imitates mannerisms and activities • May be aggressive • Recognizes self in mirror • "No" is favorite word • Parallel play	• Use of pronouns • Parents understand most • Two-word sentences • Uses 250 words • Identifies body parts by pointing
Age 3	• Rides tricycle • Stacks 9 cubes (36 mo) • Alternates feet going up stairs • Bowel and bladder control (toilet training) • Draws recognizable figures • Catches ball with arms • Cuts paper with scissors • Unbuttons buttons	• Fixed gender identity • Gender-specific play • Understands "taking turns" • Knows full name	• Complete sentences • Uses 900 words • Understands 3600 words • Strangers can understand • Recognizes common objects in pictures • Can answer, "Tell me what we wear on our feet?" "Which block is bigger?"

Table 1.4. Child Development Milestones

MCAT Concept Check 1.6:

Before you move on, assess your understanding of the material with these questions.

1. Describe the process of neurulation.

   _____

2. For each of the primitive reflexes below, briefly describe the observed behavior.

Primitive Reflex	Behavior
Rooting	
Moro	
Babinski	
Grasping	

3. What are the two main themes that dictate the stages of motor development in early childhood?

   1._____

   2._____

Conclusion

Behavioral psychology is the study of all physical and mental actions based on the response of the body to external stimuli, specifically the activity of the nervous and endocrine systems. The nervous system is a complex organization of structures and neurons that communicate and coordinate information. The endocrine system, in conjunction with the nervous system, controls human behavior. Aside from neurotransmitter and hormonal control of behavior, certain behaviors are genetically passed from generation to generation, as are many other physical traits. The genetic aspects of behavior are thought to interact with the learned components of behavior. Human behavior is also studied as it correlates to the development from embryo to fetus to infant and well into adolescence and adulthood. The development of motor skills and social behavior is seen to progress at a consistent rate across the species.

In the next chapter, our focus will be on the neurological systems used to interact with the world—most notably, those systems that exist for sensation and perception of the environment. These include vision, hearing, smell and taste, somatosensation, and others.

CONCEPT SUMMARY

A Brief History of Neuropsychology

- **Neuropsychology** is the study of the connection between the nervous system and behavior. It most often focuses on the functions of various brain regions.

Organization of the Human Nervous System

- There are three types of neurons in the nervous system: **sensory** (**afferent**) neurons, **motor** (**efferent**) neurons, and **interneurons.**
- **Reflex arcs** use the ability of interneurons in the spinal cord to relay information to the source of stimuli while simultaneously routing it to the brain.
- The nervous system is made up of the **central nervous system** (**CNS**; brain and spinal cord) and **peripheral nervous system** (**PNS**; most cranial and spinal nerves).
  - The PNS is divided into the **somatic** (voluntary) and **autonomic** (automatic) divisions.
  - The autonomic system is further divided into the **parasympathetic** (rest-and-digest) and **sympathetic** (fight-or-flight) branches.

Organization of the Brain

- The brain has three subdivisions: hindbrain, midbrain, and forebrain.
  - The **hindbrain** contains the cerebellum, medulla oblongata, and reticular formation.
  - The **midbrain** contains the inferior and superior colliculi.
  - The **forebrain** contains the thalamus, hypothalamus, basal ganglia, limbic system, and cerebral cortex.
- Methods of studying the brain include studying humans and animals with lesions, electrical stimulation and activity recording (including **electroencephalography [EEG]**), and **regional cerebral blood flow**.

Parts of the Forebrain

- The **thalamus** is a relay station for sensory information.
- The **hypothalamus** maintains homeostasis and integrates with the endocrine system through the **hypophyseal portal system** that connects it to the **anterior pituitary**.
- The **basal ganglia** smoothen movements and help maintain postural stability.
- The **limbic system**, which contains the septal nuclei, amygdala, and hippocampus, controls emotion and memory.
  - The **septal nuclei** are involved with feelings of pleasure, pleasure-seeking behavior, and addiction.
  - The **amygdala** controls fear and aggression.

- The **hippocampus** consolidates memories and communicates with other parts of the limbic system through an extension called the **fornix**.
- The **cerebral cortex** is divided into four lobes: frontal, parietal, occipital, and temporal.
  - The **frontal lobe** controls executive function, impulse control, long-term planning, motor function, and speech production.
  - The **parietal lobe** controls sensations of touch, pressure, temperature, and pain; spatial processing; orientation; and manipulation.
  - The **occipital lobe** controls visual processing.
  - The **temporal lobe** controls sound processing, speech perception, memory, and emotion.
- The brain is divided into two **cerebral hemispheres**, left and right. In most individuals, the left hemisphere is the dominant hemisphere for language.

Influences on Behavior

- **Neurotransmitters** are released by neurons to carry a signal to another neuron or effector (a muscle fiber or a gland).
  - **Acetylcholine** is used by the somatic nervous system (to move muscles), the parasympathetic nervous system, and the central nervous system (for alertness).
  - **Dopamine** maintains smooth movements and steady posture.
  - **Endorphins** and **enkephalins** act as natural painkillers.
  - **Epinephrine** and **norepinephrine** maintain wakefulness and alertness, and mediate fight-or-flight responses. Epinephrine tends to act as a hormone, and norepinephrine tends to act more classically as a neurotransmitter.
  - **γ-Aminobutyric acid** (**GABA**) and **glycine** act as brain "stabilizers."
  - **Glutamate** acts as an excitatory neurotransmitter in the brain.
  - **Serotonin** modulates mood, sleep patterns, eating patterns, and dreaming.
- The endocrine system is tied to the nervous system through the hypothalamus and the anterior pituitary, as well as a few other hormones.
  - **Cortisol** is a stress hormone released by the adrenal cortex.
  - **Testosterone** and **estrogen** mediate libido; testosterone also increases aggressive behavior. Both are released by the adrenal cortex. In males, the testes also produce testosterone. In females, the ovaries also produce estrogen.
  - **Epinephrine** and **norepinephrine** are released by the adrenal medulla and cause physiological changes associated with the sympathetic nervous system.
- **Nature *vs.* nurture** is a classic debate regarding the relative contributions of genetics (nature) and environment (nurture) to an individual's traits. For most traits, both nature and nurture play a role. The relative effects of each can be studied.

- o **Family studies** look at the relative frequency of a trait within a family compared to the general population.

- o **Twin studies** compare concordance rates between monozygotic (identical) and dizygotic (fraternal) twins.

- o **Adoption studies** compare similarities between adopted children and their adoptive parents, relative to similarities with their biological parents.

Development

- The nervous system develops through neurulation, in which the notochord stimulates overlying ectoderm to fold over, creating a **neural tube** topped with **neural crest** cells.

  - o The **neural tube** becomes the central nervous system (CNS).

  - o The **neural crest** cells spread out throughout the body, differentiating into many different tissues.

- **Primitive reflexes** exist in infants and should disappear with age. Most primitive reflexes serve (or served, in earlier times) a protective role. They can reappear in certain nervous system disorders.

  - o In the **rooting reflex**, the infant turns his or her head toward anything that brushes the cheek.

  - o In the **Moro reflex**, the infant extends the arms, then slowly retracts them and cries in response to a sensation of falling.

  - o In the **Babinski reflex**, the big toe is extended and the other toes fan in response to the brushing of the sole of the foot.

  - o In the **grasping reflex**, the infant grabs anything put into his or her hand.

- Developmental milestones give an indication of what skills and abilities a child should have at a given age. Most children adhere closely to these milestones, deviating by only one or two months.

  - o Gross and fine motor abilities progress head to toe and core to periphery.

  - o Social skills shift from parent-oriented to self-oriented to other-oriented.

  - o Language skills become increasingly complex.

ANSWERS TO CONCEPT CHECKS

1.1

1.
- Franz Gall: phrenology; associated development of a trait with growth of its relevant part of the brain.
- Pierre Flourens: extirpation/ablation; concluded that different brain regions have specific functions.
- William James: "father of American psychology"; pushed for importance of studying adaptations of the individual to his or her environment.
- John Dewey: credited with the landmark article on functionalism; argued for studying the entire organism as a whole.
- Paul Broca: correlated pathology with specific brain regions, such as speech production from Broca's area.
- Hermann von Helmoltz: measured speed of a nerve impulse.
- Sir Charles Sherrington: inferred the existence of synapses.

1.2

1. The central nervous system includes the brain and spinal cord. The peripheral nervous system includes most of the cranial and spinal nerves and sensors.

2. Afferent (sensory) neurons bring signals from a sensor to the central nervous system. Efferent (motor) neurons bring signals from the central nervous system to an effector.

3. The somatic nervous system is responsible for voluntary actions; most notably, moving muscles. The autonomic nervous system is responsible for involuntary actions, like heart rate, bronchial dilation, dilation of the eyes, exocrine gland function, and peristalsis.

4. The sympathetic nervous system promotes a fight-or-flight response, with increased heart rate and bronchial dilation, redistribution of blood to locomotor muscles, dilation of the eyes, and slowing of digestive and urinary functions. The parasympathetic nervous system promotes rest-and-digest functions, slowing heart rate and constricting the bronchi, redistributing blood to the gut, promoting exocrine secretions, constricting the pupils, and promoting peristalsis and urinary function.

1.3

1.

Subdivision	Functions
Hindbrain	Balance, motor coordination, breathing, digestion, general arousal processes (sleeping and waking); "vital functioning"
Midbrain	Receives sensory and motor information from the rest of the body; reflexes to auditory and visual stimuli
Forebrain	Complex perceptual, cognitive, and behavioral processes; emotion and memory

2. Methods used for mapping the brain include studying humans with brain lesions, extirpation, stimulation or recording with electrodes (cortical mapping, single-cell electrode recordings, electroencephalogram [EEG]), and regional cerebral blood flow (rCBF).

1.4

1. 1–A, 2–H, 3–F, 4–E, 5–C, 6–I, 7–G, 8–D, 9–B

2.

Lobe	Function
Frontal	Executive function, impulse control, long-term planning (prefrontal cortex), motor function (primary motor cortex), speech production (Broca's area)
Parietal	Sensation of touch, pressure, temperature, and pain (somatosensory cortex); spatial processing, orientation, and manipulation
Occipital	Visual processing
Temporal	Sound processing (auditory cortex), speech perception (Wernicke's area), memory, and emotion (limbic system)

1.5

1. 1–F, 2–E, 3–D, 4–A, 5–B, 6–G, 7–C

2. The hypothalamus controls release of pituitary hormones; the pituitary is the "master gland" that triggers hormone secretion in many other endocrine glands. The adrenal medulla produces adrenaline (epinephrine), which causes sympathetic nervous system effects throughout the body. The adrenal cortex produces cortisol, a stress hormone. The adrenal cortex and testes produce testosterone, which is associated with libido.

3. Nature is defined as heredity, or the influence of inherited characteristics on behavior. Nurture refers to the influence of environment and physical surroundings on behavior. It has long been debated whether nature or nurture has the larger influence; it is a complicated situation, but for most traits, both exert some influence.

4.

Study	Sample Group	Control Group
Family study	Family of genetically related individuals	Unrelated individuals (general population)
Twin study	Monozygotic (MZ, identical) twins	Dizygotic (DZ, fraternal) twins
Adoption study	Adoptive family (relative to adopted child)	Biological family (relative to adopted child)

1.6

1. Neurulation occurs when a furrow is produced from ectoderm overlying the notochord and consists of the neural groove and two neural folds. As the neural folds grow, the cells at their leading edge are called neural crest cells. When the neural folds fuse, this creates the neural tube, which will form the CNS.

2.

Primitive Reflex	Behavior
Rooting	Turns head toward direction of any object touching the cheek
Moro	In response to sudden head movement, arms extend and slowly retract; baby usually cries
Babinski	Extension of big toe and fanning of other toes in response to brushing the sole of the foot
Grasping	Holding onto any object placed in the hand

3. Gross motor development proceeds from head to toe, and from the core to the periphery.

SHARED CONCEPTS

Discrete Practice Questions

Consult your online resources for Full-Length Exams and Passage-Based Questions (for certain chapters).

1. Which of the following is true regarding nerve cells?
   A. Sensory neurons are also referred to as efferent neurons.
   B. Interneurons are also referred to as afferent neurons.
   C. Motor neurons transmit information from receptors to the brain.
   D. Sensory neurons transmit information from receptors to the brain.

2. Which component of the nervous system is NOT involved in the initial reflexive response to pain?
   A. Spinal cord
   B. Cerebral cortex
   C. Interneuron
   D. Motor neuron

3. A child has experienced nervous system damage and can no longer coordinate the movements to dribble a basketball, although she can still walk in an uncoordinated fashion. Which region of the central nervous system was most likely affected?
   A. Forebrain
   B. Midbrain
   C. Hindbrain
   D. Spinal cord

4. The temporal lobe deals with all of the following EXCEPT:
   A. language comprehension.
   B. memory.
   C. emotion.
   D. motor skills.

5. Which part of the brain deals with both homeostasis and emotions?
   A. Cerebellum
   B. Pons
   C. Hypothalamus
   D. Thalamus

6. Which of the following activities would most likely be completed by the right hemisphere of a left-handed person?
   A. Finding a car in a parking lot
   B. Learning a new language
   C. Reading a book for pleasure
   D. Jumping rope with friends

7. Which of the following is/are true with regard to neurulation?
   I. The neural tube differentiates from endoderm.
   II. The neural tube becomes the peripheral nervous system.
   III. Neural crest cells migrate from their original site.
   A. I only
   B. III only
   C. II and III only
   D. I, II, and III

8. Which of the following neurotransmitters is NOT classified as a catecholamine?
   A. Epinephrine
   B. Norepinephrine
   C. Dopamine
   D. Acetylcholine

9. If the amount of acetylcholinesterase, an enzyme that breaks down acetylcholine, is increased, which of the following would likely be the result?

   A. Weakness of muscle movements
   B. Excessive pain or discomfort
   C. Mood swings and mood instability
   D. Auditory and visual hallucinations

10. The adrenal glands do all of the following EXCEPT:

    A. promote the fight-or-flight response via estrogen.
    B. produce stress responses via cortisol.
    C. produce both hormones and neurotransmitters.
    D. release estrogen in males and testosterone in females.

11. A disorder of the pineal gland would most likely result in which of the following disorders?

    A. High blood pressure
    B. Diabetes
    C. Insomnia
    D. Hyperthyroidism

12. Which of the following neurotransmitters is associated with both schizophrenia and Parkinson's disease?

    A. GABA
    B. Serotonin
    C. Dopamine
    D. Enkephalins

13. In a personality survey, which set of twins would be expected to score most similarly?

    A. Identical twins raised in different homes
    B. Fraternal twins raised in different homes
    C. Identical twins raised in the same home
    D. Fraternal twins raised in the same home

14. During a physical examination, a physician brushes the bottom of the foot of a fifty-year-old patient with multiple sclerosis. Her toes are observed to curl toward the bottom of her foot, with no fanning of the toes. This response is:

    A. abnormal, and evidence that she is exhibiting a primitive reflex.
    B. normal, and evidence that she is exhibiting a primitive reflex.
    C. abnormal, and evidence that she is not exhibiting a primitive reflex.
    D. normal, and evidence that she is not exhibiting a primitive reflex.

15. Which of the following fine motor tasks would one expect to see first in an infant?

    A. Grasping for objects with two fingers
    B. Following objects with the eyes
    C. Scribbling with a crayon
    D. Moving a toy from one hand to the other

Explanations to Discrete Practice Questions

1. D

Sensory neurons are also referred to as afferent neurons, while motor neurons are also referred to as efferent neurons, eliminating **choices (A)** and **(B)**. Motor neurons transmit motor information from the brain to the body, contrary to **choice (C)**, and sensory neurons transmit sensory information from receptors to the brain.

2. B

The cerebral cortex is not involved in the initial reflexive response to pain. Instead, the sensory receptors send information to the interneurons in the spinal cord, which stimulate a motor neuron to allow quick withdrawal. While the brain does ultimately get the signal, the reflexive withdrawal has already occurred by that time.

3. C

The hindbrain is responsible for balance and motor coordination, which would be necessary for dribbling a basketball. The midbrain, **choice (B)**, manages sensorimotor reflexes that also promote survival. The forebrain, **choice (A)**, is associated with emotion, memory, and higher-order cognition. The spinal cord, **choice (D)**, is likely not damaged as the child can still walk.

4. D

The temporal lobes have many functions, but motor skills are not associated with this area. The temporal lobes contain Wernicke's area, which is responsible for language comprehension, **choice (A)**. The temporal lobes also function in emotion and memory, **choices (B)** and **(C)**, because they contain the amygdala and hippocampus. Motor skills are associated with the frontal lobe (primary motor cortex), basal ganglia (smooth movements), and cerebellum (coordination).

5. C

The hypothalamus is responsible for homeostatic and emotional functions. The cerebellum, **choice (A)**, is responsible for maintaining posture and balance while the pons, **choice (B)**, is above the medulla and contains sensory and motor tracts between the cortex and the medulla. The thalamus, **choice (D)**, acts as a relay station for sensory information.

6. A

The right hemisphere is usually the nondominant hemisphere, even in left-handed individuals. Sense of direction is an ability of the nondominant hemisphere. The other answer choices are all abilities attributed to the dominant hemisphere.

7. B

Neurulation occurs when the notochord causes differentiation of overlying ectoderm into the neural tube and neural crest cells. The neural tube ultimately becomes the central nervous system (brain and spinal cord), and neural crest cells migrate to other sites in the body to differentiate into a number of different tissues. Thus, only statement III is true.

8. D

Acetylcholine is not a catecholamine; however epinephrine, norepinephrine, and dopamine are.

9. A

If there were increased amounts of acetylcholinesterase, more acetylcholine would be degraded, lowering acetylcholine levels in the body. Low levels of acetylcholine would result in weakness or paralysis of muscles. Pain, **choice (B)**, could result if one were injured and endorphins were found in low levels. Mood swings, **choice (C)**, could be a result of varying levels of serotonin. Hallucinations, **choice (D)**, have been seen to result from high levels of dopamine.

10. A

The adrenal glands do promote the fight-or-flight response, but through epinephrine and norepinephrine, not estrogen. The adrenal cortex produces both estrogen and testosterone in both sexes, as mentioned in **choice (D)**, thus serving as a source of estrogen in males and testosterone in females.

11. C

The pineal gland is responsible for producing melatonin, which controls the body's circadian rhythm. Insomnia would be a disturbance of this circadian rhythm, and may be attributable to a pineal gland disorder in some cases. Hypertension, diabetes, and hyperthyroidism would be unrelated to issues with the pineal gland.

12. C

Schizophrenia is associated with high levels of dopamine or high sensitivity to dopamine. Parkinson's disease is associated with destruction of the dopaminergic neurons in the basal ganglia.

13. C

Personality is seen to be somewhat hereditary, as monozygotic, or identical, twins have been seen to express more of the same personality traits. However, environment is also a factor. Thus, identical twins raised in the same home would be expected to have the most similar personalities.

14. D

The Babinski reflex is a primitive reflex that refers to an extension of the big toe accompanied by fanning of the other toes. It is normal in infants, but should disappear with time—certainly by the time a child begins to walk. In a fifty-year-old woman, the Babinski reflex would be abnormal. However, despite her neurological illness, this patient is exhibiting a normal response to the brushing of her foot; that is, she is not showing the Babinski reflex.

15. B

Motor skills tend to develop from the core toward the periphery. Following objects with the eyes occurs around four weeks of age. The other actions all require movements of the hand, which do not occur in an organized fashion until later.

2

Sensation and Perception

In This Chapter

Chapter Profile

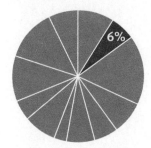

The content in this chapter should be relevant to about 6% of all questions about the Behavioral Sciences on the MCAT.

This chapter covers material from the following AAMC content category:

6A: Sensing the environment

Introduction

It's your first time visiting Europe. You can't wait to see the glorious, ornate architecture, sample the local cuisine, and listen to the traditional music. You want to take in the "sights and sounds" of this society; that is, have a sensory experience of this culture. To truly experience any location (or vacation!), your sensory receptors—for vision, hearing, taste, smell, and somatosensation—gather all of the information from the world around you, and your brain filters and processes that information to focus your attention on its most salient details. This is a complex interplay between many sensory networks, composed of sensory processes, neural tracts, and the brain itself.

You finally land in your European destination and begin to explore. You turn the corner on one street and are suddenly overwhelmed with a odd feeling of familiarity. *But . . . I've never been here before!* you think as the strange sensation of *déjà vu* sets in. Everything just seems "right": the signs are in the "right" place, the cars look familiar, and everything is bizarrely "where you expect." *Déjà vu* (French: "already seen") comes from many sources; in one form, it is believed to come from processing information faster than expected. When we process an image (or other sensory input) for the first time, it actually takes longer than the next time we are exposed to that same stimulus. Thus, an exposure to the same scenery at an earlier time through a movie or television show may have primed you for *déjà vu*.

But we don't feel *déjà vu* every time we see an image again; that's where memory comes in—a topic we'll discuss in Chapter 3 of *MCAT Behavioral Sciences Review*. Indeed, it is the brain's sensory receptors saying, *Yes, you have seen this before!* in tandem with the memory system saying, *But I don't know when or where!* that contributes to this phenomenon of *déjà vu*.

In this chapter, we will focus on the concepts of sensation and its associated receptors, including the eye and hair cells in the ear, as well as perception and the complex brain functions associated with processing sensory information. We'll briefly touch on the other sensory modalities, including vestibular sense, taste, smell, somatosensation, and kinesthetic sense, and consider the roles they play in helping us interact with the world.

2.1 Sensation *vs.* Perception

LEARNING GOALS

After Chapter 2.1, you will be able to:

- Explain the pathway for a stimulus to reach conscious perception
- Connect the common sensory receptors to their functions
- Describe absolute threshold, threshold of conscious perception, and difference threshold
- Explain Weber's law and signal detection theory
- Describe how sensory adaptation affects a difference threshold

In common parlance, we often use the terms "sensation" and "perception" interchangeably, as synonyms. However, in the field of psychology, these two terms have very specific definitions and are commonly contrasted. **Sensation** more appropriately aligns with **transduction**, which is the conversion of physical, electromagnetic, auditory, and other information from our internal and external environment to electrical signals in the nervous system. Sensation is performed by receptors in the peripheral nervous system, which forward the stimuli to the central nervous system in the form of action potentials and neurotransmitters. Sensation can therefore be thought of as a raw signal, which is unfiltered and unprocessed until it enters the central nervous system.

Perception, on the other hand, refers to the processing of this information to make sense of its significance. These complex manipulations include both external sensory experience and the internal activities of the brain and spinal cord. Perception thus helps us make sense of the world. The difference between sensation and perception is key to the challenge of creating artificial intelligence: we can easily create sensors for robots to pick up information from their environment, but teaching them how to comprehend and respond to that information is far more challenging.

Sensory processing is a common topic on the MCAT; you should understand not only the definitions of these terms, but be able to apply the concepts herein to your own day-to-day sensory experiences.

SENSORY RECEPTORS

Sensory receptors are neurons that respond to stimuli and trigger electrical signals. Some of these stimuli originate outside of the body, and are referred to as **distal stimuli** prior to reaching the body, as they are part of the "outside" world. For example, a campfire is a distal stimulus. The photons that reach the observer's rods and cones, as well as the heat the observer feels, are proximal stimuli. **Proximal stimuli** directly interact with and affect the sensory receptors, and inform the observer about the presence of distal stimuli. Sensory receptors may encode multiple aspects of a stimulus. For example, photoreceptors respond to light and can encode not only the brightness of the light, but also its color and shape. The relationship between the physical nature of stimuli and the sensations and perceptions they evoke is studied in the field of **psychophysics**.

In order to inform the central nervous system, the signals from these stimuli must pass through specific sensory pathways. In each case, different types of receptors—generally nerve endings or specific sensory cells—receive the stimulus and transmit the data to the central nervous system through sensory ganglia. **Ganglia** are collections of neuron cell bodies found outside the central nervous system. Once transduction occurs, the electrochemical energy is sent along neural pathways to various **projection areas** in the brain, which further analyze the sensory input.

Sensory receptors differ from one sense to another. There are over a dozen recognized sensory receptors, but the MCAT is unlikely to test even half of those. The most heavily tested receptors include:

- Photoreceptors: respond to electromagnetic waves in the visible spectrum (sight)
- Hair cells: respond to movement of fluid in the inner ear structures (hearing, rotational and linear acceleration)
- Nociceptors: respond to painful or noxious stimuli (somatosensation)
- Thermoreceptors: respond to changes in temperature (thermosensation)
- Osmoreceptors: respond to the osmolarity of the blood (water homeostasis)
- Olfactory receptors: respond to volatile compounds (smell)
- Taste receptors: respond to dissolved compounds (taste)

THRESHOLDS

Perception, like sensation, is closely tied to the biology and physiology of interpreting the world around us. However, unlike sensation, perception is inextricably linked to experience and both internal and external biases. Sensations are relayed to the brain, which perceives the significance of the stimulus; for example, determining

Mnemonic

Distal = in the **distance**
Proximal = in close **proximity**

whether something is hot or cold. The same sensation can produce radically different perceptions in different people, and because these variations must be explained by central nervous system activity, perception is considered a part of psychology.

A good example of the psychological element of perception is a **threshold**—the minimum amount of a stimulus that renders a difference in perception. For example, the temperature may noticeably change from warm to cool when the sun sets, but subtle fluctuations in temperature throughout the day are generally unnoticeable because they are below the difference threshold. If sound increases 10 dB (ten times the sound intensity), this is usually very obvious; if it increased only 0.1 dB, it may be too small to detect. There are three main types of thresholds: the absolute threshold, the threshold of conscious perception, and the difference threshold.

Absolute Threshold

The **absolute threshold** is the minimum of stimulus energy that is needed to activate a sensory system. It is therefore a threshold in sensation, not in perception. Sounds of extremely low intensity may still cause slight vibrations in the sensory receptors of the inner ear, but these may not be significant enough to be converted to an action potential through transduction. While most human sensory systems are extremely sensitive, all systems also have this minimum sensory level below which the stimulus will not be transduced to the central nervous system. For example, the absolute threshold for sweet taste is a teaspoon of sucrose dissolved in two gallons of water. On a clear, dark night with no other lights shining, the eye can just detect the light of one candle burning thirty miles away. When we are talking about an absolute threshold, we're talking about how bright, loud, or intense a stimulus must be before it is sensed.

Threshold of Conscious Perception

It is possible for sensory systems to send signals to the central nervous system without a person perceiving them. This may be because the stimulus is too subtle to demand our attention, or may last for too brief of a duration for the brain to fully process the information. Thresholds can also be called **limina**. Thus, **subliminal perception** often refers to the perception of a stimulus below a given threshold. Usually, this term refers to the threshold of conscious perception. Note the difference between the absolute threshold and the threshold for conscious perception: a stimulus below the absolute threshold will not be transduced, and thus never reaches the central nervous system. A stimulus below the threshold of conscious perception arrives at the central nervous system, but does not reach the higher-order brain regions that control attention and consciousness. Contrary to common thinking, there is actually little practical value to using subliminal perception to sell products.

One common way to analyze this limit in human perceptive ability is to use **discrimination testing,** also referred to as **psychophysical discrimination testing**. A participant is presented with a stimulus that is varied slightly, and then is asked to identify whether there is a difference in the second stimulus. The difference between the current stimulus and the original is increased until the participant

MCAT Expertise

On the MCAT, thresholds will frequently be used in conjunction with subjects in studies. Be on the lookout for experimental design questions when thresholds appear in a passage.

Key Concept

The absolute threshold is the minimum intensity at which a stimulus will be transduced (converted into action potentials).

Bridge

You already know one of the absolute thresholds from the discussion of sound in Chapter 7 of *MCAT Physics and Math Review*. Remember that I_0 $(10^{-12}\frac{W}{m^2})$ in the equation for sound level is the absolute threshold of normal human hearing.

reports noticing a change. For example, a participant may be shown a shade of blue and asked to indicate when the shade has actually changed as the experimenter displays shades that are increasingly different from the reference blue.

Difference Threshold

The **difference threshold** or **just-noticeable difference** (**jnd**) refers to the minimum difference in magnitude between two stimuli before one can perceive this difference. For example, most individuals without formal ear training find it impossible to discriminate between two sound waves at 440 Hz and 441 Hz. While they are different frequencies, the perception of the tones is that they are the same. In this range of sound frequencies, the just-noticeable difference is about 3 Hz; thus, most individuals just begin to hear a difference between sound waves at 440 Hz and 443 Hz.

While the jnd was given as 3 Hz above, it is far more important to focus on the ratio between the change in stimulus and its original value, rather than the actual difference between the frequencies. Thus, the jnd for sound frequency is more accurately quantified as 0.68 percent (3 Hz ÷ 440 Hz). This relationship has been formalized in **Weber's law**, which states that there is a constant ratio between the change in stimulus magnitude needed to produce a jnd and the magnitude of the original stimulus. Thus, for higher-magnitude stimuli, the actual difference must be larger to produce a jnd. If we've calculated the jnd as 0.68 percent for sound frequency, then an individual would be expected to be able to discriminate between sounds at 1000 Hz and 1006.8 Hz (6.8 Hz = 0.68% of 1000 Hz), but not between 1000 Hz and 1003 Hz (3 Hz = 0.3% of 1000 Hz). Weber's law appears to be accurate for all sensory modalities, except at the extremely high and low ends of each range.

SIGNAL DETECTION THEORY

Perception of stimuli can also be affected by nonsensory factors, such as experiences (memory), motives, and expectations. This concept is termed **signal detection theory**, which focuses on the changes in our perception of the same stimuli depending on both internal (psychological) and external (environmental) context. For example, how loud would someone need to yell your name in a crowd to get your attention? Part of the answer comes from psychology: If you heard something that sounds vaguely like your name, would you likely acknowledge it or not? The answer is not merely a yes or no, but would depend on the size of the crowd; your expectation of being called; social factors, like the makeup of the crowd and your comfort with the other individuals; and personality: highly sociable, extroverted individuals tend to hear their names more easily than quieter, introverted individuals.

Signal detection theory also allows us to explore **response bias**, which refers to the tendency of subjects to systematically respond to a stimulus in a particular way due to nonsensory factors. A basic signal detection experiment consists of many trials;

MCAT Expertise

When the MCAT brings up Weber's law, questions will usually give a numerical relationship and then ask for it to be applied; typically, it simply amounts to applying a ratio.

Real World

On the surface, signal detection experiments would appear to be easy tasks—shouldn't an individual easily be able to tell if he or she perceived something or not? However, consider the thought processes that occur when you're quietly studying in the library with your phone on silent and you suddenly think you may have heard a buzz. *Is my phone ringing?* you wonder. You freeze in place and wait for another buzz; even if it doesn't come, you may still be so convinced you heard a signal that you still check your phone. Perception is not a passive matter!

during each trial, a stimulus (signal) may or may not be presented. Trials in which the signal is presented are called **catch trials**, whereas those in which the signal is not presented are called **noise trials**. After each trial, the subject is asked to indicate whether or not a signal was given. There are therefore four possible outcomes for each trial, as illustrated in Figure 2.1: **hits**, in which the subject correctly perceives the signal; **misses**, in which the subject fails to perceive a given signal; **false alarms**, in which the subject seems to perceive a signal when none was given; and **correct negatives**, in which the subject correctly identifies that no signal was given. A significant proportion of misses or false alarms gives an indication of response bias in the subject.

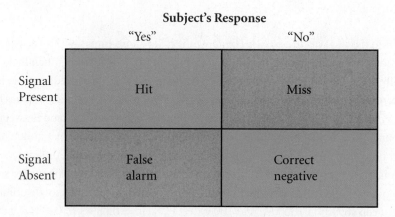

Figure 2.1. Possible Outcomes from a Signal Detection Experiment Trial

ADAPTATION

Our detection of a stimulus can change over time through **adaptation**. Adaptation can have both a physiological (sensory) component and a psychological (perceptual) component. For example, the pupils of the eyes will dilate in the dark and constrict in the light to make our vision more similar in different environments as part of physiological adaptation. In loud environments, we contract small muscles in the middle ear to reduce the amount of vibration of the ossicles, reducing sound intensity. We also adapt to somatosensory stimuli; cold water no longer seems so cold once our bodies "get used to it." Once we're dressed, we stop feeling the clothes on our bodies until we have a reason to think about them. Adaptation is one way the mind and body try to focus attention on only the most relevant stimuli, which are usually changes in the environment around us.

MCAT Concept Check 2.1:

Before you move on, assess your understanding of the material with these questions.

1. What is the pathway for a stimulus to reach conscious perception?

_____

2. Match each sensory receptor to its function:

1. Hair cell	A. Sense painful or bothersome physical stimuli
2. Nociceptor	B. Sense changes in temperature
3. Olfactory receptor	C. Sense electromagnetic radiation in the visible range
4. Osmoreceptor	
5. Photoreceptor	D. Sense changes in blood concentration
6. Taste receptor	E. Sense volatile chemicals
7. Thermoreceptor	F. Sense motion of fluid in the inner ear
	G. Sense dissolved chemicals

3. For each of the thresholds below, provide a brief description:

- Absolute threshold:

_____

- Threshold of conscious perception:

_____

- Difference threshold:

_____

4. What aspect of thresholds do Weber's law and signal detection theory focus on?

- Weber's law:

_____

- Signal detection theory:

_____

5. How does sensory adaptation affect a difference threshold?

_____

2.2 Vision

LEARNING GOALS

After Chapter 2.2, you will be able to:

- List the functions of the parts of the eye, including the cornea, pupil, iris, ciliary body, canal of Schlemm, lens, retina, and sclera
- Describe parallel processing
- Identify the cell types responsible for color, shape, and motion detection
- Recall the structures in the visual pathway:

Vision is a highly adapted sense in human beings. With the ability to sense brightness, color, shape, and movement, and then to integrate this information to create a cohesive three-dimensional model of the world, the visual pathways are extremely important to everyday life. In fact, vision is the only sense to which an entire lobe of the brain is devoted: the occipital lobe.

STRUCTURE AND FUNCTION OF THE EYE

The anatomy of the eye is shown in Figure 2.2.

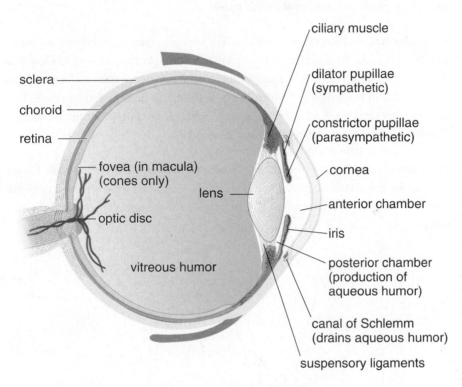

Figure 2.2. Anatomy of the Eye

The eye is a specialized organ used to detect light in the form of photons. Most of the exposed portion of the eye is covered by a thick structural layer known as the **sclera**, or the white of the eye. The sclera does not cover the frontmost portion of the eye, the cornea. The eye is supplied with nutrients by two sets of blood vessels: the **choroidal vessels**, a complex intermingling of blood vessels between the sclera and the retina, and the **retinal vessels**. The innermost layer of the eye is the **retina**, which contains the actual photoreceptors that transduce light into electrical information the brain can process.

When entering the eye, light passes first through the **cornea**, a clear, domelike window in the front of the eye, which gathers and focuses the incoming light. The front of the eye is divided into the **anterior chamber**, which lies in front of the iris, and the **posterior chamber** between the iris and the lens. The **iris**, which is the colored part of the eye, is composed of two muscles: the **dilator pupillae**, which opens the pupil under sympathetic stimulation; and the **constrictor pupillae**, which constricts the pupil under parasympathetic stimulation. The iris is continuous with the **choroid**, as is the **ciliary body**, which produces the **aqueous humor** that bathes the front part of the eye before draining into the **canal of Schlemm**. The **lens** lies right behind the iris and helps control the refraction of the incoming light. Contraction of the

ciliary muscle, a component of the ciliary body, is under parasympathetic control. As the muscle contracts, it pulls on the **suspensory ligaments** and changes the shape of the lens, a phenomenon known as **accommodation**. Behind the lens lies the **vitreous**, a transparent gel that supports the retina.

The **retina** is in the back of the eye and is like a screen consisting of neural elements and blood vessels. Its function is to convert incoming photons of light to electrical signals. It is actually considered part of the central nervous system and develops as an outgrowth of brain tissue. The **duplexity** or **duplicity theory of vision** states that the retina contains two kinds of photoreceptors: those specialized for light-and-dark detection and those specialized for color detection.

The retina is made up of approximately 6 million cones and 120 million rods. **Cones** are used for color vision and to sense fine details. Cones are most effective in bright light and come in three forms, which are named for the wavelengths of light they best absorb, as shown in Figure 2.3.

Figure 2.3. Relative Absorption of the Three Types of Cones at Different Wavelengths
The cones are named for the wavelengths at which they have highest light absorption: short (S, also called blue), medium (M, green), and long (L, red).

Mnemonic

Cones are for color vision. **Rods** function best in "**rod**uced" light.

In reduced illumination, **rods** are more functional and only allow sensation of light and dark because they all contain a single pigment called **rhodopsin**. Rods have low sensitivity to details and are not involved in color vision, but permit night vision.

While there are many more rods than cones in the human eye, the central section of the retina, called the macula, has a high concentration of cones; in fact, its centermost point, called the **fovea**, contains only cones. As one moves further away from the fovea, the concentration of rods increases while the concentration of cones decreases. Therefore, visual acuity is best at the fovea, and the fovea is most sensitive in normal daylight vision. There is a blind spot where the optic nerve leaves the eye, as there are no photoreceptors here, as shown in Figure 2.4.

Macula

Fovea

Optic disk

Figure 2.4. Specialized Regions of the Retina

The connection between the rods and cones and the optic nerve is not direct. There are several layers of neurons in between, as shown in Figure 2.5: bipolar cells, ganglion cells, horizontal cells, and amacrine cells. Rods and cones connect with **bipolar cells**, which highlight gradients between adjacent rods or cones. Bipolar cells synapse with **ganglion cells**, which group together to form the **optic nerve**. These bipolar, horizontal, amacrine, and ganglion cells fall "in between" the rods and cones and the optic nerve, and are located in front of the rods and cones closer to the front of the eye. This means that information is being transmitted "forward" towards the lens from the rod and cone cells, through a series of integration steps, until the signal reaches the ganglion cells. Because there are many, many more receptors than ganglion cells, each ganglion cell has to represent the combined activity of many rods and cones. This results in a loss of details as information from the photoreceptors is combined. As the number of receptors that converge through the bipolar neurons onto one ganglion cell increases, the resolution decreases. On average, the number of cones converging onto an individual ganglion cell is smaller than for rods. Therefore, color vision has a greater sensitivity to fine detail than black-and-white vision does.

Amacrine and **horizontal cells** receive input from multiple retinal cells in the same area before the information is passed on to ganglion cells. They can thereby accentuate slight differences between the visual information in each bipolar cell. These cells are important for edge detection, as they increase our perception of contrasts.

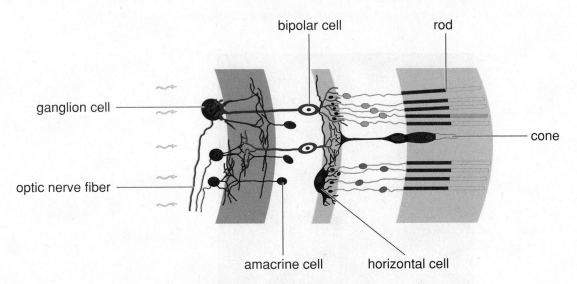

Figure 2.5. Cells of the Retina

VISUAL PATHWAYS

Visual pathways refer to both the physical anatomical connections between the eyes and the brain and the flow of visual information along these connections. As demonstrated in Figure 2.6, each eye's right visual field projects onto the left half of each eye's retina and each eye's left visual field projects onto the right half of each eye's retina. As the signal travels through the optic nerves toward the brain, the first significant event occurs at the **optic chiasm**. Here, the fibers from the nasal half (closer to the nose) of each retina cross paths. These fibers carry the temporal visual field (further toward the side of the head) from each eye. Because the temporal fibers (which carry the nasal visual field) do *not* cross in the chiasm, this reorganization means that all fibers corresponding to the left visual field from both eyes project into the right side of the brain, and all fibers corresponding to the right visual field from both eyes project into the left side of the brain. These reorganized pathways are called **optic tracts** once they leave the optic chiasm.

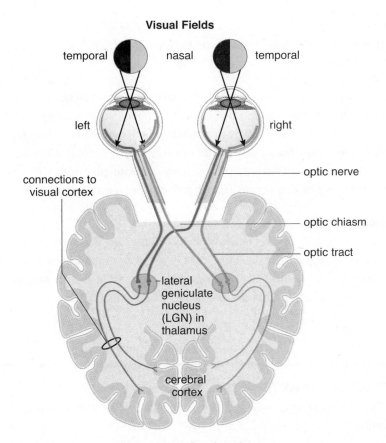

Visual Fields

temporal   nasal   temporal

left   right

optic nerve

connections to
visual cortex

optic chiasm

optic tract

lateral
geniculate
nucleus
(LGN) in
thalamus

cerebral
cortex

Figure 2.6. Visual Pathways

From the optic chiasm, the information goes to several different places in the brain: the **lateral geniculate nucleus** (**LGN**) of the **thalamus**, through radiations in the temporal and parietal lobes to the **visual cortex** in the **occipital lobe**. There are also inputs into the **superior colliculus**, which controls some responses to visual stimuli and reflexive eye movements.

PROCESSING

While being able to sense all of the light information around us is useful in its own right, we must be able to make sense of visual stimuli to be able to interact with the environment. One process that helps create a cohesive image of the world is parallel processing. **Parallel processing** is the ability to simultaneously analyze and combine information regarding color, shape, and motion. Then, these features can be compared to our memories to determine what is being viewed. For example, most people can recognize a moving car very easily from a distance because they are familiar with the usual motions and shapes of cars.

Parallel processing is not only a psychological model, but also has a correlate in neuroscience called **feature detection**. Our visual pathways contain cells specialized in detection of color, shape, or motion.

Real World

When a there is a loud, sudden sound, the superior colliculus aligns the eyes with the likely stimulus. In other words, it's the superior colliculus (as well as the sympathetic nervous system) that gives us the "deer in the headlights" appearance during the startle response.

Color

As described above, cones are responsible for color vision.

Shape

Shape refers not only to the three-dimensional geometry of an object, but also our ability to discriminate an object of interest from the background by detecting its boundaries. Shape is detected by **parvocellular cells**, which have very high color **spatial resolution**; that is, they permit us to see very fine detail when thoroughly examining an object. However, parvocellular cells can only work with stationary or slow-moving objects because they have very low **temporal resolution**.

Motion

Motion is detected by **magnocellular cells** because they have very high temporal resolution. However, magnocellular cells have low spatial resolution, so much of the rich detail of an object can no longer be seen once it is motion. Magnocellular cells therefore provide a blurry but moving image of an object.

Mnemonic

Magnocellular cells specialize in motion detection.

MCAT Concept Check 2.2:

Before you move on, assess your understanding of the material with these questions.

1. List the functions of the various parts of the eye:

   • Cornea:

   _____

   • Pupil:

   _____

   • Iris:

   _____

   • Ciliary body:

   _____

   • Canal of Schlemm:

   _____

   • Lens:

   _____

   • Retina:

   _____

   • Sclera:

   _____

2. List the structures in the visual pathway, from where light enters the cornea to the visual projection areas in the brain.

_____

3. What is parallel processing?

_____

4. In feature detection, what type of cells are responsible for color? Shape? Motion?

   • Color:

   _____

   • Shape:

   _____

   • Motion:

   _____

2.3 Hearing and Vestibular Sense

LEARNING GOALS

After Chapter 2.3, you will be able to:

- Identify the structures used to detect linear acceleration and rotational acceleration
- Explain how the structural features of the cochlea and the hair cells are able to transmit information about pitch of an incoming sound to the brain
- List the structures in the auditory pathway

The ear is a complex organ responsible not only for our sense of hearing, but also for both rotational and linear acceleration (**vestibular sense**). These senses are critically important to our ability to get around in the world, and their associated structures are encased in some of the densest bone of the body to protect them from damage.

STRUCTURE AND FUNCTION OF THE EAR

The ear is divided into three parts, as shown in Figure 2.7: the outer, middle, and inner ear. A sound wave first reaches the cartilaginous outside part of the ear, called the **pinna** or **auricle**. The main function of the pinna is to channel sound waves into the **external auditory canal**, which directs the sound waves to the **tympanic membrane (eardrum)**. The membrane vibrates in phase with the incoming sound waves. The frequency of the sound wave determines the rate at which the tympanic membrane vibrates: it moves back and forth at a high rate for high-frequency sounds and more slowly for low-frequency sounds. Louder sounds have greater **intensity**, which corresponds to an increased amplitude of this vibration.

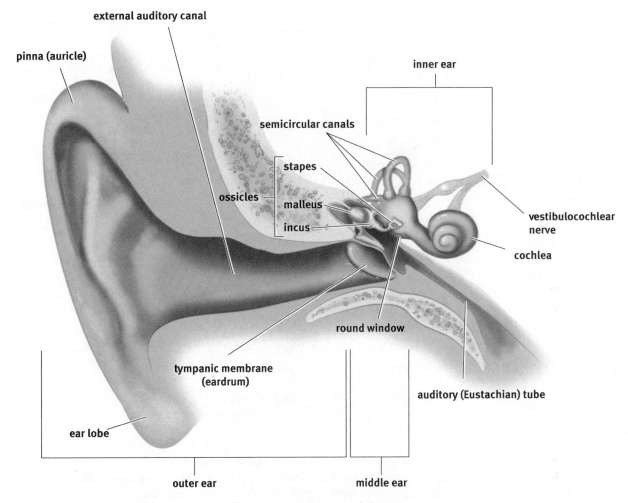

Figure 2.7. Anatomy of the Ear

The tympanic membrane divides the outer ear from the middle ear. The middle ear houses the three smallest bones in the body, called **ossicles**. The ossicles help transmit and amplify the vibrations from the tympanic membrane to the inner ear. The **malleus** (**hammer**) is affixed to the tympanic membrane; it acts on the **incus** (**anvil**), which acts on the **stapes** (**stirrup**). The baseplate of the stapes rests on the oval window of the cochlea, which is the entrance to the inner ear. The middle ear is connected to the nasal cavity via the **Eustachian tube**, which helps equalize pressure between the middle ear and the environment.

The inner ear sits within a **bony labyrinth**, which contains the **cochlea**, **vestibule**, and **semicircular canals**, as shown in Figure 2.8. These structures are continuous with each other and are mostly filled by the **membranous labyrinth**, which is bathed with a potassium-rich fluid called **endolymph**. The membranous labyrinth is suspended within the bony labyrinth by a thin layer of another fluid called **perilymph**. Perilymph simultaneously transmits vibrations from the outside world and cushions the inner ear structures.

Bridge

Remember that sound is a longitudinal wave carried through air (or another medium), which causes displacement of particles parallel to the axis of sound propagation. In other words, when a sound wave hits your eardrum, it literally causes it to oscillate back and forth because of moving air particles. Sound is discussed in Chapter 7 of *MCAT Physics and Math Review*.

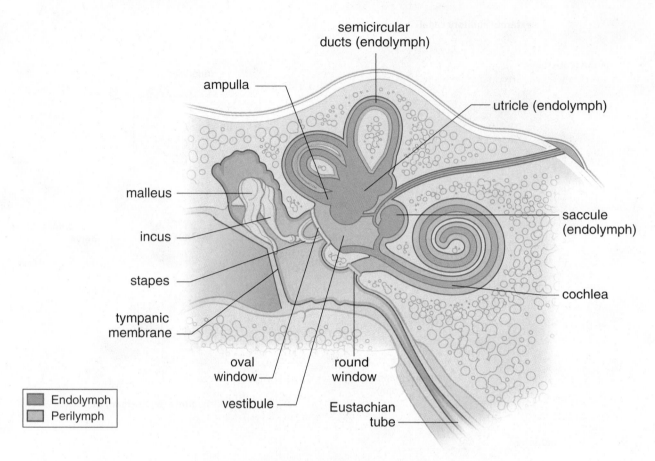

Figure 2.8. The Membranous and Bony Labyrinth
The membranous labyrinth is filled with endolymph (blue); it is suspended within
the bony labyrinth, which is filled with perilymph (purple).

Bridge

The junction between the stapes and the oval window is extremely similar to a thermodynamic gas–piston system, as described in Chapter 3 of *MCAT Physics and Math Review*. However, fluids are not as compressible as gases; therefore, the round window must be present to allow the perilymph in the cochlea to actually move back and forth with the stapedial footplate.

Cochlea

The **cochlea** is a spiral-shaped organ divided into three parts called **scalae**, as shown in Figure 2.9. All three scalae run the entire length of the cochlea. The middle scala houses the actual hearing apparatus, called the **organ of Corti**, which rests on a thin, flexible membrane called the **basilar membrane**. The organ of Corti is composed of thousands of hair cells, which are bathed in **endolymph**. On top of the organ of Corti is a relatively immobile membrane called the **tectorial membrane**. The other two scalae, filled with **perilymph**, surround the hearing apparatus and are continuous with the oval and round windows of the cochlea. Thus, sound entering the cochlea through the oval window causes vibrations in perilymph, which are transmitted to the basilar membrane. Because fluids are essentially incompressible, the **round window**, a membrane-covered hole in the cochlea, permits the perilymph to actually move within the cochlea. Like the rods and cones of the eye, the hair cells in the organ of Corti convert the physical stimulus into an electrical signal, which is carried to the central nervous system by the **auditory (vestibulocochlear) nerve**.

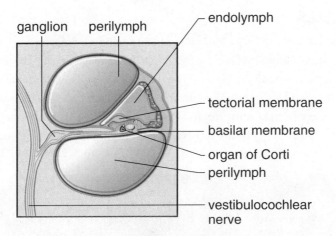

Figure 2.9. Structure of the Cochlea (Cross-Section)

Vestibule

The **vestibule** refers to the portion of the bony labyrinth that contains the **utricle** and **saccule**. These structures are sensitive to linear acceleration, so are used as part of the balancing apparatus and to determine one's orientation in three-dimensional space. The utricle and saccule contain modified hair cells covered with **otoliths**. As the body accelerates, these otoliths will resist that motion. This bends and stimulates the underlying hair cells, which send a signal to the brain.

Semicircular Canals

While the utricle and saccule are sensitive to linear acceleration, the three **semicircular canals** are sensitive to rotational acceleration. The semicircular canals are arranged perpendicularly to each other, and each ends in a swelling called an **ampulla**, where hair cells are located. When the head rotates, endolymph in the semicircular canal resists this motion, bending the underlying hair cells, which send a signal to the brain.

AUDITORY PATHWAYS

The **auditory pathways** in the brain are a bit more complex than the visual pathways. Most sound information passes through the vestibulocochlear nerve to the brainstem, where it ascends to the **medial geniculate nucleus (MGN)** of the thalamus. From there, it projects to the **auditory cortex** in the temporal lobe for sound processing. Some information is also sent to the **superior olive**, which localizes the sound, and the **inferior colliculus**, which is involved in the startle reflex and helps keep the eyes fixed on a point while the head is turned (vestibulo–ocular reflex).

Mnemonic

The lateral geniculate nucleus (LGN) is for light; the medial geniculate nucleus (MGN) is for music.

HAIR CELLS

Hair cells are named for the long tufts of **stereocilia** on their top surface, shown in Figure 2.10. As vibrations reach the basilar membrane underlying the organ of Corti, the stereocilia adorning the hair cells begin to sway back and forth within the endolymph. The swaying causes the opening of ion channels, which cause a receptor potential. Certain hair cells are also directly connected to the immobile tectorial membrane; these hair cells are involved in amplifying the incoming sound.

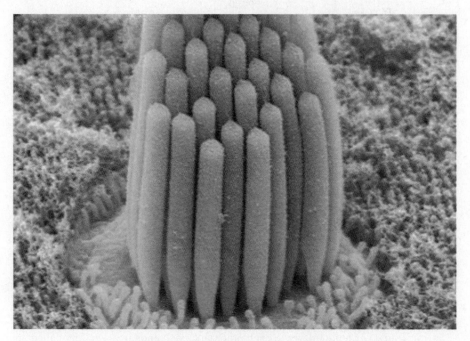

Figure 2.10. Stereocilia of a Hair Cell
Movement of fluid inside the cochlea leads to depolarization
of the neuron associated with the hair cell.

The basilar membrane changes thickness depending on its location in the cochlea. The accepted theory on sound perception is **place theory**, which states that the location of a hair cell on the basilar membrane determines the perception of pitch when that hair cell is vibrated. The highest-frequency pitches cause vibrations of the basilar membrane very close to the oval window, whereas low-frequency pitches cause vibrations at the apex, away from the oval window. Thus, the cochlea is **tonotopically** organized: which hair cells are vibrating gives the brain an indication of the pitch of the sound.

MCAT Concept Check 2.3:

Before you move on, assess your understanding of the material with these questions.

1. What structures are used to detect linear acceleration? Rotational acceleration?

   • Linear acceleration:

   _____

   • Rotational acceleration:

   _____

2. List the structures in the auditory pathway, from where sound enters the pinna to the auditory projection areas in the brain.

   _____

3. How does the organization of the cochlea indicate the pitch of an incoming sound?

   _____

2.4 Other Senses

LEARNING GOALS

After Chapter 2.4, you will be able to:

- List the structures in the olfactory pathway
- Distinguish between the chemicals detected by the nose and mouth
- Recall the four main modalities of somatosensation

While vision and hearing are, by far, the most heavily tested senses on the MCAT, the other senses are still considered fair game on Test Day. These include the chemical senses of smell and taste; somatosensation, which includes all of the modalities of "touch"; and kinesthetic sense.

SMELL

Smell is considered one of the chemical senses, which means that it responds to incoming chemicals from the outside world. Specifically, smell responds to volatile or aerosolized compounds. **Olfactory chemoreceptors** (**olfactory nerves**) are located in olfactory epithelium in the upper part of the nasal cavity. Chemical stimuli must bind to their respective chemoreceptors to cause a signal. There are a tremendous number of specific chemoreceptors, which allows us to recognize subtle differences in similar scents, such as lavender and jasmine.

Smell can also carry interpersonal information through the medium of **pheromones**. Pheromones have debatable effects on humans, but play an enormous role in many animals' social, foraging, and sexual behavior. Pheromones are secreted by one person or animal, and once bonded with chemoreceptors, compel or urge another to behave in a specific way.

As is true with all senses, there is a defined **olfactory pathway** to the brain. Odor molecules are inhaled into the nasal passages and then contact the olfactory nerves in the olfactory epithelium. These receptor cells are activated, sending signals to the **olfactory bulb**. These signals are then relayed via the **olfactory tract** to higher regions of the brain, including the limbic system.

TASTE

As a sense, taste is often simpler than we imagine. There are five basic tastes: sweet, sour, salty, bitter, and *umami* (savory). Flavor is not synonymous with taste, but rather refers to the complex interplay between smell and taste, which can be affected by nonchemical stimuli like texture and the individual's mood.

Tastes are also detected by **chemoreceptors**; however, unlike olfactory chemoreceptors, taste chemoreceptors are sensitive to dissolved compounds. Saltiness, for example, is a reaction to alkali metals, and is generally triggered by the sodium found in table salt. Sourness, on the other hand, is a reaction to acid, such as lemon juice or vinegar. Sweet, bitter, and savory flavors are also triggered by specific molecules binding to receptors. The receptors for taste are groups of cells called **taste buds**, which are found in little bumps on the tongue called **papillae**. Taste information travels from taste buds to the brainstem, and then ascend to the **taste center** in the thalamus before traveling to higher-order brain regions.

SOMATOSENSATION

Somatosensation is often reduced to "touch" when listed as a sense, but is actually quite complex. It is usually described as having four modalities: pressure, vibration, pain, and temperature. There are at least five different types of receptors that receive tactile information, including:

- **Pacinian corpuscles:** respond to deep pressure and vibration
- **Meissner corpuscles:** respond to light touch
- **Merkle cells (discs):** respond to deep pressure and texture
- **Ruffini endings:** respond to stretch
- **Free nerve endings:** respond to pain and temperature

Transduction occurs in the receptors, which send the signal to the central nervous system where it eventually travels to the **somatosensory cortex** in the parietal lobe.

There are three additional concepts related to touch perception that are important to know: two-point thresholds, physiological zero, and gate theory of pain. A **two-point threshold** refers to the minimum distance necessary between two points of stimulation on the skin such that the points will be felt as two distinct stimuli. The size of the two-point threshold depends on the density of nerves in the particular area of skin being tested.

Temperature is judged relative to **physiological zero**, or the normal temperature of the skin (between 86 and 97°F). Thus, an object feels "cold" because it is under physiological zero; an object feels "warm" because it is above physiological zero.

Pain perception is part of the somatosensory system and can result from signals sent from a variety of sensory receptors, most commonly **nociceptors**. Pain also relies on thresholds, which may vary greatly from person to person. For example, the idea of what temperature of water is "so hot it hurts" may vary by several degrees between individuals. The **gate theory of pain** proposes that there is a special "gating" mechanism that can turn pain signals on or off, affecting whether or not we perceive pain. In this theory, the spinal cord is able to preferentially forward the signals from other touch modalities (pressure, temperature) to the brain, thus reducing the sensation of pain. Gate theory has been superseded by other theories, but still provides a useful model of understanding touch processing at the spinal cord level.

KINESTHETIC SENSE

Kinesthetic sense is also called **proprioception**, and refers to the ability to tell where one's body is in space. For example, even with your eyes closed, you could still describe the location and position of your hand. The receptors for proprioception are found mostly in muscle and joints, and play critical roles in hand–eye coordination, balance, and mobility.

Real World

The gate theory of pain explains why rubbing an injury (like bumping your knee on a table) seems to reduce the pain of the injury.

MCAT Concept Check 2.4:

Before you move on, assess your understanding of the material with these questions.

1. List the structures in the olfactory pathway, from where odor molecules enter the nose to where olfactory signals project in the brain.

   _____

   _____

2. Both smell and taste are sensitive to chemicals. What is different about the types of chemicals each one can sense?

_____

_____

3. What are the four main modalities of somatosensation?

1. _____

2. _____

3. _____

4. _____

2.5 Object Recognition

High-Yield

LEARNING GOALS

After Chapter 2.5, you will be able to:

- Compare and contrast bottom-up processing and top-down processing
- Describe each of the Gestalt principles: proximity, similarity, good continuation, subjective contours, closure, and pragnanz

Modern theories of object recognition assume at least two major types of psychological processing: bottom-up processing and top-down processing. **Bottom-up (data-driven) processing** refers to object recognition by parallel processing and feature detection, as described earlier. Essentially, the brain takes the individual sensory stimuli and combines them together to create a cohesive image before determining what the object is. **Top-down (conceptually driven) processing** is driven by memories and expectations that allow the brain to recognize the whole object and then recognize the components based on these expectations. In other words, top-down processing allows us to quickly recognize objects without needing to analyze their specific parts. Neither system is sufficient by itself: if we only performed bottom-up processing, we would be extremely inefficient at recognizing objects; every time we looked at an object, it would be like looking at it for the first time. On the other hand, if we only performed top-down processing, we would have difficulty discriminating slight differences between similar objects. This distinction is also partially responsible for the feeling of *déjà vu* described in the introduction to this chapter: when we believe we are experiencing something for the first time, we expect to rely on bottom-up processing; however, when the mind finds that it is able to recognize an experience more quickly than expected (through top-down processing), it searches for a reason for this recognition. In other words, *déjà vu* is often evoked when we have recognition without an obvious reason: *I know that guy from some where . . . but where?* The distinction between top-down and bottom-up processing is relevant for all senses, but is most commonly applied in the context of vision.

Perceptual organization refers to the ability to use these two processes, in tandem with all of the other sensory clues about an object, to create a complete picture or idea. Most of the images we see in everyday life are incomplete; often, we may only be able to see a part of an object and must infer what the rest of the object looks like. By using what information is available in terms of depth, form, motion, constancy, and other clues, we can often "fill in the gaps" using Gestalt principles.

Depth perception can rely on both monocular and binocular cues (processes that involve one or both eyes, respectively). Monocular cues include the relative size of objects, partial obscuring of one object by another, the convergence of parallel lines at a distance, position of an object in the visual field, and lighting and shadowing. The primary binocular cues are the slight differences in images projected on the two retinas and the angle required between the two eyes to bring an object into focus.

The **form** of an object is usually determined through parallel processing and feature detection, and the motion of an object is perceived through magnocellular cells, as described earlier. **Constancy** refers to the idea that we perceive certain characteristics of objects to remain the same, despite differences in the environment. For example, we perceive a white piece of paper as essentially the same color whether it is illuminated by fluorescent lights, incandescent bulbs, or sunlight—this is called color constancy. We also have constancy for brightness, size, and shape, depending on context.

GESTALT PRINCIPLES

Gestalt principles generally follow the same basic idea: these are ways for the brain to infer missing parts of a picture when a picture is incomplete. There are dozens of Gestalt principles, but the highest-yield are summarized below and can be visualized in Figure 2.11.

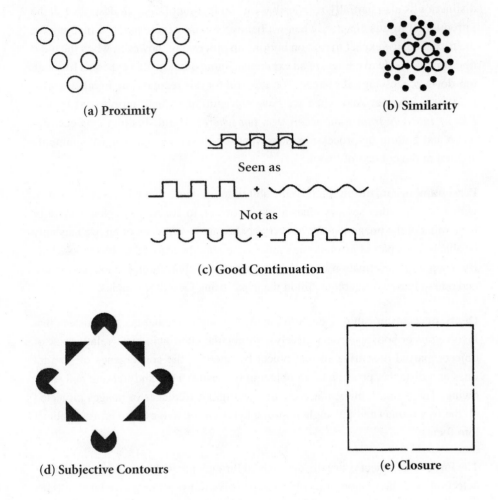

Figure 2.11. Gestalt Principles

The **law of proximity** says that elements close to one another tend to be perceived as a unit. In Figure 2.11a, we do not see ten unrelated dots; rather, we see a triangle and a square, each composed of a certain number of dots. The **law of similarity** says that objects that are similar tend to be grouped together. In Figure 2.11b, we see the big hollow dots as being distinct from the others, forming a triangle against a background of small filled-in dots. The **law of good continuation** says that elements that appear to follow in the same pathway tend to be grouped together. That is, there is a tendency to perceive continuous patterns in stimuli rather than abrupt changes. As seen in Figure 2.11c, our mind tends to break down this complex figure into a sawtooth line and a wavy line, rather than two lines that contain both sawtooth and wavy elements. Some researchers have argued that the phenomena of subjective contours may arise from this law. **Subjective contours** have to do with perceiving contours and, therefore, shapes that are not actually present in the stimulus. In Figure 2.11d, subjective contours lead to the perception of a white diamond on a black square with its corners lying on the four circles. Finally, the **law of closure** says that when a space is enclosed by a contour it tends to be perceived as a complete figure. Closure also refers to the fact that certain figures tend to be perceived as more complete (or closed) than they really are. In Figure 2.11e, we don't see four right angles; instead, we see a square, even though the four sides aren't complete. All these laws operate to create the most stable, consistent, and simplest figures possible within a given visual field. Taken altogether, the Gestalt principles are governed by the **law of prägnanz**, which says that perceptual organization will always be as regular, simple, and symmetric as possible.

MCAT Concept Check 2.5:

Before you move on, assess your understanding of the material with these questions.

1. How is sensory information integrated in bottom-up processing? Top-down processing?

    *   Bottom-up processing:

        _____

    *   Top-down processing:

        _____

2. Briefly describe each of the Gestalt principles below:

Gestalt Principle	Description
Proximity	
Similarity	
Good continuation	
Subjective contours	
Closure	
Prägnanz	

Conclusion

The sensory systems described in this chapter are key to your success on Test Day. Not only are the eye, ear, and other senses high-yield in their own right, but connections to topics in physics, biology, research design, and other concepts in the behavioral sciences make these key topics for passages. But sensation is only one part of the system; we must then take this raw information and process it in the brain to truly perceive the world around us. We use complex neurological pathways to integrate and sort sensory information. We then process it through multiple systems, analyzing individual features and components of the environment while building expectations based on our memories and past experiences. We fill in gaps in our sensorium using Gestalt principles. And all that reaches our conscious awareness is the final product: a cohesive concept of the world around us.

You've completed your vacation in Europe. You used your rods and cones to see the sites, your chemoreceptors to taste and smell the local food, your hair cells to listen to the local music, and your kinesthetic and vestibular senses to help navigate through physical spaces. As you get ready to board the plane for home, all you're left with are your memories—a topic we'll turn to in the next chapter.

CONCEPT SUMMARY

Sensation *vs.* Perception

- **Sensation** is the conversion, or transduction, of physical, electromagnetic, auditory, and other information from the internal and external environment into electrical signals in the nervous system.

- **Perception** is the processing of sensory information to make sense of its significance.

- **Sensory receptors** are nerves that respond to stimuli and trigger electrical signals.
  - Sensory neurons are associated with **sensory ganglia**: collections of cell bodies outside the central nervous system.
  - Sensory stimuli are transmitted to **projection areas** in the brain, which further analyze the sensory input.
  - Common sensory receptors include photoreceptors, hair cells, nociceptors, thermoreceptors, osmoreceptors, olfactory receptors, and taste receptors.

- A **threshold** is the minimum stimulus that causes a change in signal transduction.
  - The **absolute threshold** is the minimum of stimulus energy that is needed to activate a sensory system.
  - The **threshold of conscious perception** is the minimum of stimulus energy that will create a signal large enough in size and long enough in duration to be brought into awareness.
  - The **difference threshold** or **just-noticeable difference** (**jnd**) is the minimum difference in magnitude between two stimuli before one can perceive this difference.
  - **Weber's law** states that the jnd for a stimulus is proportional to the magnitude of the stimulus, and that this proportion is constant over most of the range of possible stimuli.

- **Signal detection theory** refers to the effects of nonsensory factors, such as experiences, motives, and expectations, on perception of stimuli.
  - Signal detection experiments allow us to look at **response bias**. In a signal detection experiment, a stimulus may or may not be given, and the subject is asked to state whether or not the stimulus was given. There are four possible outcomes: hits, misses, false alarms, or correct negatives.

- **Adaptation** refers to a decrease in response to a stimulus over time.

Vision

- The eye is an organ specialized to detect light in the form of photons.
  - The **cornea** gathers and filters incoming light.
  - The **iris** divides the front of the eye into the **anterior** and **posterior chambers**. It contains two muscles, the **dilator** and **constrictor pupillae**, which open and close the **pupil**.

- o The **lens** refracts incoming light to focus it on the retina and is held in place by **suspensory ligaments** connected to the **ciliary muscle**.
- o The ciliary body produces **aqueous humor**, which drains through the **canal of Schlemm**.
- o The retina contains rods and cones. **Rods** detect light and dark; **cones** come in three forms (short-, medium-, and long-wavelength) to detect colors.
- o The retina contains mostly cones in the **macula**, which corresponds to the central visual field. The center of the macula is the **fovea**, which contains only cones.
- o Rods and cones synapse on **bipolar cells**, which synapse on **ganglion cells**. Integration of the signals from ganglion cells and edge-sharpening is performed by **horizontal** and **amacrine cells**.
- o The bulk of the eye is supported by the **vitreous** on the inside and the **sclera** and **choroid** on the outside.
- The visual pathway starts from the eye, and travels through the **optic nerves**, **optic chiasm**, **optic tracts**, **lateral geniculate nucleus** (**LGN**) of the thalamus, and **visual radiations** to get to the **visual cortex**.
  - o The optic chiasm contains fibers crossing from the nasal side of the retina (temporal visual fields) of both eyes.
  - o The visual radiations run through the temporal and parietal lobes.
  - o The visual cortex is in the occipital lobe.
- Vision, like all senses, is processed through **parallel processing**: the ability to simultaneously analyze and combine information regarding color, shape, and motion. Color is detected by cones.
  - o Shape is detected by **parvocellular cells**, with high spatial resolution and low temporal resolution.
  - o Motion is detected by **magnocellular cells**, with low spatial resolution and high temporal resolution.

Hearing and Vestibular Sense
- The ear is divided into the outer, middle, and inner ear.
  - o The **outer ear** consists of the **pinna (auricle)**, **external auditory canal**, and **tympanic membrane**.
  - o The **middle ear** consists of the **ossicles**: **malleus** (hammer), **incus** (anvil), and **stapes** (stirrup). The footplate of the stapes rests on the **oval window** of the cochlea. The middle ear is connected to the nasal cavity by the **Eustachian tube**.
  - o The **inner ear** contains the **bony labyrinth**, within which is the **membranous labyrinth**. The bony labyrinth is filled with **perilymph**; the membranous labyrinth is filled with **endolymph**. The membranous labyrinth consists of the **cochlea**, which detects sound; **utricle** and **saccule**, which detect linear acceleration; and **semicircular canals**, which detect rotational acceleration.

- The auditory pathway starts from the cochlea and travels through the **vestibulocochlear nerve** and **medial geniculate nucleus** (**MGN**) of the thalamus to get to the **auditory cortex** in the temporal lobe.
- Sound information also projects to the **superior olive**, which localizes the sound, and the **inferior colliculus**, which is involved in the startle reflex.

Other Senses

- Smell is the detection of volatile or aerosolized chemicals by the **olfactory chemoreceptors** (**olfactory nerves**) in the olfactory epithelium.
  - The olfactory pathway starts from the olfactory nerves and travels through the **olfactory bulb** and **olfactory tract** to get to higher-order brain areas, such as the limbic system.
  - Pheromones are chemicals given off by animals that have an effect on social, foraging, and sexual behavior in other members of that species.
- Taste is the detection of dissolved compounds by **taste buds** in **papillae**. It comes in five modalities: sweet, sour, salty, bitter, and *umami* (savory).
- **Somatosensation** refers to the four touch modalities: pressure, vibration, pain, and temperature.
  - A **two-point threshold** is the minimum distance necessary between two points of stimulation on the skin such that the points will be felt as two distinct stimuli.
  - **Physiological zero** is the normal temperature of the skin to which objects are compared to determine if they feel "warm" or "cold."
  - **Nociceptors** are responsible for pain perception. The **gate theory of pain** states that pain sensation is reduced when other somatosensory signals are present.
- **Kinesthetic sense** (**proprioception**) refers to the ability to tell where one's body is in three-dimensional space.

Object Recognition

- **Bottom-up** (**data-driven**) **processing** refers to recognition of objects by parallel processing and feature detection. It is slower, but less prone to mistakes.
- **Top-down** (**conceptually driven**) **processing** refers to recognition of an object by memories and expectations, with little attention to detail. It is faster, but more prone to mistakes.
- Perceptual organization refers to our synthesis of stimuli to make sense of the world, including integration of depth, form, motion, and constancy.
- **Gestalt principles** are ways that the brain can infer missing parts of a picture when a picture is incomplete.
  - The **law of proximity** says that elements close to one another tend to be perceived as a unit.
  - The **law of similarity** says that objects that are similar appear to be grouped together.

- The **law of good continuation** says that elements that appear to follow the same pathway tend to be grouped together.
- **Subjective contours** refers to the perception of nonexistent edges in figures, based on surrounding visual cues.
- The **law of closure** says that when a space is enclosed by a group of lines, it is perceived as a complete or closed line.
- The **law of prägnanz** says that **perceptual organization** will always be as regular, simple, and symmetric as possible.

ANSWERS TO CONCEPT CHECKS

2.1

1. Sensory receptor → afferent neuron → sensory ganglion → spinal cord → brain (projection areas)

2. 1–F, 2–A, 3–E, 4–D, 5–C, 6–G, 7–B

3. Absolute threshold is the minimum stimulus that can evoke an action potential in a sensory receptor. Threshold of conscious perception is the minimum stimulus that can evoke enough action potentials for a long enough time that the brain perceives the stimulus. The difference threshold (just-noticeable difference) is the minimum difference between two stimuli that can be detected by the brain.

4. Weber's law explains that just-noticeable differences are best expressed as a ratio, which is constant over most of the range of sensory stimuli. Signal detection theory concerns the threshold to sense a stimulus, given obscuring internal and external stimuli.

5. Adaptation generally raises the difference threshold for a sensory response; as one becomes used to small fluctuations in the stimulus, the difference in stimulus required to evoke a response must be larger.

2.2

1. Cornea: gathers and focuses the incoming light
   Pupil: allows passage of light from the anterior to posterior chamber
   Iris: controls the size of the pupil
   Ciliary body: produces aqueous humor; accommodation of the lens
   Canal of Schlemm: drains aqueous humor
   Lens: refracts the incoming light to focus it on the retina
   Retina: detects images
   Sclera: provides structural support

2. Cornea → pupil → lens → vitreous → retina (rods and cones → bipolar cells → ganglion cells) → optic nerve → optic chiasm → optic tract → lateral geniculate nucleus (LGN) of thalamus → radiations through parietal and temporal lobes → visual cortex (occipital lobe)

3. Parallel processing is the ability to simultaneously analyze color, shape, and motion of an object and to integrate this information to create a cohesive image of the world. Parallel processing also calls on memory systems to compare a visual stimulus to past experiences to help determine the object's identity.

4. Cones are responsible for color. Parvocellular cells are responsible for shape. Magnocellular cells are responsible for motion.

2.3

1. Linear acceleration is detected by the utricle and saccule. Rotational acceleration is detected by the semicircular canals.

2. Pinna → external auditory canal → tympanic membrane → malleus → incus → stapes → oval window → perilymph in cochlea → basilar membrane → hair cells → vestibulocochlear nerve → brainstem → medial geniculate nucleus (MGN) of thalamus → auditory cortex (temporal lobe)

3. The basilar membrane is tonotopically organized: high-pitched sounds cause vibrations at the base of the cochlea, whereas low-pitched sounds cause vibrations at the apex of the cochlea.

2.4

1. Nostril → nasal cavity → olfactory chemoreceptors (olfactory nerves) on olfactory epithelium → olfactory bulb → olfactory tract → higher-order brain regions, including limbic system

2. Smell is sensitive to volatile or aerosolized compounds; taste is sensitive to dissolved compounds.

3. The four main modalities of somatosensation are pressure, vibration, pain, and temperature.

2.5

1. Bottom-up processing requires each component of an object to be interpreted through parallel processing, and then integrated into one cohesive whole. Top-down processing starts with the whole object and, through memory, creates expectations for the components of the object.

2.

Gestalt Principle	Description
Proximity	Components close to one another tend to be perceived as a unit.
Similarity	Components that are similar (in color, shape, size) tend to be grouped together.
Good continuation	Components that appear to follow in the same pathway tend to be grouped together; abrupt changes in form are less likely than continuation of the same pattern.
Subjective contours	Edges or shapes that are not actually present can be implied by the surrounding objects (especially if good continuation is present).
Closure	A space enclosed by a contour tends to be perceived as a complete figure; such figures tend to be perceived as more complete (or closed) than they really are.
Prägnanz	Perceptual organization will always be as regular, simple, and symmetric as possible.

SHARED CONCEPTS

Discrete Practice Questions

Consult your online resources for Full-Length Exams and Passage-Based Questions (for certain chapters).

1. A weight lifter is just able to tell the difference between 100 and 125 pounds. According to Weber's law, the lifter would notice a difference between:

   A. 125 and 150 pounds.
   B. 5 and 6 pounds.
   C. 25 and 35 pounds.
   D. 225 and 275 pounds.

2. A man is at a party with his wife. There is loud music in the background and the location is crowded. While listening to the music he hears what he believes to be his wife's laughter and turns around to investigate. The man is exhibiting:

   A. feature detection.
   B. bottom-up processing.
   C. vestibular sense.
   D. signal detection.

3. A woman is at a restaurant and orders a spicy entrée. After the first bite, she experiences burning in her mouth and becomes concerned that her food is too hot for her. The next few bites are similarly uncomfortable, but after a while the spiciness seems to subside somewhat, and by the end of the meal, she doesn't notice the spice level. The end of the meal experience is best described as:

   A. adaptation.
   B. signal detection.
   C. a difference threshold.
   D. pain perception.

4. Which sensory receptors send signals in response to tissue damage?

   A. Chemoreceptors
   B. Nociceptors
   C. Osmoreceptors
   D. Photoreceptors

5. Which part of the eye is responsible for gathering and focusing light?

   A. Cornea
   B. Pupil
   C. Iris
   D. Retina

6. A man is looking for change to do laundry. He decides to look under the seats of his car. He uses a flashlight but is still unable to get more than an obscured look at the space below. There are various items such as wrappers and papers, but the man sees the glint of silver from an object laying flat and determines it to be a coin. To make this determination, this man used:

   A. signal detection.
   B. sensory adaptation.
   C. feature detection.
   D. kinesthetic sense.

7. Upon which part of the eye are images projected and transduced into electrical signals?

   A. Cornea
   B. Pupil
   C. Retina
   D. Lens

8. The ability to sense stimuli against one's own skin is known as:

   A. somatosensation.
   B. kinesthetic sense.
   C. vestibular sense.
   D. chemoreception.

9. Which of the following is NOT a taste modality?

   A. Sweet
   B. Floral
   C. Savory
   D. Bitter

10. Which of the following best describes the difference between endolymph and perilymph?

    A. Endolymph is found in the vestibule, while perilymph is found in the cochlea.

    B. Endolymph is found in the cochlea, while perilymph is found in the vestibule.

    C. Endolymph is found in the membranous labyrinth, while perilymph is found in the bony labyrinth.

    D. Endolymph is found in the bony labyrinth, while perilymph is found in the membranous labyrinth.

11. Chemicals that compel behavior after binding with chemoreceptors are known as:

    A. pheromones.

    B. olfactory receptors.

    C. somatostimuli.

    D. papillae.

12. Prolonged vitamin B_{12} deficiency can be associated with subacute combined degeneration of the spinal cord. Patients with this disease have difficulty walking because they lose the ability to feel where their feet are in space. This represents a loss of:

    A. vestibular sense.

    B. kinesthetic sense.

    C. parallel processing.

    D. feature detection.

13. A person proofreading a paper reads over a long, misspelled word in which an "e" is replaced with an "o." The person does not recognize the error and reads the word as correct. Which of the following could explain why the proofreader read the word as correct?

    A. Parallel processing

    B. Feature detection

    C. Top-down processing

    D. Bottom-up processing

14. A corporate logo uses five unconnected angles equally spaced in a circular fashion. When viewed, it appears to be a star. Which of the following is the logo artist using to create a complete pattern to viewers?

    A. Bottom-up processing

    B. Top-down processing

    C. Gate theory

    D. Gestalt principles

15. A patient comes in with a tumor of the pituitary gland which has grown upward into the optic chiasm and caused a visual field defect. The most likely defect from compression of the optic chiasm is:

    A. complete blindness in one eye.

    B. loss of the upper visual fields in both eyes.

    C. loss of the nasal visual fields in both eyes.

    D. loss of the temporal visual fields in both eyes.

Explanations to
Discrete Practice Questions

1. C

Weber's law posits that thresholds are proportional. Going from 100 to 125 pounds is a 25 percent increase. **Choice (C)** is a 40 percent increase while all the rest are all under 25 percent.

2. D

The man is discerning a specific noise within a field of many noises. This is the definition of signal detection. In an experimental setup, his response would be considered a hit if his wife was indeed laughing; his response would be considered a false alarm if his wife was not laughing.

3. A

The spicy food can be considered an extreme stimulus because it eclipses what the woman believes she can handle in terms of heat. However, after experiencing the stimulus over and over, the experience of spice drops to barely perceptible. This is sensory adaptation: a reduction in response to a stimulus over time.

4. B

Nociceptors are important for pain sensation, which would be expected during tissue damage. Chemoreceptors, **choice (A)**, respond to chemicals, whether volatile or aerosolized (olfaction) or dissolved (taste). Osmoreceptors, **choice (C)**, respond to changes in blood osmolarity, and photoreceptors, **choice (D)**, respond to light.

5. A

The cornea is responsible for gathering and focusing light. The iris and pupil, **choices (B)** and **(C)**, are both involved in regulating the amount of light coming into the eye but not in focusing it. The retina, **choice (D)**, transduces the light into electrical signals that are sent to the brain. The lens serves a similar function to the cornea and would also be a valid answer to this question.

6. C

This man was able to distinguish the coin from other items by recognizing specific features of the coin; in this case, it was the glint of the metal surface and its position in the car. This phenomenon is called feature detection.

7. C

The retina is the part of the eye upon which images are projected. Rods and cones in the retina then convert the electromagnetic radiation into electrical signals.

8. A

Somatosensation refers to the various modalities of touch: pressure, vibration, temperature, and pain. Kinesthetic sense, **choice (B)**, refers to the ability to tell where one's body is in space. Vestibular sense, **choice (C)**, refers to the detection of linear and rotational acceleration in the middle ear. Finally, chemoreception, **choice (D)**, refers to sensing chemicals in the environment.

9. B

The five tastes are sweet, sour, salty, bitter, and *umami*. Floral would be related to smell rather than taste.

10. C

Endolymph is the potassium-rich fluid that bathes the hair cells of the inner ear, all of which are found within the membranous labyrinth. Perilymph is found in the space between the membranous labyrinth and the bony labyrinth. Both the membranous labyrinth and bony labyrinth contribute to the cochlea and the vestibule, eliminating **choices (A)** and **(B)**.

11. A

Pheromones are the volatile chemicals given off by organisms that bind with olfactory chemoreceptors and influence behavior. It is debatable if pheromones serve a role in humans, but are known to affect foraging and sexual behavior in some animals.

12. B

Kinesthetic sense, or proprioception, refers to the ability to tell where body parts are in three-dimensional space. The sensors for proprioception are found predominantly in the muscles and joints. Loss of vestibular sense, **choice (A)**, would also cause difficulty walking, but this would be due to a sense of dizziness or vertigo, not an inability to feel one's feet.

13. C

The proofreader used a larger pattern to identify the word and expected to see an "e," thus missing the error. This is related to top-down processing; the proofreader used recognition and expectations, which led to missing a detail. Bottom-up processing, **choice (D)**, would be the analysis of each detail individually before creating a cohesive image.

14. D

Gestalt principles are the basis for many optical illusions and include the tendency of people to see continuity even when lines are unconnected. Specifically, this logo appears to rely on the law of closure to create one complete star from five nontouching angles.

15. D

The optic chiasm houses the crossing fibers from each optic nerve. Specifically, the fibers coming from the nasal half of the retina in each eye cross in the chiasm to join the optic tract on the opposite side. Remember that the lens of the eye causes inversion, so images on the nasal half of the retina actually originate in the temporal visual field. This condition is called bitemporal hemianopsia.

Learning and Memory

In This Chapter

Chapter Profile

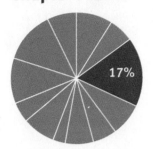

17%

The content in this chapter should be relevant to about 17% of all questions about the Behavioral Sciences on the MCAT.

This chapter covers material from the following AAMC content categories:

6B: Making sense of the environment

7C: Attitude and behavior change

Introduction

A college student sits hunched over a desk in a quiet library, poring over a small stack of textbooks. It's 11 p.m. the night before the organic chemistry midterm, and he has what seems to be a near endless list of reactions to commit to memory before tomorrow. The situation seems bleak, but he has been here before and has taken every precaution to make sure that this study session will be successful: he knows that the coffee he's drinking will keep him awake and that the quiet of the library will reduce distractions and allow him to concentrate. It's stressful, to be sure, but he has been able to study this way before and do quite well, reinforcing his current set of behaviors. He makes his way through a set of flashcards—reactants on one side, products on the other—and while he is able to identify most of them, he misses a few, placing those cards on a separate pile to be reviewed later. He knows this rehearsal will most likely help him for tomorrow, but will he be able to recall this information again for the final in two months? He takes another sip of coffee and tries to put everything else out of his mind, focusing intently on the information in front of him.

Sound familiar? If you're like most students, you've found yourself in a similar scenario at least once. In this chapter, we'll discuss the ways in which we both memorize new information and learn new behaviors. In doing so, you'll not only be directly preparing to answer MCAT questions about this content, but you might also learn a few new tricks to help you to effectively commit all of the MCAT content to memory, a skill that will be helpful both now and later in your career as a doctor.

3.1 Learning

LEARNING GOALS

After Chapter 3.1, you will be able to:

- Apply principles of habituation, dishabituation, and sensitization to real life scenarios
- Identify the conditioned stimulus, unconditioned stimulus, conditioned response, and unconditioned response in a Pavlovian learning paradigm
- Distinguish between negative reinforcement, positive reinforcement, negative punishment, and positive punishment
- Predict how reinforcement schedule will affect relative frequency of behavioral response in an operant conditioning scenario

To a psychologist, **learning** refers specifically to the way in which we acquire new behaviors. To understand learning, we must start with the concept of a stimulus. A **stimulus** can be defined as anything to which an organism can respond, including all of the sensory inputs we discussed in Chapter 2 of *MCAT Behavioral Sciences Review*. The combination of stimuli and responses serves as the basis for all behavioral learning.

Responses to stimuli can change over time depending on the frequency and intensity of the stimulus. For instance, repeated exposure to the same stimulus can cause a decrease in response called **habituation**. This is seen in many first-year medical students: students often have an intense physical reaction the first time they see a cadaver or treat a severe laceration, but as they get used to these stimuli, the reaction lessens until they are unbothered by these sights.

The opposite process can also occur. **Dishabituation** is defined as the recovery of a response to a stimulus after habituation has occurred. Dishabituation is often noted when, late in the habituation of a stimulus, a second stimulus is presented. The second stimulus interrupts the habituation process and thereby causes an increase in response to the original stimulus. Imagine, for example, that you're taking a long car trip and driving for many miles on a highway. After a while, your brain will get used to the sights, sounds, and sensations of highway driving: the dashed lines dividing the lanes, the sound of the engine and the tires on the road, and so on. Habituation has occurred. At some point you use an exit ramp, and these sensations change. As you merge onto the new highway, you pay more attention to the sensory stimuli coming in. Even if the stimuli are more or less the same as on the previous highway, the presentation of a different stimulus (using the exit ramp) causes dishabituation and a new awareness of—and response to—these stimuli. Dishabituation is temporary and always refers to changes in response to the original stimulus, not the new one.

Learning, then, is a change in behavior that occurs in response to a stimulus. While there are many types of learning, the MCAT focuses on two types: associative learning and observational learning.

ASSOCIATIVE LEARNING

Associative learning is the creation of a pairing, or association, either between two stimuli or between a behavior and a response. On the MCAT, you'll be tested on two such kinds of learning: classical and operant conditioning.

CLASSICAL CONDITIONING

Classical conditioning is a type of associative learning that takes advantage of biological, instinctual responses to create associations between two unrelated stimuli. For many people, the first name that comes to mind for research in classical conditioning is Ivan Pavlov. His experiments on dogs were not only revolutionary, but also provide a template for the way the MCAT will test classical conditioning.

Classical conditioning works, first and foremost, because some stimuli cause an innate or reflexive physiological response. For example, we reflexively salivate when we smell bread baking in an oven, or we may jump or recoil when we hear a loud noise. Any stimulus that brings about such a reflexive response is called an **unconditioned stimulus**, and the innate or reflexive response is called an **unconditioned response**. Many stimuli do not produce a reflexive response and are known as **neutral stimuli**. Neutral stimuli can be referred to as **signaling stimuli** if they have the potential to be used as a conditioning stimulus.

In Pavlov's experiment, the unconditioned stimulus was meat, which would cause the dogs to salivate reflexively, and the neutral stimulus was a ringing bell. Through the course of the experiment, Pavlov repeatedly rang the bell before placing meat in the dogs' mouths. Initially, the dogs did not react much when they only heard the bell ring without receiving meat. However, after this procedure was repeated several times, the dogs began to salivate when they heard the bell ring. In fact, the dogs would salivate even if Pavlov only rang the bell and did not deliver any meat. Pavlov thereby turned a neutral stimulus into a **conditioned stimulus**: a normally neutral

Key Concept

Dishabituation is the recovery of a response to a stimulus, usually after a different stimulus has been presented. Note that the term refers to changes in response to the original stimulus, not the new one.

stimulus that, through association, now causes a reflexive response called a **conditioned response**. Classical conditioning, then, is the process of taking advantage of a reflexive, unconditioned stimulus to turn a neutral stimulus into a conditioned stimulus, as shown in Figure 3.1. This process is also referred to as **acquisition**.

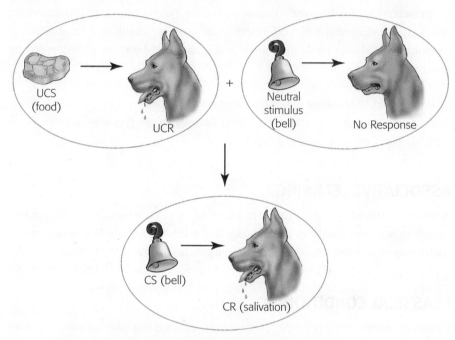

Figure 3.1. Classical Conditioning
UCS = unconditioned stimulus, UCR = unconditioned response,
CS = conditioned stimulus, CR = conditioned response

MCAT Expertise

On the MCAT, the key to telling conditioned and unconditioned responses apart will be to look at which stimulus is causing them: unconditioned stimuli cause an unconditioned response, while conditioned stimuli cause a conditioned response.

Notice that the stimuli change in this experiment, but the response is the same throughout. Because salivation in response to food is natural and requires no conditioning, it is an unconditioned response in this context. On the other hand, when paired with a conditioned stimulus, salivation is considered a conditioned response.

Just because a conditioned response has been acquired does not mean that it is permanent. If the conditioned stimulus is presented without the unconditioned stimulus enough times, the organism can become habituated to the conditioned stimulus and **extinction** occurs. If the bell rings often enough without the dog getting meat, the dog may stop salivating when the bell sounds. Interestingly, even this extinction of a response is not always permanent; after some time, if an extinct conditioned stimulus is presented again, a weak conditioned response can sometimes be exhibited, a phenomenon called **spontaneous recovery**.

There are a few processes that can modify the response to a conditioned stimulus after acquisition has occurred. **Generalization** is a broadening effect by which a stimulus similar enough to the conditioned stimulus can also produce the conditioned response. In one famous experiment, researchers conditioned a child called Little Albert to be afraid of a white rat by pairing the presentation of the rat with a loud noise. Subsequent tests showed that Little Albert's conditioning had generalized such that he also exhibited a fear response to a white stuffed rabbit, a white sealskin coat, and even a man with a white beard.

Finally, in **discrimination**, an organism learns to distinguish between two similar stimuli. This is the opposite of generalization. Pavlov's dogs could have been conditioned to discriminate between bells of different tones by having one tone paired with meat, and another presented without meat. In this case, association could have occurred with one tone but not the other.

MCAT Expertise

Classical conditioning is a favorite topic on the MCAT. Expect at least one question to describe a Pavlovian experiment and ask you to identify the role of one of the stimuli or responses described.

OPERANT CONDITIONING

Whereas classical conditioning is concerned with instincts and biological responses, **operant conditioning** links voluntary behaviors with consequences in an effort to alter the frequency of those behaviors. Just as the MCAT will test you on the difference between conditioned and unconditioned responses and stimuli, it will ask you to distinguish between reinforcement and punishment too. Operant conditioning is associated with B. F. Skinner, who is considered the father of **behaviorism**, the theory that all behaviors are conditioned. The four possible relationships between stimulus and behavior are summarized in Figure 3.2.

	Stimulus	
	Added	Removed
Behavior Continues	Positive reinforcement	Negative reinforcement
Behavior Stops	Positive punishment	Negative punishment

Figure 3.2. Terminology of Operant Conditioning

Reinforcement

Reinforcement is the process of increasing the likelihood that an individual will perform a behavior. Reinforcers are divided into two categories. **Positive reinforcers** increase a behavior by adding a positive consequence or incentive following the desired behavior. Money is an example of a common and strong positive reinforcer: employees will continue to work if they are paid. **Negative reinforcers** act similarly in that they increase the frequency of a behavior, but they do so by removing something unpleasant. For example, taking an aspirin reduces a headache, so the next time you have a headache, you are more likely to take one. Negative reinforcement is often confused with punishment, which will

Real World

This concept of learning by consequence forms the foundation for behavioral therapies for many disorders including phobias, anxiety disorders, and obsessive–compulsive disorder.

be discussed in the next section, but remember that the frequency of the behavior is the distinguishing factor: any reinforcement—positive or negative—increases the likelihood that a behavior will be performed.

Negative reinforcers can be subdivided into escape learning and avoidance learning, which differ in the timing of the unpleasant stimulus. Taking aspirin is an example of **escape learning**: the role of the behavior is to reduce the unpleasantness of something that already exists, like a headache. **Avoidance learning**, on the other hand, is meant to prevent the unpleasantness of something that has yet to happen. In fact, you are practicing avoidance right now: you are studying to avoid the unpleasant consequence of a poor score on the MCAT. When you do well on Test Day, that success will positively reinforce the behavior of studying for the next major exam of your medical career: the United States Medical Licensing Examination® (USMLE®)!

Classical and operant conditioning can be used hand-in-hand. For example, dolphin trainers take advantage of reinforcers when training dolphins to perform tricks. Sometimes, the trainers will feed the dolphin a fish after it performs a trick. The fish can be said to be a **primary reinforcer** because the fish is a treat that the dolphin responds to naturally. Dolphin trainers also use tiny handheld devices that emit a clicking sound. This clicker would not normally be a reinforcer on its own, but the trainers use classical conditioning to pair the clicker with fish to elicit the same response. The clicker is thus a **conditioned reinforcer**, which is sometimes called a **secondary reinforcer**. Eventually, the dolphin may even associate the presence of the trainer with the possibility of reward, making the presence of the trainer a **discriminative stimulus**. A discriminative stimulus indicates that reward is potentially available in an operant conditioning paradigm.

Punishment

In contrast to reinforcement, **punishment** uses conditioning to reduce the occurrence of a behavior. **Positive punishment** adds an unpleasant consequence in response to a behavior to reduce that behavior; for example, in some countries a thief may be flogged for stealing, which is intended to stop him from stealing again. **Negative punishment** is the reduction of a behavior when a stimulus is removed. For example, a parent may forbid her child from watching television as a consequence for bad behavior, with the goal of preventing the behavior from happening again.

Reinforcement Schedules

The presence or absence of reinforcing or punishing stimuli is just a part of the story. The rate at which desired behaviors are acquired is also affected by the schedule being used to affect those behaviors. Reinforcement schedules have two different factors: whether the schedule is fixed or variable, and whether the schedule is based on a ratio or an interval.

- **Fixed-ratio (FR) schedules** reinforce a behavior after a specific number of performances of that behavior. For example, in a typical operant conditioning experiment, researchers might reward a rat with a food pellet every third time it presses a bar in its cage. **Continuous reinforcement** is a fixed-ratio schedule in which the behavior is rewarded every time it is performed.
- **Variable-ratio (VR) schedules** reinforce a behavior after a varying number of performances of the behavior, but such that the average number of performances to receive a reward is relatively constant. With this type of reinforcement schedule, researchers might reward a rat first after two button presses, then eight, then four, then finally six.
- **Fixed-interval (FI) schedules** reinforce the first instance of a behavior after a specified time period has elapsed. For example, once our rat gets a pellet, it has to wait 60 seconds before it can get another pellet. The first lever press after 60 seconds gets a pellet, but subsequent presses during those 60 seconds accomplish nothing.
- **Variable-interval (VI) schedules** reinforce a behavior the first time that behavior is performed after a varying interval of time. Instead of waiting exactly 60 seconds, for example, our rat might have to wait 90 seconds, then 30 seconds, then three minutes. In each case, once the interval elapses, the next press gets the rat a pellet.

Of these schedules, variable-ratio works the fastest for learning a new behavior, and is also the most resistant to extinction. The effectiveness of the various reinforcement schedules is demonstrated in Figure 3.3.

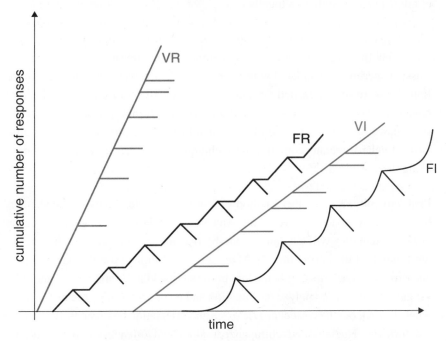

Figure 3.3. Reinforcement Schedules
Hatches correspond to instances of reinforcement. The start of each line corresponds to time zero for that schedule.

Mnemonic

VR stands for **V**ariable-**R**atio, but it can also stand for **V**ery **R**apid and **V**ery **R**esistant to extinction.

Real World

Gambling (and gambling addiction) is so difficult to extinguish because most gambling games are based on variable-ratio schedules. While the probability of winning the jackpot on any individual pull of a slot machine is the same, we get caught in the idea that the next pull will be the "right one."

There are a few things to note in this graph. First, variable-ratio schedules have the fastest response rate: the rat will continue pressing the bar quickly with the hope that the next press will be the "right one." Also note that fixed schedules (fixed-ratio and fixed-interval) often have a brief moment of no responses after the behavior is reinforced: the rat will stop hitting the lever until it wants another pellet, once it has figured out what behavior is necessary to receive the pellet.

One final idea associated with operant conditioning is the concept of shaping. **Shaping** is the process of rewarding increasingly specific behaviors. For example, if you wanted to train a bird to spin around in place and then peck a key on a keyboard, you might first give the bird a treat for turning slightly to the left, then only for turning a full 90 degrees, then 180, and so on. Then you might only reward this behavior if done near the keyboard until eventually the bird is only rewarded once the full set of behaviors is performed. While it may take some time, the use of shaping in operant conditioning can allow for the training of extremely complicated behaviors.

Cognitive and Biological Factors in Associative Learning

It would be incorrect to say that classical and operant conditioning are the only factors that affect behavior, nor would it be correct to say that we are all mindless and robotic, unable to resist the rewards and punishments that occur in our lives. Since Skinner's initial perspectives, it has been found that many cognitive and biological factors are at work that can change the effects of associative learning or allow us to resist them altogether.

Many organisms undergo **latent learning**; that is, learning that occurs without a reward but that is spontaneously demonstrated once a reward is introduced. The classic experiment associated with latent learning involves rats running a maze. Rats that were simply carried through the maze and then incentivized with a food reward for completing the maze on their own performed just as well—and in some cases better—than those rats that had been trained to run the maze using more standard operant conditioning techniques by which they were rewarded along the way.

Problem solving is another method of learning that steps outside the standard behaviorist approach. Think of the way young children put together a jigsaw puzzle: often, they will take pieces one-by-one and try to make them fit together until they find the correct match. Many animals will also use this kind of trial-and-error approach, testing behaviors until they yield a reward. As we get older, we gain the ability to analyze the situation and respond correctly the first time, as when we seek out the correct puzzle piece and orientation based on the picture we are forming. Humans and chimpanzees alike will often avoid trial-and-error learning and instead take a step back, observe the situation, and take decisive action to solve the challenges they face.

Not all behaviors can be taught using operant conditioning techniques. Many animals are predisposed to learn (or not learn) behaviors based on their own natural abilities and instincts. Animals are most able to learn behaviors that coincide with their natural behaviors: birds naturally peck when searching for food, so rewarding them with food in response to a pecking-based behavior works well. This predisposition is known as **preparedness**. Similarly, it can be very difficult to teach animals behaviors that work against their natural instincts. For example, researchers used behavioral techniques to try to train raccoons to place coins in a piggy bank. Their efforts were unsuccessful, as the raccoons would pick up the coins, rub them together, and dip them into the bank before pulling them back out. The researchers concluded that the task they were trying to train the raccoons to perform was conflicting with their natural food-gathering instinct, which was to rub seeds together and wash them in a stream to clean them before eating. This difficulty in overcoming instinctual behaviors is called **instinctive drift**. The researchers had far better luck training the raccoons to place a ball in a basketball net, as the ball was too large to trigger the food-washing instinct.

OBSERVATIONAL LEARNING

Observational learning is the process of learning a new behavior or gaining information by watching others. The most famous and perhaps most controversial study into observational learning is Albert Bandura's Bobo doll experiment, in which children watched an adult in a room full of toys punching and kicking an inflatable clown toy. When the children were later allowed to play in the room, many of them ignored the other toys in the room and inflicted similar violence on the Bobo doll just as they had seen the adult do. It's important to note that observational learning is not simply imitation because observational learning can be used to teach individuals to avoid behavior as well. In later iterations of the Bobo doll experiment, children who watched the adult get scolded after attacking the Bobo doll were less likely to be aggressive toward the Bobo doll themselves.

Like associative learning, there are a few neurological factors that affect observational learning. The most important of these are **mirror neurons**. These neurons are located in the frontal and parietal lobes of the cerebral cortex and fire both when an individual performs an action and when that individual observes someone else performing that action. Mirror neurons are largely involved in motor processes, but additionally are thought to be related to empathy and vicarious emotions; some mirror neurons fire both when we experience an emotion and also when we observe another experiencing the same emotion. Mirror neurons also play a role in imitative learning by a number of primates, as shown in Figure 3.4.

Real World

The connection between violent video games and aggressive behavior is still under active debate. While there are many interest groups on both sides of the controversy, the American Academy of Pediatrics (a major medical society) published one report in which they attributed a 13 to 22% increase in aggressive behavior to observational learning from video games.

Figure 3.4. Use of Mirror Neurons in a Macaque
Many neonatal primates imitate facial expressions using mirror neurons.

Research suggests that observational learning through **modeling** is an important factor in determining an individual's behavior throughout his or her lifetime. People learn what behaviors are acceptable by watching others perform them. Much attention is focused on violent media or domestic abuse as models for antisocial behavior, but prosocial modeling can be just as powerful. Of course, observational learning is strongest when a model's words are consistent with his or her actions. Many parents adopt a *Do as I say, not as I do* approach when teaching their children, but research suggests that children will disproportionately imitate what the model *did*, rather than what the model *said*.

MCAT Concept Check 3.1:

Before you move on, assess your understanding of the material with these questions.

1. Which of the following might cause a person to eat more food during a meal: eating each course separately and moving to the next only when finished with the current course, or interrupting the main course several times by eating side dishes?

   _____

   _____

2. A college student plays a prank on his roommate by popping a balloon behind the roommate's head after every time he makes popcorn. Before long, the smell of popcorn makes the roommate nervous. Which part of the story corresponds to each of the classical conditioning concepts below?

   • Conditioned stimulus:

   _____

   • Unconditioned stimulus:

   _____

   • Conditioned response:

   _____

   • Unconditioned response:

   _____

3. What is the difference between negative reinforcement and positive punishment? Provide an example of each.

   • Negative reinforcement:

   _____

   _____

   • Positive punishment:

   _____

   _____

3.2 Memory

High-Yield

LEARNING GOALS

After Chapter 3.2, you will be able to:

*   Order the three modes of encoding from strongest to weakest
*   Distinguish between maintenance rehearsal and elaborative rehearsal
*   Predict how learning environments may impact recall
*   Describe factors and phenomena that can lead to flaws in memory
*   Define each type of human memory:

While learning is mostly concerned with behavior, the study of memory focuses on how we gain the knowledge that we accumulate over our lifetimes. The formation of memories can be divided into three major processes: encoding, storage, and retrieval.

ENCODING

Encoding refers to the process of putting new information into memory. Much of the information that we gain is passively absorbed from the environment. As you walk down the street, you are constantly bombarded with information that seeps into your brain: you notice the temperature; you keep track of the route that you're taking; you might stop at a coffee shop and realize that the same barista has been working each day this week. All of this information is gained without effort and is thus said to be the result of **automatic processing**.

There are, however, times when we must actively work to gain information. In studying for the MCAT, for example, you may create flashcards to memorize the enzymes of digestion or the functions of endocrine hormones. This active memorization is known as **controlled (effortful) processing**.

MCAT Expertise

Do not allow yourself to study for the MCAT using automatic processing! Just reading the text "to get through it" won't cut it for the MCAT. Engage with the text: fill out the MCAT Concept Checks, write notes in the margins, ask yourself questions. Scientific studies of learning have demonstrated, time and time again, that controlled processing improves comprehension, retention, and speed and accuracy on Test Day.

With practice, controlled processing can become automatic. Think back to a time when you were learning a foreign language. At first, each word required a great deal of processing to decipher: you had to hear the word and consciously translate it into your native language in order to understand what was being said. This took an amount of time and effort that was probably difficult to maintain for prolonged periods. However, as you gained more experience with the language, this process became easier until you may have been able to understand those same words intuitively, without having to think very hard about them at all. At that point, this skill that once required controlled processing became automatic.

There are a few different ways that we encode the meaning of information that requires controlled processing. We can visualize it (**visual encoding**), store the way it sounds (**acoustic encoding**), or put it into a meaningful context (**semantic encoding**). Of these three, semantic encoding is the strongest and visual encoding is the weakest. When using semantic encoding, the more vivid the context, the better. In fact, we tend to recall information best when we can put it into the context of our own lives, a phenomenon called the **self-reference effect**.

Of course, grouping information into a meaningful context is only one trick that we can use to aid in encoding. Another such aid is **maintenance rehearsal**, which is the repetition of a piece of information to either keep it within working memory (to prevent forgetting) or to store it in short-term and eventually long-term memory— topics discussed in the next section.

Mnemonics are another common way to memorize information, particularly lists. As you've seen in your Kaplan study materials, mnemonics are often acronyms or rhyming phrases that provide a vivid organization of the information we are trying to remember. Two other mnemonic techniques are commonly employed by memory experts. The **method of loci** involves associating each item in the list with a location along a route through a building that has already been memorized. For example, in memorizing a grocery list, someone might picture a carton of eggs sitting on their door step, a person spilling milk in the front hallway, a giant stick of butter in the living room, and so on. Later, when the person wishes to recall the list, they simply take a mental walk through the locations and recall the images they formed earlier. Similarly, the **peg-word** system associates numbers with items that rhyme with or resemble the numbers. For example, one might be associated with the sun, two with a shoe, three with a tree, and so on. As groundwork, the individual memorizes their personal peg-list. When another list needs to be memorized, the individual can simply pair each item in the list with their peg-list. In this example, the individual may visualize eggs being fried by the sun (1), a pair of shoes (2) filled with milk, and a tree (3) with leaves made of butter. Because of the serial nature of both the method-of-loci and peg-word systems, they are very useful for memorizing large lists of objects in order.

Finally, **chunking** (sometimes referred to as **clustering**) is a memory trick that involves taking individual elements of a large list and grouping them together into groups of elements with related meaning. For example, consider the following list of

Real World

The purpose of the Real World sidebars in your *MCAT Review* books is semantic encoding: by putting content into a meaningful context, retention of the information is improved. Most of our Real World sidebars are related to medicine because of the self-reference effect.

16 letters: E-N-A-L-P-K-C-U-R-T-R-A-C-S-U-B. Memorizing the list in order by rote might prove difficult until we realize that we can reverse the items and group them into meaningful chunks: BUS, CAR, TRUCK, PLANE.

STORAGE

Following encoding, information must be stored if it is to be remembered. There are several types of memory storage.

Sensory Memory

The first and most fleeting kind of memory storage is **sensory memory**, which consists of both **iconic** (visual) and **echoic** (auditory) memory. Sensory memory lasts only a very short time (generally under one second), but within that time our eyes and ears take in an incredibly detailed representation of our surroundings that we can recall with amazing precision. Sensory memories are maintained by the major projection areas of each sensory system, such as the occipital lobe (vision) and temporal lobe (hearing). Of course, sensory memory fades very quickly, and unless the information is attended to, it will be lost.

The nature of sensory memory can be demonstrated experimentally. Consider the following procedure: a research participant is presented with a three-by-three array of letters, such as that presented in Figure 3.5, that is flashed onto a screen for a mere fraction of a second. When asked to list all of the letters she saw, the participant is able to correctly identify three or four (a procedure known as **whole-report**). However, when asked to list the letters of a particular row immediately after the presentation of the stimulus (known as **partial-report**), she can do so with 100 percent accuracy, no matter which row is chosen. This is iconic memory in action: in the time it takes to list out a few of the items, the entire list fades, yet it is clear that all of the letters do make their way into iconic memory because any small subset can be recalled at will.

Figure 3.5. A Sample 3-by-3 Array for Studying Sensory Memory

Short-Term Memory

Of course, we do pay attention to some of the information that we are exposed to, and that information enters our **short-term memory**. Similar to sensory memory, short-term memory fades quickly, over the course of approximately 30 seconds without rehearsal. In addition to having a limited duration, short-term memories are also limited in capacity to approximately seven items, usually stated as the **7 ± 2 rule**. As discussed in the previous section, the capacity of short-term memory can be increased by clustering information, and the duration can be extended using maintenance rehearsal. Short-term memory is housed primarily in the **hippocampus**, which is also responsible for the consolidation of short-term memory into long-term memory.

Working Memory

Working memory is closely related to short-term memory and is similarly supported by the hippocampus. It enables us to keep a few pieces of information in our consciousness simultaneously and to manipulate that information. To do this, one must integrate short-term memory, attention, and executive function; accordingly, the frontal and parietal lobes are also involved. This is the form of memory that allows us to do simple math in our heads.

Long-Term Memory

With enough rehearsal, information moves from short-term to long-term memory, an essentially limitless warehouse for the knowledge that we are then able to recall on demand, sometimes for the rest of our lives. One of the ways that information is consolidated into long-term memory is **elaborative rehearsal**. Unlike maintenance rehearsal, which is simply a way of keeping the information at the forefront of consciousness, elaborative rehearsal is the association of the information to knowledge already stored in long-term memory. Elaborative rehearsal is closely tied to the self-reference effect noted earlier; those ideas that we are able to relate to our own lives are more likely to find their way into our long-term memory. While long-term memory is primarily controlled by the hippocampus, it should be noted that memories are moved, over time, back to the cerebral cortex. Thus, very long-term memories—our names and birthdates, the faces of our parents—are generally not affected by damage to the hippocampus.

There are two types of long-term memory. **Implicit** (**nondeclarative** or **procedural**) **memory** consists of our skills and conditioned responses. **Explicit** (**declarative**) **memory** consists of those memories that require conscious recall. Explicit memory can be further divided into **semantic memory** (the facts that we know) and **episodic memory** (our experiences). Interestingly, memory disorders can affect one type of memory but leave others alone. For example, a patient with amnesia might not remember the time he learned to ride a bicycle or the names of the parts of a bicycle (episodic and semantic memories, respectively) but may, to his surprise, retain the skill of riding a bicycle when given one. The various major categories of memory are summarized in Figure 3.6.

Real World

Have you ever looked at a picture of a simple unfinished puzzle, and been able to fit the pieces together mentally? This skill is explained by one of the major theories that underlies working memory, which includes the concept of a visuospatial sketchpad. The visuospatial sketchpad was proposed by Baddeley and Hitch as part of their three-part working memory model along with the other two components they proposed: the central executive and the phonological loop. The visuospatial sketchpad explains our ability to not only store visual and spatial information, but to manipulate it as well.

MCAT Expertise

Although semantic and episodic memory are differentiated and can be separate, they can also co-occur. For example, one type of explicit memory with components of both episodic and semantic memory is flashbulb memory—the detailed recollection of stimuli surrounding an important event.

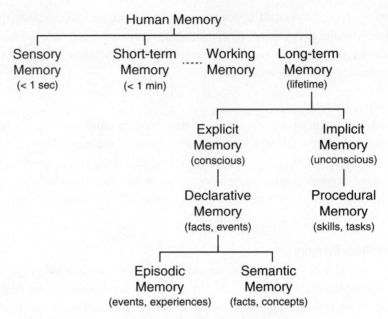

Figure 3.6. Types of Memory

RETRIEVAL

Of course, memories that are stored are of no use unless we can pull them back out to use them. **Retrieval** is the name given to the process of demonstrating that something that has been learned has been retained. Most people think about retrieval in terms of **recall**, or the retrieval and statement of previously learned information, but learning can be additionally demonstrated by recognizing or quickly relearning information.

Recognition, the process of merely identifying a piece of information that was previously learned, is far easier than recall. This difference is something you can take advantage of because the MCAT, as a multiple-choice test, is largely based on recognizing information. If the MCAT were a fill-in-the-blank style exam, your approach to studying would have to be vastly different and far more in-depth.

Relearning is another way of demonstrating that information has been stored in long-term memory. In studying the memorization of lists, Hermann Ebbinghaus found that his recall of a list of short words he had learned the previous day was often quite poor. However, he was able to rememorize the list much more quickly the second time through. Ebbinghaus interpreted this to mean that the information had been stored, even though it wasn't readily available for recall. Through additional research, he discovered that the longer the amount of time between sessions of relearning, the greater the retention of the information later on. Ebbinghaus dubbed this phenomenon the **spacing effect**, and it helps to explain why cramming is not nearly as effective as spacing out studying over an extended period of time.

Real World

Think back to elementary school. How many of your classmates do you think you could list? Chances are, not many. On the other hand, glancing through your class photo, you would probably recognize the vast majority of your former classmates. This gap is the difference between recall and recognition.

Recalling a fact at a moment's notice can be difficult. Fortunately, the brain has ways of organizing information so that it can take advantage of environmental cues to tell it where to find a given memory. Psychologists think of memory not as simply a stockpile of unrelated facts, but rather as a network of interconnected ideas. The brain organizes ideas into a **semantic network**, as shown in Figure 3.7, in which concepts are linked together based on similar meaning, not unlike an Internet encyclopedia wherein each page includes links for similar topics. For example, the concept of *red* might be closely linked to other colors, like *orange* and *green*, as well as objects, like *fire engine* and *roses*. When one node of our semantic network is activated, such as seeing the word *red* on a sign, the other linked concepts around it are also unconsciously activated, a process known as **spreading activation**. Spreading activation is at the heart of a retrieval cue known as **priming**, in which recall is aided by first being presented with a word or phrase that is close to the desired semantic memory.

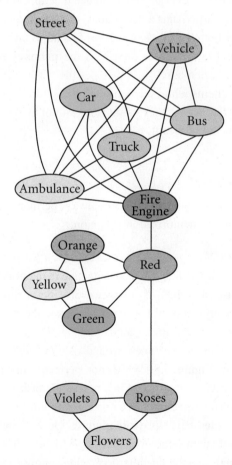

Figure 3.7. An Example Semantic Network
In spreading activation, the concept of *red* will also unconsciously
activate other linked concepts.

Context effects are another common retrieval cue. Memory is aided by being in the physical location where encoding took place. Psychologists have shown a person will score better when they take an exam in the same room in which they learned the information. Context effects can go even further than this; facts learned underwater are better recalled when underwater than when on land.

Similarly, a person's mental state can also affect recall. This retrieval cue is called **state-dependent memory,** alternately referred to as a **state-dependent effect**. People who learn facts or skills while intoxicated, for example, will show better recall or proficiency when performing those same tasks while intoxicated as compared to performing them while sober. Emotions work in a similar way: being in a foul mood primes negative memories, which in turn work to sustain the foul mood. So not only will memory be better for information learned when in a similar mood, but recall of negative or positive memories will lead to the persistence of the mood.

Finally, the **serial position effect** is a retrieval cue that appears while learning lists. When researchers give participants a list of items to memorize, the participants have much higher recall for both the first few and last few items on the list. The tendency to remember early and late items is known as the **primacy** and **recency effect**, respectively. However, when asked to remember the list later, people show strong recall for the first few items while recall of the last few items fades. Psychologists interpret this to mean that the recency effect is a result of the last items still being in short-term memory on initial recall.

FORGETTING

Unfortunately, even long-term memory is not always permanent. Several phenomena can result in the loss of memorized information.

Brain Disorders

There are several disorders that can lead to decline in memory. The most common is **Alzheimer's disease**, which is a degenerative brain disorder thought to be linked to a loss of acetylcholine in neurons that link to the hippocampus, although its exact causes are not well understood. Alzheimer's is marked by progressive **dementia** (a loss of cognitive function) and memory loss, with atrophy of the brain, as shown in Figure 3.8. While not perfectly linear, memory loss in Alzheimer's disease tends to proceed in a retrograde fashion, with loss of recent memories before distant memories. Microscopic findings of Alzheimer's include **neurofibrillary tangles** and β-amyloid plaques. One common phenomenon that occurs in individuals with middle- to late-stage Alzheimer's is **sundowning**, an increase in dysfunction in the late afternoon and evening.

Bridge

The β-amyloid plaques of Alzheimer's disease are incorrectly folded copies of the amyloid precursor protein, in which insoluble β-pleated sheets form and then deposit in the brain. Protein folding is discussed in detail in Chapter 1 of *MCAT Biochemistry Review*.

Figure 3.8. Findings of Alzheimer's Disease

Korsakoff's syndrome is another form of memory loss caused by thiamine deficiency in the brain. The disorder is marked by both **retrograde amnesia** (the loss of previously formed memories) and **anterograde amnesia** (the inability to form new memories). Another common symptom is **confabulation**, or the process of creating vivid but fabricated memories, typically thought to be an attempt made by the brain to fill in the gaps of missing memories.

Agnosia is the loss of the ability to recognize objects, people, or sounds, though usually only one of the three. Agnosia is usually caused by physical damage to the brain, such as that caused by a stroke or a neurological disorder such as multiple sclerosis.

Decay

Of course, not all memory loss is due to a disorder. Often, memories are simply lost naturally over time as the neurochemical trace of a short-term memory fades. In his word memorization experiment, Ebbinghaus noted what he called a "curve of forgetting," as shown in Figure 3.9. For a day or two after learning the list, recall fell sharply but then leveled off.

Figure 3.9. Ebbinghaus's Curve of Forgetting

Interference

Another common reason for memory loss is **interference** (also referred to as an **interference effect**), a retrieval error caused by the existence of other, usually similar, information. Interference can be classified by its direction. When we experience **proactive interference**, old information is interfering with new learning. For example, think back to a time when you moved to a new address. For a short time, you may have had trouble recalling individual pieces of the new address because you were so used to the old one. Similarly, Ebbinghaus found that with each successive list he learned, his recall for new lists decreased over time, an effect he attributed to interference caused by older lists.

Retroactive interference is when new information causes forgetting of old information. For example, at the beginning of a school year, teachers learning a new set of students' names often find that they can no longer remember the names of the previous year's students. One way of preventing retroactive interference is to reduce the number of interfering events, which is why it is often best to study in the evening about an hour before falling asleep (although this also depends on your personal style!).

Aging and Memory

Contrary to popular belief, aging does not necessarily lead to significant memory loss; while there are many individuals whose memory fades in old age, this is not always the case. In fact, studies show that there is a larger range of memory ability for 70-year-olds than there is for 20-year-olds. There are, however, some trends that can be demonstrated when evaluating the memories of older individuals. When asked about the most pivotal events in their lives, people in their 70s and 80s tend to say that their most vivid memories are of events that occurred in their teens and 20s, a fact that psychologists interpret to mean that this time is a peak period for encoding in a person's life.

3: Learning and Memory

Even for the elderly, certain types of memory remain quite strong. People tend not to demonstrate much degeneration in recognition or skill-based memory as they age. Even certain types of recall will remain strong for most people; semantically meaningful material can be easily learned and recalled, most likely due to older individuals having a larger semantic network than their younger counterparts. **Prospective memory** (remembering to perform a task at some point in the future) remains mostly intact when it is event-based—that is, primed by a trigger event, such as remembering to buy milk when walking past the grocery store. On the other hand, time-based prospective memory, such as remembering to take a medication every day at 7:00 a.m., does tend to decline with age.

MEMORY CONSTRUCTION

We often think of memory as a record of our experiences or a kind of video recording that is stored to be accessed later. Nothing could be further from the truth: memory can be faulty to the point where two people can recall the same event as occurring in completely different ways. In fact, memories are influenced heavily by our thoughts and feelings both while the event is occurring and later during recall. We've already discussed confabulation, a phenomenon in which we fill in gaps in our memories such that, over time and with enough rehearsal, our memories of the event can change drastically. Confabulation is one example of the creation of **false memories**, but our memories can also be affected by outside sources as well.

One such phenomenon is the **misinformation effect**. In a famous experiment, participants were shown several pictures including one of a car stopped at a yield sign. Later, they were presented with written descriptions of the pictures, some of which contained misinformation, such as describing a car stopped at a stop sign. When asked to recall the details of the pictures, many participants insisted on having seen a stop sign in the picture.

The misinformation effect can also be seen at the point of recall. In another experiment, participants were shown a video of an automobile accident. Some participants were then asked, *How fast were the cars moving when they collided?*, while others were asked about the accident using more descriptive language such as *How fast were the cars moving when they crashed?* Those participants who were asked the question with leading language were much more likely to overstate the severity of the accident than those who had been asked the question with less descriptive language.

Source-monitoring error involves confusion between semantic and episodic memory: a person remembers the details of an event, but confuses the context under which those details were gained. Source-monitoring error often manifests when a person hears a story of something that happened to someone else, and later recalls the story as having happened to him- or herself.

Real World

During a Congressional Medal of Honor ceremony in 1983, Ronald Reagan relayed a vivid story about a heroic World War II pilot who received a posthumous medal. Skeptical reporters, unaware of any incident matching the details of Reagan's story, checked into the story and found that the pilot had existed—in the 1944 movie *A Wing and a Prayer*. Reagan had remembered the details of the pilot's heroic actions but had forgotten their source.

MCAT Concept Check 3.2:

Before you move on, assess your understanding of the material with these questions.

1. List the three modes in which information can be encoded, from strongest to weakest.

   1._____

   2._____

   3._____

2. In what ways is maintenance rehearsal different from elaborative rehearsal?

   _____

   _____

3. In terms of recall, why might it be a bad idea to study for the MCAT while listening to music?

   _____

   _____

4. What are some factors that might cause eyewitness courtroom testimony to be unreliable?

3.3 Neurobiology of Learning and Memory

LEARNING GOALS

After Chapter 3.3, you will be able to:

- Describe neuroplasticity and changes that occur throughout the human lifespan
- Recall the terms involved with removing and strengthening memory connections

Even as you read this text, your brain is changing. Memory, and therefore learning, involves changes in brain physiology, such that with each new concept you learn your brain is altering its synaptic connections in response. You may have heard that it is far easier for children to learn a new language than it is for adults. Indeed, the cliché *you can't teach an old dog new tricks*, while not strictly true, does have its roots in neurobiology.

As infants, we are born with many more neurons than we actually need. As our brains develop, neural connections form rapidly in response to stimuli via a phenomenon called **neuroplasticity**. In fact, the brains of young children are so plastic that they can reorganize drastically in response to injury, as evidenced by studies of children who have had entire hemispheres of their brains removed to prevent severe seizures. The remaining hemisphere will change to take over functions of the missing parts of the brain, allowing these children to grow up to lead essentially normal lives. While our brains do maintain a degree of plasticity throughout our lives, adult brains display nowhere near the degree of plasticity as those of a child. Another way our brains change is through a process called **synaptic pruning**. As we grow older, weak neural connections are broken while strong ones are bolstered, increasing the efficiency of our brains' ability to process information.

This concept of plasticity is important because it is closely linked to learning and memory. As you learned in Chapter 4 of *MCAT Biology Review*, stimuli cause activation of neurons, which release their neurotransmitters into the synaptic cleft. These neurotransmitters continue to stimulate activity until degradation, reuptake, or diffusion out of the synaptic cleft. In the interim, this neural activity forms a memory trace that is thought to be the cause of short-term memory. As discussed earlier, if the stimulus isn't repeated or rehearsed, the memory trace disappears, and the consequence is the loss of the short-term memory. However, as the stimulus is repeated, the stimulated neurons become more efficient at releasing their neurotransmitters and at the same time receptor sites on the other side of the synapse increase, increasing receptor density. This strengthening is known as **long-term potentiation**, and is believed to be the neurophysiological basis of long-term memory.

As described in the previous section, a memory begins its life as a sensory memory in the projection area of a given sensory modality. This sensory memory is brief, unless maintained in consciousness and moved, as a short-term memory, into the hippocampus in the temporal lobe. The memory can then be manipulated through working memory while in the hippocampus (in tandem with the frontal and parietal lobes), and even stored for later recall. Over very long periods of time, memories are gradually moved from the hippocampus back to the cerebral cortex. Note that this general pathway is a drastic oversimplification of the complex interplay of brain regions involved in memory, but is a useful paradigm for Test Day.

MCAT Concept Check 3.3:

Before you move on, assess your understanding of the material with these questions.

1. What is neuroplasticity? How does neuroplasticity change during life?

   _____

   _____

2. What is the term for removing weak neural connections? What is the term for strengthening memory connections through increased neurotransmitter release and receptor density?

   • Removing weak connections:

   _____

   • Strengthening connections:

   _____

Conclusion

In this chapter, we discussed two very important ways that we react to our environments. We are constantly receiving input from the world around us, and the way we memorize that information depends greatly on both the nature of the information and its importance to us individually. That information can also have a profound effect on us, causing us to increase or decrease the frequency of certain behaviors, sometimes without our conscious knowledge. Because the concepts of learning and memory are both used heavily in research, we can expect the MCAT to place many of its passages testing these topics within an experimental context.

CONCEPT SUMMARY

Learning

- **Habituation** is the process of becoming used to a stimulus. **Dishabituation** can occur when a second stimulus intervenes, causing a resensitization to the original stimulus.

- **Associative learning** is a way of pairing together stimuli and responses, or behaviors and consequences.

- In **classical conditioning**, an unconditioned stimulus that produces an instinctive, unconditioned response is paired with a neutral stimulus. With repetition, the neutral stimulus becomes a conditioned stimulus that produces a conditioned response.

- In **operant conditioning**, behavior is changed through the use of consequences.

  o **Reinforcement** increases the likelihood of a behavior.

  o **Punishment** decreases the likelihood of a behavior.

  o The schedule of reinforcement affects the rate at which the behavior is performed. Schedules can be based either on a ratio of behavior to reward or on an amount of time, and can be either fixed or variable. Behaviors learned through variable-ratio schedules are the hardest to extinguish.

- **Observational learning**, or **modeling**, is the acquisition of behavior by watching others.

Memory

- **Encoding** is the process of putting new information into memory. It can be **automatic** or **effortful**. Semantic encoding is stronger than both acoustic and visual encoding.

- **Sensory** and **short-term memory** are transient and are based on neurotransmitter activity. **Working memory** requires short-term memory, attention, and executive function to manipulate information.

- **Long-term memory** requires elaborative rehearsal and is the result of increased neuronal connectivity.

  o **Explicit (declarative) memory** stores facts and stories.

  o **Implicit (nondeclarative) memory** stores skills and conditioning effects.

- Facts are stored via **semantic networks**.

- **Recognition** of information is stronger than **recall**.

- **Retrieval** of information is often based on **priming** interconnected nodes of the semantic network.

- Memories can be lost through disorders such as Alzheimer's disease, Korsakoff's syndrome, or agnosia; decay; or interference.

- Memories are highly subject to influence by outside information and mood both at the time of encoding and at recall.

Neurobiology of Learning and Memory

- Both learning and memory rely on changes in brain chemistry and physiology, the extent of which depends on **neuroplasticity**, which decreases as we age.

- **Long-term potentiation**, responsible for the conversion of short-term to long-term memory, is the strengthening of neuronal connections resulting from increased neurotransmitter release and adding of receptor sites.

ANSWERS TO CONCEPT CHECKS

3.1

1. Eating each course of a meal before moving on to the next causes habituation; each bite causes less pleasurable stimulation, so people feel less desire to keep eating. On the other hand, mixing up the courses of a meal causes dishabituation for taste, which would cause people to eat more overall.

2. The conditioned stimulus is the smell of popcorn. The unconditioned stimulus is the popping of the balloon. The conditioned response is nervousness (fear) in response to the presence of popcorn. The unconditioned response is fear in response to the popping of the balloon.

3. Negative reinforcement causes an increase of a given behavior by removing something unpleasant, while positive punishment reduces behavior by adding something unpleasant. Examples will vary, but common negative reinforcers include medicines that reduce pain or avoiding uncomfortable situations to reduce anxiety. Common examples of positive punishments include spankings or getting detention in school for bad behavior.

3.2

1. Of the three modes in which information can be encoded, semantic is the strongest, followed by acoustic. Visual is the weakest.

2. Maintenance rehearsal is the repetition of information to keep it within short-term memory for near-immediate use. Elaborative rehearsal is the association of information to other stored knowledge, and is a more effective way to move information from short-term to long-term memory.

3. Because you will be taking the MCAT in a quiet room, studying under similar circumstances will aid recall due to context effects. Music may also compete for attention, reducing your ability to focus on the relevant study material.

4. Several factors can affect the accuracy of eyewitness testimony, including the manner in which questions are asked; the nature of information shared with the witness by police, lawyers, and other witnesses following the event; the misinformation effect; source-monitoring error; and the amount of time elapsed between the event and the trial. Even watching crime dramas, the news, or witnessing similar events can cause source-monitoring error.

3.3

1. Neuroplasticity is the ability of the brain to form new connections rapidly. The brain is most plastic in young children, and plasticity quickly drops off after childhood.

2. Pruning is the term for removing weak neural connections. Long-term potentiation is the strengthening of memory connections through increased neurotransmitter release and receptor density.

SHARED CONCEPTS

Discrete Practice Questions

Consult your online resources for Full-Length Exams and Passage-Based Questions (for certain chapters).

1. Researchers repeatedly startle a participant with a loud buzzer. After some time, the participant stops being startled by the buzzer. If the researchers interrupt the study with the sound of pans banging together, which of the following would likely be observed?

   A. Increased startle response to the buzzer
   B. Decreased startle response to the buzzer
   C. No change in the response to the buzzer
   D. Generalization to previously nonaversive stimuli

2. Many pets will run toward the kitchen when they hear the sound of a can opener opening a can of pet food. The sound of the can opener is a:

   A. conditioned response.
   B. unconditioned response.
   C. conditioned stimulus.
   D. unconditioned stimulus.

3. A person suffers from food poisoning after eating a spoiled orange, and later finds that the smell of lemon and other citrus fruits make her nauseated. This is an example of:

   A. acquisition.
   B. generalization.
   C. discrimination.
   D. negative reinforcement.

4. Which of the following processes would increase the likelihood of a behavior?

   A. Extinction
   B. Negative punishment
   C. Positive punishment
   D. Avoidance learning

5. A credit card company begins applying an interest rate to credit card accounts in response to late payments. This is an example of:

   A. positive reinforcement because the bank will now make more money.
   B. negative reinforcement because the bank is adding a fee to motivate the person to pay their bills.
   C. positive punishment because the bank is adding a fee to reduce the incidence of late payments.
   D. negative punishment because the bank is decreasing the amount the person has to pay.

6. A rat is trained to press a lever to obtain food under a fixed-interval schedule. Which of the following behaviors would the rat most likely exhibit?

   A. Pressing the lever continuously whenever it is hungry.
   B. Pressing the lever exactly once and waiting for the food pellet before pressing it again.
   C. Pressing the lever slowly at first, but with increasing frequency as the end of the interval approaches.
   D. None of the above; the association formed by fixed-interval schedules is too weak to increase behavior.

7. Which of the following is true of teaching an animal a complicated, multistage behavior?

   I. The individual parts of the behavior should not run counter to the animal's natural instincts.
   II. The behaviors must be tied to a food reward of some kind.
   III. Rewarding individual parts of the behavior on their own interferes with reinforcement of the entire behavior.

   A. I only
   B. I and III only
   C. II and III only
   D. I, II, and III

8. Which of the following is true of controlled processing?

    A. It is the means through which information enters short-term memory.

    B. Information that requires controlled processing cannot become automatic.

    C. It always requires active attention to the information being encoded.

    D. Most information we can later recall is encoded using controlled processing.

9. Which of the following methods of encoding is most conducive to later recall?

    A. Semantic

    B. Visual

    C. Iconic

    D. Acoustic

10. Which of the following would be most likely to be stored in long-term memory?

    A. A list of nonsense words

    B. A list of the dates of birth of 15 randomly selected people

    C. A list of the names of musicians in an individual's favorite bands

    D. A list of the dates of battles in the Peloponnesian War

11. An individual memorizes a shopping list by associating each item with an image that corresponds with a number. This individual is using which of the following mnemonics?

    A. Clustering

    B. Method of loci

    C. Elaborative rehearsal

    D. Peg-words

12. A researcher uses a partial-report procedure after presenting participants with an array of nine numbers for a fraction of a second. Which of the following is the most likely result of this procedure?

    A. The participants will be able to recall any of the rows or columns in great detail but only immediately after presentation.

    B. The participants will only be able to recall the first few numbers in the array due to the serial position effect.

    C. The participants will be able to recall approximately seven of the numbers for a few seconds following presentation of the stimulus.

    D. The participants will not be able to recall any of the numbers verbally, but will be able to draw the full array under hypnosis.

13. Which of the following is an example of a semantic memory?

    A. Having the ability to drive a car

    B. Knowing the parts of a car engine

    C. Remembering the experience of learning to drive

    D. Associating a car with other vehicles in a semantic network

14. Which of the following is an example of a circumstance that could cause a state-dependent recall effect?

    I. The individual is outside on a rainy day.

    II. The individual is high on marjiuana.

    III. The individual is in a manic episode.

    A. I only

    B. III only

    C. II and III only

    D. I, II, and III

15. Which of the following would elderly individuals be most likely to have trouble recalling?

    A. The circumstances of meeting his or her significant other in college

    B. A doctor's appointment scheduled for 1:00 p.m.

    C. The names of the characters in his or her favorite television show

    D. That a library book needs to be returned when passing by the library on a morning walk

Explanations to Discrete Practice Questions

1. A

After a while, the participant became habituated to the sound of the buzzer. Introducing a new stimulus, such as the banging pans, should dishabituate (resensitize) the original stimulus, causing a temporary increase in response to the sound of the buzzer.

2. C

The sound of a can opener would not normally produce a response on its own, making it a stimulus that must have been conditioned by association with food.

3. B

Generalization is the process by which similar stimuli can produce the same conditioned response. Here, the response to the taste and smell of oranges has generalized to that of all citrus.

4. D

Avoidance learning is a type of negative reinforcement in which a behavior is increased to prevent an unpleasant future consequence. Extinction, **choice (A)**, is a decreased response to a conditioned stimulus when it is no longer paired with an unconditioned stimulus. Punishment, **choices (B)** and **(C)**, lead to decreased behaviors in operant conditioning.

5. C

Because the credit card company wishes to decrease the behavior of late bill payment, this is a punishment, so we can eliminate **choices (A)** and **(B)**. The company is adding something unpleasant by adding an additional fee, and is hoping to reduce the occurrence of late payments (the target behavior), making **choice (C)** a match. The person is now having to pay additional money, making **choice (D)** an opposite answer.

6. C

In a fixed-interval schedule, the desired behavior is rewarded the first time it is exhibited after the fixed interval has elapsed. Both fixed-interval and fixed-ratio schedules tend to show this phenomenon: almost no response immediately after the reward is given, but the behavior increases as the rat gets close to receiving the reward.

7. A

Complicated, multistage behaviors are typically taught through shaping, so statement III must not be part of the correct answer. Reinforcers do not necessarily need to be food-based, and instinctive drift can interfere with learning of complicated behaviors; therefore, only statement I is accurate.

8. C

This is the definition of controlled processing and is the only answer choice that is necessarily true of controlled processing. Effortful processing is used to create long-term memories, and—with practice—can become automatic, invalidating **choices (A)** and **(B)**. Most of our day-to-day activities are processed automatically, making **choice (D)** incorrect.

9. A

Semantic encoding, or encoding based on the meaning of the information, is the strongest of the methods of encoding. Visual encoding, **choice (B)**, is the weakest, and acoustic encoding, **choice (D)**, is intermediate between the two. Iconic memory, **choice (C)**, is a type of sensory memory.

10. C

The self-reference effect indicates that information that is most meaningful to an individual is the most likely to be memorized. **Choice (C)** is the most personally relevant to the individual memorizing the list.

11. D

The association of words on a list to a preconstructed set of ideas is common to both the method-of-loci and peg-word mnemonics. Method-of-loci systems, **choice (B)**, associate items with locations, while peg-word systems use images associated with numbers.

12. A

Partial-report procedures, in which the individual is asked to recall a specific portion of the stimulus, are incredibly accurate, but only for a very brief time. This is a method of studying sensory (specifically, iconic) memory. Both the serial position effect, **choice (B)**, and the 7 ± 2 rule, **choice (C)**, are characteristics of short-term memory.

13. B

Semantic memory is the category of long-term memory that refers to recall of facts, rather than experiences or skills. Be careful not to confuse semantic memory with semantic networks, **choice (D)**, which are the associations of similar concepts in the mind to aid in their retrieval.

14. C

State-dependent recall is concerned with the internal rather than external states of the individual. As such, both statements II and III are examples of state-dependent circumstances, while statement I might cause a context effect instead.

15. B

Elderly individuals have the most trouble with time-based prospective memory, which is remembering to do an activity at a particular time. Other forms of memory are generally preserved, or may decline slightly but less significantly than time-based prospective memory.

Cognition, Consciousness, and Language

In This Chapter

Chapter Profile

8%

The content in this chapter should be relevant to about 8% of all questions about the Behavioral Sciences on the MCAT.

This chapter covers material from the following AAMC content category:

6B: Making sense of the environment

Introduction

As we think and move through the world, we often take our brains for granted. As you read, speak, ponder, make decisions, and perform complex motor functions, your brain is rapidly using electrical and chemical impulses to encode, store, and retrieve information. Most of these processes occur without your awareness or conscious thought. Imagine going to the grocery store. You fill your cart while comparing prices, assessing the produce, and planning what meals to make in the near future. After the cashier totals your purchases, you pull out a debit card, punch in a PIN, and leave with your groceries. While you were shopping in that grocery store, your brain was busy taking in all of the information around it and deciding which stimuli required attention. At the same time, you were making conscious decisions about your purchases, likely daydreaming, and maybe even singing along to music playing in the background. But, to our awareness, this was still just a simple trip to the store because most of the time, we don't even notice the tremendous processing power of our brain as we navigate the world.

But in some ways, this capacity for simultaneous conscious thought, daydreaming, and decision-making is what makes us human. Many of these functions are under the province of the frontal lobe, which—in comparison to other species on this planet—is disproportionately large in *H. sapiens sapiens*. Our frontal lobe enables us to eschew instantaneous reward and to seek out delayed gratification, like studying for the MCAT to get that high score you deserve. The frontal lobe also controls our production of language, which permits us to transmit ideas between individuals, cultures, and time. Finally, the frontal lobe helps us coordinate our thinking by deciding which stimuli deserve our attention. These are functions that are indispensible to our daily functioning and will be the focus of this chapter.

4.1 Cognition

LEARNING GOALS

After Chapter 4.1, you will be able to:

- List the steps in the information processing model of cognition
- Describe the effects of aging, heredity, and environment on cognitive function
- Recall Piaget's four stages of cognitive development and their key features

---

The study of **cognition** looks at how our brains process and react to the incredible information overload presented to us by the world. Cognition, overall, is not a uniquely human trait, but we are certainly the most advanced species on the planet in terms of complex thought. As described in the introduction, the frontal lobe is disproportionately large in our subspecies; a comparison to our recent anthropological ancestors demonstrates that our skull is shaped to accommodate this enlarged lobe, as shown in Figure 4.1.

Figure 4.1. Skulls of *H. sapiens* (left) and *H. neanderthalensis* (right)

INFORMATION PROCESSING MODEL

In the 1950s, much of science and engineering turned toward the production of computers and artificial intelligence. It was noted that certain steps were required in order to use a computer to store and process information. First, the information must be encoded in a language that the computer understands. Then, the information must be stored in such a way that it can be found later. Finally, the computer must be able to retrieve that information when required.

Psychologists took this model of information processing and applied it to the human brain. They theorized that the brain is somewhat like a computer. It must encode information into a series of chemical and electrical signals. Then, the brain must be able to store this information such that it can be retrieved when needed. Then, there must be a process by which the brain is able to retrieve information.

The manner in which information is encoded, stored, and retrieved has been a consistent source of debate. One prominent theory, Paivio's **dual-coding theory**, states that both verbal association and visual images are used to process and store information. For example, the word "dad" can recall some information, and the picture of "dad" can recall that same information. The fact that we can code this information two different ways builds redundancy and increases the chance that the information can be retrieved and used effectively when cued, much like search engine optimization within a computer program.

However, the human brain is not a computer. While the computer analogy creates a simple paradigm by which information is processed by the brain, it does not tell the whole story. The human brain doesn't just handle information in the form of facts: it also handles emotions, sensations such as smell and taste, as well as memories. As discussed in Chapter 3 of *MCAT Behavioral Sciences Review*, encoding, storage, and retrieval are often flavored by context and emotion.

> **Bridge**
>
> The key memory processes of encoding, storage, and retrieval are covered in Chapter 3 of *MCAT Behavioral Sciences Review*.

The **information processing model** has four key components, or pillars:

- Thinking requires sensation, encoding, and storage of stimuli.
- Stimuli must be analyzed by the brain (rather than responded to automatically) to be useful in decision-making.
- Decisions made in one situation can be extrapolated and adjusted to help solve new problems (also called situational modification).
- Problem solving is dependent not only on the person's cognitive level, but also on the context and complexity of the problem.

COGNITIVE DEVELOPMENT

Cognitive development is the development of one's ability to think and solve problems across the lifespan. Interestingly, during childhood, cognitive development is limited by the pace of brain maturation. Early cognitive development includes

Key Concept

Piaget's stages of cognitive development:
- Sensorimotor
- Preoperational
- Concrete operational
- Formal operational

learning control of one's own body as well as learning how to interact with and manipulate the environment. Early cognitive development is characterized by mastering the physical environment. As physical tasks are mastered, a new challenge looms for a developing child: abstract thinking. As discussed in Chapter 1 of *MCAT Behavioral Sciences Review*, social skills also develop during the lifetime.

As you will see during our review of Piaget's stages of cognitive development, the development of the ability to think abstractly is developed throughout childhood. The development of abstract thinking is also dependent upon increases in working memory and mental capacities. As the brain develops, the ability to process information in an abstract manner also develops.

Piaget's Stages of Cognitive Development

Jean Piaget was one of the most influential figures in developmental psychology. Piaget insisted that there are qualitative differences between the way that children and adults think, and thus divided the lifespan into four stages of cognitive development: sensorimotor, preoperational, concrete operational, and formal operational. Piaget believed that passage through each of these stages was a continuous and sequential process in which completion of each stage prepares the individual for the stage that follows.

Before delving into the actual stages, we have to look at how Piaget explained learning. According to Piaget, infants learn mainly through instinctual interaction with the environment. For example, infants possess a grasping reflex. Through experience with this reflex, the infant learns that it is possible to grasp objects. Piaget referred to these organized patterns of behavior and thought as schemata. A **schema** can include a concept (What is a *dog*?), a behavior (What do you do when someone asks you your name?), or a sequence of events (What do you normally do in a sit-down restaurant?). As a child proceeds through the stages, new information has to be placed into the different schemata. Piaget theorized that new information is processed via **adaptation**. According to Piaget, adaptation to information comes about by two complementary processes: assimilation and accommodation. **Assimilation** is the process of classifying new information into existing schemata. If the new information does not fit neatly into existing schemata, then accommodation occurs. **Accommodation** is the process by which existing schemata are modified to encompass this new information.

The first stage is the **sensorimotor stage**, starting at birth and lasting until about two years of age. In this stage, a child learns to manipulate his or her environment in order to meet physical needs. Two different types of **circular reactions**, named for their repetitive natures, begin. **Primary circular reactions** are the repetition of a body movement that originally occurred by chance, such as sucking the thumb; usually, the behavior is repeated because the child finds it soothing. **Secondary circular reactions** occur when manipulation is focused on something outside the body, such as repeatedly throwing toys from a high chair. These behaviors are often repeated because the child gets a response from the environment (such as a parent picking up the dropped toy). The key milestone that ends the sensorimotor stage is the development of **object permanence**, which is the understanding that objects continue to exist even when out of view. This is the idea behind "peek-a-boo," shown in Figure 4.2. This game is so entertaining to young infants because they lack object permanence. Each time the adult reveals him- or herself, the child interprets it as though he or she has just come into existence. Object permanence marks the beginning of **representational thought**, in which the child has begun to create mental representations of external objects and events.

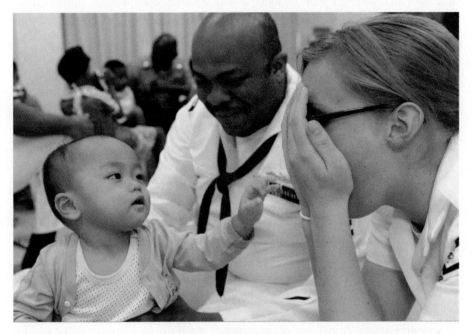

Figure 4.2. Peek-a-Boo
This game depends on the child being in the sensorimotor stage, prior to the development of object permanence.

The **preoperational stage** lasts from about two to seven years of age, and is characterized by symbolic thinking, egocentrism, and centration. **Symbolic thinking** refers to the ability to pretend, play make-believe, and have an imagination. **Egocentrism** refers to the inability to imagine what another person may think or feel. **Centration** is the tendency to focus on only one aspect of a phenomenon, or inability to understand the concept of **conservation**. For example, a child can be presented with two identical quantities of pizza: on one plate is a single large slice, while the other plate has the exact same quantity in two slices. A child in this stage will be unable to tell that the quantities are equal and will focus mainly on the number of slices on the plate rather than the actual quantity.

The **concrete operational stage** lasts from about 7 to 11 years of age. In this stage, children can understand conservation and consider the perspectives of others. Additionally, they are able to engage in logical thought as long as they are working with concrete objects or information that is directly available. These children have not yet developed the ability to think abstractly.

The **formal operational stage** starts around 11 years of age, and is marked by the ability to think logically about abstract ideas. Generally coinciding with adolescence, this stage is marked by the ability to reason about abstract concepts and problem solve. The difference between this type of thought and concrete operations is illustrated by Piaget's pendulum experiment. Children were given a pendulum in which they could vary the length of the string, the weight of the pendulum, the force of the push, and the initial angle of the swing. They were asked to find out what determined the frequency of the swing. Children in the concrete operational stage manipulated the variables at random and even distorted the data to fit preconceived hypotheses. Adolescents, on the other hand, were able to hold all variables but one constant at a given time, proceeding methodically to discover that only the length of the string affects the frequency.

Role of Culture in Cognitive Development

Cognitive development is very much related to culture, as one's culture will determine what one is expected to learn. Some cultures will place a higher value on social learning, including cultural traditions and roles, while other cultures will value knowledge. In addition, one's culture will also influence the rate of cognitive development as children are treated very differently from culture to culture.

Lev Vygotsky, a prominent educational psychologist, proposed that the engine driving cognitive development is the child's internalization of his or her culture, including interpersonal and societal rules, symbols, and language. As a child develops, her skills and abilities are still in formative stages. With help from adults or other children, those skills can develop further. That help may come in the form of instruction from a teacher or even watching another child perform the skill.

Cognitive Changes in Late Adulthood

Aging brings about many changes in cognition. Reaction time increases steadily in early adulthood, and time-based prospective memory—the ability to remember to perform a task at a specific time in the future—also declines with age. Intellectual changes also occur; however, IQ changes have been found to be misleading. Early research into the field of intelligence and aging indicated that a substantial decline in IQ occurred between the ages of 30 and 40. In order to further elucidate what specific changes were occurring, intelligence itself was separated into two subtypes: fluid intelligence and crystallized intelligence. **Fluid intelligence** consists of problem-solving skills, while **crystallized intelligence** is more related to use of learned skills and knowledge. Fluid intelligence was shown to peak in early adulthood, while crystallized intelligence peaked in middle adulthood. Regardless, both types of intelligence have been shown to decline with age.

Bridge

Culture has profound effects on cognitive development, as well as social structure, rules, and mores. Culture is discussed in detail in Chapter 11 of *MCAT Behavioral Sciences Review*.

Bridge

Lev Vygotsky is also a key figure in the psychology of identity. Along with Kohlberg, Freud, and Erikson, he proposed a staged system of identity formation. These theorists are discussed in Chapter 6 of *MCAT Behavioral Sciences Review*.

Decline in intellectual abilities in adulthood has been linked with how long an older adult retains the ability to function in what is known as **activities of daily living** (eating, bathing, toileting, dressing, and ambulation). It appears, however, that this decline is not uniform. Certain characteristics, such as higher level of education, more frequent performance of intellectual activities, socialization, and a stimulating environment have been found to be protective against intellectual decline.

Intellectual decline is not always benign. Some types of intellectual decline, especially those resulting in dementia, are very common and indicate a progressive loss of function beyond that of old age. **Dementia** often begins with impaired memory, but later progresses to impaired judgment and confusion. Personality changes are also very common as dementia progresses. The most common cause of dementia is Alzheimer's disease. Vascular (multi-infarct) dementia, caused by high blood pressure and repeated microscopic clots in the brain, is also a very common cause. It is also important to note that people with dementia often require full-time supportive care in order to carry out activities of daily living. This causes tremendous stress on families, including children and spouses of those with dementia, as the care for the person with dementia often falls on family members.

HEREDITY, ENVIRONMENT, AND BIOLOGIC FACTORS

Cognition can be affected by a wide variety of conditions. These may include actual problems with the brain itself (organic brain disorders), genetic and chromosomal conditions, metabolic derangements, and long-term drug use. The environment can also affect both cognitive development and day-to-day cognition.

Parenting styles may influence cognitive development by reward, punishment, or indifference for an emerging skill. In addition, genetics can predispose to a state that may make cognitive development difficult. For example, many genetic and chromosomal diseases such as Down's syndrome and Fragile X syndrome are associated with delayed cognitive development. Antisocial personality disorder has also been shown to have a strong genetic component. The presence of genes for this disorder may make it difficult for a child to appreciate the rights of others.

Intellectual disabilities in children can also be caused by chemical exposures, illness, injury, or trauma during birth. Alcohol use during pregnancy can cause fetal alcohol syndrome, which results in slowed cognitive development and distinct craniofacial features, shown in Figure 4.3. Infections in the brain may result in electrical abnormalities and slowed development. Complications during birth—especially those causing reduced oxygen delivery to the brain—may also affect cognition. Finally, reduced cognition can also occur following trauma to the brain, as occurs with shaken baby syndrome.

Real World

Alzheimer's disease accounts for approximately 60 to 80% of all dementia cases.

Skin folds at the corner of the eye

Low nasal bridge

Short nose

Indistinct philtrum (groove between nose and upper lip)

Small head circumference

Small eye opening

Small midface

Thin upper lip

Figure 4.3. Craniofacial Features of Fetal Alcohol Syndrome

Real World

The delirium associated with alcohol withdrawal, called *delirium tremens*, can be life threatening. As a depressant, alcohol is the only major drug of abuse in which both overdose and withdrawal can be lethal.

However, not all cognitive decline in adulthood is slow. If there has been a rapid decline in cognition, this may be the result of delirium. **Delirium** is rapid fluctuation in cognitive function that is reversible and caused by medical (nonpsychological) causes. It can be caused by a variety of issues, including electrolyte and pH disturbances, malnutrition, low blood sugar, infection, a drug reaction, alcohol withdrawal, and pain.

MCAT Concept Check 4.1:

Before you move on, assess your understanding of the material with these questions.

1. The three steps in the information processing model are:

    1. _____

    2. _____

    3. _____

2. An elderly man is taken to his doctor by his daughter. His daughter says that during the past two days, he has been speaking to his wife who has been deceased for four years. Prior to that, he was completely normal. The elderly man most likely has:

    _____

3. List Piaget's four stages of cognitive development, and the key features of each.

Stage	Key Features

4.2 Problem Solving and Decision-Making

LEARNING GOALS

After Chapter 4.2, you will be able to:

- Identify examples of functional fixedness, mental sets, trial-and-error problem solving, algorithms, and deductive reasoning
- Recall key fallacies and biases, including base rate fallacy, disconfirmation principle, confirmation bias, overconfidence, and belief perseverance
- Describe models of intellectual functioning and tests of intellectual ability
- Explain the availability and representativeness heuristics

Every day you are faced with problems. Many of these problems you solve without any real conscious thought about what is happening. However, much like the scientific method, problem solving itself has a process. First, we must frame the problem; that is, create a mental image or schematic of the issue. Then, we generate potential solutions and begin to test them. These potential solutions may be derived from a **mental set**, which is the tendency to approach similar problems in the same way. Once solutions have been tested, we evaluate the results, considering other potential solutions that may have been easier or more effective in some way.

Problem solving can be impeded by an inappropriate mental set, as well as by functional fixedness, which is demonstrated by Duncker's candle problem. Consider the following scenario: You walk into a room and see a box of matches, some tacks, and a candle. Your task is to mount the candle on the wall so that it can be used without the wax dropping on the floor. Before reading on, try to solve the problem.

Most people find the task challenging. You might have thought of tacking the candle to the wall, but that solution doesn't work because the wax would still drop to the floor. The key is to realize that the matchbox can serve not just as a container for the matches, but as a holder for the candle. The solution, therefore, is to tack the box to the wall and put the candle in the box. **Functional fixedness** can thus be defined as the inability to consider how to use an object in a nontraditional manner.

TYPES OF PROBLEM SOLVING

In psychology, different approaches to problem solving include trial-and-error, algorithms, deductive reasoning, and inductive reasoning.

Key Concept

The first step in problem solving (framing the problem) may seem obvious; however, when we get "stuck" on a problem, it is most often because the manner in which we have framed the problem is inefficient or not useful.

Trial-and-Error

Trial-and-error is a less sophisticated type of problem solving in which various solutions are tried until one is found that seems to work. While an educated approach may be used, this type of problem solving is usually only effective when there are relatively few possible solutions.

Algorithms

An **algorithm** is a formula or procedure for solving a certain type of problem. Algorithms can be mathematical or a set of instructions, designed to automatically produce the desired solution.

Deductive Reasoning

Deductive (top-down) reasoning starts from a set of general rules and draws conclusions from the information given. An example of deductive reasoning is a logic puzzle, as shown in Figure 4.4. In these puzzles, one has to synthesize a list of logical rules to come up with the single possible solution to the problem.

	Black	Turnip	Spade	Bob	Patch	Toby	1	2	3
Jim	●	X	X	●	X	X	X	●	X
Tylor	X	●	X	X			X	X	●
Mike	X	X	●	X			●	X	X
1					X	X	●		
2						X			
3				X		X			
Bob			X						
Patch									
Toby									

Figure 4.4. A Logic Puzzle Grid
Logic puzzles are applications of deductive reasoning in which only one possible solution can be deduced based on the information given.

Inductive Reasoning

Inductive (bottom-up) reasoning seeks to create a theory via generalizations. This type of reasoning starts with specific instances, and then draws a conclusion from them.

HEURISTICS, BIASES, INTUITION, AND EMOTION

We make decisions every day. Some are insignificant: *What should I wear today?* Others are very important: *Where am I going to apply to medical school?* Decision-making is a complicated process, but we use a number of tools, such as heuristics, biases, intuition, and emotions, to speed up or simplify the process. While useful from a time and complexity standpoint, these tools can also lead us to short-sighted or problematic solutions.

Heuristics

Heuristics are simplified principles used to make decisions; they are colloquially called **rules of thumb**. The **availability heuristic** is used when we try to decide how likely something is. When we use this heuristic, we make our decisions based on how easily similar instances can be imagined. Often, the use of this heuristic leads us to a correct decision, but not always. As an example, answer the following question: *Are there more words in the English language that start with the letter "K" or that have "K" as their third letter?*

Most people respond that there are more words that begin with the letter "K" than have "K" as their third letter. In fact, there are actually at least twice as many words in English that have "K" as the third letter than begin with "K." Most people approach this question by trying to think of words that fit into each category. Because we're so used to classifying words by their first letter, it is easier to think of words beginning with "K." Thus, in this case, the availability heuristic tends to lead to an incorrect answer.

The **representativeness heuristic** involves categorizing items on the basis of whether they fit the prototypical, stereotypical, or representative image of the category. For example, consider a standard coin that is flipped ten times in a row and lands on heads every time. What is the probability of the coin landing on heads the next time? Mathematically, the probability must still be 50 percent, but most individuals will either overestimate the probability based on the pattern that has been established, or underestimate the probability with the logic that the number of heads and tails must "even out." Hence, like the availability heuristic, the use of the representativeness heuristic can sometimes lead us astray. Using prototypical or stereotypical factors while ignoring actual numerical information is called the **base rate fallacy**.

While heuristics can lead us astray, they are essential to speedy and effective decision-making. Heuristics are often used by experts in a given field. For instance, to win at chess, one must be able to think several moves ahead. On any particular turn, there may be 15 or 20 possible moves, each one of which may have multiple consequences; analyzing every possibility would take far too long. There are heuristics, however, that can quickly rule out some of the possible moves: the king must be protected, it is generally good to control the center squares, and pieces should not be put in danger when possible. In this way, heuristics provide a more efficient—although sometimes inaccurate—method for problem solving.

MCAT Expertise

Detail questions on the MCAT often have wrong answer choices that are stated in the passage, but that fail to answer the question posed. According to the availability heuristic, students who do not truly problem solve on MCAT questions will be tempted by these familiar-sounding answers merely because they can recall that statement being mentioned in the passage. Don't forget to use your Outline effectively, as described in Chapter 4 of *MCAT Critical Analysis and Reasoning Skills Review*!

Bias and Overconfidence

When a potential solution to a problem fails during testing, this solution should be discarded. This is known as the **disconfirmation principle**: the evidence obtained from testing demonstrated that the solution does not work. However, the presence of a confirmation bias may prevent an individual from eliminating this solution. **Confirmation bias** is the tendency to focus on information that fits an individual's beliefs, while rejecting information that goes against them. Confirmation bias also contributes to **overconfidence**, or a tendency to erroneously interpret one's decisions, knowledge, and beliefs as infallible. The similar phenomenon of **belief perseverance** refers to the inability to reject a particular belief despite clear evidence to the contrary. Together, confirmation bias, overconfidence, and belief perseverance can seriously impede a person's analysis of available evidence.

Intuition

Intuition can be defined as the ability to act on perceptions that may not be supported by available evidence. Often, people may have beliefs that are not necessarily supported by evidence, but that a person "feels" to be correct. Intuition is often developed by experience. For example, an emergency room physician, over the course of seeing thousands of patients with chest pain, may develop a keen sense of which patients are actually having a heart attack without even looking at an electrocardiogram (EKG) or a patient's vital signs. This intuition can be more accurately described by the **recognition-primed decision model**: the doctor's brain is actually sorting through a wide variety of information to match a pattern. Over time, the doctor has gained an extensive level of experience that he or she is able to access without awareness.

Emotion

Emotion is the subjective experience of a person in a certain situation. How a person feels often influences how a person thinks and makes decisions. For example, a person who is angry is often more likely to engage in more risky decision-making. In addition, emotions in decision-making are not limited to the emotion experienced while the decision is being made; emotions that a person *expects* to feel from a particular decision are also involved. For example, if a person believes a car will make them feel more powerful, he or she may be more likely to purchase that car.

INTELLECTUAL FUNCTIONING

Intellectual functioning is a highly studied area of psychology. How is intelligence defined? What makes someone more intelligent than someone else? These are multifaceted questions that are difficult to answer; however, theorists have proposed models for some aspects of intelligence.

Multiple Intelligences

There has been much debate concerning the definition of intelligence. Howard Gardner's theory of **multiple intelligences** is one of the most all-encompassing definitions, with seven defined types of intelligence: linguistic, logical–mathematical, musical, visual–spatial, bodily–kinesthetic, interpersonal, and intrapersonal. Gardner argues that Western culture values the first two abilities over the others. After all, linguistic ability and logical–mathematical ability are the two abilities tested on traditional intelligence quotient (IQ) tests.

Variations in Intellectual Ability

There are a number of tests and studies that have historically attempted to quantify intelligence. A founding concept behind these tests is Spearman's "g factor," or general intelligence factor. The theory behind the existence of a g factor is based on the observation that performance on different cognitive tasks is in many cases positively correlated, indicating an underlying factor or variable is playing a role. This underlying variable of intelligence is often measured with standardized tests that generate an **intelligence quotient** (**IQ**) for the test taker. IQ tests were largely pioneered by Alfred Binet in the early twentieth century. A professor at Stanford University took Binet's work and created what is known as the **Stanford–Binet IQ test**. While later iterations of the test use different methodologies to arrive at a score, it is useful to know the original formula for calculating IQ:

$$IQ = \frac{\text{mental age}}{\text{chronological age}} \times 100$$

Equation 4.1

Using this equation, a four-year-old with intelligence abilities at the level of the average six-year-old would have an IQ of 150. The distribution of IQ scores from the original study of the Stanford–Binet IQ test is shown in Figure 4.5.

Figure 4.5. Distribution of IQ Scores for Children 5 to 14 Years of Age
Mean = 100; SD = 15

Some theorists have argued heavily for intelligence as a hereditary trait, most notably Galton in his novel *Hereditary Genius*. In reality, variations in intellectual ability can be attributed to many determinants, including genes, environment, and educational experiences. Intellectual ability does appear to run in families, which may be due to both genetics and the environment; some environments are simply more enriching than others. Parental expectations, socioeconomic status, and nutrition have all been shown to correlate with intelligence.

The educational system plays a significant role in the development of intelligence. Children who attend school tend to have greater increases in IQ, and IQ actually decreases slightly during summer vacations. Early intervention in childhood also improves IQ, especially for children in low-enrichment environments. Finally, both intellectually gifted and cognitively disabled children benefit from specialized educational environments. For cognitively disabled students, this is often defined as the least restrictive environment, in which they are encouraged to participate as much as possible in the regular mainstream classroom, with individualized help as needed.

MCAT Concept Check 4.2:

Before you move on, assess your understanding of the material with these questions.

1. A child plays with a tool set, noting that a nail can only be hit with a hammer. When a friend suggests that the handle of a screwdriver can be used to a hit a nail, the child passionately objects. This is an example of:

   _____

2. A doctor uses a flow chart to treat a patient with sepsis. Given its use in problem solving, a flowchart is an example of a(n):

   _____

3. A patient in a mental health facility believes that the sky is pink. Despite several trips outside, the patient still declares the sky is pink. Which psychological principle does this represent?

   _____

4. Provide a brief definition of the availability and representativeness heuristics.
   - Availability heuristic:

     _____

   - Representativeness heuristic:

     _____

4.3 Consciousness

Consciousness is one's level of awareness of both the world and one's own existence within that world.

STATES OF CONSCIOUSNESS

The accepted states of consciousness are alertness, sleep, dreaming, and altered states of consciousness. Technically, sleep and dreaming are also considered altered states, but we will consider these states separately from hypnosis, meditation, and drug-induced altered states of consciousness. Altered states of consciousness may also result from sickness, dementia, delirium, and coma.

ALERTNESS

Alertness is a state of consciousness in which we are awake and able to think. In this state, we are able to perceive, process, access information, and express that information verbally. In the alert state, we also experience a certain level of physiological arousal. Cortisol levels tend to be higher, and electroencephalogram (EEG) waves indicate a brain in the waking state.

Alertness is maintained by neurological circuits in the prefrontal cortex at the very front of the brain. Fibers from the prefrontal cortex communicate with the **reticular formation**, a neural structure located in the brainstem, to keep the cortex awake and alert. A brain injury that results in disruption of these connections results in coma.

SLEEP

Sleep is important to consider while studying for the MCAT or any other major exam. While it may be tempting to pull all-nighters in an attempt to maximize your test score, this may not be the best strategy for success. In fact, long-term sleep deprivation has been linked with diminished cognitive performance as well as the development of chronic diseases such as diabetes and obesity.

Stages of Sleep

Sleep is studied by recording brain wave activity occurring during the course of a night's sleep. This is done with **electroencephalography**, or **EEG**, which records an average of the electrical patterns within different portions of the brain. There are four characteristic EEG patterns correlated with different stages of waking and sleeping: beta, alpha, theta, and delta waves. There is a fifth wave that corresponds to REM sleep, which is the time during the night when we have most of our dreams. These sleep stages form a complete cycle lasting about 90 minutes.

Beta and alpha waves characterize brain wave activity when we are awake and are shown in Figure 4.6. **Beta waves** have a high frequency and occur when the person is alert or attending to a mental task that requires concentration. Beta waves occur when neurons are randomly firing. **Alpha waves** occur when we are awake but relaxing with our eyes closed, and are somewhat slower than beta waves. Alpha waves are also more synchronized than beta waves.

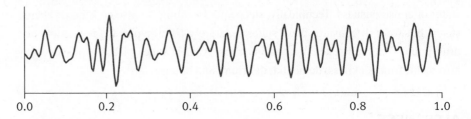

Figure 4.6. Beta (top) and Alpha (bottom) Waves on EEG
Beta and alpha waves are seen during alertness.

As soon as you doze off, you enter **Stage 1**, which is detected on the EEG by the appearance of **theta waves**, shown in Figure 4.7. At this point, EEG activity is characterized by irregular waveforms with slower frequencies and higher voltages.

Figure 4.7. Theta Waves
Theta waves are seen during Stage 1 and 2 sleep.

As you fall more deeply asleep, you enter **Stage 2**. The EEG shows theta waves along with **sleep spindles** and **K complexes**, shown in Figure 4.8.

Figure 4.8. Sleep Spindle and K Complex in Stage 2 Sleep

As you fall even more deeply asleep, you enter **Stages 3** and **4**, also known as **slow-wave sleep** (**SWS**). EEG activity grows progressively slower until only a few sleep waves per second are seen. These low-frequency, high-voltage sleep waves are called **delta waves**, shown in Figure 4.9. During these stages, it becomes especially difficult to rouse someone from sleep. SWS has been associated with cognitive recovery and memory consolidation, as well as increased growth hormone release.

Figure 4.9. Delta Waves of Slow-Wave Sleep

Mnemonic

Remember the sequential order of
these brain waves—beta, alpha, theta,
delta—by combining their first letters to
form **BAT-D** and remember that a **bat**
sleeps during the **d**ay.

Stages 1 through 4 are all part of **non-rapid eye movement (NREM) sleep**; **rapid eye movement (REM) sleep** is interspersed between cycles of the NREM sleep stages. In this stage, arousal levels reach that of wakefulness, but the muscles are paralyzed. It is also called **paradoxical sleep** because one's heart rate, breathing patterns, and EEG mimic wakefulness, but the individual is still asleep. This is the stage in which dreaming is most likely to occur and is also associated with memory consolidation. Recent studies have associated REM more with procedural memory consolidation and SWS with declarative memory consolidation.

Sleep Cycles and Changes to Sleep Cycles

A **sleep cycle** refers to a single complete progression through the sleep stages. The makeup of a sleep cycle changes during the course of the night, as shown in Figure 4.10. Early in the night, SWS predominates as the brain falls into deep sleep and then into more wakeful states. Later in the night, REM sleep predominates.

Figure 4.10. Hypnogram of Sleep Cycles

Over the lifespan, the length of the sleep cycle increases from approximately 50 minutes in children to 90 minutes in adults. Children also spend more time in SWS than adults. Changes to sleep cycles from disrupted sleep or disordered work schedules can cause many health problems. Disruption of SWS and REM can result in diminished memory. Sleep deprivation also causes diminished cognitive performance, although the person who is sleep-deprived is unlikely to recognize that performance has been subpar. Sleep deprivation also negatively affects mood, problem solving, and motor skills.

Sleep and Circadian Rhythms

Our daily cycle of waking and sleeping is regulated by internally generated rhythms or **circadian rhythms**. In humans and other animals, the circadian rhythm approximates a 24-hour cycle that is somewhat affected by external cues such as light. Biochemical signals underlie circadian rhythms. Sleepiness can partially be attributed to blood levels of **melatonin**, a serotonin-derived hormone from the **pineal gland**. The retina has direct connections to the hypothalamus, which controls the pineal gland; thus, decreasing light can cause the release of melatonin.

Cortisol, a steroid hormone produced in the **adrenal cortex**, is also related to the sleep–wake cycle. Its levels slowly increase during early morning because increasing light causes the release of **corticotropin releasing factor** (**CRF**) from the hypothalamus. CRF causes release of **adrenocorticotropic hormone** (**ACTH**) from the anterior pituitary, which stimulates cortisol release. Cortisol contributes to wakefulness.

Dreaming

Philosophers and those interested in the human experience have hypothesized about the purpose, meaning, and function of dreaming since antiquity. The ancient Egyptians believed that dreams were messages sent from the supernatural world to tell of future events. The Greeks believed dreams to carry messages from the gods, but the dream required the help of a priest to interpret. Dreams have long been a subject of wonder.

Most dreaming occurs during REM; however, soon after we enter Stage 2 sleep, our mental experience starts to shift to a dreamlike state. Throughout the night, approximately 75% of dreaming occurs during REM. REM dreams tend to be longer and more vivid than those experienced during NREM sleep.

While the purpose and meaning of dreams is not fully understood, a few theories have been proposed. In the **activation–synthesis theory**, dreams are caused by widespread, random activation of neural circuitry. This activation can mimic incoming sensory information, and may also consist of pieces of stored memories, current and previous desires, met and unmet needs, and other experiences. The cortex then tries to stitch this unrelated information together, resulting in a dream that is both bizarre and somewhat familiar. In the **problem-solving dream theory**, dreams are a way to solve problems while you are sleeping. Dreams are untethered by the rules of the real world, and thus allow interpretation of obstacles differently than during waking hours. Finally, in the **cognitive process dream theory**, dreams are merely the sleeping counterpart of stream-of-consciousness. Just as you may be thinking about an upcoming weekend trip when your consciousness quickly shifts to your upcoming MCAT Test Day, so too does the content of a dream rapidly shift and change. Ultimately, the question is less *Which group is right?* and more *How can we unify these theories?* The study of dreaming is limited by the difference between the brain and the mind: dreaming must have a neurological component, but is still highly subjective. **Neurocognitive models of dreaming** seek to unify biological and psychological perspectives on dreaming by correlating the subjective, cognitive experience of dreaming with measurable physiological changes.

Bridge

The hypothalamic–pituitary–adrenal axis is an example of how the endocrine system can regulate behavior. The endocrine system is discussed in Chapter 5 of *MCAT Biology Review*.

Bridge

Other psychologists have proposed explanations for dreams. One of the most notable is Freud, who separated dreams into their *manifest content* (what one actually sees and hears) and their *latent content* (the underlying significance of these dream elements). Freud's model of personality is discussed in Chapter 6 of *MCAT Behavioral Sciences Review*.

Sleep Disorders

Sleep disorders are divided into two categories: dyssomnias and parasomnias. **Dyssomnias** refer to disorders that make it difficult to fall asleep, stay asleep, or avoid sleep, and include insomnia, narcolepsy, and sleep apnea. **Parasomnias** are abnormal movements or behaviors during sleep, and include night terrors and sleepwalking. Most sleep disorders occur during NREM sleep.

Insomnia is difficulty falling asleep or staying asleep. It is the most common sleep disorder and may be related to anxiety, depression, medications, or disruption of sleep cycles and circadian rhythms. **Narcolepsy**, in contrast, is a condition characterized by lack of voluntary control over the onset of sleep. The symptoms of narcolepsy are unique, and include **cataplexy**, a loss of muscle control and sudden intrusion of REM sleep during waking hours, usually caused by an emotional trigger; **sleep paralysis**, a sensation of being unable to move despite being awake; and **hypnagogic** and **hypnopompic hallucinations**, which are hallucinations when going to sleep or awakening. Another dyssomnia is **sleep apnea**, which is an inability to breathe during sleep. People with this disorder awaken often during the night in order to breathe. Sleep apnea can be either obstructive or central. Obstructive sleep apnea occurs when a physical blockage in the pharynx or trachea prevents airflow; central sleep apnea occurs when the brain fails to send signals to the diaphragm to breathe.

Night terrors, which are most common in children, are periods of intense anxiety that occur during slow-wave sleep. Children will often thrash and scream during these terrors, and will show signs of sympathetic overdrive, with a high heart rate and rapid breathing. Because these usually occur during SWS, the child experiencing the episode is very difficult to wake, and usually does not remember the dream the next morning. **Sleepwalking**, or **somnambulism**, also usually occurs during SWS. Some sleepwalkers may eat, talk, have sexual intercourse, or even drive great distances while sleeping with absolutely no recollection of the event. Most return to their beds and awake in the morning, with no knowledge of their nighttime activities. Contrary to popular belief, awakening a sleepwalker will not harm the person; however, it is generally suggested to quietly guide the sleepwalker back to bed to avoid disturbing SWS.

Sleep deprivation can result from as little as one night without sleep, or from multiple nights with poor-quality, short-duration sleep. Sleep deprivation results in irritability, mood disturbances, decreased performance, and slowed reaction time. Extreme deprivation can cause psychosis. While one cannot make up for lost sleep, people who are permitted to sleep normally after sleep deprivation often exhibit **REM rebound**, an earlier onset and greater duration of REM sleep compared to normal.

Mnemonic

Hypna**g**o**g**ic hallucinations occur when one is **go**ing to bed. Hypno**pom**pic hallucinations occur when one is **pop**ping up out of bed.

HYPNOSIS

Hypnosis, named after the Greek god of sleep, *Hypnos*, was first documented in the eighteenth century. **Hypnosis** can be defined as a state in which a person appears to be in control of his or her normal functions, but is in a highly suggestible state. In other words, a hypnotized person easily succumbs to the suggestions of others. Hypnosis starts with **hypnotic induction**, in which the hypnotist seeks to relax the subject and increase the subject's level of concentration. Then, the hypnotist can suggest perceptions or actions to the hypnotized person. In practice, hypnosis is not the same as its sensationalized version in the media, in which a hypnotist will snap his fingers and cause an individual to exhibit bizarre behavior. Rather, hypnosis has been used successfully for pain control, psychological therapy, memory enhancement, weight loss, and smoking cessation. Brain imaging has indicated that hypnotic states are indeed real; however, effective hypnosis requires a willing personality and lack of skepticism on the part of the patient.

MEDITATION

Defining **meditation** can be tricky and is highly dependent on the practitioner of meditation and his or her beliefs. Meditation has been a central practice in the religions of Buddhism, Hinduism, Taoism, Judaism, and others. Meditation usually involves quieting of the mind for some purpose, whether spiritual, religious, or related to stress reduction. In the secular Western tradition, meditation is often used for counseling and psychotherapy because it produces a sense of relaxation and relief from anxiety and worrying. To that end, meditation causes physiological changes such as decreased heart rate and blood pressure. On EEG, meditation resembles Stage 1 sleep with theta and slow alpha waves.

MCAT Concept Check 4.3:

Before you move on, assess your understanding of the material with these questions.

1. For each of the sleep stages below, list its EEG waveforms and main features.

Stage	EEG Waves	Features
Awake		
Stage 1		
Stage 2		
Stage 3		
Stage 4		
REM		

Bridge

Hypnosis has been used to recover repressed memories of trauma; however, these memories are not admissible in a court of law. This is because the suggestible state of hypnotism makes an individual vulnerable to creating false memories, which can be perceived as completely real. False memories are discussed in Chapter 3 of *MCAT Behavioral Sciences Review*.

MCAT Expertise

Recent studies have demonstrated that mindful meditation not only improves psychological well-being, but may even help improve test scores and student performance. Take time for yourself while studying for the MCAT; keep your mind calm to keep it sharp.

2. Which two hormones are most associated with maintaining circadian rhythms?

• _____

• _____

3. What is the difference between a dyssomnia and a parasomnia? Provide an example of each.

• Dyssomnia:

_____

• Parasomnia:

_____

4.4 Consciousness-Altering Drugs High-Yield

LEARNING GOALS

After Chapter 4.4, you will be able to:

• List the drugs (or drug classes) known to increase GABA activity in the brain
• Recall the drugs (or drug classes) known to upregulate dopamine, norepinephrine, or serotonin activity
• Identify the three main structures in the mesolimbic reward pathway and the primary neurotransmitter of the pathway

Consciousness-altering drugs are generally described in four different groups: depressants, stimulants, opiates, and hallucinogens. Biologically speaking, marijuana has depressant, stimulant, and hallucinogenic effects, and will be considered separately.

DEPRESSANTS

Depressants reduce nervous system activity, resulting in a sense of relaxation and reduced anxiety. Of the depressants, alcohol is certainly the most common.

Alcohol

Alcohol has several different effects on the brain. It increases activity of the GABA receptor, a chloride channel that causes hyperpolarization of the membrane, as shown in Figure 4.11. This causes generalized brain inhibition, resulting in diminished arousal at moderate doses. Behavior may seem less inhibited because the centers of the brain that prevent inappropriate behavior are also depressed. Alcohol also increases dopamine levels, causing a sense of mild euphoria. At higher doses, brain activity becomes more disrupted. Logical reasoning and motor skills are affected, and fatigue may result. One of the main effects on logical reasoning is the inability to recognize consequences of actions, creating a short-sighted view of the world called **alcohol myopia**. Alcohol use is implicated in many automobile accidents, homicides (for both perpetrator and victim), and hospital admissions. Intoxication with alcohol is often measured using blood alcohol level.

Figure 4.11. GABA Receptor
GABA is the primary inhibitory neurotransmitter in the brain; its receptor is a chloride channel that causes hyperpolarization of the membrane.

Alcohol is one of the most widely abused drugs. Alcoholism rates tend to be higher for those of lower socioeconomic status (SES), but low-SES alcoholics tend to enter recovery sooner and at higher rates. Alcoholism tends to run in families, and children of alcoholics are also likely to suffer from major depressive disorder. Long-term consequences of alcoholism include cirrhosis and liver failure, pancreatic damage, gastric or duodenal ulcers, gastrointestinal cancer, and brain disorders including

Wernicke–Korsakoff Syndrome, caused by a deficiency of thiamine (vitamin B_1) and characterized by severe memory impairment with changes in mental status and loss of motor skills.

Barbiturates and Benzodiazepines

Barbiturates were historically used as anxiety-reducing (anxiolytic) and sleep medications, but have mostly been replaced by **benzodiazepines**, which are less prone to overdose. Barbiturates include *amobarbital* and *phenobarbital*; benzodiazepines include *alprazolam*, *lorazepam*, *diazepam*, and *clonazepam*. These drugs also increase GABA activity, causing a sense of relaxation. However, both of these drug types can be highly addictive. If taken with alcohol, overdoses of barbiturates or benzodiazepines may result in coma or death.

STIMULANTS

Stimulants cause an increase in arousal in the nervous system. Each drug increases the frequency of action potentials, but does so by different mechanisms.

Amphetamines

Amphetamines cause increased arousal by increasing release of dopamine, norepinephrine, and serotonin at the synapse and decreasing their reuptake. This increases arousal and causes a reduction in appetite and decreased need for sleep. Physiological effects include an increase in heart rate and blood pressure. Psychological effects include euphoria, hypervigilance (being "on edge"), anxiety, delusions of grandeur, and paranoia. Prolonged use of high doses of amphetamines can result in stroke or brain damage. Users often suffer from withdrawal after discontinuation, leading to depression, fatigue, and irritability.

Cocaine

Cocaine originates from the coca plant, grown in the high-altitude regions of South America. Cocaine can be purified from these leaves or created synthetically. Cocaine also decreases reuptake of dopamine, norepinephrine, and serotonin, although by a different mechanism. The effects of cocaine intoxication and withdrawal are therefore similar to amphetamines, as listed above. Cocaine also has anesthetic and vasoconstrictive properties, and is therefore sometimes used in surgeries in highly vascularized areas, such as the nose and throat. These vasoconstrictive properties can also lead to heart attacks and strokes when used recreationally. **Crack** is a form of cocaine that can be smoked. With quick and potent effects, this drug is highly addictive.

Ecstasy (3,4-methylenedioxy-*N*-methylamphetamine, MDMA)

Ecstasy, commonly called "E," acts as a hallucinogen combined with an amphetamine. As a designer amphetamine, its mechanism and effects are similar to other amphetamines. Physiologically, ecstasy causes increased heart rate, increased blood pressure, blurry vision, sweating, nausea, and hyperthermia.

Psychologically, ecstasy causes feelings of euphoria, increased alertness, and an overwhelming sense of well-being and connectedness. Ecstasy is an example of a club or rave drug, and is often packaged in colorful pills, as shown in Figure 4.12.

Figure 4.12. Pills of Ecstasy (MDMA)

OPIATES AND OPIOIDS

Derived from the poppy plant, **opium** has been used and abused for centuries. Today, we have numerous drugs, used both recreationally and therapeutically, derived from opium. Naturally occurring forms, called **opiates**, include *morphine* and *codeine*. Semisynthetic derivatives, called **opioids**, include *oxycodone, hydrocodone*, and *heroin*. These compounds bind to opioid receptors in the peripheral and central nervous system, causing a decreased reaction to pain and a sense of euphoria. Overdose, however, can cause death by respiratory suppression, in which the brain stops sending signals to breathe.

Heroin, or *diacetylmorphine*, was originally created as a substitute for morphine. However, once injected, the body rapidly metabolizes heroin to morphine. Usually smoked or injected, heroin was once the most widely abused opioid; however, this designation has shifted to prescription opioids like oxycodone and hydrocodone. Treatment for opioid addiction may include use of *methadone*, a long-acting opioid with lower risk of overdose.

HALLUCINOGENS

Hallucinogens include drugs such as **lysergic acid diethylamide (LSD)**, shown in Figure 4.13, *peyote, mescaline, ketamine*, and *psilocybin*-containing mushrooms. The exact mechanism of most hallucinogens is unknown, but is thought to be a complex interaction between various neurotransmitters, especially serotonin. These drugs typically cause distortions of reality and fantasy, enhancement of sensory experiences, and introspection. Physiologic effects include increased heart rate and blood pressure, dilation of pupils, sweating, and increased body temperature.

Figure 4.13. Sheet of LSD Blotter Paper
Like ecstasy, LSD is often a club drug sold on colorful paper.

MARIJUANA

Marijuana, shown in Figure 4.14, primarily refers to the leaves and flowers of two plant species: *Cannabis sativa* and *Cannabis indica*. It has been the subject of many news reports in the last few years as many states move toward the legalization of marijuana for medical or recreational use. While talks about the legal status of marijuana in the United States are fairly recent, marijuana has been used for centuries, with the earliest known accounts originating from approximately 3 B.C.E.

Figure 4.14. Cannabis

The active chemical in marijuana is known as **tetrahydrocannabinol (THC)**. THC exerts its effects by acting at cannabinoid receptors, glycine receptors, and opioid receptors. How these receptors interact to create the "high" achieved from marijuana use is unknown. It is known, however, that THC inhibits GABA activity and indirectly increases dopamine activity (causing pleasure). Physiological effects are mixed, including eye redness, dry mouth, fatigue, impairment of short-term memory, increased heart rate, increased appetite, and lowered blood pressure. Psychologically, effects seem to fall into the categories of stimulant, depressant, and hallucinogen.

DRUG ADDICTION

Drug addiction is highly related to the **mesolimbic reward pathway**, one of four dopaminergic pathways in the brain, as shown in Figure 4.15. This pathway includes the **nucleus accumbens (NAc)**, the **ventral tegmental area (VTA)**, and the connection between them called the **medial forebrain bundle (MFB)**. This pathway is normally involved in motivation and emotional response, and its activation accounts for the positive reinforcement of substance use. This addiction pathway is activated by all substances that produce psychological dependence. Gambling and falling in love also activate this pathway.

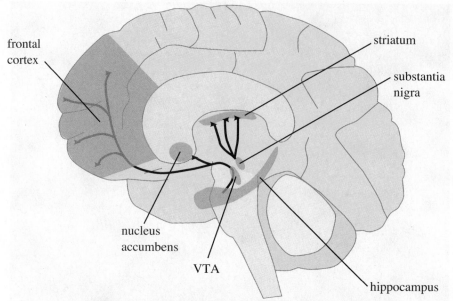

Figure 4.15. Dopaminergic Pathways in the Brain
The reward pathway is composed of the nucleus accumbens, ventral tegmental area (VTA), and the medial forebrain bundle between them (not labeled).

MCAT Concept Check 4.4:

Before you move on, assess your understanding of the material with these questions.

1. Which four drugs (or drug classes) are known to increase GABA activity in the brain?

   - _____

   - _____

   - _____

   - _____

2. Which three drugs (or drug classes) are known to increase dopamine, norepinephrine, and serotonin activity in the brain?

   - _____

   - _____

   - _____

3. What are the three main structures in the mesolimbic reward pathway? What is this pathway's primary neurotransmitter?

- Structure:

  _____

- Structure:

  _____

- Structure:

  _____

- Neurotransmitter:

  _____

4.5 Attention

LEARNING GOALS

After Chapter 4.5, you will be able to:

- Compare and contrast controlled processing and automatic processing
- Describe the role of the "filter" used in selective attention

Attention refers to concentrating on one aspect of the sensory environment, or **sensorium**. While this definition is straightforward, an understanding of how attention works and the mechanism by which we can shift our attention from one set of stimuli to another is still somewhat unclear.

SELECTIVE ATTENTION

Selective attention is focusing on one part of the sensorium while ignoring other stimuli. It therefore acts as a filter between sensory stimuli and our processing systems. If a stimulus is attended to, it is passed through a filter and analyzed further. If the stimulus is not attended to, it is lost. In its original conceptualization, selective attention was viewed as an all-or-nothing process: if we choose a particular stimulus to give our attention to, the other stimuli are lost. However, recent evidence indicates that this is not the case.

Imagine this: You are at a party, talking with a friend. However, your ears perk up when you hear your name spoken halfway across the room. Even though you were engaged in conversation and presumably paying attention, you were able to perceive your name being mentioned. This is sometimes called the **cocktail party phenomenon** and is evidence of a different interpretation of selective attention. Selective attention is probably more of a filter that allows us to focus on one thing while allowing other stimuli to be processed in the background. Only if the other stimuli are particularly important—one's name being mentioned, a sudden flash of light, pain—do we shift our attention to them.

DIVIDED ATTENTION

Divided attention is the ability to perform multiple tasks at the same time. Most new or complex tasks require undivided attention, and utilize **controlled (effortful) processing**, discussed in Chapter 3 of *MCAT Behavioral Sciences Review*. In contrast, familiar or routine actions can be performed with **automatic processing**, which permits the brain to focus on other tasks with divided attention. Consider learning to drive: at first, drivers intensely grip the steering wheel and pay undivided attention to the road ahead. But as you become more accustomed to driving, you can relegate some aspects of driving—like knowing how hard to push on the pedal—to automatic processing. This lets a driver perform secondary tasks such as changing the radio station. That being said, automatic processing is far from perfect. It does not allow for innovation or rapid response to change, which may contribute to the high incidence of car accidents that result from distracted driving.

MCAT Concept Check 4.5:

Before you move on, assess your understanding of the material with these questions.

1. Compare and contrast controlled (effortful) processing and automatic processing:

   - Controlled (effortful) processing:

   _____

   - Automatic processing:

   _____

2. Briefly describe the function of the "filter" used in selective attention:

   _____

   _____

K

4.6 Language

LEARNING GOALS

After Chapter 4.6, you will be able to:

- Recall the expected milestones of language development and the ages at which they should occur
- Identify the primary characteristics of the nativist, behaviorist, and social interactionist theories of language development
- Describe the symptoms and brain regions associated with Broca's, Wernicke's, and conduction aphasia

Whether it is written, spoken, or signed, **language** is fundamental to the creation of communities. As humans began to live in groups, the ability to communicate became essential. Division of labor and a sense of shared history require that the meaning of the language be the same for all speakers of the language.

COMPONENTS OF LANGUAGE

There are five basic components of language: phonology, morphology, semantics, syntax, and pragmatics.

Phonology

Phonology refers to the actual sound of language. There are about 40 speech sounds or **phonemes** in English, although many more exist in other languages, as shown in Figure 4.16. Children must learn to produce and recognize the sounds of language, separating them from environmental noises and other human-created sounds, like coughing. They must also learn when subtle differences between speech sounds represent a change in meaning or not; the pronunciation of a word varies between people. The ability to make this distinction is called **categorical perception**, and is an auditory example of **constancy**, as described in Chapter 2 of *MCAT Behavioral Sciences Review*.

International Phonetic Alphabet

Plosive		Tap or Flap		Lateral Fricative	
Name	**Text**	**Name**	**Text**	**Name**	**Text**
Voiceless bilabial	p	Voiced alveolar	ɾ	Voiceless alveolar	ɬ
Voiced bilabial	b	Voiced retroflex	ɽ	Voiced alveolar	ɮ
Voiceless alveolar	t	**Fricative**		**Approximant**	
Voiced alveolar	d	**Name**	**Text**	**Name**	**Text**
Voiceless retroflex	ʈ	Voiceless bilabial	ɸ	Voiced labiodental	ʋ
Voiced retroflex	ɖ	Voiced bilabial	β	Voiced alveolar	ɹ
Voiceless palatal	c	Voiceless labiodental	f	Voiced retroflex	ɻ
Voiced palatal	ɟ	Voiced labiodental	v	Voiced palatal	j
Voiceless velar	k	Voiceless dental	θ	Voiced velar	ɰ
Voiced velar	g	Voiced dental	ð	**Lateral Approximant**	
Voiceless uvular	q	Voiceless alveolar	s	**Name**	**Text**
Voiced uvular	ɢ	Voiced alveolar	z	Voiced alveolar	l
Voiceless glottal	ʔ	Voiceless postalveolar	ʃ	Voiced retroflex	ɭ
Nasal		Voiced postalveolar	ʒ	Voiced palatal	ʎ
Name	**Text**	Voiceless retroflex	ʂ	Voiced velar	ʟ
Voiced bilabial	m	Voiced retroflex	ʐ	**Clicks**	
Voiced labiodental	ɱ	Voiceless palatal	ç	**Name**	**Text**
Voiced alveolar	n	Voiced palatal	ʝ	Bilabial	ʘ
Voiced retroflex	ɳ	Voiceless velar	x	Dental	ǀ
Voiced palatal	ɲ	Voiced velar	ɣ	(Post)alveolar	ǃ
Voiced velar	ŋ	Voiceless uvular	χ	Palatoalveolar	ǂ
Voiced uvular	ɴ	Voiced uvular	ʁ	Alveolar lateral	ǁ
Trill		Voiceless pharyngeal	ħ		
Name	**Text**	Voiced pharyngeal	ʕ		
Voiced bilabial	ʙ	Voiceless glottal	h		
Voiced alveolar	r	Voiced glottal	ɦ		
Voiced uvular	ʀ	Voiceless dorso-palatal	ɧ		

Figure 4.16. The International Phonetic Alphabet
The IPA is an unambiguous system of writing all of the known phonemes of all human languages.

Morphology

Morphology refers to the structure of words. Many words are composed of multiple building blocks called **morphemes**, each of which connotes a particular meaning. Consider the word *redesigned*, which can be broken into three morphemes: *re–*, indicating *to do again*; *–design–*, the verb root; and *–ed*, indicating an action in the past.

Semantics

Semantics refers to the association of meaning with a word. A child must learn that certain combinations of phonemes represent certain physical objects or events, and that words may refer to entire categories, such as *women*, while others refer to specific members of categories, such as *mommy*. One can see this skill developing in young children as they may refer to all women as *mommy*.

Syntax

Syntax refers to how words are put together to form sentences. A child must notice the effects of word order on meaning: *Nathan has only three pieces of candy* has a very different meaning than *Only Nathan has three pieces of candy.*

Pragmatics

Finally, **pragmatics** refers to the dependence of language on context and pre-existing knowledge. In other words, the manner in which we speak may differ depending on the audience and our relationship to that audience. Imagine asking to share a seat on a bus. Depending on whom we ask, we may word this request in wildly different ways. To a stranger, we may be more formal: *Pardon me, do you mind if I share this seat?* To a close friend, we may be less so: *Hey, move over!* Pragmatics are also affected by **prosody**—the rhythm, cadence, and inflection of our voices.

LANGUAGE DEVELOPMENT

To effectively interact with society, a child must learn to communicate through language, whether oral or signed. An important precursor to language is **babbling**. Almost without exception, children—including deaf children—spontaneously begin to babble during their first year. For hearing children, babbling reaches its highest frequency between nine and twelve months. For deaf children, verbal babbling ceases soon after it begins.

The timeline of language acquisition is fairly consistent among children. From 12 to 18 months, children add about one word per month. Starting around 18 months, an "explosion of language" begins in which the child quickly learns dozens of words, and uses each word with varying inflection and gestures to convey a desired meaning. For example, a child may ask, *Apple?* while pointing at an apple in a bowl of fruit, in an effort to request an apple. The same child may also point to a piece of fruit in a grocery store and ask, *Apple?* in an attempt to distinguish between an apple and some other fruit. For children at this age, gestures, inflection, and context are essential for the parent or caregiver to identify the meaning.

Between 18 and 20 months of age, children begin to combine words. The child in the previous example may say, *Eat apple* to tell a caregiver that he would like to eat an apple. In the grocery store, the same child may ask, *That apple?* to distinguish between fruit. In this way, context and gesture becomes less important as the ability to assemble sentences develops.

By the age of two or three years, children can speak in longer sentences. Vocabulary grows exponentially. As a child creates longer sentences, grammatical errors increase as the child internalizes the complex rules of grammar. These include **errors of growth** in which a child applies a grammatical rule (often a morpheme)

> ## Key Concept
>
> Timeline of language acquisition:
> - 9 to 12 months: babbling
> - 12 to 18 months: about one word per month
> - 18 to 20 months: "explosion of language" and combining words
> - 2 to 3 years: longer sentences (3 words or more)
> - 5 years: language rules largely mastered

Real World

Pediatricians often monitor language development to determine if there is a developmental delay. For example, a two-year-old child who uses fewer than 10 words has a significant developmental delay and should be referred for speech therapy. This would also prompt a search for other developmental issues.

in a situation where it does not apply: *runned* instead of *ran*, or *funner* instead of *more fun*. Interestingly, parents are less likely to correct errors of grammar than errors of word choice.

For the most part, language is substantially mastered by the age of five. The acquisition of language appears easy for most children, which has led to significant speculation on exactly how this occurs.

Nativist (Biological) Theory

The **nativist (biological) theory**, largely credited to linguist Noam Chomsky, advocates for the existence of some innate capacity for language. Chomsky is known for his study of **transformational grammar**. He focused on syntactic transformations, or changes in word order that retain the same meaning; for example, *I took the MCAT vs. The MCAT was taken by me*. Chomsky noted that children learn to make such transformations effortlessly at an early age. He therefore concluded that this ability must be innate. In this theory, this innate ability is called the **language acquisition device (LAD)**, a theoretical pathway in the brain that allows infants to process and absorb language rules.

Nativists believe in a **critical period** for language acquisition between two years and puberty. If no language exposure occurs during this time, later training is largely ineffective. This came to light through an unfortunate test case: a victim of child abuse. This child had been isolated from all human contact from age two to thirteen, when she was discovered by authorities. Even with later language exposure, she was unable to master many rules of language, although she was able to learn some aspects of syntax. This may indicate that there is a sensitive period for language development, rather than a critical period. A **sensitive period** is a time when environmental input has maximal effect on the development of an ability. Most psychologists consider the sensitive period for language development to be before the onset of puberty.

Learning (Behaviorist) Theory

The **learning (behaviorist) theory**, proposed by B. F. Skinner, explained language acquisition by operant conditioning. Very young babies are capable of distinguishing between phonemes of all human languages, but by six months of age, show a strong preference for phonemes in the language spoken by their parents. Skinner explained language acquisition by **reinforcement**. That is, parents and caregivers repeat and reinforce sounds that sound most like the language spoken by the parents. Thus, over time, the infant perceives that certain sounds have little value and are not reinforced, while other sounds have value and are reliably reinforced by parents and caregivers. While this may account for the development of words and speech, many psycholinguists point out that this theory cannot fully explain the explosion in vocabulary that occurs during early childhood.

Social Interactionist Theory

The **social interactionist theory** of language development focuses on the interplay between biological and social processes. That is, language acquisition is driven by the child's desire to communicate and behave in a social manner, such as interacting with caretakers and other children. Interactionist theory allows for the role of brain development in the acquisition of language. As the biological foundation for language develops and children are exposed to language, the brain groups sounds and meanings together. Then, as the child interacts with others, certain brain circuits are reinforced, while others are de-emphasized, resulting in atrophy of those circuits.

INFLUENCE OF LANGUAGE ON COGNITION

Psycholinguistics has long focused on the relationship between language and thinking. Linguist Benjamin Whorf proposed the **Whorfian hypothesis**, also called the **linguistic relativity hypothesis**, which suggests that our perception of reality—the way we think about the world—is determined by the content of language. In essence, language affects the way we think rather than the other way around. For instance, the Inuit language has a wide variety of names for different types of snow, whereas the English language has very few. Therefore, according to the Whorfian hypothesis, Inuits are better at discriminating subtleties between different types of snow than English speakers are. This is a somewhat controversial notion that depends on the definition of "a word," but most linguists agree that language can influence how we think to some degree. Word choice, inflection, context, and speaker all play a role in our perception of a message. In addition, language often provides an original framework for understanding information. A more expansive framework with more specific vocabulary allows for more sophisticated processing of that information and enhanced communication of that information to others.

BRAIN AREAS AND LANGUAGE

Two different areas of the brain are responsible for speech production and language comprehension, as shown in Figure 4.17. Both, however, are located in the dominant hemisphere, which is usually the left hemisphere. **Broca's area**, located in the inferior frontal gyrus of the frontal lobe, controls the motor function of speech via connections with the motor cortex. **Wernicke's area**, located in the superior temporal gyrus of the temporal lobe, is responsible for language comprehension. Broca's area and Wernicke's area are connected by the **arcuate fasciculus**, a bundle of axons that allows appropriate association between language comprehension and speech production.

Figure 4.17. Brain Areas Associated with Language
Blue = Broca's area; Green = Wernicke's area. Other colored regions are associated with other aspects of language beyond the scope of the MCAT (yellow = supramarginal gyrus; orange = angular gyrus; light pink = primary auditory cortex).

Aphasia is a deficit of language production or comprehension. Much of what we know regarding language and aphasia is through observations of people with damage to speech-related areas. When damage occurs to Broca's area, speech comprehension is intact but the patient will have a reduced or absent ability to produce spoken language. This is known as **Broca's (expressive) aphasia**. These patients are often very frustrated because they are stuck with the sensation of having every word on the tip of their tongue.

On the other hand, when Wernicke's area is damaged, motor production and fluency of speech is retained but comprehension of speech is lost. This is known as **Wernicke's (receptive) aphasia**. Because speech comprehension is lost, these patients speak nonsensical sounds and inappropriate word combinations devoid of meaning. Patients with Wernicke's aphasia often believe that they are speaking and understanding perfectly well, even though the people around them have no comprehension of what is being said. This can also be very frustrating to patients.

Finally, if the arcuate fasciculus is affected, the resulting aphasia is known as **conduction aphasia**. Because Broca's and Wernicke's areas are unaffected, speech production and comprehension are intact. However, the patient is unable to repeat something that has been said because the connection between these two regions has been lost. This is a very rare form of aphasia.

MCAT Concept Check 4.6:

Before you move on, assess your understanding of the material with these questions.

1. For each of the ages below, list the expected milestone(s) of language development:

Age	Milestone(s)
9 to 12 months	
12 to 18 months	
18 to 20 months	
2 to 3 years	
5 years	

2. For each of the theories of language acquisition below, what is the primary motivation or trigger for language development?

   - Nativist (Biological):

   _____

   - Learning (Behaviorist):

   _____

   - Social interactionist:

   _____

3. Briefly describe the clinical features of each type of aphasia listed below:

   - Broca's aphasia:

   _____

   - Wernicke's aphasia

   _____

   - Conduction aphasia:

   _____

Conclusion

One of the biggest questions that psychology and biology seek to answer is how the brain, an organ consisting of lipids, water, and neurotransmitters, becomes the mind. Cognition and consciousness allow us to think about who we are, where we are, and what we are doing at a given moment, and this all occurs due to a complex interaction between individual neurons within the brain. Not only do we experience consciousness, but our behaviors are also intricately intertwined with physiological brain function. Language is one of the most complex cognitive processes, requiring intact comprehension and production mechanisms, and an understanding of the rules of our native language.

As much as we research what the mind is and how it works, there is as much interest in *why* we do what we do and how we *feel* about it. This is the function of motivation (both internal and external) and emotion, which we will explore in detail in the next chapter.

CONCEPT SUMMARY

Cognition

- Thought is more than just that of which we are conscious. The brain processes and makes decisions about the importance of various stimuli below the level of conscious awareness.

- The **information processing model** states that the brain encodes, stores, and retrieves information much like a computer.

- The ability to think abstractly develops over the life span. Early cognitive development is limited by brain maturation. Culture, genes, and environment also influence cognitive development.

- **Piaget's stages of cognitive development** are sensorimotor, preoperational, concrete operational, and formal operational.

  - The **sensorimotor stage** focuses on manipulating the environment to meet physical needs through **circular reactions**. **Object permanence** ends this stage.

  - The **preoperational stage** focuses on **symbolic thinking**, **egocentrism**, and **centration**.

  - The **concrete operational stage** focuses on understanding the feelings of others and manipulating physical (concrete) objects.

  - The **formal operational stage** focuses on abstract thought and problem solving.

- A mild level of cognitive decline while aging is normal; significant changes in cognition may signify an underlying disorder.

- Biological factors that affect cognition include organic brain disorders, genetic and chromosomal conditions, metabolic derangements, and drug use.

Problem Solving and Decision-Making

- **Problem solving** requires identification and understanding of the problem, generation of potential solutions, testing of potential solutions, and evaluation of results.

  - A **mental set** is a pattern of approach for a given problem. An inappropriate mental set may negatively impact problem solving.

  - **Functional fixedness** is the tendency to use objects only in the way they are normally utilized, which may create barriers to problem solving.

- Types of problem solving include **trial-and-error**, **algorithms**, **deductive reasoning** (deriving conclusions from general rules), and **inductive reasoning** (deriving generalizations from evidence).

- Heuristics, biases, intuition, and emotions may assist decision-making, but may also lead to erroneous or problematic decisions.

  - **Heuristics** are shortcuts or rules of thumb used to make decisions.

- o **Biases** exist when an experimenter or decision maker is unable to objectively evaluate information.

- o **Intuition** is a "gut feeling" regarding a particular decision. However, intuition can often be attributed to experience with similar situations.

- o Emotional state often plays a role in decision-making.

- Gardner's theory of **multiple intelligences** proposes seven areas of intelligence including: linguistic, logical–mathematical, musical, visual–spatial, bodily–kinesthetic, interpersonal, and intrapersonal.

- Variations in intellectual ability can be attributed to combinations of environment, education, and genetics.

Consciousness

- States of consciousness include alertness, sleep, dreaming, and altered states of consciousness.

- **Alertness** is the state of being awake and able to think, perceive, process, and express information. **Beta** and **alpha waves** predominate on **electroencephalography (EEG)**.

- **Sleep** is important for health of the brain and body.

  - o **Stage 1** is light sleep and is dominated by **theta waves** on EEG. **Stage 2** is slightly deeper and includes theta waves, **sleep spindles**, and **K complexes**.

  - o **Stages 3** and **4** are deep (**slow-wave**) sleep (**SWS**). **Delta waves** predominate on EEG. Most sleep disorders occur during Stage 3 and 4 **non-rapid eye movement (NREM) sleep**. Dreaming in SWS focuses on consolidating declarative memories.

  - o **Rapid eye movement (REM) sleep** is sometimes called **paradoxical sleep**: the mind appears close to awake on EEG, but the person is asleep. Eye movements and body paralysis occur in this stage. Dreaming in REM focuses on consolidating procedural memories.

  - o The **sleep cycle** is approximately 90 minutes for adults; the normal cycle is Stage 1–2–3–4–3–2–REM or just 1–2–3–4–REM, although REM becomes more frequent toward the morning.

  - o Changes in light in the evening trigger release of **melatonin** by the **pineal gland**, resulting in sleepiness. **Cortisol** levels increase in the early morning and help promote wakefulness. **Circadian rhythms** normally trend around a 24-hour day.

  - o Most **dreaming** occurs during REM, but some dreaming occurs during other sleep stages. There are many different models that attempt to account for the content and purpose of dreaming.

  - o Sleep disorders include **dyssomnias**, such as insomnia, narcolepsy, sleep apnea, and sleep deprivation; and **parasomnias**, such as night terrors and sleepwalking (somnambulism).

- **Hypnosis** is a state of consciousness in which individuals appear to be in control of their normal faculties but are in a highly suggestible state. Hypnosis is often used for pain control, psychological therapy, memory enhancement, weight loss, and smoking cessation.
- **Meditation** involves a quieting of the mind and is often used for relief of anxiety. It has also played a role in many of the world's religions.

Consciousness-Altering Drugs

- Consciousness-altering drugs are grouped by effect into depressants, stimulants, opiates, and hallucinogens.
  - **Depressants** include alcohol, barbiturates, and benzodiazepines. They promote or mimic GABA activity in the brain.
  - **Stimulants** include amphetamines, cocaine, and ecstasy. They increase dopamine, norepinephrine, and serotonin concentration at the synaptic cleft.
  - **Opiates** and **opioids** include heroin, morphine, opium, and prescription pain medications such as oxycodone and hydrocodone. They can cause death by respiratory depression.
  - **Hallucinogens** include lysergic acid diethylamide (LSD), peyote, mescaline, ketamine, and psilocybin-containing mushrooms.
  - **Marijuana** has depressant, stimulant, and hallucinogenic effects. Its active ingredient is **tetrahydrocannabinol**.
- Drug addiction is mediated by the **mesolimbic pathway**, which includes the **nucleus accumbens**, **medial forebrain bundle**, and **ventral tegmental area**. Dopamine is the main neurotransmitter in this pathway.

Attention

- **Selective attention** allows one to pay attention to a particular stimulus while determining if additional stimuli in the background require attention.
- **Divided attention** uses **automatic processing** to pay attention to multiple activities at one time.

Language

- Language consists of phonology, morphology, semantics, syntax, and pragmatics.
  - **Phonology** refers to the actual sound of speech.
  - **Morphology** refers to the building blocks of words, such as rules for pluralization (*–s* in English), past tense (*–ed*), and so forth.
  - **Semantics** refers to the meaning of words.
  - **Syntax** refers to the rules dictating word order.
  - **Pragmatics** refers to the changes in language delivery depending on context.

- Theories of language development focus on different reasons or motivations for language acquisition.

  o The **nativist (biological) theory** explains language acquisition as being innate and controlled by the **language acquisition device (LAD)**.

  o The **learning (behaviorist) theory** explains language acquisition as being controlled by operant conditioning and reinforcement by parents and caregivers.

  o The **social interactionist theory** explains language acquisition as being caused by a motivation to communicate and interact with others.

- The **Whorfian (linguistic relativity) hypothesis** states that the lens through which we view and interpret the world is created by language.

- Speech areas in the brain are found in the dominant hemisphere, which is usually the left.

  o The motor function of speech is controlled by **Broca's area**. Damage results in **Broca's aphasia**, a nonfluent aphasia in which generating each word requires great effort.

  o Language comprehension is controlled by **Wernicke's area**. Damage results in **Wernicke's aphasia**, a fluent, nonsensical aphasia with lack of comprehension.

  o The **arcuate fasciculus** connects Wernicke's area and Broca's area. Damage results in **conduction aphasia**, marked by the inability to repeat words heard despite intact speech generation and comprehension.

ANSWERS TO CONCEPT CHECKS

4.1

1. The three steps in the information processing model are encoding, storage, and retrieval.
2. The elderly man most likely has delirium. The time course is incompatible with the slow decline of dementia.
3.

Stage	Key Features
Sensorimotor	Focuses on manipulating environment for physical needs; circular reactions; ends with object permanence
Preoperational	Symbolic thinking, egocentrism, and centration
Concrete operational	Understands conservation and the feelings of others; can manipulate concrete objects logically
Formal operational	Can think abstractly and problem solve

4.2

1. Functional fixedness
2. Algorithm
3. Belief perseverance
4. The availability heuristic is used for making decisions based on how easily similar instances can be imagined. The representativeness heuristic is used for making decisions based on how much a particular item or situation fits a given prototype or stereotype.

4.3

1.

Stage	EEG Waves	Features
Awake	Beta and alpha	Able to perceive, process, access information, and express that information verbally
Stage 1	Theta	Light sleep and dozing
Stage 2	Theta	Sleep spindles and K complexes
Stage 3	Delta	Slow-wave sleep; dreams; declarative memory consolidation; sleep disorders occur in this stage
Stage 4	Delta	Slow-wave sleep; dreams; declarative memory consolidation; sleep disorders occur in this stage
REM	Mostly beta	Appears awake physiologically; dreams; procedural memory consolidation; body is paralyzed

2. The two hormones most associated with maintaining circadian rhythms are melatonin and cortisol.
3. Dyssomnias are disorders in which the duration or timing of sleep is disturbed. Examples include insomnia, narcolepsy, and sleep apnea. Parasomnias are disorders in which abnormal behaviors occur during sleep. Examples include night terrors and sleepwalking (somnambulism).

4.4

1. Drugs known to increase GABA activity in the brain include alcohol, barbiturates, benzodiazepines, and marijuana.

2. Drugs known to increase dopamine, norepinephrine, and serotonin activity in the brain include amphetamines, cocaine, and ecstasy (MDMA). Ecstasy is a designer amphetamine; it is mentioned separately here because of its hallucinogenic properties.

3. The three main structures in the mesolimbic reward pathway are the nucleus accumbens, medial forebrain bundle, and ventral tegmental area. The neurotransmitter of this pathway is dopamine.

4.5

1. Controlled (effortful) processing is used when maintaining undivided attention on a task, and is usually used for new or complex actions. Automatic processing is used for less critical stimuli in divided attention, and is usually used for familiar or repetitive actions.

2. The filter in selective attention permits us to focus on one set of stimuli while scanning other stimuli in the background for important information (such as our name or a significant change in the environment).

4.6

1.

Age	Milestone(s)
9 to 12 months	Babbling
12 to 18 months	Increase of about one word per month
18 to 20 months	"Explosion of language" and combining words (two-word sentences)
2 to 3 years	Longer sentences of three or more words
5 years	Language rules largely mastered

2. The primary trigger in the nativist theory is an innate ability to pick up language via the language acquisition device. In the learning theory, it is operant conditioning with reinforcement by parents and caregivers. In the social interactionist theory, it is a desire to communicate and act socially.

3. Broca's aphasia is marked by difficulty producing language, with hesitancy and great difficulty coming up with words. Wernicke's aphasia is fluent, but includes nonsensical sounds and words devoid of meaning; language comprehension is lost. Conduction aphasia is marked by difficulty repeating speech, with intact speech production and comprehension.

EQUATION TO REMEMBER

(4.1) **Stanford–Binet intelligence quotient:** $\text{IQ} = \dfrac{\text{mental age}}{\text{chronological age}} \times 100$

SHARED CONCEPTS

Behavioral Sciences Chapter 1
Biology and Behavior

Behavioral Sciences Chapter 3
Learning and Memory

Behavioral Sciences Chapter 6
Identity and Personality

Behavioral Sciences Chapter 11
Social Structure and Demographics

Biology Chapter 4
The Nervous System

Critical Analysis and Reasoning Skills Chapter 6
Formal Logic

Discrete Practice Questions

Consult your online resources for Full-Length Exams and Passage-Based Questions (for certain chapters).

1. Which of the following terms describes how existing schemata are modified to incorporate new information?

    A. Assimilation
    B. Adaptation
    C. Affirmation
    D. Accommodation

2. Which of the following of Piaget's stages of cognitive development occur before adolescence?

    I. Preoperational
    II. Sensorimotor
    III. Formal operational

    A. I only
    B. II only
    C. I and II
    D. II and III

3. A student is volunteering in a hospital with a stroke center. When asked what he believes is the prevalence of stroke among those greater than 65 years old, the student states that it is probably about 40% even though data analysis indicates that it is significantly lower. What accounts for this error?

    A. Deductive reasoning
    B. Representativeness heuristic
    C. Base rate fallacy
    D. Confirmation bias

4. Which of the following types of intelligence is NOT described by Gardner's theory of multiple intelligences?

    A. Fluid intelligence
    B. Bodily–kinesthetic intelligence
    C. Visual–spatial intelligence
    D. Linguistic intelligence

5. EEG waveforms during REM sleep most resemble which of the following states of consciousness?

    A. Alertness
    B. Slow-wave sleep
    C. Stage 1 sleep
    D. Meditation

6. Which of the following indicates the pattern of sleep stages during a complete sleep cycle early in the night?

    A. 1–2–3–4–1–2–REM
    B. 1–2–3–4–3–2–REM
    C. 4–3–2–1–2–3–REM
    D. 4–3–2–4–3–1–REM

7. Increases in which of the following hormones cause sleepiness?

    A. Cortisol
    B. Growth hormone
    C. Melatonin
    D. Oxytocin

8. Which theory of dreaming states that dreams and thoughts during wakeful periods use the same stream-of-consciousness system?

    A. Activation–synthesis theory
    B. Problem-solving theory
    C. Cognitive process theory
    D. Neurocognitive theory

9. A 19-year old college student is picked up by campus police after shoplifting a large bag of corn chips and a dozen ice cream sandwiches. His eyes are bloodshot. During questioning, he repeatedly asks for water because his mouth is dry, and he cannot stop giggling. What is the psychoactive substance in the drug this student has most likely recently taken?

   A. Alprazolam
   B. 3,4-Methylenedioxy-*N*-methylamphetamine
   C. Diacetylmorphine
   D. Tetrahydrocannabinol

10. Language consists of multiple components. Which of the following involves the order in which words are put together?

   A. Phonology
   B. Semantics
   C. Syntax
   D. Pragmatics

11. A child speaks in sentences of at least 3 words, but makes grammatical errors including misuse of the past tense. How old is this child likely to be?

   A. 14 months
   B. 22 months
   C. 30 months
   D. 5 years

12. Which language theory states that language development occurs due to preferential reinforcement of certain phonemes by parents and caregivers?

   A. Nativist theory
   B. Learning theory
   C. Social interactionist theory
   D. Neurocognitive theory

13. A stroke patient comprehends speech but cannot properly move her mouth to form words. Which of the following brain areas is likely affected?

   A. Broca's area
   B. Wernicke's area
   C. Arcuate fasciculus
   D. Superior temporal gyrus

14. A nine-year-old girl is brought to the pediatrician. Her parents describe that any time she is startled, she appears to collapse and fall asleep. She also complains of waking up in the morning unable to move. Which sleep disorder should be suspected?

   A. Insomnia
   B. Sleep deprivation
   C. Narcolepsy
   D. Sleep apnea

15. During which of the following stages does dreaming occur?

   I. Stage 3
   II. Stage 4
   III. REM

   A. I only
   B. II only
   C. III only
   D. I, II, and III

Explanations to Discrete Practice Questions

1. D

Jean Piaget hypothesized that new information is processed by adaptation, **choice (B)**. Adaptation is too broad of an answer because it includes both assimilation, **choice (A)**, and accommodation, **choice (D)**. Assimilation is incorporation of new information into existing schemata. If the new information doesn't fit, then accommodation occurs. Accommodation is the modification of existing schemata to account for new information and is thus the correct answer.

2. C

The sensorimotor, preoperational, and concrete operational stages occur prior to adolescence. The formal operational stage generally coincides with adolescence.

3. C

The base rate fallacy occurs when prototypical or stereotypical factors are used for analysis rather than actual data. Because the student is volunteering in a hospital with a stroke center, he sees more patients who have experienced a stroke than would be expected in a hospital without a stroke center. Thus, this experience changes his perception and results in base rate fallacy. Deductive reasoning, **choice (A)**, refers to drawing conclusions by integrating different pieces of evidence. The representativeness heuristic, **choice (B)**, involves categorization and classification based on how well an individual example fits its category. Confirmation bias, **choice (D)**, occurs when a person only seeks information that reinforces his or her opinions.

4. A

Fluid intelligence consists of problem-solving skills and is not one of Gardner's seven multiple intelligences. Gardner's theory lists linguistic, logical–mathematical, musical, visual–spatial, bodily–kinesthetic, interpersonal, and intrapersonal intelligences.

5. A

EEG during REM is composed mainly of beta waves, which are present during alertness. SWS, **choice (B)**, consists mainly of delta waves, which are not typically present during REM sleep. Stage 1 sleep, **choice (C)**, consists mainly of theta waves. Meditation, **choice (D)**, is quieting of the mind, and consists mainly of slow alpha and theta waves.

6. B

Early in the evening, sleep cycles include deepening of sleep (Stages 1–2–3–4), followed either by lightening of sleep (Stages 4–3–2) and then REM, or just directly moving from Stage 4 into REM. Later in the evening, the cycle may be shortened as slow-wave sleep becomes less common.

7. C

As light diminishes throughout the day, the pineal gland increases secretion of melatonin, resulting in sleepiness. Cortisol levels, **choice (A)**, increase throughout the early morning, resulting in wakefulness. Growth hormone secretion, **choice (B)**, peaks during slow-wave sleep. Oxytocin, **choice (D)**, is associated with uterine contractions in childbirth, milk letdown, and bonding behavior.

8. C

Cognitive theorists proposed in the cognitive process dream theory that wakeful and dreaming states use the same mental systems within the brain, particularly stream-of-consciousness. The activation–synthesis theory, **choice (A)**, states that dreams are caused by widespread, random activation of neural circuitry. The problem-solving dream model, **choice (B)**, indicates that dreams are used to solve problems while sleeping due to untethering of dreams from obstacles perceived while awake. The neurocognitive theorists, **choice (D)**, seek to unify cognitive and biological perspectives by correlating the subjective dream experience with the physiological experience of dreaming.

9. D

The description of the student matches the clinical features of marijuana (cannabis) use: hunger (presumably, based on his loot), redness of the eyes, dry mouth, and euphoria. Marijuana may also cause an increased heart rate, short-term memory loss, paranoia, and—in high doses—hallucinations. Tetrahydrocannabinol is the primary active substance in marijuana.

10. C

Syntax refers to how words are put together to form sentences and create meaning. Phonology, **choice (A)**, refers to the actual sounds of a language. Semantics, **choice (B)**, refers to the association of meaning with a word. Pragmatics, **choice (D)**, refers to changes in usage, wording, and inflection based on context.

11. C

A child who speaks in three-word sentences but has not yet mastered most of the fundamental rules of language, including past tense, is likely to be between two and three years old.

12. B

Learning theory, largely based on the work of B. F. Skinner, states that parents reinforce phonemes that sound most like their language, resulting in preferential preservation of these phonemes. Nativist theory, **choice (A)**, posits a critical period during which language acquisition occurs. Social interactionist theory, **choice (C)**, indicates that language develops via interaction with parents and caregivers as well as a desire of the child to communicate. Neurocognitive theory, **choice (D)**, is concerned with the subjective experience of dreaming and the physiology of dreaming.

13. A

Broca's area governs the motor function of language. A stroke that affects Broca's area will leave receptive language intact, but word formation will be affected. A stroke affecting Wernicke's area, **choice (B)**, will make it so the individual is unable to comprehend speech. A stroke affecting the arcuate fasciculus, **choice (C)**, will result in an inability to repeat words heard but spontaneous language production is intact. The superior temporal gyrus, **choice (D)**, is where Wernicke's area is located.

14. C

The patient and her parents are describing cataplexy (a sudden loss of muscle tone and intrusion of REM sleep during waking hours, usually in response to a startling or emotional trigger) and sleep paralysis (an inability to move despite being awake, usually when waking up in the morning). These symptoms are highly suggestive of narcolepsy; in fact, some consider cataplexy to be pathognomonic for (absolutely indicative of) the disorder.

15. D

About 75% of dreaming occurs during REM, but dreams occur in all other stages of sleep as well. More bizarre dreams are likely to occur during REM.

Motivation, Emotion, and Stress

In This Chapter

Chapter Profile

The content in this chapter should be relevant to about 6% of all questions about the Behavioral Sciences on the MCAT.

This chapter covers material from the following AAMC content categories:

6C: Responding to the world

7A: Individual influences on behavior

Introduction

She has developed a heart condition, has suffered substantial bone density decreases, has esophageal and stomach ulcers, and has lost 25 percent of her body mass: she is affected by anorexia nervosa. As a career model, she has been put under extreme pressure in the workplace to look a certain way. Over time, this pressure motivated her to lose weight in an unhealthy manner. In her case, she was motivated by feelings of disgust and guilt that go directly against the body's basic needs. A combination of stress from her job and peers, intrinsic and extrinsic motivation, and negative emotions resulted in what could be a life-threatening condition.

In this chapter we'll discuss motivation, emotion, and stress. We will look at factors that influence motivation, the components of emotion, and the stressors that lead to the stress response. We will also look at theories used to explain these processes and associated behaviors. The physiological, cognitive, and behavioral elements will be examined in order to understand the role that these topics play in everyday life. Exploring these ideas will enable us to tackle any question related to these concepts on Test Day.

5.1 Motivation

> **LEARNING GOALS**
>
> After Chapter 5.1, you will be able to:
>
> - Describe the sources of motivation posited by instinct theory, arousal theory, drive reduction theory, and the need-based theories
> - Order Maslow's proposed hierarchy of needs from most to least essential
> - Apply opponent-process theory to drug use and withdrawal

Motivation is the purpose, or driving force, behind our actions. The word derives from the Latin *movere*, meaning "to move." There are many examples of motivation in our everyday lives. As you sit, studying for the MCAT, you realize you are thirsty, so you reach for your water bottle. When you realize it is empty, the need to quench your thirst drives you to get up, walk to the kitchen, and fill the bottle with water. Thus, the physical state of thirst motivated an action. The desire to go to medical school and become a physician has motivated you to complete required undergraduate coursework, strive for a competitive GPA, participate in extracurricular activities, and dedicate your time to study for a standardized test. The goal of staying fit and healthy motivates many to spend hours in the gym, while the initial discomfort of physical activity might motivate others to stay sedentary. Motivation can be directed toward minimizing pain, maximizing pleasure, or it can be rooted in a particular physical need such as eating, drinking, sleeping, or sex.

Real World

Intrinsic motivation can be reduced by introducing external reward into a scenario. In one study, children were given art supplies and told to draw. Some children were told they would receive a gold ribbon for their drawing, while others were not. Those who knew of the potential reward were driven by extrinsic motivation and spent less time drawing, acting only to receive the reward. Children who did not know about the reward drew for the sake of drawing—by intrinsic motivation—and spent more time drawing.

Motivation can be categorized based on what drives people to act. These drives can be external forces, such as rewards and punishments, or internal forces, where the behavior is personally gratifying. External forces, coming from outside oneself, create extrinsic motivation. **Extrinsic motivation** can include rewards for showing a desired behavior or avoiding punishment if the desired behavior is not achieved. Examples of such motivation include working hard at your job for praise from your boss, practicing regularly for a sport so that you will perform strongly in an upcoming game, or studying for months on end to achieve a high score on the MCAT. Each of these acts result in external, tangible rewards. Extrinsic motivation can also include doing chores to avoid punishment and working to avoid being fired. Competition is a strong form of external motivation because a person is incentivized to beat others and not only to win, perform, or achieve for him- or herself. Motivation that comes from within oneself is referred to as **intrinsic motivation**. This can be driven by interest in a task or pure enjoyment. A student who takes interest in the subject matter at hand and has the goal of mastering the content is driven by intrinsic motivation, while the goal of achieving high grades is considered extrinsic.

The primary views of motivation include instincts that elicit natural behavior, the desire to maintain optimal levels of arousal, the drive to reduce uncomfortable states, and the goal of satisfying physiological and psychological needs.

INSTINCT THEORY

Early attempts to understand the basis of motivation focused on **instincts**, which are innate, fixed patterns of behavior in response to stimuli. For example, wolves are instinctively pack creatures that naturally follow the alpha male of their group. Additionally, they are highly territorial creatures, protecting areas that are much larger than needed to hunt and dwell. This protection includes scent-marking, howling, and direct aggressive attacks on intruders. Humans also have instinctive behavior; for example, thumb sucking is an instinctual response to stress in babies that is aimed at self-soothing. As discussed in Chapter 1 of *MCAT Behavioral Sciences Review*, primitive reflexes like the grasp reflex, shown in Figure 5.1, are also instinctual. Note that some instincts last for the entire lifetime, while others may appear or disappear with age.

Figure 5.1. The Grasp Reflex
Primitive reflexes are examples of instincts, seen in infants,
that extinguish with age.

Key Concept

An instinct is an innate, fixed pattern of behavior in response to a stimulus. It may be consistent throughout life, or it may appear or disappear with time.

According to the **instinct theory** of motivation, people are driven to do certain behaviors based on evolutionarily programmed instincts. This theory was one of the first to describe motivation and was derived from Darwin's theory of evolution. William James, the father of modern psychology, was one of the first to write about human instincts in his 1890 publication of *Principles of Psychology*. He stated that humans were driven by many instincts, possibly more than any other animal studied. James suggested that human actions are derived from 20 physical instincts, including suckling and locomotion, and 17 mental instincts, including curiosity and fearfulness. However, he said that many of these instincts were in direct conflict with each other and could be overridden by experience. Arguably the greatest proponent of instinct theory was William McDougall, who proposed that humans were driven to all thoughts and behaviors by 18 distinctive instincts, including flight and acquisition. James and McDougall postulated that the instincts of suckling and carrying food to the mouth result in naturally motivating one to eat.

AROUSAL THEORY

Another factor that influences motivation is **arousal**, the psychological and physiological state of being awake and reactive to stimuli. Arousal involves the brainstem, autonomic nervous system, and endocrine system, and plays a vital role in behavior and cognition.

Arousal theory states that people perform actions in order to maintain an optimal level of arousal: seeking to increase arousal when it falls below their optimal level, and to decrease arousal when it rises above their optimum level. Additionally, the **Yerkes–Dodson law** postulates a U-shaped function between the level of arousal and performance. This law states that performance is worst at extremely high and low levels of arousal and optimal at some intermediate level, as depicted in Figure 5.2. The optimal level of arousal varies between different types of tasks: lower levels are optimal for highly cognitive tasks, while higher levels are optimal for activities that require physical endurance and stamina. Further, simple tasks generally require slightly higher arousal than complex tasks.

Real World

While a moderate level of arousal is optimal for performance, certain individuals seek out higher levels of arousal. These people may seek out dangerous activities, such as skydiving or bungee jumping, and are considered *adrenaline junkies*. These individuals are sometimes found to have lower levels of monoamine oxidase (MAO), which breaks down catecholamines. Low levels of MAO result in higher neurotransmitter levels, which may lead to motivation to experience high levels of arousal.

Figure 5.2. Yerkes–Dodson Law

DRIVE REDUCTION THEORY

Drives are defined as internal states of tension that activate particular behaviors focused on goals. Drives are thought to originate within an individual without requiring any external factors to motivate behavior. In other words, drives help humans survive by creating an uncomfortable state, ensuring motivation to eliminate this state or to relieve the internal tension created by unmet needs. **Primary drives**, including the need for food, water, and warmth, motivate us to sustain bodily processes in homeostasis. **Homeostasis** is the regulation of the internal environment to maintain an optimal, stable set of conditions. In homeostatic regulation, external factors are encountered, and the system will react to push the system back to its optimal state.

Homeostasis is usually controlled by **negative feedback** loops. A common real-life example of a negative feedback loop is a thermostat. A thermostat is set to a desired temperature, and then sensors monitor the air temperature in relation to this desired temperature. If the air temperature gets too cold, the heater will turn on; if the temperature gets too warm, the heater will turn off. Negative feedback loops in the body operate the same way. When our bodies are lacking nutrients and energy, feedback systems release hormones like ghrelin that create a hunger drive and motivate eating. After we consume food, feedback is sent to the brain to turn off the hunger drive through hormones like leptin. Hunger is a complex feedback system involving these hormones, receptors in the walls of the stomach, levels of glucose (maintained by the liver), and insulin and glucagon levels (released by the pancreas). The concentrations of many hormones of the endocrine system are regulated by three-organ "axes," such as the hypothalamic–pituitary–adrenal axis shown in Figure 5.3.

Real World

One well-characterized drive is the hunger (food) drive, which has been studied for over 60 years. The hunger drive is a primary drive, in that food is necessary for life. Given the necessity of food to life, many species possess multiple processes that drive the individual to consume food. These biological processes include tie-ins to the sense of smell and taste, which were demonstrated by smany studies, notably those of Janowitz and Grossman.

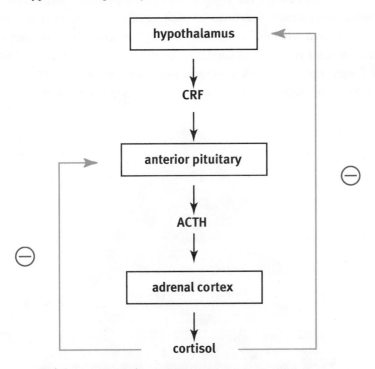

Figure 5.3. Negative Feedback in the Endocrine System

Key Concept

Primary drives are those that motivate us to sustain necessary biological processes. Secondary drives are those that motivate us to fulfill nonbiological, emotional, or "learned" desires.

Bridge

Drive reduction theory can be applied to motivation in terms of learning, and is commonly used to define motivational states within behavioral conditioning. Conditioning and learning are discussed in Chapter 3 of *MCAT Behavioral Sciences Review*.

Additional drives that are not directly related to biological processes are called **secondary drives**. These drives are thought to stem from learning. The drive to matriculate into medical school and become a physician is an example of a secondary drive. Secondary drives also include certain emotions, such as the desire for nurturing, love, achievement, and aggression.

Drive reduction theory explains that motivation is based on the goal of eliminating uncomfortable states. Theorists hypothesize that certain physiological conditions result in a negative internal environment. This internal environment then drives motivation and seeks homeostasis in order to reduce the uncomfortable internal state.

NEED-BASED THEORIES

Needs are also motivators that influence human behavior. Through this lens, motivation can be described as how we allocate our energy and resources to best satisfy these needs. Motivation thus determines which behaviors are most important to pursue, how much effort will be taken, and for how long the effort will be maintained.

Abraham Maslow observed that certain needs will yield a greater influence on our motivation and established what is referred to as **Maslow's hierarchy of needs**. Maslow classified needs into five groups, and assigned different levels of priority to each group. The hierarchy is typically displayed as a pyramid, as shown in Figure 5.4, where the most primitive, essential, and important needs are at the base. The first four levels of the pyramid correspond to physiological needs, safety and security, love and belonging, and self-esteem. The highest level of the pyramid corresponds to self-actualization, or the need to realize one's fullest potential. Maslow theorized that if the lowest level of need is not met, motivation to meet that need will be the highest priority. Once that need is met, if additional needs exist, they will be satisfied based on priority. For example, a person's most basic motivation will be to satisfy physiological needs, followed by the need to establish a safe and secure environment.

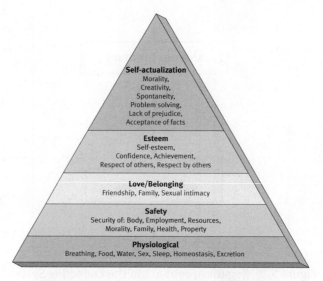

Figure 5.4. Maslow's Hierarchy of Needs

Another need-based motivational theory is the **self-determination theory (SDT)**. SDT emphasizes the role of three universal needs: autonomy, the need to be in control of one's actions and ideas; competence, the need to complete and excel at difficult tasks; and relatedness, the need to feel accepted and wanted in relationships. Theorists explain that these three needs must be met in order to develop healthy relationships with oneself and others.

ADDITIONAL THEORIES AND APPLICATIONS

There are two other theories of motivation that you want to know for the MCAT: incentive theory and expectancy-value theory. **Incentive theory** explains that behavior is motivated not by need or arousal, but by the desire to pursue rewards and to avoid punishments. **Expectancy–value theory** states that the amount of motivation needed to reach a goal is the result of both the individual's expectation of success in reaching the goal and the degree to which he or she values succeeding at the goal.

There are many motivations that stem from biology but that are impacted by additional psychological and sociocultural factors. One of the strongest natural motivations is hunger. However, people often eat for the sheer pleasure of the act, a motivation that has led to obesity occurring at alarming rates in the United States. Societal and cultural norms can determine what types of foods one eats and when. For example, some cultures have a traditional diet very high in fat and participate in many social activities involving food. At the other extreme, anorexia nervosa is also correlated to biological and cultural factors. It has been observed that those suffering from the disease are more likely to suffer from personality disorders as well. The prevalence of anorexia in the United States has increased significantly in the last several decades as the societal concept of beauty has changed from more full-bodied idols to extremely thin cultural icons.

Opponent-Process Theory

Motivations are considered destructive if they result in harm to oneself. For example, drug abusers can be motivated to take drugs by the pleasure experienced when taking the drug or by the removal of withdrawal symptoms. While there are many "hard" drugs available, the most commonly used psychoactive substances in the United States are caffeine, nicotine, and alcohol. A theory of motivation that explains continuous drug use is the **opponent-process theory**. This theory explains that when a drug is taken repeatedly, the body will attempt to counteract the effects of the drug by changing its physiology. For example, the body will counteract repeated use of alcohol, a depressant, by increasing arousal. The problem with this reaction is that it will last longer than the drug, resulting in withdrawal symptoms that are exactly opposite the effects of alcohol: sensations of anxiety, jitteriness, and irritability. The withdrawal created by this mechanism can create a physical dependence on the drug. Opponent-process theory can also explain **tolerance**, a decrease in perceived drug effect over time. Cultural and demographic factors also affect drug use. Young adults are the most likely age group to smoke, with a decline in smoking rates seen as the group ages. Smoking is also seen more commonly in disadvantaged socioeconomic groups. Across the globe, smoking rates are highest in Eastern Europe; this creates visibility, leading to additional pressure or desire to smoke in these communities.

Sexual Motivation

Sexual motivation is another area that has been widely studied. In 1948, Alfred Kinsey reported his findings on sexual behavior from interviews with people from a broad range of sociocultural backgrounds. Kinsey hoped to identify what sexual behaviors people were participating in, how often, with whom, and at what age they began. William Masters and Virginia Johnson published another important study of sexual motivation. The study involved physiological measurement of sexual arousal, proving that men and women experience similar physical responses. The most notable differences seen between the sexes were based on cultural influences and learned behavior.

Physiologically, humans are motivated to sexual behavior based on the secretion of estrogens, progesterone, and androgens. There is a strong correlation between hormone concentration and sexual desire. Another biological factor for sexual motivation is smell. Certain odors have been shown to increase sexual desire and activity. Pleasure and the interpretation of pleasure is also a key player in sexual motivation and one that is highly influenced by culture. One study measured physiological arousal based on watching sexually explicit videos. The results showed that both men and women experienced the same levels of arousal, but women more often reported being unaroused or having feelings of disgust based on subjective interviews. This study demonstrated that cognition plays a role in sexual motivation. Additionally, culture and society influence what is deemed appropriate sexual behavior, the age at which it is deemed appropriate, and with whom. Cultural norms and conditioning influence the desire for sexual interaction, or lack thereof.

MCAT Concept Check 5.1:

Before you move on, assess your understanding of the material with these questions.

1. For each of the theories listed below, what creates motivation?

Theory	Factor for Motivation
Instinct theory	
Arousal theory	
Drive reduction theory	
Need-based theories	

2. List Maslow's hierarchy of needs in decreasing priority:

- _____

- _____

- _____

- _____

- _____

3. Based on opponent-process theory, what clinical features would be expected with withdrawal from cocaine use?

_____

5.2 Emotion

LEARNING GOALS

After Chapter 5.2, you will be able to:

- Describe the three elements of emotion: psychological response, behavioral response, and cognitive response
- Recall the seven universal facially expressed emotions
- Compare and contrast the James–Lange, Cannon–Bard, and Schachter–Singer theories of emotion
- Identify the names and functions of the parts of the limbic system:

Emotion is a natural instinctive state of mind derived from one's circumstances, mood, or relationships with others. The word emotion is derived from the same Latin word as motivation. What does psychology have to tell us about emotions?

THREE ELEMENTS OF EMOTION

There are three elements of an emotion: the physiological response, the behavioral response, and the cognitive response.

Physiological Response

When a feeling is first experienced, arousal is stimulated by the autonomic nervous system. The physiological component includes changes in heart rate, breathing rate, skin temperature, and blood pressure. While it may be hard to recognize these changes and associate them with an emotion in everyday life, these changes have been detected in laboratory settings. Some emotions, such as fear, aggression, and embarrassment, are associated with more pronounced physiological changes than others.

Behavioral Response

The behavioral component of an emotion includes facial expressions and body language. For example, a smile, a friendly hand gesture, or even a subtle head tilt toward someone are commonly recognized as warm and happy signals. On the other hand, a frown, slumping of the shoulders, and looking downward are recognized as sad or downtrodden signals.

Cognitive Response

Finally, the cognitive component of emotion is the subjective interpretation of the feeling being experienced. Determination of one's emotion is largely based on memories of past experiences and perception of the cause of the emotion.

UNIVERSAL EMOTIONS

Darwin made the argument that emotions are a result of evolution; thus, emotions and their corresponding expressions are universal. He explained that all humans evolved the same set of facial muscles to show the same expressions when communicating emotion, regardless of their society or culture. This sparked an ongoing discussion of the relationship between emotion and culture among psychologists and sociologists. Paul Ekman described a set of basic emotions that are recognized by societies around the world, and further identified that six emotions are associated with consistent facial expressions across cultures. Ekman and other psychologists have revised this list; one of the more well-recognized sets consists of seven universal facially expressed emotions and includes: happiness, sadness, contempt, surprise, fear, disgust, and anger. These emotions correspond to the distinctive facial expressions explained in Table 5.1 and depicted in Figure 5.5.

MCAT Expertise

The AAMC lists fear, anger, happiness, surprise, joy, disgust, and sadness as universal emotions. Given the lack of consensus in the scientific community, the MCAT is more likely to test the topic conceptually.

Emotion	Facial Expression Cues
Happiness	Smile, wrinkling around eyes, raised cheeks
Sadness	Frown, inner eyebrows pulled up and together
Contempt	One corner of the mouth pulled upwards
Surprise	Eyes widen, eyebrows pulled up and curved, jaw opens
Fear	Eyes widen, eyebrows pulled up and together, lips pulled toward ears
Disgust	Nose wrinkling and/or raising of upper lip
Anger	Glaring, eyebrows pulled down and together, lips pressed together

Table 5.1. Seven Universal Emotions

Figure 5.5.   Seven Universal Emotions
First row: happiness, sadness, contempt, surprise; second row: fear, disgust, anger.

While emotions are experienced universally, it is argued that they can be affected greatly by culture. Cultural dissimilarities in emotion include varying reactions to similar events, differences in the emotional experience itself, the behavior exhibited in response to an emotion, and the perception of that emotion by others within the society.

ADAPTIVE ROLE OF EMOTION

In accordance with Darwin's thoughts on universal emotion, the evolutionary perspective states that everything we do, think, and feel is based on specialized functional programs designed for any problem we encounter. These programs are functionally coordinated in order to produce a cohesive response. Emotions are thought to be evolutionary adaptations due to situations encountered over the evolutionary history of the human species that guide sensory processing, physiological response, and behavior. Further, different emotions are thought to have evolved during different periods in history. Among the earliest to develop were primal emotions, such as fear; other, more evolutionarily progressive emotions include social emotions, such as guilt and pride.

THEORIES OF EMOTION

Early psychologists believed that the cognitive component of emotion led to the physiological component, which then produced the behavioral component. In other words, the feeling of anger started with perception of a negative stimulus, which caused physiological changes, such as increased skin temperature, which then resulted in behavior, such as yelling. This explanation assumes that feeling precedes arousal, which precedes action.

James–Lange Theory

William James, the founder of functionalist theory, viewed the progression of these emotional elements differently. Around the same time, Carl Lange developed a theory of emotion similar to that of James's. The explanation developed by the two is referred to as the **James–Lange theory of emotion**. According to the theory, a stimulus results first in physiological arousal, which leads to a secondary response in which the emotion is labeled. James believed that when peripheral organs receive information and respond, that response is then labeled as an emotion by the brain. For example, a car cutting you off on the highway is a stimulus for elevated heart rate and blood pressure, increased skin temperature, and dry mouth. These physiological responses result in the cognitive labeling of anger: *I must be angry because my skin is hot and my blood pressure is high.* By extension, an emotion would not be processed without feedback from the peripheral organs; this theory predicts that individuals who cannot mount a sympathetic response, like patients with spinal cord injuries, should show decreased levels of emotion. Subsequent studies have proven this claim to be false; spinal cord injury subjects continue to show the same level of emotion after their injuries as before.

Cannon–Bard Theory

Walter Cannon and Philip Bard developed another scheme for explaining emotional components, referred to as the **Cannon–Bard theory of emotion**. In an attempt to test the James–Lange theory, Cannon studied the expression of emotion and its relationship to feedback from the sympathetic nervous system using cats whose afferent nerves had been severed. He hypothesized that physiological arousal and feeling an emotion occur at the same time, not in sequence. Thus, severing the feedback should not alter the emotion experienced. In this theory, a person will respond with action after experiencing the emotion both mentally and physically. Bard, a student of Cannon's, further explained that when exposed to a stimulus, sensory information is received and sent to both the cortex and the sympathetic nervous system simultaneously by the thalamus. Thus, the Cannon–Bard theory of emotion, depicted in Figure 5.6, states that the cognitive and physiological components of emotion occur simultaneously and result in the behavioral component of emotion, or action: *I am afraid because I see a snake and my heart is racing . . . Let me out of here!*

While critics of the James–Lange theory cite the severed afferent nerve study as support for the Cannon–Bard theory, there are also weaknesses in this theory. The Cannon–Bard theory fails to explain the vagus nerve, a cranial nerve that functions as a feedback system, conveying information from the peripheral organs back to the central nervous system.

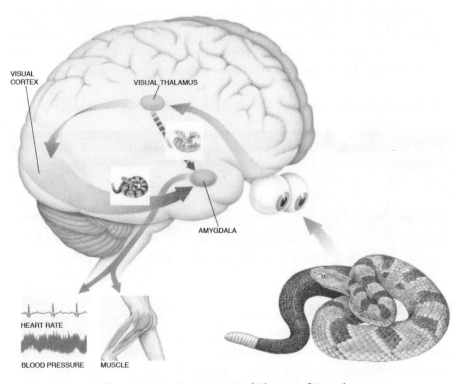

VISUAL CORTEX

VISUAL THALAMUS

AMYGDALA

HEART RATE

BLOOD PRESSURE   MUSCLE

Figure 5.6.   Cannon–Bard Theory of Emotion
Visual stimuli pass through the thalamus and rough information is sent to the amygdala (fear) and the sympathetic nervous system (arousal). Action (muscle contraction) quickly follows. The visual cortex can either strengthen or quell this fear response once it has identified the stimulus.

Schachter–Singer Theory

A third theory is the **Schachter–Singer theory of emotion**, also termed the **cognitive arousal theory** or the **two-factor theory**. It states that both arousal and the labeling of arousal based on environment must occur in order for an emotion to be experienced: *I am excited because my heart is racing and everyone else is happy.* What is unique to the Schachter–Singer theory is this aspect of cognitive

MCAT Expertise

The MCAT will expect that you have a solid understanding of the differences in emotional processing described by each of the three theories of emotion. It is best to mentally sort these theories by "first response" and "second response" to the stimulus.

appraisal: to feel an emotion, one must consciously analyze the environment in relation to nervous system arousal. To study this, Stanley Schachter and Jerome Singer gave injections of epinephrine or placebo to groups of subjects that were either informed, ignorant, or misinformed. They also manipulated external cues in the study by having an actor act either happy or angry. They observed that epinephrine did result in increased physiological arousal; however, they also discovered that the environment and cognitive processing affected the emotion experienced by the subjects. The misinformed and ignorant groups experienced the highest levels of emotion. Schachter and Singer explained this by stating that a subject experiencing physiological arousal with no explanation or with a misleading explanation will attribute that arousal to the surrounding environment, and label herself as happy or angry based on the behavior of the actor. In other words, the presence of unexpected arousal plus an environment that encourages a particular emotion is sufficient to create that emotion in the subject. Contrarily, the informed group knew to expect physiological arousal from the drug, and thus attributed their feelings to being side effects, rather than emotions.

The three theories of emotion discussed in this section are summarized in Table 5.2.

Theory		First Response	Second Response
James–Lange		Nervous system arousal	Conscious emotion
Cannon–Bard	Stimulus	Nervous system arousal and conscious emotion	Action
Schachter–Singer		Nervous system arousal and cognitive appraisal	Conscious emotion

Table 5.2. Theories of Emotion

THE LIMBIC SYSTEM

Experiencing emotion is a complex process involving many parts of the brain. The most notable of these circuits is the **limbic system**, a complex set of structures that reside below the cerebrum on either side of the thalamus, as shown in Figure 5.7. The system is made up of the amygdala, thalamus, hypothalamus, hippocampus and fornix, septal nuclei, and parts of the cerebral cortex; it plays a large role in both motivation and emotion.

Figure 5.7.   The Limbic System

The **amygdala** is a small round structure that signals the cortex about stimuli related to attention and emotions. The amygdala processes the environment, detects external cues, and learns from the person's surroundings in order to produce emotion. This region is associated with fear and also plays a role in human emotion through interpretation of facial expressions.

The **thalamus** functions as a preliminary sensory processing station and routes information to the cortex and other appropriate areas of the brain. The **hypothalamus**, located below the thalamus, synthesizes and releases a variety of neurotransmitters. It serves many homeostatic functions, and is involved in modulating emotion. Indeed, by controlling the neurotransmitters that affect mood and arousal, the hypothalamus largely dictates emotional states.

The **hippocampus**, within the temporal lobe, is primarily involved in creating long-term memories. Along with the functions of the amygdala and hypothalamus, the storage and retrieval of emotional memories is key in producing an emotional response. The hippocampus also aids in creating context for stimuli to lead to an emotional experience. As described in Chapter 3 of *MCAT Behavioral Sciences Review*, memory systems can be divided into two categories: explicit and implicit. When an emotion is experienced, sensory systems transmit this information into both the explicit memory system, primarily controlled by the hippocampus in the medial temporal lobe, and the implicit memory system, controlled by the amygdala. Both memory systems are used for both the formation and retrieval of emotional memories, as shown in Figure 5.8. The conscious (explicit) memory is the memory of experiencing the actual emotion: remembering that you were happy at your high school graduation or that you were sad when you lost a loved one is explicit memory. Note that these are episodic memories: they are more properly considered memories *about* emotions than stored emotions. The unconscious (implicit) memory is referred to as **emotional memory**; this is the storage of the actual feelings of emotion associated with an event. When experiencing a similar event later on, these emotions may be retrieved. Thus, explicit memory of the emotion produces a conscious memory of

Real World

When specific areas of the limbic system are stimulated during brain surgery, patients have described sensations such as happiness, contentment, and pleasure; in other areas, they report fear and anxiety.

Real World

Research on rats has shown that when the amygdalae are damaged, the rats can no longer be classically conditioned to establish new fears. Similar effects have also been seen in humans wherein damage to this region prevents fear conditioning. This has been measured by autonomic nervous system responses as well as functional imaging.

the experience, and implicit memory determines the expression of past emotions. This distinction can be further identified when looking at individuals with posttraumatic stress disorder (PTSD). The explicit memory is the "story" of the event: what happened, where it occurred, who was involved, the fact that the scenario was traumatic, and so forth. The implicit memory corresponds to the sensations of unease and anxiety when put back into a similar environment.

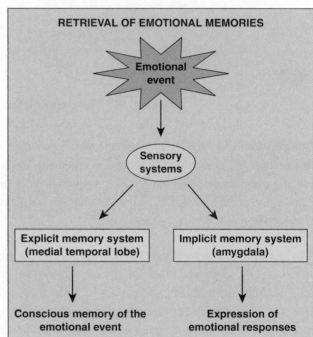

Figure 5.8. Formation and Retrieval of Emotional Memories

The ability to distinguish and interpret others' facial expressions is primarily controlled by the temporal lobe, with some input from the occipital lobe. This function is lateralized: the right hemisphere is more active when discerning facial expressions than the left. There are also gender differences: women demonstrate more activation of these brain areas than men. This ability is present but weak in children and develops into adulthood; adults are much more effective at identifying both positive and negative emotions.

The **prefrontal cortex** is the anterior portion of the frontal lobes and is associated with planning intricate cognitive functions, expressing personality, and making decisions. The prefrontal cortex also receives arousal input from the brainstem, coordinating arousal and cognitive states. It has been demonstrated that the left prefrontal cortex is associated with positive emotions and the right prefrontal cortex with negative emotions. The **dorsal prefrontal cortex** is associated with attention and cognition, while the **ventral prefrontal cortex** connects with regions of the brain responsible for experiencing emotion. Specifically, the **ventromedial prefrontal cortex**, shown in Figure 5.9, is thought to play a substantial role in decision-making and controlling emotional responses from the amygdala.

Real World

One of the most notable studies on prefrontal cortex function is that of Phineas Gage. Gage was involved in an accident in which a metal rod pierced his brain, destroying the left frontal lobe. Gage's memory, speech, and motor skills were unaffected, but his personality was dramatically altered. Post-accident, Gage displayed irritable and impatient behavior, which inhibited his ability to complete simple tasks.

Figure 5.9. Ventromedial Prefrontal Cortex
The ventromedial prefrontal cortex is highlighted in blue.

As described earlier, the **autonomic nervous system** is also related to emotion; specific physiological reactions are associated with specific emotions. Skin temperature, heart rate, breathing rate, and blood pressure are all affected when experiencing emotion. Decreased skin temperature is detected in subjects experiencing fear, while increased skin temperature is associated with anger. Increased heart rate is observed in subjects experiencing both anger and fear, while decreased heart rate is observed in happy subjects. Heart rate variability is another factor used to determine emotion. Decreased heart rate variability is associated with stress, frustration, and anger. Blood pulse volume increases with anger or stress, and decreases with sadness or relaxation. Skin conductivity is directly correlated with sympathetic arousal; however, a specific emotion cannot be identified by skin response. Diastolic blood pressure is increased to the greatest degree by anger, followed by fear, sadness, and happiness.

MCAT Concept Check 5.2:

Before you move on, assess your understanding of the material with these questions.

1. What are the three elements of emotion? Provide a brief description of each.

   • _____

   • _____

   • _____

2. What are the seven universal emotions?

   • _____

   • _____

   • _____

   • _____

   • _____

   • _____

   • _____

3. Compare and contrast the James–Lange, Cannon–Bard, and Schachter–Singer theories of emotion:

James–Lange Theory	Cannon–Bard Theory	Schachter–Singer Theory

4. What is the function of each part of the limbic system listed below?

   • Amygdala:

   _____

   • Thalamus:

   _____

   • Hypothalamus:

   _____

   • Hippocampus:

   _____

   • Ventromedial prefrontal cortex:

   _____

5.3 Stress

LEARNING GOALS

After Chapter 5.3, you will be able to:

- Distinguish between primary and secondary appraisals of stress
- Recall the three stages of general adaptation syndrome and the physiological changes associated with each stage
- Recognize common stressors and effective techniques for management of stress

---

In all aspects of life, at all times of day, we must make decisions, overcome challenges, and continue forward. While some of these decisions are small, others require planning and adaptation to new circumstances. Behavior of others and the perception of our surroundings affect our behavior and mental state, at times in a negative manner. It is our response to challenging events, be they physical, emotional, cognitive, or behavioral, that defines **stress**.

COGNITIVE APPRAISAL OF STRESS

Cognitive appraisal is the subjective evaluation of a situation that induces stress. This process consists of two stages. Stage 1, or **primary appraisal**, is the initial evaluation of the environment and the associated threat. This appraisal can be identified as irrelevant, benign–positive, or stressful. If primary appraisal reveals a threat, stage 2 appraisal begins. **Secondary appraisal** is directed at evaluating whether the organism can cope with the stress. This appraisal involves the evaluation of three things: harm, or damage caused by the event; threat, or the potential for future damage caused by the event; and challenge, or the potential to overcome and possibly benefit from the event. Individuals who perceive themselves as having the ability to cope with the event experience less stress than those who don't. In general, appraisal and stress level are personal, as individuals have different skills, abilities, and coping mechanisms. For example, while a spider might incite fear and stress in some, it would result in irrelevant appraisal in others. Some situations require ongoing monitoring through constant **reappraisal**, such as the perception of being followed.

MCAT Expertise

The MCAT will expect you to know the two stages of stress appraisal: primary and secondary. Primary appraisal is the initial examination, which results in the identification of the stress as irrelevant, benign–positive, or stressful. If identified as a threat, secondary appraisal is an evaluation of one's ability to cope with the stress.

TYPES OF STRESSORS

A **stressor** is a biological element, external condition, or event that leads to a stress response. The severity of stressors can range from minimal or irritating hassles, like temporarily lost keys, to catastrophic scenarios, such as an impending natural disaster. Common stressors include:

- Environmental factors: uncomfortable temperature, loud sounds, inclement weather
- Daily events: running late, losing items, unexpected occurrences
- Workplace or academic setting: assignments, hierarchical interactions, time managment
- Social expectations: demands placed on oneself by society, family, and friends
- Chemical and biological stressors: diet, alcohol, drugs, viruses, allergies, medications, medical conditions

Stressors are classified as either causing distress or causing eustress. **Distress** occurs when experiencing unpleasant stressors, whereas eustress is a result of positive conditions. **Eustress** can include life events such as graduating from college, achieving a high score on the MCAT, getting married, or buying a house. While they are positive, any event requiring a person to change or adapt his or her lifestyle leads to stress. Stress level can be measured in "life change units" in a system called the **social readjustment rating scale**.

Stressors can also be psychological. Pressure, control, predictability, frustration, and conflict are all forms of psychological stress. Pressure is experienced when expectations or demands are put in place from external sources; this produces a feeling of urgency to complete tasks, perform actions, or display particular behaviors. The ability to control one's surroundings typically reduces stress levels; the inability to control a situation or event increases stress. In a study of nursing home patients, it was observed that those who had the most control of their daily environment displayed more active, positive, and social behavior. Predictability also plays a role in stress levels. For example, firefighters and policeman who cannot predict their daily scenarios experience higher levels of stress on the job. Frustration, which occurs when attaining a goal or need is prevented, increases stress. These frustration stresses can be external, such as not getting a raise, or internal, such as a disability interfering with everyday life. Finally, conflict stresses arise from the need to make a choice. Approach–approach conflict refers to the need to choose between two desirable options. Avoidance–avoidance conflicts are choices between two negative options. Approach–avoidance conflicts deal with only one choice, goal, or event, but the outcome could have both positive and negative elements. For instance, while a job promotion might mean more money or status, it also comes with increased responsibility, potential for longer working hours, and increased pressure.

PHYSIOLOGICAL RESPONSE TO STRESSORS

When subjected to stress, the body initially responds via the sympathetic nervous system. The "fight-or-flight" response initiates an increase in heart rate and decrease in digestion, with all available energy being reserved for reacting to the stressful event. The sequence of physiological responses developed by Hans Selye is called the **general adaptation syndrome** and consists of three distinct stages, as shown in Figure 5.10.

Figure 5.10. Three Stages of Stress Response

First is **alarm**, or the initial reaction to a stressor and the activation of the sympathetic nervous system. Shortly thereafter, the hypothalamus stimulates the pituitary to secrete adrenocorticotropic hormone (ACTH). This hormone stimulates the adrenal glands to produce cortisol, which maintains the steady supply of blood sugar needed to respond to stressful events. The hypothalamus also activates the adrenal medulla, which secretes epinephrine and norepinephrine to activate the sympathetic nervous system. The next stage is **resistance**, in which the continuous release of hormones allows the sympathetic nervous system to remain engaged to fight the stressor. Last, a person will experience **exhaustion** when the body can no longer maintain an elevated response with sympathetic nervous system activity. At this point, individuals become more susceptible to illnesses and medical conditions (such as ulcers and high blood pressure), organ systems can begin to deteriorate (including heart disease), and in extreme cases, death can result. Some of the positive and negative effects of stress are shown in Figure 5.11.

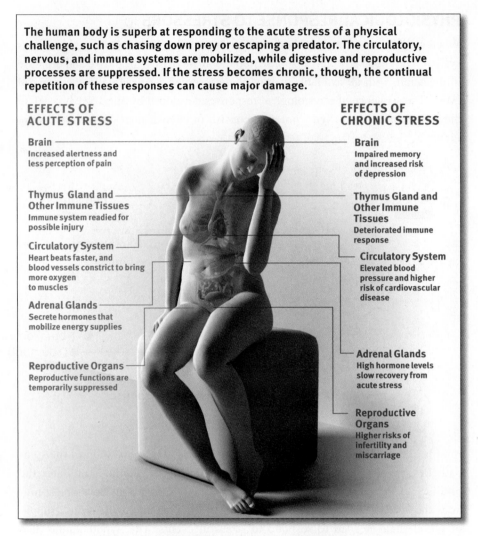

The human body is superb at responding to the acute stress of a physical challenge, such as chasing down prey or escaping a predator. The circulatory, nervous, and immune systems are mobilized, while digestive and reproductive processes are suppressed. If the stress becomes chronic, though, the continual repetition of these responses can cause major damage.

EFFECTS OF ACUTE STRESS

Brain
Increased alertness and less perception of pain

Thymus Gland and Other Immune Tissues
Immune system readied for possible injury

Circulatory System
Heart beats faster, and blood vessels constrict to bring more oxygen to muscles

Adrenal Glands
Secrete hormones that mobilize energy supplies

Reproductive Organs
Reproductive functions are temporarily suppressed

EFFECTS OF CHRONIC STRESS

Brain
Impaired memory and increased risk of depression

Thymus Gland and Other Immune Tissues
Deteriorated immune response

Circulatory System
Elevated blood pressure and higher risk of cardiovascular disease

Adrenal Glands
High hormone levels slow recovery from acute stress

Reproductive Organs
Higher risks of infertility and miscarriage

Figure 5.11. Positive and Negative Effects of Stress

EMOTIONAL AND BEHAVIORAL RESPONSES TO STRESS

Beyond the effects on the human body, stress also takes a psychological toll on people who are unable to reduce their stress levels. On the emotional level, elevated stress can result in individuals feeling irritable, moody, tense, fearful, and helpless. They may also have difficulties with concentration and memory. Negative behavior responses to stress include withdrawing from others, difficulties at work or at school, substance use, aggression, and suicide. Additionally, chronic stress can lead to mental health disorders, such as anxiety and depression.

COPING AND STRESS MANAGEMENT

Strategies for coping with stress fall into two groups. Problem-focused strategies involve working to overcome a stressor, such as reaching out to family and friends for social support, confronting the issue head-on, and creating and following a plan of problem-solving actions. Emotionally focused strategies center on changing one's feelings about a stressor. They include taking responsibility for the issue, engaging in self-control, distancing oneself from the issue, engaging in wishful thinking, and using positive reappraisal to focus on positive outcomes instead of the stressor. Some coping strategies are adaptive, and reduce stress in a healthy way. A stressed person could, for example, reach out to a loved one for help as a support-seeking coping strategy. However, coping strategies may also be maladaptive and include detrimental tactics, such as turning to drugs or alcohol.

Individuals can also engage in stress management to reduce their stress levels. Exercise is a powerful stress management tool that not only improves health and well-being, but also enhances mood. Exercise releases endorphins, opioid neuropeptides that act as "feel-good" neurotransmitters. Relaxation techniques, including meditation, diaphragmatic breathing, and progressive muscle relaxation have also been found to reduce stress. Additionally, studies have shown that engaging in a spiritual practice helps to manage stress.

MCAT Expertise

Use these coping and stress management techniques to boost your performance (and mood) on Test Day!

MCAT Concept Check 5.3:

Before you move on, assess your understanding of the material with these questions.

1. What are the key features of primary and secondary cognitive appraisal of stress?

   • Primary appraisal:

   _____

   • Secondary appraisal:

   _____

2. What are the three stages of the general adaptation syndrome? What physiological changes are evident in each stage?

Stage	Physiological Changes

3. What are some common stressors? What are some effective techniques for managing stress?

   • Common stressors:

   _____

   • Stress management techniques:

   _____

   _____

   _____

Conclusion

The ability to strive for our goals and desires, be it for internal or external reasons, is an important aspect of psychology and behavior. Motivation is the mechanism used to meet our needs, act toward an end goal, and ultimately survive. While there are many factors that influence motivation, including instincts, arousal, drives, and needs, they all result in action to obtain perceived rewards, fulfill needs, or avoid perceived punishments. Emotion is a complex process resulting in physiological, cognitive, and behavioral elements, described in different fashions by the James–Lange, Cannon–Bard, and Schachter–Singer theories of emotion. Many components of the nervous system play a role in experiencing emotions, including the seven universal emotions. The response of the body and mind to challenges defines stress. Stress appraisal has phases that identify and allow the body to respond to the stressor encountered. The physical and mental response to stress can be severe, but there are many management and coping mechanisms commonly used to reduce the level of stress experienced.

Hopefully this chapter has left you motivated to keep working toward that goal of an excellent MCAT score and becoming the doctor you deserve to be. Studying for the MCAT certainly introduces a significant stress, but effective stress management techniques and a solid foundation in MCAT content and strategy will turn Test Day into eustress. Just keep your eyes on that white coat, an important garment that will some day be part of your identity—a topic we'll explore in the next chapter.

CONCEPT SUMMARY

Motivation

- **Motivation** is the purpose, or driving force, behind our actions.

- Motivation can be **extrinsic**, based on external circumstances; or **intrinsic**, based on internal drive or perception.

- The primary factors that influence emotion are instincts, arousal, drives, and needs.

  o **Instincts** are innate, fixed patterns of behavior in response to stimuli. In the **instinct theory** of motivation, people perform certain behaviors because of these evolutionarily programmed instincts.

  o In the **arousal theory**, people perform actions to maintain **arousal**, the state of being awake and reactive to stimuli, at an optimal level. The **Yerkes–Dodson law** shows that performance is optimal at a medium level of arousal.

  o **Drives** are internal states of tension that beget particular behaviors focused on goals.

  o Primary drives are related to bodily processes; secondary drives stem from learning and include accomplishments and emotions. **Drive reduction theory** states that motivation arises from the desire to eliminate drives, which create uncomfortable internal states.

  o Satisfying **needs** may also drive motivation. **Maslow's hierarchy of needs** prioritizes needs into five categories: physiological needs (highest priority), safety and security, love and belonging, self-esteem, and self-actualization (lowest priority).

  o **Self-determination theory** emphasizes the role of three universal needs: autonomy, competence, and relatedness.

- **Incentive theory** explains motivation as the desire to pursue rewards and avoid punishments.

- **Expectancy–value theory** states that the amount of motivation for a task is based on the individual's expectation of success and the amount that success is valued.

- **Opponent-process theory** explains motivation for drug use: as drug use increases, the body counteracts its effects, leading to tolerance and uncomfortable withdrawal symptoms.

- Sexual motivation is related to hormones as well as cultural and social factors.

Emotion

- **Emotion** is a state of mind, or feeling, that is subjectively experienced based on circumstances, mood, and relationships.

- The three components of emotion are **cognitive** (subjective), **behavioral** (facial expressions and body language), and **physiological** (changes in the autonomic nervous system).

- The **seven universal emotions** are happiness, sadness, contempt, surprise, fear, disgust, and anger.
- There are multiple theories of emotion, based on the interactions of the three components of emotion.
  - In the **James–Lange theory**, nervous system arousal leads to a cognitive response in which the emotion is labeled.
  - In the **Cannon–Bard theory**, the simultaneous arousal of the nervous system and cognitive response lead to action.
  - In the **Schachter–Singer theory**, nervous system arousal and interpretation of context lead to a cognitive response.
- The **limbic system** is the primary nervous system component involved in experiencing emotion.
  - The **amygdala** is involved with attention and fear, helps interpret facial expressions, and is part of the intrinsic memory system for emotional memory.
  - The **thalamus** is a sensory processing station.
  - The **hypothalamus** releases neurotransmitters that affect mood and arousal.
  - The **hippocampus** creates long-term explicit (episodic) memories.
  - The **prefrontal cortex** is involved with planning, expressing personality, and making decisions. The **ventral prefrontal cortex** is critical for experiencing emotion; the **ventromedial prefrontal cortex**, specifically, is involved in controlling emotional responses from the amygdala and decision-making.

Stress

- The physiological and cognitive response to challenges or life changes is defined as **stress**.
- Stress appraisal has two stages:
  - **Primary appraisal** is classifying a potential stressor as irrelevant, benign–positive, or stressful.
  - **Secondary appraisal** is directed at evaluating if the organism can cope with the stress, based on harm, threat, and challenge.
- A **stressor** is anything that leads to a stress response and can include environment, daily events, workplace or academic settings, social expectations, chemicals, and biological stressors. Psychological stressors include pressure, control, predictability, frustration, and conflict.
- Stressors can lead to **distress** or **eustress**.
- The three stages of the **general adaptation syndrome** are alarm, resistance, and exhaustion.
- Stress management can include psychological, behavioral, and spiritual aspects.

ANSWERS TO CONCEPT CHECKS

5.1

1.

Theory	Factor for Motivation
Instinct theory	Instincts: innate, fixed patterns of behavior in response to stimuli
Arousal theory	Maintaining a constant level of arousal, the psychological and physiological state of being awake and reactive to stimuli
Drive reduction theory	Drives: internal states of tension or discomfort that can be relieved with a particular action
Need-based theories	Needs: factors necessary for physiological function or emotional fulfillment

2. Physiological needs, safety and security, love and belonging, self-esteem, self-actualization

3. Cocaine is a stimulant, causing euphoria, restlessness, increased heart rate, increased temperature, and anxiety. According to opponent-process theory, cocaine withdrawal should be the opposite: depressed mood, fatigue, decreased heart rate, decreased temperature, and apathy.

5.2

1. The three elements of emotion include the following:
   - Physiological response (autonomic nervous system): heart rate, breathing rate, skin temperature, blood pressure
   - Behavioral response: facial expressions, body language
   - Cognitive response: subjective interpretation, memories of past experiences, perception of cause of emotion

2. The seven universal emotions are happiness, sadness, contempt, surprise, fear, disgust, and anger.

3.

James–Lange Theory	Cannon–Bard Theory	Schachter–Singer Theory
• Stimulus leads to physiological arousal • Arousal leads to cognitive labeling of emotion • *I must be angry because my skin is hot and my blood pressure is high* • Requires connection between sympathetic nervous system and brain	• Stimulus leads to physiological arousal and feeling of emotion • Thalamus processes sensory information, sends it to cortex and sympathetic nervous system • Action is secondary response to stimulus • *I am afraid because I see a snake and my heart is racing . . . Let me out of here!* • Does not explain vagus nerve	• Both arousal and labeling based on environment required to feel an emotion • *I am excited because my heart is racing and everyone else is happy*

4. The amygdala is involved with attention and emotions (specifically fear), helps interpret facial expressions, and is part of the intrinsic memory system for emotional memory. The thalamus is a sensory processing station. The hypothalamus releases neurotransmitters that affect mood and arousal. The hippocampus creates long-term explicit memories (episodic memories). The ventromedial prefrontal cortex is involved in decision-making and controlling emotional responses from the amygdala.

5.3

1. Primary appraisal is categorizing the stressor as irrelevant, benign–positive, or stressful. Secondary appraisal is the evaluation of the ability of the organism to cope with that stress.

2.

Stage	Physiological Changes
Alarm	Activation of sympathetic nervous system, release of ACTH and cortisol, stimulation of adrenal medulla to secrete epinephrine and norepinephrine
Resistance	Continuous release of hormones activates sympathetic nervous system
Exhaustion	Can no longer maintain elevated sympathetic nervous system activity, more susceptible to illness and medical conditions, organ systems deteriorate, death

3. Common stressors include environmental or physical discomfort, daily events, workplace or academic setting, social expectations, and chemical and biological stressors. Effective stress management techniques include exercise, relaxation techniques (meditation, diaphragmatic breathing, progressive muscle relaxation), spiritual practice, and many more.

SHARED CONCEPTS

Behavioral Sciences Chapter 1
Biology and Behavior

Behavioral Sciences Chapter 3
Learning and Memory

Behavioral Sciences Chapter 7
Psychological Disorders

Biology Chapter 4
The Nervous System

Biology Chapter 5
The Endocrine System

Biology Chapter 10
Homeostasis

Discrete Practice Questions

Consult your online resources for Full-Length Exams and Passage-Based Questions (for certain chapters).

1. A college student strives for excellent grades and hopes to graduate with a better GPA than his brother. This type of motivation is considered:

   A. extrinsic motivation.
   B. intrinsic motivation.
   C. a primary drive.
   D. a secondary drive.

2. When practicing her recital song at home, a teenage girl sounds perfectly in pitch to her family and friends. However, when performing at the recital in front of a large audience of peers, strangers, and coaches, her pitch and tone are off, resulting in a poor performance. This second performance is best explained by:

   A. drive reduction theory.
   B. instinct approach theory.
   C. Maslow's hierarchy of needs.
   D. the Yerkes–Dodson law.

3. Seeking homeostasis to reduce an uncomfortable internal state is associated with which motivational theory?

   A. Drive reduction theory
   B. Instinct theory
   C. Arousal theory
   D. Incentive theory

4. People from cultures around the world can identify which of the following emotions?

   A. Happiness, sadness, and surprise
   B. Happiness, anger, and apathy
   C. Sadness, anticipation, and happiness
   D. Excitement, anger, and disgust

5. Experiencing emotion involves three components, which are:

   A. behavioral, reactionary, and cognitive.
   B. emotional, physical, and mental.
   C. physiological, cognitive, and behavioral.
   D. emotional, cognitive, and behavioral.

6. The statement "I noticed my heart racing and breathing rate increasing when I saw a bear, so I am afraid," corresponds most closely with which theory of emotion?

   A. Schachter–Singer theory
   B. Yerkes–Dodson theory
   C. Cannon–Bard theory
   D. James–Lange theory

7. Which theory of motivation is most significantly informed by Darwin's theory of evolution?

   A. Arousal theory
   B. Drive reduction theory
   C. Instinct theory
   D. Incentive theory

8. Simultaneous processing of conscious emotions and physiological activation is the defining feature of which theory of emotion?

   A. Schachter–Singer theory
   B. James–Lange theory
   C. Incentive theory
   D. Cannon–Bard theory

9. All of the following brain regions are primarily responsible for the experience of emotions EXCEPT the:

    A. amygdala.
    B. prefrontal cortex.
    C. basal ganglia.
    D. thalamus.

10. A person with high left frontal lobe activity is most likely experiencing which emotion?

    A. Happiness
    B. Sadness
    C. Surprise
    D. Disgust

11. Determination of the intensity and risk of a stressor occurs during which stage(s) of stress appraisal?

    A. Primary appraisal only
    B. Secondary appraisal only
    C. Both primary and secondary appraisal
    D. Neither primary nor secondary appraisal

12. A medical student is feeling a high level of stress due to upcoming exams and pressure from his family to engage in activities at home. He chooses to go the gym for a workout to help himself relax. This workout is which type of stress?

    A. Hassle
    B. Frustration
    C. Distress
    D. Eustress

13. Which type of conflict is associated with the LEAST amount of stress?

    A. Approach–approach conflict
    B. Avoidance–avoidance conflict
    C. Approach–avoidance conflict
    D. Avoidance–escape conflict

14. While cleaning your house, you notice a large spider on the wall by your head and feel your heart rate jump up and your skin temperature grow warm. Which stage of stress response are you experiencing?

    A. Alarm
    B. Resistance
    C. Exhaustion
    D. Homeostasis

15. Each of the following responses to stress is considered maladaptive EXCEPT:

    A. drug use.
    B. social withdrawal.
    C. progressive muscle relaxation.
    D. avoiding the stressor.

Explanations to Discrete Practice Questions

1. A

Due to the competitive nature of the motivation, this is considered extrinsic motivation. Extrinsic motivation is based on external conditions, including perceived reward or fear of punishment. In this case, the reward is beating his brother. There is no suggestion of an uncomfortable internal state or tension, which is an aspect of drives, eliminating **choices (C)** and **(D)**.

2. D

The Yerkes–Dodson law states that there is an optimal level of arousal necessary to perform. If levels of arousal are too high, poor performance can result. In the case of this girl performing at her recital, her arousal level is very high as a result of nervousness and anxiety, resulting in a poor performance.

3. A

Drive reduction theory is the theory that one will act to eliminate uncomfortable internal states known as drives. The body will push toward equilibrium, or homeostasis.

4. A

The seven universal emotions are happiness, sadness, contempt, surprise, fear, disgust, and anger.

5. C

The three components of emotion are the physiological (changes in the autonomic nervous system), cognitive (subjective interpretation of an emotion), and behavioral (facial expressions and body language) responses.

6. D

Experiencing a physiological reaction to a stimulus and then labeling that response as emotion is in line with the James–Lange theory of emotion. In the statement, seeing the bear is the stimulus, an increase in heart rate and breathing rate is the physiological reaction, and identifying this as fear is the emotion experienced.

7. C

According to Darwin's theory of evolution, all species have instincts that help them survive. The instinct theory of motivation states that people are motivated to act based on instincts that they are programmed to exhibit.

8. D

The Cannon–Bard theory of emotion is based on the premise that conscious feelings and physiological components of emotion are experienced at exactly the same time. In this theory, this combination then leads to action. This is commonly confused with the Schachter–Singer theory, **choice (A)**, in which nervous system arousal occurs and then is labeled based on the context provided by the environment.

9. C

The amygdala, prefrontal cortex, and thalamus all play a role in the experience of emotions. The basal ganglia are involved in smooth movement and are not primarily responsible for the experience of emotions.

10. A

The left frontal lobe is associated with positive feelings, corresponding with joy and happiness. The right frontal lobe is associated with negative feelings, such as sadness and disgust, **choices (B)** and **(D)**.

11. B

Secondary appraisal of stress is the stage at which the ability of the organism to cope with the stressor is evaluated. This is based on the harm, threat, and challenge of the stressor, which are all correlated with its intensity. Primary appraisal is simply the initial determination of whether there is a negative association at all, not its intensity.

12. D

A positive stressor creates eustress. Because working out is used to relax, it is considered a eustress. Hassle, **choice (A)**, and frustration, **choice (B)**, are both types of distress, **choice (C)**, or negative stressors.

13. A

Approach–approach conflict is one in which both results are good outcomes. While one must be chosen, neither choice results in a negative outcome: for example, choosing between two desserts. Avoidance–escape conflict, **choice (D)**, is not a recognized form of conflict; these two terms are related to types of negative reinforcers.

14. A

The initial reaction to stress, which is activation of the sympathetic nervous system, is the alarm stage of stress response.

15. C

Progressive muscle relaxation is a relaxation technique demonstrated to help reduce stress in a manner that is beneficial to the body and psyche. The other methods described here, including avoidance of the stressor, **choice (D)**, serve to increase stress or merely change the source of the stress.

Identity and Personality

6

In This Chapter

Chapter Profile

The content in this chapter should be relevant to about 7% of all questions about the Behavioral Sciences on the MCAT.

This chapter covers material from the following AAMC content categories:

7A: Individual influences on behavior

8A Self-identity

Introduction

Social psychologists are concerned with how our social lives influence the ways in which we perceive ourselves. Specifically, researchers have focused on the influence that other people's views, our social roles, and our group memberships have on our perceptions of who we are.

Who are you? If you're like most people, you could probably answer that question in many different ways. You might list your physical characteristics, your family relationships, your emotional tendencies, or your skills and talents. In fact, many introductory psychology courses include an exercise in which students are asked to make a list of answers to the question *Who am I?* Completing this list gives these students a glimpse into their identity and personality. These ideas form the core of the study of psychology, in which the central goal is explaining our thoughts and behaviors. In this chapter, we'll discuss both of these concepts and review the key theorists and their approaches to answering the question of who we are.

6.1 Self-Concept and Identity

> ## LEARNING GOALS
>
> After Chapter 6.1, you will be able to:
>
> - Distinguish between self-concept and identity
> - Recall the factors that contribute to different types of identity, such as gender and ethnic identity
> - Predict how a person would explain an event to themselves based on their locus of control

When you look in the mirror, whom do you see? If you're studying to take the MCAT, chances are some descriptors that come to mind include *student, intelligent, future doctor*, and so on. Our own internal list of answers to the question *Who am I?* form our **self-concept**. Many of the ways in which we define ourselves fall under the classification of a **self-schema**; that is, a self-given label that carries with it a set of qualities. For example, the *athlete* self-schema usually carries the qualities of youth, physical fitness, and dressing and acting in certain ways, although these qualities may change depending on culture, socioeconomic status, and personal beliefs. The idea of self-concept goes beyond these self-schemata; it also includes our appraisal of who we used to be and who we will become: our past and future selves.

Sometimes the terms self-concept and identity are used interchangeably, but psychologists generally use them to refer to two different but closely related ideas. Social scientists define **identity** as the individual components of our self-concept related to the groups to which we belong. Whereas we have one all-encompassing self-concept, we have multiple identities that define who we are and how we should behave within any given context. Religious affiliation, sexual orientation, personal relationships, and membership in social groups are just a few of the identities that sum to create our self-concept. In fact, our individual identities do not always need to be compatible. Are you the same person when interacting with your friends as you are when you interact with coworkers or family? For most people the answer is *no*; they take on a particular identity in different social situations.

TYPES OF IDENTITY

While there are many different types of identity, the MCAT—for historical or social reasons—tends to focus on some forms of identity more than others.

Gender Identity

Gender identity describes a person's appraisal of him- or herself on scales of masculinity and femininity. While these concepts were long thought to be two extremes on a single continuum, theorists have reasoned that they must be two separate dimensions because individuals can achieve high scores on scales of both masculinity and femininity. **Androgyny** is defined as the state of being simultaneously very masculine and very feminine, while those who achieve low scores on both scales are referred to as **undifferentiated**. Gender identity is usually well established by age three, although it may morph and change over time. Some theories, such as the theory of **gender schema**, hold that key components of gender identity are transmitted through cultural and societal means.

Keep in mind that gender identity is not necessarily tied to biological sex or sexual orientation, although in most Western cultures these concepts are seen as closely related. While it is typical of most cultures to view gender as a strictly binary concept, many cultures consider a third gender. For example, the people of Samoa refer to androgynous but biologically male individuals as *fa'afafine*. To the Samoans, the *fa'afafine* are seen as an important social caste and are accepted as equals, although this is not always the case for third genders across all cultures.

Ethnic and National Identity

Ethnic identity refers to one's ethnic group, in which members typically share a common ancestry, cultural heritage, and language. Many social psychologists study the ways in which our ethnic identity influences our perspectives of ourselves. In a 1947 study, Kenneth and Mamie Clark explored ethnic self-concepts among ethnically white and black children using a doll preference task: the experimenter showed each child a black doll and a white doll, and asked the child a series of questions about how the child felt about the dolls. The majority of both white and black children preferred the white doll. This study was important because it highlighted the negative effects of racism and minority group status on the self-concept of black children at the time. However, subsequent research using improved methodology (for example, randomizing the ethnicity of the experimenter), has shown that black children hold more positive views of their own ethnicity; this may also represent societal changes at large.

While ethnicity is largely an identity into which we are born, **nationality** is based on political borders. National identity is the result of shared history, media, cuisine, and national symbols such as a country's flag. Nationality need not be tied to one's ethnicity or even to legal citizenship. Symbols play an important role in both ethnic and national identity: symbols of Jewish ethnicity are shown in Figure 6.1a, while symbols of American nationality are shown in Figure 6.1b.

Real World

Transgender individuals, for whom gender identity does not match biological sex, have been a heavily stigmatized group in American culture. In fact, it was not until the publication of the DSM-5 in 2013 that gender identity disorder was formally removed as a diagnosis. The DSM-5 includes the diagnosis gender dysphoria, which is given only to individuals for whom gender identity causes significant psychological stress.

(a)

(b)

Figure 6.1. Ethnic and National Symbols
(a) Jewish ethnicity; (b) American nationality.

Other Types of Identity

Of course, there are many more categories through which we evaluate our identity. We compare ourselves to others in terms of age, class, religious affiliation, sexual orientation, and so on. Aspects of these other identities are explored in other parts of *MCAT Behavioral Sciences Review*.

It is important to know that there are several factors that determine which identity will be enacted in particular situations. It is believed that our identities are organized according to a **hierarchy of salience**, such that we let the situation dictate which identity holds the most importance for us at any given moment. For instance, male and female college students in same-sex groups are less likely to list gender in their self-descriptions than students in mixed-gender groups. Furthermore, researchers have found that the more salient the identity, the more we conform to the role expectations of the identities. Salience is determined by a number of factors, including the amount of work we have invested into the identity, the rewards and gratification associated with the identity, and the amount of self-esteem we have associated with the identity.

SELF-EVALUATION

Our individual self-concept plays a very important role in the way we evaluate and feel about ourselves. **Self-discrepancy theory** maintains that each of us has three selves. Our self-concept makes up our **actual self**, the way we see ourselves as we currently are. Our **ideal self** is the person we would like to be, and our **ought self** is our representation of the way others think we should be. Generally, the closer these three selves are to one another, the higher our **self-esteem** or self-worth will be.

Those with low self-esteem don't necessary view themselves as worthless, but they will be far more critical of themselves. As a result, they take criticism from others poorly and typically believe that people will only accept them if they are successful. Research also shows that they are more likely to use drugs, to be pessimistic, and to give up when facing frustration than their counterparts with high self-esteem.

While self-esteem is the measure of how we feel about ourselves, **self-efficacy** is our belief in our ability to succeed. Self-efficacy can vary by activity for individuals; we all can think of situations in which we hold the belief that we are able to be effective and, conversely, those in which we feel powerless. Of course, we are more motivated to pursue those tasks for which our self-efficacy is high, but we can get into trouble when it is too high. **Overconfidence** can lead us to take on tasks for which we are not ready, leading to frustration, humiliation, or sometimes even personal injury. Self-efficacy can also be depressed past the point of recovery. In one study (which certainly could not be replicated under current ethical guidelines), dogs were divided into three groups. The first was a control group in which the dogs were simply strapped into a harness. In the second group, dogs were similarly strapped into a harness but subjected to painful electrical shocks, which they could stop by pressing a lever. Dogs in the third group were similarly harnessed and shocked, but were powerless to control the administration of the shock. Dogs in the first two groups recovered from the experience quickly; the third group soon stopped trying to escape the shock and acted as if they were helpless to avoid the pain of the experience, even when offered opportunities to avoid being shocked. Only when the dogs were forcibly removed from their cages did they change their expectations about their control over the electrical shocks and took action to escape their predicament. This phenomenon is called **learned helplessness** and is considered one possible model of clinical depression.

Locus of control is another core self-evaluation that is closely related to self-concept. **Locus of control** refers to the way we characterize the influences in our lives. People with an internal locus of control view themselves of controlling their own

Bridge

Remember that *esteem* is one of Maslow's hierarchy of needs (#4 in priority). This model is discussed in Chapter 5 of *MCAT Behavioral Sciences Review*.

Bridge

Locus of control and cognitive dissonance are integral to attribution theory. In order to preserve self-esteem, we often see our successes as a direct result of our efforts and our failures as the result of uncontrollable outside influences. Attribution theory is discussed in Chapter 10 of *MCAT Behavioral Sciences Review*.

MCAT Expertise

Effective MCAT students review full-length exams with an internal locus of control: *What can I do to prepare myself better for the next practice test?* An external locus of control prevents students from actually gaining anything from their practice: *Oh, that was just a stupid question.*

fate, whereas those with an external locus of control feel that the events in their lives are caused by luck or outside influences. For example, a runner who loses a race may attribute the cause of the loss internally (*I didn't train hard enough*) or externally (*My shoes didn't fit and the track was wet*).

All of these ideas work hand-in-hand to influence the way we feel about ourselves. The happiest among us are those who have high self-esteem, view themselves as effective people, feel that they are in control of their destinies, and see themselves as living up to their own expectations of who they would like to be.

MCAT Concept Check 6.1:

Before you move on, assess your understanding of the material with these questions.

1. What is the difference between self-concept and identity?

   _____

2. List three factors that contribute to a person's ethnic identity. How are these factors different from those that determine national identity?

   1. _____
   2. _____
   3. _____

   • National identity:

   _____

3. A high school student fails a history test. How might a student with an internal locus of control interpret this event? What about a student with an external locus of control?

   • Internal:

   _____

   • External:

   _____

6.2 Formation of Identity

High-Yield

LEARNING GOALS

After Chapter 6.2, you will be able to:

- Identify the three major phases of Kohlberg's theory of moral development and their central tenets
- Explain, and distinguish between, the theories of identity of Erikson, Freud, Vygotsky, and Kohlberg

Psychologists generally agree that we are not born with our self-concept and identity in place and fully developed. As young children, our identities are largely defined by our relationship to our parents. As we move into adolescence, we begin to develop into unique individuals, deciding who we want to be when on our own. Several theorists have proposed stages through which we develop. They vary in scope with respect to both the aspects of our identity they describe and their timespan, but they all have one thing in common: the MCAT loves to test on them!

FREUD: PSYCHOSEXUAL DEVELOPMENT

Sigmund Freud was a pioneer in charting personality and emotional growth. For Freud, human psychology and human sexuality were inextricably linked. In fact, Freud made the assertion that far from lying dormant until puberty, the **libido** (sex drive) is present at birth. Freud believed that libidinal energy and the drive to reduce libidinal tension were the underlying dynamic forces that accounted for human psychological processes.

Freud hypothesized five distinct stages of psychosexual development, summarized in Table 6.1 at the end of this section. In each stage, children are faced with a conflict between societal demands and the desire to reduce the libidinal tension associated with different erogenous zones of the body. Each stage differs in the manner in which libidinal energy is manifested and the way in which the libidinal drive is met. **Fixation** occurs when a child is overindulged or overly frustrated during a stage of development. In response to the anxiety caused by fixation, the child forms a personality pattern based on that particular stage, which persists into adulthood as a functional mental disorder known as a **neurosis**.

The first stage is the **oral stage** (0 to 1 year). During this stage, gratification is obtained primarily through putting objects into the mouth, biting, and sucking. Libidinal energy is centered on the mouth. An orally fixated adult would likely exhibit excessive dependency.

MCAT Expertise

Though revolutionary at the time, Freud's theories have largely been discredited. They do, however, provide an interesting window into the history of personality theory. Expect the MCAT to test these ideas from a historical context, usually prefaced by *According to Freud's theory of psychosexual development...*

Bridge

Freud's stages of psychosocial development are based on the same principles as drive reduction theory, as discussed in Chapter 5 of *MCAT Behavioral Sciences Review*: libidinal energy creates internal tension, which we aim to reduce through certain behaviors.

Next is the **anal stage** (1 to 3 years), during which the libido is centered on the anus and gratification is gained through the elimination and retention of waste materials. Toilet training occurs during this stage. Fixation during this stage would lead to either excessive orderliness (*anal-retentiveness*) or sloppiness in the adult.

The **phallic** or **Oedipal stage** (3 to 5 years) centers on resolution of the **Oedipal conflict** for male children or the analogous **Electra conflict** for female children. In Freud's view, the male child envies his father's intimate relationship with his mother and fears castration at his father's hands. He wishes to eliminate his father and possess his mother, but the child feels guilty about these wishes. To successfully resolve the conflict, he deals with his guilty feelings by identifying with his father, establishing his sexual identity, and internalizing moral values. Also, the child to a large extent de-eroticizes, or **sublimates** his libidinal energy. This may be expressed through collecting objects or focusing on schoolwork. Freud did not elaborate much on the Electra complex, although he theorized a similar desire. Because females cannot have castration fear (instead, they are thought to have **penis envy**), girls are expected to exhibit less stereotypically female behavior and be less morally developed in this theory.

Once the libido is sublimated, the child has entered the stage called **latency**, which lasts until puberty is reached.

For Freud, the final stage is the **genital stage**, beginning in puberty and lasting through adulthood. According to Freud, if prior development has proceeded correctly, the person should enter into healthy heterosexual relationships at this point. However, if sexual traumas of childhood have not been resolved, such behaviors as homosexuality, asexuality, or fetishism may result.

Stage	Description
Oral	Libidinal energy centered on the mouth; fixation can lead to excessive dependency
Anal	Toilet training occurs during this time; fixation can lead to excessive orderliness or messiness
Phallic	Oedipal or Electra conflict is resolved during this stage
Latency	Libido is largely sublimated during this stage
Genital	Begins at puberty; if previous stages have been successfully resolved, the person will enter into normal heterosexual relationships

Table 6.1. Freud's Stages of Psychosexual Development

ERIKSON: PSYCHOSOCIAL DEVELOPMENT

Erik Erikson's stages of personality development are based on a series of crises that derive from conflicts between needs and social demands. As such, psychosocial theory emphasizes emotional development and interactions with the social environment. According to Erikson, it is possible to fail at resolving the conflict central to any given stage of development, but this does not mean that mastery of each stage is required to move on to the next. Instead, Erikson viewed successful resolution of a stage, marked by answering an essential existential question, to imbue an individual with skills and traits that are carried through subsequent stages. Erikson's stages are summarized in Table 6.2 at the end of this section.

The first such conflict is that of **trust *vs.* mistrust** (0 to 1 year). If resolved successfully, the child will come to trust his environment as well as himself. If mistrust wins out, the child will often be suspicious of the world, possibly throughout his life.

The second conflict is **autonomy *vs.* shame and doubt** (1 to 3 years). The favorable outcome here is feeling able to exert control over the world and to exercise choice as well as self-restraint. The unfavorable outcome is a sense of doubt and a persistent external locus of control.

The next conflict confronted is **initiative *vs.* guilt** (3 to 6 years). Favorable outcomes include a sense of purpose, the ability to initiate activities, and the ability to enjoy accomplishment. If guilt wins out, the child will be so overcome by the fear of punishment that the child may either unduly restrict himself, or may overcompensate by showing off.

If the conflict of **industry *vs.* inferiority** (6 to 12 years) is resolved favorably, the child will feel competent, be able to exercise his or her abilities and intelligence in the world, and be able to affect the world in the way that the child desires. Unfavorable resolution results in a sense of inadequacy, a sense of inability to act in a competent manner, and low self-esteem.

During adolescence (12 to 20 years), the conflict of **identity *vs.* role confusion** emerges. This stage encompasses what Erikson termed **physiological revolution**. The favorable outcome is fidelity, the ability to see oneself as a unique and integrated person with sustained loyalties. Unfavorable outcomes are confusion about one's identity and an amorphous personality that shifts from day to day.

The main crisis of young adulthood (20 to 40 years) is **intimacy *vs.* isolation**. Favorable outcomes are love, the ability to have intimate relationships with others, and the ability to commit oneself to another person and to one's own goals. If this crisis is not favorably resolved, there will be an avoidance of commitment, alienation, and distancing of oneself from others and one's ideals. Isolated individuals are either withdrawn or capable of only superficial relationships with others.

The conflict of middle age (40 to 65 years) is **generativity *vs.* stagnation**. The successful resolution of this conflict results in an individual capable of being a productive, caring, and contributing member of society. If this crisis is not overcome, one acquires a sense of stagnation and may become self-indulgent, bored, and self-centered with little care for others.

Real World

The conflict of identity *vs.* role confusion has some positive effects: teenagers identifying their interests, gravitating toward friends who share these interests, and creating a sense of whom they want to be. On the other hand, this conflict can lead to the formation of cliques, bullying, and significant peer pressure. The increase of online and in-person bullying among adolescents has led to a number of programs to ease this crisis, such as *StopBullying.gov* and the *It Gets Better* campaign.

Finally, old age (above 65 years) brings about the crisis of **integrity *vs.* despair**. If favorably resolved, we will see wisdom, which Erikson defined as detached concern with life itself, with assurance in the meaning of life, dignity, and an acceptance of the fact that one's life has been worthwhile, along with a readiness to face death. If not resolved favorably, there will be feelings of bitterness about one's life, a feeling that life has been worthless, and at the same time, fear over one's own impending death.

Erikson's Stage (Crisis)	Age	Existential Question
Trust *vs.* mistrust	0 to 1 year	Can I trust the world?
Autonomy *vs.* shame and doubt	1 to 3 years	Is it okay to be me?
Initiative *vs.* guilt	3 to 6 years	Is it okay for me to do, move, and act?
Industry *vs.* inferiority	6 to 12 years	Can I make it in the world of people and things?
Identity *vs.* role confusion	12 to 20 years	Who am I? What can I be?
Intimacy *vs.* isolation	20 to 40 years	Can I love?
Generativity *vs.* stagnation	40 to 65 years	Can I make my life count?
Integrity *vs.* despair	65 years to death	Is it okay to have been me?

Table 6.2. Erikson's Stages of Psychosocial Development

KOHLBERG: MORAL REASONING

Lawrence Kohlberg's theory of personality development focuses not on resolving conflicts or urges, but rather on the development of moral thinking. Kohlberg reasoned that, as our cognitive abilities grow, we are able to think about the world in more complex and nuanced ways, and this directly affects the ways in which we resolve moral dilemmas and perceive the notion of right and wrong.

Kohlberg's observations about moral reasoning were based on responses of subjects to hypothetical moral dilemmas. One often-cited example is the *Heinz dilemma*. In this scenario, a man named Heinz has a wife who is dying of a rare disease. There is a druggist in the town who invented a drug that could cure the disease. It costs him $200 to produce, yet he sells it for $2000. Heinz cannot afford this price, so he goes to the druggist and asks him if he would lower the price, a request that the druggist refuses. Desperate to save his wife, Heinz breaks into the druggist's office one night and steals the medication. Kohlberg presented dilemmas such as this one to volunteers and asked them to explain whether the characters in the story acted morally and why or why not. Kohlberg wasn't interested in the participants' appraisal of the actions as right or wrong, as he believed either answer could be justified. Instead, he was far more interested in the reasoning behind the appraisal. Based on the participants' responses, Kohlberg organized moral reasoning into six distinct stages ranging from the concrete to the abstract. He then organized these stages into three phases consisting of two stages each. Kohlberg's stages are summarized in Table 6.3.

Preconventional morality, the first of these phases, is typical of preadolescent thinking and places an emphasis on the consequences of the moral choice. Stage one (**obedience**) is concerned with avoiding punishment (*If I steal the drug, I'll go to jail*), while stage two (**self-interest**) is about gaining rewards (*I need to save my wife because I want to spend more of my life with her*). Stage two is often called the **instrumental relativist stage** because it is based on the concepts of reciprocity and sharing: *I'll scratch your back, you scratch mine.*

The second phase is **conventional morality**, which begins to develop in early adolescence when individuals begin to see themselves in terms of their relationships to others. This phase is based on understanding and accepting social rules. Stage three (**conformity**) places emphasis on the "good boy, nice girl" orientation in which a person seeks the approval of others (*I should not steal the drug because stealing is wrong*). Stage four (**law and order**) maintains the social order in the highest regard (*If everyone stole things they couldn't afford, people who produce those items would not be able to continue their business*).

The third phase is **postconventional morality**, which describes a level of reasoning that Kohlberg claimed not everyone was capable of and is based on social mores, which may conflict with laws. Stage five (**social contract**) views moral rules as conventions that are designed to ensure the greater good, with reasoning focused on individual rights (*Everyone has a right to live; businesses have a right to profit from their products*). Finally, stage six (**universal human ethics**) reasons that decisions should be made in consideration of abstract principles (*It is wrong for one person to hold another's life for ransom*).

Kohlberg viewed these stages as a progression in which each stage is adopted and then abandoned for the next as the individual progresses. In other words, we all begin in stage one and progress to varying degrees as our thinking matures.

Kohlberg is not without his critics. Some argue that postconventional morality describes views that are more prevalent in individualistic societies and is therefore biased against collectivist cultures. Similarly, Kohlberg's research was only performed using male subjects, which may cloud differences in reasoning patterns between men and women.

Key Concept

Conventional morality corresponds to normal adult moral reasoning. Preconventional is therefore expected in children, and postconventional is expected in a smaller subset of adults with more advanced moral reasoning skills than the average population.

Phase	Age	Stages
Preconventional morality	Preadolescence	1: Obedience 2: Self-interest
Conventional morality	Adolescence to adulthood	3: Conformity 4: Law and order
Postconventional morality	Adulthood (if at all)	5: Social contract 6: Universal human ethics

Table 6.3. Kohlberg's Stages of Moral Development

Bridge

Kohlberg and Vygotsky's theories of cognitive development were both heavily influenced by Piaget's work in this area, discussed in Chapter 4 of *MCAT Behavioral Sciences Review*.

VYGOTSKY: CULTURAL AND BIOSOCIAL DEVELOPMENT

Like Kohlberg, Lev Vygotsky's work was focused on understanding cognitive development. For Vygotsky, the engine driving cognitive development was the child's internalization of various aspects of the culture: rules, symbols, language, and so on. As the child internalized these various interpersonal and cultural rules, her cognitive activity developed accordingly.

Vygotsky is known for his concept of the **zone of proximal development**, referring to those skills and abilities that have not yet fully developed but are in the process of development. Gaining these skills successfully requires the help of a "more knowledgeable other," typically an adult. For example, a child may struggle to ride a bicycle on her own, but with the help and guidance of a parent she may be successful. Vygotsky would say that this skill is currently within the child's zone of proximal development.

THE INFLUENCE OF OTHERS ON IDENTITY

Our personalities do not form in a vacuum; we are as much a product of those around us as a product of our own internal growth and development. Albert Bandura, who was also the psychologist behind the Bobo doll experiment described in Chapter 3 of *MCAT Behavioral Sciences Review*, claimed that observational learning contributes greatly to our future behaviors.

Young children observe and encode the behaviors they see in others, and may later imitate these behaviors. Children are more likely to imitate behaviors performed by someone who is like them: for example, young children will reliably mimic behaviors performed by their same-sex siblings. A child's first models are her parents, but as the child grows and forms more relationships, other role models emerge. Siblings, teachers, and the media all play an important role in modeling behavior for a developing child, but by adolescence, peers become the most important role models in a person's life.

As children grow, they become more able to see the identities of others as different from their own. They might experiment with other identities by taking on the roles of others, such as when children play *house* or *school*. Such **role-taking** is good practice for later in life, when a child begins to understand the perspectives and roles of others. Eventually, children become able to see how others perceive them and to imagine themselves from the outside. The ability to sense how another's mind works—for example, understanding how a friend is interpreting a story while you tell it—is referred to as **theory of mind**. Once this ability has developed, we begin to recognize and react to how others think about us. We become aware of judgments from the outside world and react to these judgments. Our reactions to how others perceive us can be varied—maintaining, modifying, downplaying, or accentuating different aspects of our personality. This construct, which relies on others reflecting our *selves* back to *ourselves*, is appropriately called the **looking-glass self**.

A related concept is a **reference group**. Our self-concept often depends on whom we are comparing ourselves to. For example, as of 2012, the average annual salary for a physician in the United States was about $200,000. Compared to the national median household salary (approximately $50,000), these individuals were quite well off. However, only 11 percent considered themselves "rich." Why? Many physicians live in higher socioeconomic areas, and their responses may thus be biased by comparison to those around them.

MCAT Concept Check 6.2:

Before you move on, assess your understanding of the material with these questions.

1. Each of the following theorists evaluates an individual and determines that the person has failed in completing one of the theorist's developmental stages. What would each say is the most likely outcome for this person?

   • Freud:

   _____

   • Erikson:

   _____

   • Kohlberg:

   _____

2. Name and briefly describe the three major phases of Kohlberg's theory of moral development.

Phase	Description

6.3 Personality

> ## LEARNING GOALS
>
> After Chapter 6.3, you will be able to:
>
> - Describe how personality is defined by the psychoanalytic, humanistic, type, behaviorist, social cognitive, biological, and trait perspectives
> - List the traits described by the Eysencks' PEN theory
> - List the Big Five personality traits
> - Recall the roles of the id, ego, and superego in the psychoanalytic perspective of personality

We've seen that identity is the way we define ourselves. **Personality**, while similar, describes the set of thoughts, feelings, traits, and behaviors that are characteristic of an individual across time and different locations. In a way, identity describes who we are, while personality describes how we act and react to the world around us. There are many different theories of personality, and different theorists within each category espouse sometimes conflicting views in an attempt to describe behavior. Like the various theories of development discussed earlier in this chapter, some of these ideas have been discredited, and so will only be tested on the MCAT from a historical perspective.

We can categorize theories of personality into four areas: psychoanalytic (psychodynamic), humanistic (phenomenological), type and trait, and behaviorist. There are great differences between and within these divisions in how personality is defined and how abnormal personalities are explained.

THE PSYCHOANALYTIC PERSPECTIVE

MCAT Expertise

The psychoanalytic perspective, much like other Freudian and Jungian theories within psychology, has been largely discredited and has fallen from common use. However, it is useful as a contrast to other theories of personality, and is included within testable materials as laid out by the AAMC.

The **psychoanalytic** or **psychodynamic theories of personality** contain some of the most widely varying perspectives on behavior, but they all have in common the assumption of unconscious internal states that motivate the overt actions of individuals and determine personality. The most noteworthy supporter of the psychoanalytic theory is Freud.

Sigmund Freud

Freud's contribution to the study of personality was his structural model, which involved three major entities: the id, ego, and superego, illustrated in Figure 6.2.

The **id** consists of all the basic, primal, inborn urges to survive and reproduce. It functions according to the **pleasure principle**, in which the aim is to achieve immediate gratification to relieve any pent-up tension. The **primary process** is the id's response to frustration: *obtain satisfaction now, not later*. Mental imagery, such as daydreaming or fantasy, that fulfills this need for satisfaction is termed **wish fulfillment**.

Real World

If a person is hungry and food is unavailable, wish fulfillment—fantasizing or daydreaming about food—helps relieve some of the tension created by the pleasure principle.

Figure 6.2. Freud's Topographic Model of the Mind

Because this mental image cannot effectively reduce tension on a permanent basis, the **ego** comes into play. The ego operates according to the **reality principle**, taking into account objective reality as it guides or inhibits the activity of the id and the id's pleasure principle. This guidance is referred to as the **secondary process**. The aim of the reality principle is to postpone the pleasure principle until satisfaction can actually be obtained. It must be emphasized that while the ego suspends the workings of the primary process, it does so only to meet the demands of objective reality. The mutual give and take of the ego and reality promotes the growth of perception, memory, problem solving, thinking, and reality testing. The ego can be understood to be the organizer of the mind: it receives its power from—and can never be fully independent of—the id.

Real World

When stuck in traffic, our id may desire to honk loudly at the cars in front of us, or to even pull over to the shoulder of the highway and drive recklessly past the congestion. Our ego knows that this would be unwise, and may advise us to breathe deeply and change the radio station to something calming instead.

The ego is also responsible for moderating the desires of the superego. Whereas the id's desires are basic needs, those of the superego are refined and focused on the ideal self. The **superego** is the personality's perfectionist, judging our actions and responding with pride at our accomplishments and guilt at our failures. The superego can be divided into two subsystems, both of which are a reflection of the morals taught to a child by his caregivers. The conscience is a collection of the improper actions for which a child is punished, and the **ego-ideal** consists of those proper actions for which a child is rewarded. Ultimately, a system of right and wrong substitutes for parental rewards and punishments.

Freud also stated that our access to the id, ego, and superego falls into three main categories: thoughts to which we have conscious access, thoughts that we aren't currently aware of (**preconscious**), and thoughts that have been repressed (**unconscious**). Note that the term *subconscious* is often erroneously used to refer to Freud's unconscious mind.

Freud postulated that our behaviors are also influenced by instincts. To Freud, an **instinct** is an innate psychological representation of a biological need. Instincts are the propelling aspects of Freud's dynamic theory of personality, and fall into two types: life and death instincts. Life instincts, referred to as *Eros*, promote an individual's quest for survival through thirst, hunger, and sexual needs. Death instincts, referred to as *Thanatos*, represent an unconscious wish for death and destruction. *Thanatos* was proposed by Freud as a response to his observations of victims of trauma reenacting or focusing on their traumatic experiences.

The ego's recourse for relieving anxiety caused by the clash of the id and super-ego is through **defense mechanisms**. All defense mechanisms have two common characteristics: first, they deny, falsify, or distort reality; second, they operate unconsciously. There are eight main defense mechanisms: repression, suppression, regression, reaction formation, projection, rationalization, displacement, and sublimation.

Repression is the ego's way of forcing undesired thoughts and urges to the unconscious, and underlies many of the other defense mechanisms, the aim of which is to disguise threatening impulses that may find their way back from the unconscious. While repression is mostly an unconscious forgetting, **suppression** is a more deliberate, conscious form of forgetting.

Regression is reversion to an earlier developmental state. Faced with stress, older children may return to earlier behaviors such as thumb sucking, throwing temper tantrums, or clinging to their mothers.

Key Concept

While repression is unconscious forgetting (such as that which may occur after traumatic events), suppression is a conscious form of forgetting: *I'm not going to think about that right now.*

When individuals suppress urges by unconsciously converting them into their exact opposites, they are taking advantage of **reaction formation**. For example, a man pining after a female celebrity he knows he will never meet may outwardly express hatred for the celebrity as a way of reducing the stress caused by his unrequited feelings.

Projection is the defense mechanism by which individuals attribute their undesired feelings to others. *I hate my parents* might, for example, turn into *My parents hate me*. Projection is an important part of personality analysis. Tests that make use of projection to gain insight into a client's mind are common in psychoanalytic therapy. For example, the **Rorschach inkblot test**, shown in Figure 6.3, relies on the assumption that the client projects his or her unconscious feelings onto the shape.

Figure 6.3. Card #10 from the Rorschach Inkblot Test

Similarly, the **thematic apperception test** consists of a series of pictures that are presented to the client, who is asked to make up a story about each one. The story, presumably, will elucidate the client's own unconscious thoughts and feelings.

Rationalization is the justification of behaviors in a manner that is acceptable to the self and society. Drivers who engage in reckless feats such as the Cannonball Run (a race from Los Angeles to New York for which the current record is just under 33 hours) might justify their dangerous pursuits by saying, both to themselves and others: *I'm in complete control, and besides, there are plenty of dangerous drivers on the road. What difference will one more make?*

Displacement describes the transference of an undesired urge from one person or object to another. Someone angry at her boss may hold her tongue at work but snap at her spouse when she gets home.

Finally, **sublimation** is the transformation of unacceptable urges into socially acceptable behaviors. Freud might say that pent-up sexual urges may be sublimated into a drive for business success or artistic creativity.

The descriptions of the most commonly tested defense mechanisms, as well as examples, are provided in Table 6.4.

Defense Mechanism	Description	Example
Repression	Unconsciously removing an idea or feeling from consciousness	A man who survived six months in a concentration camp cannot recall anything about his life during that time period
Suppression	Consciously removing an idea or feeling from consciousness	A terminally ill cancer patient puts aside his anxiety to enjoy a family gathering
Regression	Returning to an earlier stage of development	A husband speaks to his wife in "baby talk" when telling her bad news
Reaction formation	An unacceptable impulse is transformed into its opposite	Two coworkers fight all the time because they are actually very attracted to each other
Projection	Attribution of wishes, desires, thoughts, or emotions to someone else	A man who has committed adultery is convinced his wife is cheating on him, despite a lack of evidence
Rationalization	Justification of attitudes, beliefs, or behaviors	A murderer who claims that, while killing is wrong, his victim "deserved it"
Displacement	Changing the target of an emotion, while the feelings remain the same	When sent to his room as a punishment, a child begins to punch and kick his pillow
Sublimation	Channeling of an unacceptable impulse in a socially acceptable direction	A boss who is attracted to his employee becomes her mentor and advisor

Table 6.4. Commonly Tested Defense Mechanisms

Carl Jung

Later psychoanalytic theories have given more emphasis to interpersonal, sociological, and cultural influences, while maintaining their link with the psychoanalytic tradition. Carl Jung preferred to think of libido as psychic energy in general, not just psychic energy rooted in sexuality. Jung identified the ego as the conscious mind, and he divided the unconscious into two parts: the **personal unconscious**, similar to Freud's notion of the unconscious, and the collective unconscious. The **collective unconscious** is a powerful system that is shared among all humans and considered to be a residue of the experiences of our early ancestors. Its building blocks are images of common experiences, such as having a mother and a father. These images invariably have an emotional element, and are referred to as **archetypes** in Jung's theory. You can see an example of two archetypal images in Figure 6.4: God and the Devil.

Figure 6.4. Jungian Archetypes: God and the Devil
Archetypes are underlying forms or concepts that give rise to archetypal images, which may differ somewhat between cultures.

There are several important Jungian archetypes. The **persona** is likened to a mask that we wear in public, and is the part of our personality that we present to the world. Like our identity, Jung described the persona as adaptive to our social interactions, emphasizing those qualities that improve our social standing and suppressing our other, less desirable qualities. The **anima** (feminine) and the **animus** (masculine) describe sex-inappropriate qualities—in other words, feminine behaviors in males and masculine behaviors in females. For example, in Jung's theory, the anima is the suppressed female quality in males that explains emotional behavior (described by Jung as a *man's inner woman*), while the animus is the analogous male quality of females that explains power-seeking behavior (*a woman's inner man*).

The **shadow** archetype is responsible for the appearance of unpleasant and socially reprehensible thoughts, feelings, and actions in our consciousness. The **self**, to Jung, was the point of intersection between the collective unconscious,

Key Concept

Important Jungian archetypes:
- Persona—the aspect of our personality we present to the world
- Anima—a "man's inner woman"
- Animus—a "woman's inner man"
- Shadow—unpleasant and socially reprehensible thoughts, feelings, and actions in our consciousness

the personal unconscious, and the conscious mind. The self strives for unity. Jung symbolized the self as a *mandala* (Sanskrit: "circle"), shown in Figure 6.5. Jung saw the mandala, a symbol of the universe in Buddhism and Hinduism, as the mythic expression of the self: the reconciler of opposites and the promoter of harmony.

Figure 6.5. Tibetan Mandala
Jung saw the self as a mandala: the promoter of unity, balance, and harmony
between the conscious mind, personal unconscious,
and collective unconscious.

Jung described three dichotomies of personality:

- Extraversion (E, orientation toward the external world) *vs.* introversion (I, orientation toward the inner, personal world)
- Sensing (S, obtaining objective information about the world) *vs.* intuiting (N, working with information abstractly)
- Thinking (T, using logic and reason) *vs.* feeling (F, using a value system or personal beliefs)

In most individuals, both sides of each dichotomy are present to some degree, but one tends to dominate. Jung's work laid the groundwork for creation of the **Myers–Briggs Type Inventory** (**MBTI**), a classic personality test. Each of Jung's three dichotomies, and a fourth—judging (J, preferring orderliness) *vs.* perceiving (P, preferring spontaneity)—is labeled as a specific personality type, as shown in Figure 6.6.

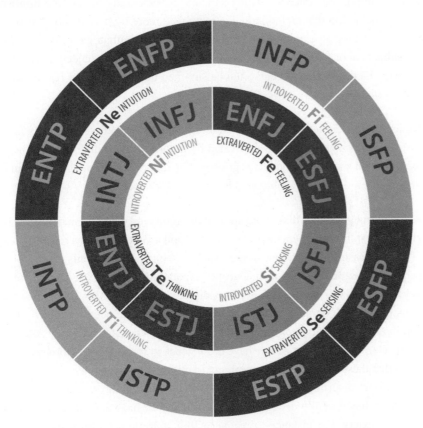

Figure 6.6. Myers–Briggs Type Inventory Personality Types

Other Psychoanalysts

Freud's theories were controversial but well-meaning attempts to describe personality. As with most psychological movements, psychoanalysis gained a following of theorists who learned from and often disagreed with its original tenets. In opposition to many of Freud's key ideas, later psychoanalysts often emphasized social rather than sexual motivations for behavior. Jung can be counted among these, as can Alfred Adler, whose theory focused on the immediate social imperatives of family and society and their effects on unconscious factors.

Adler was the originator of the concept of the **inferiority complex**: an individual's sense of incompleteness, imperfection, and inferiority both physically and socially. According to Adler, striving for superiority drives the personality. This striving enhances the personality when it is oriented toward benefiting society, but yields disorder when it is selfish.

The notions of the creative self and style of life were also important to Adler's theory. The **creative self** is the force by which each individual shapes his uniqueness and establishes his personality. **Style of life** represents the manifestation of the creative self and describes a person's unique way of achieving superiority. The family environment is crucial in molding the person's style of life.

Another important concept in Adler's theory of personality is **fictional finalism**. This is the notion that an individual is motivated more by his expectations of the future than by past experiences. According to Adler, human goals are based on the subjective or fictional estimate of life's values rather than objective data from the past. Fictional finalism can often be summed up by the phrase *Life would be perfect if only…*

Notice the difference between Freud, Jung, and Adler. Whereas Freud's major assumption is that behavior is motivated by inborn instincts and Jung's principal axiom is that a person's conduct is governed by inborn archetypes, Adler assumes that people are primarily motivated by striving for superiority.

Karen Horney, another dissenting student of Freud's, likewise argued that personality is a result of interpersonal relationships, and adamantly disagreed with many of Freud's assumptions about women such as the concept of penis envy. Horney postulated that individuals with neurotic personalities are governed by one of ten **neurotic needs**. Each of these needs is directed toward making life and interactions bearable. Examples of these neurotic needs are the need for affection and approval, the need to exploit others, and the need for self-sufficiency and independence. While healthy people have these needs to some degree, Horney emphasized that these needs become problematic if they fit at least one of four criteria: that they are disproportionate in intensity, that they are indiscriminate in application, that they partially disregard reality, or that they have a tendency to provoke intense anxiety. For instance, someone with a neurotic need for self-sufficiency and independence would go to great extremes to avoid being obligated to someone else in any way. As the central focus of the person's life, it would be a neurotic need and not a healthy one.

Horney's primary concept is that of basic anxiety. This is based on the premise that a child's early perception of self is important and stems from a child's relationship with his or her parents. Inadequate parenting can cause vulnerability and helplessness, which Horney termed **basic anxiety**, while neglect and rejection cause anger known as **basic hostility**. To overcome basic anxiety or basic hostility and attain a degree of security, the child uses three strategies in his or her relationships with others: moving toward people to obtain the goodwill of people who provide security; moving against people, or fighting them to obtain the upper hand; and moving away, or withdrawing, from people. These three strategies are the general headings under which the ten neurotic needs fall. Healthy people use all three strategies, depending on the situation. However, the highly threatened child will use one of these strategies rigidly and exclusively, and carries this strategy into adulthood.

Object relations theory also falls under the realm of psychodynamic theories of personality. In this context, *object* refers to the representation of parents or other caregivers based on subjective experiences during early infancy. These objects then persist into adulthood and impact our interactions with others, including the social bonds we create and our predictions of others' behavior.

THE HUMANISTIC PERSPECTIVE

In direct contrast to the psychoanalysts, who focus on "sick" individuals and their troubling urges, **humanistic** or **phenomenological theorists** focus on the value of individuals and take a more person-centered approach, describing those ways in which healthy people strive toward self-realization. Humanism is often associated with **Gestalt therapy**, in which practitioners tend to take a holistic view of the self, seeing each individual as a complete person rather than reducing him to individual behaviors or drives. For the humanists, our personality is the result of the conscious feelings we have for ourselves as we attempt to attain our needs and goals.

Kurt Lewin's **force field theory** puts very little stock in constraints on personalities such as fixed traits, habits, or structures such as the id, ego, and superego. Further, Lewin focused little on an individual's past or future, focusing instead on situations in the present. Lewin defined the field as one's current state of mind, which was simply the sum of the forces (influences) on the individual at that time. If the focus of humanistic psychology is exploring how an individual reaches self-realization, then these forces could be divided into two large groups: those assisting in our attainment of goals and those blocking the path to them.

Abraham Maslow, whose hierarchy of needs is discussed in Chapter 5 of *MCAT Behavioral Sciences Review*, was a humanist who studied the lives of individuals such as Ludwig van Beethoven, Albert Einstein, and Eleanor Roosevelt, who he felt were self-actualizers and had lived rich and productive lives. He identified several characteristics that these people had in common, including a nonhostile sense of humor, originality, creativity, spontaneity, and a need for some privacy. According to Maslow, self-actualized people are more likely than people who are not self-actualized to have what he called **peak experiences**: profound and deeply moving experiences in a person's life that have important and lasting effects on the individual.

George Kelly used himself as a model to theorize about human nature, and set aside the traditional concepts of motivation, unconscious emotion, and reinforcement in his descriptions of **personal construct psychology**. Kelly thought of the individual as a scientist, a person who devises and tests predictions about the behavior of significant people in his or her life. The individual constructs a scheme of anticipation of what others will do, based on his or her knowledge, perception, and relationships with these other people. Thus, the anxious person, rather than being the victim of inner conflicts and pent-up energy (as in psychodynamic theory), is one who is having difficulty constructing and understanding the variables in the environment. According to Kelly, psychotherapy is a process of insight whereby the individual acquires new constructs that will allow him or her to successfully predict troublesome events. Then, the individual will be able to integrate these new constructs into already existing ones.

Carl Rogers is most known for his psychotherapy technique known as **client-centered**, **person-centered**, or **nondirective** therapy. Rogers believed that people have the freedom to control their own behavior, and are neither slaves to the unconscious (as the psychoanalysts would suggest), nor subjects of faulty learning (as the behaviorists would say). Rather than providing solutions or diagnoses, the person-centered therapist helps the client reflect on problems, make choices, generate solutions, take positive action, and determine his or her own destiny. Rogers was the originator of the concepts of the real and ideal self discussed earlier in the chapter, and his therapeutic techniques aimed to help clients reconcile the differences between the various selves and reduce stress-inducing incongruence. Rogers also pioneered the concept of **unconditional positive regard**, a therapeutic technique by which the therapist accepts the client completely and expresses empathy in order to promote a positive therapeutic environment.

THE TYPE AND TRAIT PERSPECTIVES

The type and trait theorists were also borne out of dissatisfaction with psychoanalysis. **Type theorists** attempt to create a taxonomy of personality types, while **trait theorists** prefer to describe individual personality as the sum of a person's characteristic behaviors. For our purposes, we will consider them together.

Early attempts at personality types are generally discredited today. The ancient Greeks, for example, devised **personality types** based on **humors** or body fluids, an imbalance of which could lead to various personality disorders, as shown in Figure 6.7.

In the early 20th century, William Sheldon proposed personality types based on body type called **somatotypes**. Sheldon presumed that all short, stocky people were jolly, all tall people were high-strung and aloof, and people in between were strong and well-adjusted. One well-known type theory divides personalities into Types A and B. Individuals with **Type A** personalities are characterized by behavior that tends to be competitive and compulsive, while someone described as **Type B** is generally laid-back and relaxed. Not surprisingly, people with Type A personalities are more prone to heart disease than those with Type B personalities, although there is not much evidence to suggest that people with Type A personalities have a higher mortality rate.

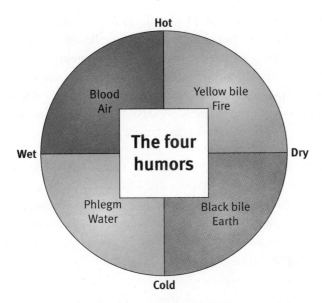

Figure 6.7. The Four Humors
Each humor was correlated with an element, an imbalance of which could lead to different personalities: blood (*sanguine*; impulsive and charismatic), bile (*choleric*; aggressive and dominant), black bile (*melancholic*; depressive and cautious), and phlegm (*phlegmatic*; relaxed and affectionate).

The Myers–Briggs Type Inventory, described earlier, also stands as a well-known example of a type theory.

Trait theorists instead use clusters of behaviors to describe individuals. Hans and Sybil Eysenck used factor analysis to group behaviors that typically occur together and assigned labels to those groups. For example, people who are more reserved and less outspoken in groups also tend to enjoy solitary activities and avoid overstimulation. These behaviors fall under the label of introversion. The Eysencks described three traits in the **PEN model**. **Psychoticism** is a measure of nonconformity or social deviance. **Extraversion** is a measure of tolerance for social interaction and stimulation. Finally, **neuroticism** is a measure of emotional arousal in stressful situations. The Eysencks reasoned that people could be distinguished from one another based on where they fell in each of these three dimensions. More recently, the PEN theory has been expanded to what is known as the **Big Five** which, as the name would suggest, uses dimensions of five traits: openness, conscientiousness, extraversion, agreeableness, and neuroticism.

Gordon Allport, primarily a trait theorist, listed three basic types of traits or dispositions: cardinal, central, and secondary. **Cardinal traits** are traits around which a person organizes his or her life. For instance, Mother Teresa's cardinal trait may be self-sacrifice. While not everyone develops a cardinal trait, everyone does have central and secondary traits. **Central traits** represent major characteristics of the personality that are easy to infer, such as honesty or charisma. **Secondary traits** are

> **Mnemonic**
>
> The Big Five Traits of Personality: **OCEAN**
> - **O**penness
> - **C**onscientiousness
> - **E**xtraversion
> - **A**greeableness
> - **N**euroticism

other personal characteristics that are more limited in occurrence: aspects of one's personality that only appear in close groups or specific social situations. A major part of Allport's theory is the concept of **functional autonomy**, in which a behavior continues despite satisfaction of the drive that originally created the behavior. A hunter, for example, may have originally hunted to obtain food to eat. However, the hunter may continue even after there is enough food simply for the enjoyment of the hunt: that which began as a means to obtain a goal became the goal itself.

David McClelland identified a personality trait that is referred to as the need for achievement (N-Ach). People who are rated high in N-Ach tend to be concerned with achievement and have pride in their accomplishments. These individuals avoid high risks (to avoid failing) and low risks (because easy tasks will not generate a sense of achievement). Additionally, they set realistic goals, and stop striving toward a goal if success is unlikely.

OTHER THEORIES OF PERSONALITY

Of course, entire textbooks can be (and in fact are) devoted to personality theorists and their ideas. The MCAT tests only the key ideas of each theory, or the concepts that overlap heavily with other topics in this text.

The **behaviorist** perspective, championed by B. F. Skinner, is based heavily on the concepts of operant conditioning, discussed in Chapter 3 of *MCAT Behavioral Sciences Review*. Skinner reasoned that personality is simply a reflection of behaviors that have been reinforced over time. Therapy, then, should focus on learning skills and changing behaviors through operant conditioning techniques. **Token economies**, for example, are often used in inpatient therapeutic settings: positive behavior is rewarded with tokens that can be exchanged for privileges, treats, or other reinforcers.

The **social cognitive** perspective takes behaviorism one step further, focusing not just on how our environment influences our behavior, but also on how we interact with that environment. Albert Bandura's concept of reciprocal determinism is a central idea to this perspective. **Reciprocal determinism** refers to the idea that our thoughts, feelings, behaviors, and environment all interact with each other to determine our actions in a given situation. People choose environments that suit their personalities, and their personalities determine how they will feel about and react to events in those environments. Locus of control is another important concept in the social cognitive perspective: some people feel more in control of their environment while others feel that their environment controls them. For a social cognitive theorist, the best predictor of future behavior is past behavior in similar situations.

On the other end of the spectrum lies the **biological** perspective, which holds that personality can be explained as a result of genetic expression in the brain. The biological and trait perspectives are closely linked, as biological theorists maintain that many traits can be shown to result from genes or differences in brain anatomy.

The dichotomy presented by the social cognitive and biological perspectives of personality is similar to another debate in psychology: whether behavior is primarily determined by an individual's personality (the **dispositional approach**) or by the environment and context (the **situational approach**). This division is investigated in depth in the section on attribution theory in Chapter 10 of *MCAT Behavioral Sciences Review*.

MCAT Concept Check 6.3:

Before you move on, assess your understanding of the material with these questions.

1. For each of the following perspectives, briefly describe how each would define personality.

    • Psychoanalytic:

    _____

    • Humanistic:

    _____

    • Type:

    _____

    • Trait:

    _____

    • Behaviorist:

    _____

    • Social cognitive:

    _____

    • Biological:

    _____

2. What are the roles of the id, ego, and superego, according to the psychoanalytic perspective?

    • Id:

    _____

    • Ego:

    _____

    • Superego:

    _____

3. What are the traits described by the Eysencks' PEN theory, and what does each describe?

   • P:

   _____

   • E:

   _____

   • N:

   _____

4. What are the Big Five personality traits?

   1. _____

   2. _____

   3. _____

   4. _____

   5. _____

Conclusion

In this chapter, we discussed two concepts that are central to the study of psychology: identity, which describes who we are, and personality, which describes the set of thoughts, feelings, traits, and behaviors that are characteristic of each of us across time and different locations. We discussed a variety of approaches to both, each with their own theorists and critics. The ideas presented in this chapter are ripe for the MCAT to test; expect questions on Test Day to ask you to identify the various perspectives and the differences between them as they apply to behavior and research.

Many of the theories of personality focus on problems in everyday life: how we cope with stresses, anxiety, and depression. In medical school, your focus will be primarily on these pathologic states of mind, or psychological disorders. It is to this extremely important topic—abnormal psychology—that we turn our attention in the next chapter.

CONCEPT SUMMARY

Self-Concept and Identity

- **Self-concept** is the sum of the ways in which we describe ourselves: in the present, who we used to be, and who we might be in the future.

- Our **identities** are individual components of our self-concept related to the groups to which we belong. Religious affiliation, sexual orientation, and ethnic and national affiliations are examples of identities.

- **Self-esteem** describes our evaluation of ourselves. Generally, the closer our **actual self** is to our **ideal self** (who we want to be) and our **ought self** (who others want us to be), the higher our self-esteem will be.

- **Self-efficacy** is the degree to which we see ourselves as being capable at a given skill or in a given situation. When placed in a consistently hopeless scenario, self-efficacy can be diminished to the point where **learned helplessness** results.

- **Locus of control** is a self-evaluation that refers to the way we characterize the influences in our lives. People with an internal locus of control see their successes and failures as a result of their own characteristics and actions, while those with an external locus of control perceive outside factors as having more of an influence in their lives.

Formation of Identity

- Freud's psychosexual stages of personality development are based on the tensions caused by the **libido**. Failure at any given stage leads to **fixation** that causes personality disorders. Freud's phases (oral, anal, phallic [Oedipal], latent, and genital) are based on the erogenous zones that are the focus of each phase of development.

- Erikson's stages of psychosocial development stem from conflicts that occur throughout life (trust *vs.* mistrust, autonomy *vs.* shame and doubt, initiative *vs.* guilt, industry *vs.* inferiority, identity *vs.* role confusion, intimacy *vs.* isolation, generativity *vs.* stagnation, integrity *vs.* despair). These conflicts are the result of decisions we are forced to make about ourselves and the environment around us at each phase of our lives.

- Kohlberg's stages of moral development describe the approaches of individuals to resolving moral dilemmas. Kohlberg believed that we progress through six stages divided into three main phases: **preconventional**, **conventional**, and **postconventional**.

- Vygotsky described development of language, culture, and skills. He proposed the idea of the **zone of proximal development**, which describes those skills that a child has not yet mastered and require a **more knowledgeable other** to accomplish.

- **Imitation** and **role-taking** are common ways children learn from others. Children first reproduce the behaviors of role models, and later learn to see the perspectives of others and practice taking on new roles.

- Our self-concept depends in part on our **reference group**, or the group to which we compare ourselves. Two individuals with the same qualities might see themselves differently depending on how those qualities compare to their reference groups.

Personality

- The **psychoanalytic** perspective views personality as resulting from unconscious urges and desires.

  o Freud's theories are based on the **id** (base urges of survival and reproduction), the **superego** (the idealist and perfectionist), and the **ego** (the mediator between the two and the conscious mind). The ego makes use of **defense mechanisms** to reduce stress caused by the urges of the id and the superego.

  o Jung assumed a **collective unconscious** that links all humans together. He viewed the personality as being influenced by **archetypes**.

  o Other psychoanalysts such as Adler and Horney have distanced themselves from Freud's theories, claiming that the unconscious is motivated by social rather than sexual urges.

- The **humanistic** perspective emphasizes the internal feelings of healthy individuals as they strive toward happiness and self-realization. Maslow's **hierarchy of needs** and Rogers's therapeutic approach of **unconditional positive regard** flow from the humanistic view of personality.

- **Type** and **trait** theorists believe that personality can be described as a number of identifiable traits that carry characteristic behaviors.

  o Type theories of personality include the ancient Greek notion of humors, Sheldon's **somatotypes**, division into **Types A** and **B**, and the **Myers–Briggs Type Inventory**.

  o The Eysencks identified three major traits which could be used to describe all individuals. The acronym for these traits is PEN: **psychoticism** (nonconformity), **extraversion** (tolerance for social interaction and stimulation), and **neuroticism** (arousal in stressful situations). Later trait theorists expanded these traits to the **Big Five**: openness, conscientiousness, extraversion, agreeableness, and neuroticism.

- o Allport identified three basic types of traits: cardinal, central, and secondary. **Cardinal traits** are the traits around which a person organizes his or her life; not everyone develops a cardinal trait. **Central traits** represent major characteristics of the personality and **secondary traits** are more personal characteristics and are limited in occurrence.

- o McClelland identified the personality trait of the need for achievement (N-Ach).

- The **social cognitive** perspective holds that individuals interact with their environment in a cycle called **reciprocal determinism**. People mold their environments according to their personalities, and those environments in turn shape our thoughts, feelings, and behaviors.

- The **behaviorist** perspective, based on the concept of operant conditioning, holds that personality can be described as the behaviors one has learned from prior rewards and punishments.

- **Biological** theorists claim that behavior can be explained as a result of genetic expression.

ANSWERS TO CONCEPT CHECKS

6.1

1. Self-concept describes the sum of all of the phrases that come to mind when we think of who we are, who we used to be, and who we may become in the future. Identity, on the other hand, describes a set of behaviors and labels we take on when in a specific group.

2. Ethnic identity is determined by common ancestry, cultural heritage, and language, among other similarities. Rather than being determined by birth, national identity is determined by the political borders of where one lives and the cultural identity of that nation.

3. A student with an internal locus of control will look for factors within him- or herself, such as not having studied hard enough. A student with an external locus of control will blame external factors such as bad luck or the test being too difficult.

6.2

1. Freud would say that the individual has become fixated in that stage, and will display the personality traits of that fixation for the rest of his or her life. Erikson would say that the individual will still move through subsequent phases, but will be lacking the skills and virtues granted by successful resolution of that stage. Kohlberg would say that the individual was incapable of reasoning at the level of failure, and that the individual would use the reasoning described in previous stages to resolve moral dilemmas.

2.

Phase	Description
Preconventional	Reasoning is based on individual rewards and punishments
Conventional	Reasoning is based on the relationship of the individual to society
Postconventional	Reasoning is based on abstract principles

6.3

1. Psychoanalytic: Personality is the result of unconscious urges and desires.
   Humanistic: Personality comes from conscious feelings about oneself resulting from healthy striving for self-realization.
   Type: Personalities are sets of distinct qualities and dispositions into which people can be grouped.
   Trait: Personalities are assembled from having different degrees of certain qualities and dispositions.
   Behaviorist: Personality is the result of behavioral responses to stimuli based on prior rewards and punishments.
   Social cognitive: Personality comes from the interactions between an individual and his or her environment.
   Biological: Personality is based on genetic influences and brain anatomy.

2. The id is the sum of our basic urges to reproduce and survive, while the superego is our sense of perfectionism and idealism. The ego mediates the anxieties caused by the actions of the id and superego by using defense mechanisms.

3. Psychoticism: nonconformity or social deviance
   Extraversion: tolerance for social interaction and stimulation
   Neuroticism: emotional arousal in stressful situations

4. The Big Five personality traits are openness, conscientiousness, extraversion, agreeableness, and neuroticism.

SHARED CONCEPTS

Discrete Practice Questions

Consult your online resources for Full-Length Exams and Passage-Based Questions (for certain chapters).

1. Each of the following is considered a part of a person's self-concept EXCEPT:

   A. the past self.
   B. the ought self.
   C. the future self.
   D. self-schemata.

2. As a gender identity, androgyny is defined as:

   A. low femininity, low masculinity.
   B. high femininity, low masculinity.
   C. low femininity, high masculinity.
   D. high femininity, high masculinity.

3. A high school student struggles consistently with math and feels that no matter how hard he studies, he "just doesn't get it." Which of the following is the most likely short-term result with respect to his ability to do math?

   A. Low self-esteem
   B. Low self-efficacy
   C. Learned helplessness
   D. An external locus of control

4. A district attorney with an internal locus of control wins an important court trial. Which of the following best represents the lawyer's attribution of the events?

   A. "I won because I made great arguments and had more experience than the defense."
   B. "I won because the jury was on my side from the beginning and believed my arguments."
   C. "I won because the defense did not adequately present their side of the case."
   D. "I shouldn't have won because I don't deserve to be successful."

5. A person keeps his desk extremely tidy and becomes very nervous whenever things are disorganized or out of place. In which of the following stages would a psychodynamic therapist say the man had become fixated?

   A. The oral stage
   B. The anal stage
   C. The phallic stage
   D. The genital stage

6. According to Erikson's stages of psychosocial development, which of the following would be the most important for a recent college graduate to accomplish?

   A. Figuring out what identities are most important to him or her
   B. Feeling like a contributing member of society
   C. Forming an intimate relationship with a significant other
   D. Finding a feeling of accomplishment in his or her life

7. Matt and Cati discuss the reasons why they avoid driving above the speed limit. Matt says that he wants to avoid a traffic fine, while Cati says that speeding is dangerous and, if everyone did it, there would be more accidents and people would get hurt. According to Kohlberg, which of the following describes the phases of moral reasoning demonstrated by Matt and Cati, respectively?

   A. Preconventional; conventional
   B. Preconventional; postconventional
   C. Conventional; preconventional
   D. Postconventional; conventional

8. A child finds that she cannot make an origami swan by herself, but is able to do so when observing and being assisted by an adult. This scenario is described in the ideas of which of the following theorists?

   A. Albert Bandura
   B. Alfred Adler
   C. B. F. Skinner
   D. Lev Vygotsky

9. Which of the following is a conclusion that can be made from research in role-taking and observational learning?

   A. Young children will only model actions performed by their parents.
   B. Celebrities and athletes are an adolescent's most important role models.
   C. Children who role-take identities that are not gender typical are more likely to take on those roles later in life.
   D. A female child is more likely to model the behavior of another female than a male.

10. A man feels extremely guilty after having an extra-marital affair. According to the psychodynamic perspective, which of the following is responsible for this anxiety?

    A. The id
    B. The ego
    C. The superego
    D. The libido

11. A woman advances through the ranks of a company, eventually becoming the CEO. Which of the following Jungian archetypes reflects this woman's drive to be successful within the company?

    A. The persona
    B. The anima
    C. The animus
    D. The shadow

12. Researchers discover that polymorphisms in the *DRD2* gene can be associated with thrill-seeking behavior, and that individuals with certain forms of the gene are more likely to become extreme athletes and have more dangerous hobbies. Which of the following theories is supported by this discovery?

    I. The social cognitive perspective
    II. The behavioral perspective
    III. The biological perspective

    A. I only
    B. III only
    C. I and III only
    D. II and III only

13. An EMT sees himself as a bit of a rebel, but is highly sociable and is able to keep calm in an emergency. This person would likely score in the lower range of which of the following traits?

    A. Psychoticism
    B. Neuroticism
    C. Extraversion
    D. Conscientiousness

14. Stockholm syndrome is a phenomenon in which a victim of a kidnapping or hostage situation may begin to identify with or even feel affection for his or her captors. A psychoanalyst might explain Stockholm syndrome by citing which of the following defense mechanisms?

    A. Reaction formation
    B. Regression
    C. Projection
    D. Displacement

15. Having struggled for years through an economic recession, a young professional begins to buy lottery tickets every Friday. "If I won the lottery," he reasons, "I'd finally have the life I've always wanted. All my stress would go away and I could live comfortably." His thoughts regarding winning the lottery are most representative of:

    A. a cardinal trait.
    B. fictional finalism.
    C. functional autonomy.
    D. unconditional positive regard.

Explanations to
Discrete Practice Questions

1. B

Self-concept is defined as the sum of all of the ways in which we see ourselves, including who we are, as in **choice (D)**, who we were in the past, **choice (A)**, and who we may become in the future, **choice (C)**. The ought self, while closely related to self-esteem, is our appraisal of how others see us and is not a part of our self-concept.

2. D

Androgyny is defined as scoring highly on scales of both femininity and masculinity. Achieving a low score on both scales, **choice (A)**, would be considered undifferentiated, while **choices (B)** and **(C)** would be described as feminine and masculine, respectively.

3. B

Because there is nothing in the question stem to suggest that this situation will fundamentally change this student's attitudes in the short term, **choices (A)** and **(D)** can be eliminated. **Choice (C)** is unlikely in the short term, as learned helplessness requires a repeated inability to have any effect on a situation over a long period of time and is much more severe, usually manifesting as depression. It is far more likely that the student will simply feel ineffective when it comes to math, which is low self-efficacy.

4. A

Because we know the lawyer has an internal locus of control, we expect her to believe that she is in control of the events that happen in her life. Both **choices (B)** and **(C)** attribute success to outside factors, representing an external locus of control. While **choice (D)** perhaps represents an attribution that could correlate to low self-esteem, it is not indicative of locus of control.

5. B

Both excessive organization and excessive sloppiness are indicative of fixation in the anal stage of psychosexual development—what is commonly referred to as anal-retentiveness.

6. C

As a postadolescent young adult, this person would be be described by Erikson as experiencing the conflict of intimacy *vs.* isolation, and so forming significant relationships with others would be a primary goal. **Choices (B)** and **(D)** represent the next two stages in life (generativity *vs.* stagnation and integrity *vs.* despair, respectively), while **choice (A)** is the conflict that Erikson would say should have been resolved in adolescence (identity *vs.* role confusion).

7. A

Matt's reasoning reflects a desire to avoid punishment, which reflects stage one in Kohlberg's preconventional phase (obedience). Cati's reasoning takes into account social order, reflecting stage four in the conventional phase (law and order).

8. D

This situation is best described by Lev Vygotsky's zone of proximal development theory, which holds that children are often unable to perform tasks by themselves, but can complete the task with the help of a more knowledgeable other.

9. D

Choice (C) has no support from role-taking research and can be eliminated. **Choices (A)** and **(B)** are both inaccurate; the Bobo doll experiment shows young children modeling behavior not performed by their parents, and teens are most influenced by their peers, not celebrities and athletes. The research does suggest, however, that children are more likely to engage in behavior modeled by individuals who are like themselves; thus, a female child is more likely to imitate behavior by another female.

10. C

The superego is responsible for moral guilt when we do not live up to our ideals. While the id and the libido, **choices (A)** and **(D)**, may be responsible for the urge to have an affair, the superego is responsible for the anxiety one feels afterward.

11. C

Jung saw the drive for power and success as typically male traits, so Jung would say this woman is exercising her "inner man." The animus is the archetype that most closely reflects this quality.

12. C

This research supports a link between genetic expression and behavior, which is a central tenet of the biological perspective. The social cognitive perspective also holds that people's behaviors and traits shape their environments, which in turn have an effect on their identity, so the discovery also supports this perspective. Behaviorism is not supported, as the discovery is not related to rewards and punishments.

13. B

As a rebel and a sociable person, this individual would score highly on both psychoticism and extraversion, respectively. Neuroticism is associated with high emotional arousal in stressful situations, so being able to keep calm in an emergency is a sign of low neuroticism. Conscientiousness, a trait associated with being hardworking and organized instead of impulsive, is not described by the question stem.

14. A

Reaction formation is a defense mechanism that converts unwanted feelings into their exact opposite. A psychodynamic theorist would say that the terror and hatred one feels toward his or her captor might be unconsciously turned into affection in an effort to reduce the stress of the situation.

15. B

Fictional finalism is comprised of internal, idealistic beliefs about the future. The assumption that winning the lottery will solve all of his problems is representative of this form of thinking. Cardinal traits, **choice (A),** are the traits around which one organizes his or her entire life. Functional autonomy, **choice (C)**, is when a behavior continues after the drive behind the behavior has ceased; for example, if this young professional continued purchasing lottery tickets after winning simply because he enjoyed them, then this behavior would have gained functional autonomy. Unconditional positive regard, **choice (D)**, is used in some forms of humanistic therapy in which the therapist believes in the internal good of the client and does not judge the client negatively for any words or actions.

Psychological Disorders

In This Chapter

Chapter Profile

3%

The content in this chapter should be relevant to about 3% of all questions about the Behavioral Sciences on the MCAT.

This chapter covers material from the following AAMC content category:

7A: Individual influences on behavior

Introduction

The progress in our understanding of hysteria has come largely through the elaboration of the so-called mechanisms by which the symptoms arise. These mechanisms have been declared to reside or to have their origin in the subconsciousness or coconsciousness. The mechanisms range all the way from the conception of Janet that the personality is disintegrated owing to lowering of the psychical tension to that of Freud, who conceives all hysterical symptoms as a result of dissociation arising through conflicts between repressed sexual desires and experiences and the various censors organized by the social life. . . . [T]he origin of the symptoms can be traced to a more simple and fairly familiar mechanism, one which, in its essence, is merely an intensification of a normal reaction of many women to marital difficulties. In other words, women frequently resort to measures which bring about an acute discomfort upon the part of their mate, through his pity, compassion and self-accusation. They resort to tears as their proverbial weapon for gaining their point.

The above is an excerpt from the *Journal of Abnormal Psychology* in 1915. Merely 100 years ago, our understanding of psychological disorders was in its infancy. Hysteria—the antiquated name for conversion disorder—was thought to result from marital discord and repressed sexual desires. We are now beginning to understand the underlying psychological and biological factors at play in a number of mental illnesses. In this chapter, we will focus on several different types of psychological disorders, their classification, causes, and frequencies.

MCAT Expertise

If you've taken a glance at the rest of this book, you might have noticed that this chapter has a low percentage of relevant content as compared to the rest of the chapters within *MCAT Behavioral Sciences Review*. While Chapter 7 materials will be tested less often than the other materials in this book, there are so many psychology questions on the MCAT that even lower-yield topics within the behavioral sciences will get you points!

7.1 Understanding Psychological Disorders

LEARNING GOALS

After Chapter 7.1, you will be able to:

- Compare and contrast the biomedical and the biopsychosocial models of psychological disorders
- Recall the most common psychological disorders in the United States

Psychological disorders are characteristic sets of thoughts, feelings, or actions that cause noticeable distress to the sufferer, cause maladaptive functioning in society, or are considered deviant by the individual's culture. Many disorders can be treated once diagnosed. The process of defining these disorders varies, and there are two main classification systems you'll need to know for the MCAT.

BIOMEDICAL *VS.* BIOPSYCHOSOCIAL APPROACHES

The first classification system to know for the MCAT is the **biomedical approach** to psychological disorders. Biomedical therapy includes interventions that rally around symptom reduction of psychological disorders. In other words, this approach assumes that any disorder has roots in biomedical disturbances, and thus the solution should also be of a biomedical nature. This view is thought of as narrower than other approaches because it fails to take into account many of the other sources of disorders, such as lifestyle and socioeconomic status. For example, heart disease clearly has roots within the mechanisms of the cardiac muscle, but the causes of these malfunctions have as much to do with biomedical causes (such as genetics) as they do with lifestyle causes (such as a diet rich in salty, fatty foods; smoking; and alcohol use). Similarly, this biomedical approach can miss some underlying sources of psychological disorders and is often more effective when supplemented with a broader approach to diagnosis and treatment.

A broader classification system commonly used for these psychological disorders is the **biopsychosocial approach**. This method assumes that there are biological, psychological, and social components to an individual's disorder. The biological component of a disorder is something in the body, like having a particular genetic syndrome. The psychological component of a disorder stems from the individual's thoughts, emotions, or behaviors. Finally, the disorder's social component results from the individual's surroundings and can include issues of perceived class in society and even discrimination or stigmatization. All three of these aspects of a disorder are considered in the biopsychosocial approach for both diagnosis and treatment.

To better understand the biopsychosocial approach, consider depression. Certain genetic factors can make an individual more or less susceptible to depressive tendencies, showing a purely biological influence on the disorder. However, from a psychological perspective, the levels of stress that the individual experiences can also contribute to the severity of the depression experienced. Finally, the social environment may provide additional stressors or support from one's career, family, and friends. Accordingly, in the biopsychosocial model, the goal is often to provide not only **direct therapy**—treatment that acts directly on the individual, such as medication or periodic meetings with a psychologist—but also **indirect therapy**, which aims to increase social support by educating and empowering family and friends of the affected individual.

CLASSIFYING PSYCHOLOGICAL DISORDERS

To aid clinicians in considering these factors, the ***Diagnostic and Statistical Manual of Mental Disorders*** (**DSM**) was created. Originally, the manual was written to collect statistical data in the United States. It is now used as a diagnostic tool in the United States and various other countries. The manual is currently in its fifth edition, which was published in May 2013, so the common abbreviation seen is DSM-5. This manual is a compilation of many known psychological disorders. The DSM-5's classification scheme is not based on theories of etiology (cause) or treatments of different disorders. Rather, it is based on descriptions of symptoms. It is used by clinicians to fit lists of compiled symptoms from a patient into a category and thus to diagnose that patient. The DSM-5 has 20 diagnostic classes of mental disorders; those that will be tested on the MCAT are discussed in this chapter.

RATES OF PSYCHOLOGICAL DISORDERS

Suffering from a mental disorder can be a lonely experience because the disorder usually occurs only in the mind of the patient. However, the rates of these psychological disorders are higher than this experience would otherwise suggest. Table 7.1 covers these rates in detail.

Real World

David Rosenhan studied whether or not it was possible to be judged sane if you are in an "insane place" (a psychiatric hospital). Rosenhan and seven other "sane" people were admitted into psychiatric hospitals by reporting auditory hallucinations. Each of these pseudopatients was diagnosed to have either schizophrenia or bipolar disorder, and each was admitted. Once admitted, they acted completely normal—but it still took an average of three weeks to be discharged, and each was still given the diagnosis of schizophrenia in remission. Once labeled, it is very hard to distance oneself from the diagnosis of mental illness.

Disorder	Percentage Affected	Number Affected (In Millions)
Any mental disorder	26.2	81.7
Specific phobia	8.7	27.1
Social anxiety disorder	6.8	21.2
Major depressive disorder	6.7	20.9
Alcohol use disorder	4.4	13.7
Posttraumatic stress disorder	3.5	10.9
Generalized anxiety disorder	3.1	9.7
Panic disorder	2.7	8.4
Bipolar disorder	2.6	8.1
Drug use disorder	1.8	5.6
Antisocial personality disorder	1.5	4.7
Borderline personality disorder	1.5	4.7
Schizophrenia	1.0	3.1
Obsessive–compulsive disorder	1.0	3.1
Agoraphobia	0.8	2.5
Anorexia nervosa	0.1	0.3
All cancers*	5.4	16.8
Diabetes*	10.7	33.3

*Note: These nonpsychological conditions are included for comparison.

Table 7.1. One-Year Prevalence Rates for Psychological Disorders in the United States

MCAT Concept Check 7.1:

Before you move on, assess your understanding of the material with these questions.

1. What is the difference between the biomedical and biopsychosocial models of psychological disorders?

   _____

2. Name three psychological disorders with greater than 2% one-year prevalence in the United States (affecting more than 1 in 50 people per year). Refer to Table 7.1 if you get stuck.

   • _____

   • _____

   • _____

7.2 Types of Psychological Disorders

LEARNING GOALS

After Chapter 7.2, you will be able to:

- List the major positive symptoms and major negative symptoms of schizophrenia
- Recall the features of major depressive episodes and manic episodes
- Distinguish between the testable mood disorders
- Relate obsession and compulsion to the symptoms of obsessive–compulsive disorder
- Describe the features and individual disorders that fall under cluster A, B, and C personality disorders

As mentioned earlier, the DSM-5 categorizes common symptoms into 20 diagnostic classes. Many of these classes represent significant revisions from the DSM-5's immediate predecessor, the DSM-IV-TR. The most heavily tested diagnostic classes on the MCAT are schizophrenia spectrum and other psychotic disorders, depressive disorders, bipolar and related disorders, anxiety disorders, obsessive–compulsive and related disorders, trauma- and stressor-related disorders, dissociative disorders, somatic symptom and related disorders, and personality disorders.

SCHIZOPHRENIA

Schizophrenia is the prototypical psychotic disorder. According to the DSM-5, individuals with a **psychotic disorder** suffer from one or more of the following conditions: delusions, hallucinations, disorganized thought, disorganized behavior, catatonia, and negative symptoms. For an individual to be given the diagnosis of schizophrenia, he or she must show continuous signs of the disturbance for at least six months, and this six-month period must include at least one month of "active symptoms" (delusions, hallucinations, or disorganized speech).

Symptoms of schizophrenia are divided into positive and negative types. **Positive symptoms** are behaviors, thoughts, or feelings added to normal behavior. Examples include delusions and hallucinations, disorganized thought, and disorganized or catatonic behavior. Positive symptoms are considered by some to be two distinct dimensions—the psychotic dimension (delusions and hallucinations) and the disorganized dimension (disorganized thought and behavior)—perhaps with different underlying causes. **Negative symptoms** are those that involve the absence of normal or desired behavior, such as disturbance of affect and avolition.

MCAT Expertise

The MCAT tests many, but not all, categories of mental disorder described within the DSM-5. Neurodevelopmental disorders, eating disorders, impulse control disorders, and sleeping disorders are not listed within the AAMC's guide to MCAT content, and as such are not included within this text.

Real World

The term schizophrenia is a relatively recent term, coined in 1911 by Eugen Bleuler. Before Bleuler, schizophrenia was called *dementia praecox*. Schizophrenia literally means "split mind" because the disorder is characterized by distortions of reality and disturbances in the content and form of thought, perception, and affect. Unfortunately, this has led to confusion with dissociative identity disorder (formerly multiple personality disorder). By *split mind*, Bleuler did not mean that the mind is split into different personalities, but that the mind is split from reality.

MCAT Expertise

The fact that delusions must be considered deviant from the society in which an individual lives provides an excellent opportunity for the MCAT to integrate mental illness and sociology. For example, a belief in shamanism—which is common in the Caribbean, Central and South America, Africa, and in some Native American tribes—would not be considered a delusion within societies that endorse shamanic medicine.

Bridge

Word salad can be seen in severe schizophrenia as well as Wernicke's (receptive) aphasia. Patients will string together unrelated words, although the prosody of the speech (its rhythm, stress, and intonation) remains intact. Aphasias are discussed in Chapter 3 of *MCAT Behavioral Sciences Review*.

Positive Symptoms

Delusions are false beliefs discordant with reality and not shared by others in the individual's culture that are maintained in spite of strong evidence to the contrary. Common delusions include delusions of reference, persecution, and grandeur. **Delusions of reference** involve the belief that common elements in the environment are directed toward the individual. For example, a person with a delusion of reference may believe that characters in a TV show are talking to him directly. **Delusions of persecution** involve the belief that the person is being deliberately interfered with, discriminated against, plotted against, or threatened. **Delusions of grandeur**, also common in bipolar I disorder, involve the belief that the person is remarkable in some significant way, such as being an inventor, historical figure, or religious icon. Other common delusions involve the concept of **thought broadcasting**, which is the belief that one's thoughts are broadcast directly from one's head to the external world, and **thought insertion**, the belief that thoughts are being placed in one's head.

Hallucinations are perceptions that are not due to external stimuli but have a compelling sense of reality. The most common form of hallucination is auditory, involving voices that the individual perceives as coming from inside or outside his or her head. Visual and tactile hallucinations are less common, but may be seen in drug use or withdrawal. Olfactory and gustatory hallucinations are even less common, but may be experienced during the aura before a seizure.

Disorganized thought is characterized by **loosening of associations**. This may be exhibited as speech in which ideas shift from one subject to another in such a way that a listener would be unable to follow the train of thought. A patient's speech may be so disorganized that it seems to have no structure—as though it were just words thrown together incomprehensibly. This is sometimes called **word salad**. In fact, a person with schizophrenia may even invent new words, called **neologisms**.

Disorganized behavior refers to an inability to carry out activities of daily living, such as paying bills, maintaining hygiene, and keeping appointments. **Catatonia** refers to certain motor behaviors characteristic of some people with schizophrenia. The patient's spontaneous movement and activity may be greatly reduced or the patient may maintain a rigid posture, refusing to be moved. At the other extreme, catatonic behavior may include useless and bizarre movements not caused by any external stimuli, **echolalia** (repeating another's words), or **echopraxia** (imitating another's actions).

Negative Symptoms

Negative symptoms of schizophrenia include **disturbance of affect** and avolition. **Affect** refers to the experience and display of emotion. Affective symptoms may include **blunting**, in which there is a severe reduction in the intensity of affect expression; **flat affect (emotional flattening)**, in which there are virtually no signs of emotional expression; or **inappropriate affect**, in which the affect is clearly discordant with the content of the individual's speech. For example, a patient with inappropriate affect may begin to laugh hysterically while describing a parent's death. Interestingly, it has become more difficult to assess the affective aspects of schizophrenia because the antipsychotic medications used in treatment frequently blunt and flatten affect as well. Finally, **avolition** is marked by decreased engagement in purposeful, goal-directed actions.

Prodromal Phase

Before schizophrenia is diagnosed, a patient often goes through a phase characterized by poor adjustment. This phase is called the **prodromal phase**. The prodromal phase is exemplified by clear evidence of deterioration, social withdrawal, role functioning impairment, peculiar behavior, inappropriate affect, and unusual experiences. This phase is followed by the active phase of symptomatic behavior. If schizophrenia development is slow, the prognosis is especially poor. If the onset of symptoms is intense and sudden, the prognosis is better.

DEPRESSIVE DISORDERS

Sadness is a natural part of life, especially in response to stressful life events like the death of a loved one. During periods of sadness, one might call him- or herself depressed. However, periodic sadness in response to life events is not a mental disorder. **Depressive disorders**, in contrast, must meet certain severity and duration requirements for diagnosis.

Major Depressive Disorder

Major depressive disorder is a **mood disorder** characterized by at least one major depressive episode. A **major depressive episode** is a period of at least two weeks with at least five of the following symptoms: prominent and relatively persistent depressed mood, loss of interest in all or almost all formerly enjoyable activities (**anhedonia**), appetite disturbances, substantial weight changes, sleep disturbances, decreased energy, feelings of worthlessness or excessive guilt (sometimes delusional), difficulty concentrating or thinking, psychomotor symptoms (feeling "slowed down"), and thoughts of death or attempts at suicide; at least one of the symptoms must be depressed mood or anhedonia. In order for major depressive disorder to be diagnosed, these symptoms must cause significant distress or impairment in functioning. As many as 15 percent of individuals with this disorder die by suicide.

A diagnosis of **persistent depressive disorder** is given to individuals who suffer from **dysthymia**, a depressed mood that isn't severe enough to meet the criteria of a major depressive episode, most of the time for at least two years. Individuals with major depressive disorder that lasts at least two years can also be given this diagnosis. Individuals with this disorder may also suffer from a combination of dysthymia and occasional major depressive episodes.

MCAT Expertise

When the MCAT tests schizophrenia, it is likely to include a connection to sociology through the *downward drift hypothesis*, which states that schizophrenia causes a decline in socioeconomic status, leading to worsening symptoms, which sets up a negative spiral for the patient toward poverty and psychosis. This is why rates of schizophrenia are much, much higher among the homeless and indigents.

Bridge

The most common first-line treatment for depression is the class of medications called selective serotonin reuptake inhibitors (SSRIs). These block the reuptake of serotonin by the presynaptic neuron, resulting in higher levels of serotonin in the synapse and relief of symptoms. The nervous system is outlined in Chapter 1 of *MCAT Behavioral Sciences Review* and Chapter 4 of *MCAT Biology Review*.

Mnemonic

Symptoms of a major depressive episode: **SIG E. CAPS**

Sadness +

- **S**leep
- **I**nterest
- **G**uilt
- **E**nergy
- **C**oncentration
- **A**ppetite
- **P**sychomotor symptoms
- **S**uicidal thoughts

Seasonal Affective Disorder

Seasonal affective disorder (SAD) is not a freestanding diagnosis in the DSM-5, but is best categorized as major depressive disorder with seasonal onset. In this case, depressive symptoms are present only in the winter months. This disorder may be related to abnormal melatonin metabolism; it is often treated with **bright light therapy**, where the patient is exposed to a bright light for a specified amount of time each day, as demonstrated with a plant in Figure 7.1.

Figure 7.1. Bright Light Therapy for Seasonal Affective Disorder

BIPOLAR AND RELATED DISORDERS

The **bipolar disorders** (formerly known as manic depression) are a major type of mood disorder characterized by both depression and mania. **Manic episodes** are characterized by abnormal and persistently elevated mood lasting at least one week with at least three of the following: increased distractibility, decreased need for sleep, inflated self-esteem or grandiosity (beliefs that one is all-powerful, famous, or wealthy), racing thoughts, increased goal-directed activity or agitation, pressured speech or increased talkativeness, and involvement in high-risk behavior. Manic episodes generally have a more rapid onset and a briefer duration than depressive episodes and may include psychosis. **Bipolar I disorder** has manic episodes with or without major depressive episodes, whereas **bipolar II disorder** has hypomania with at least one major depressive episode. In contrast to mania, **hypomania** typically does not significantly impair functioning, nor are there psychotic features, although the individual may be more energetic and optimistic. Finally, **cyclothymic disorder** consists of a combination of hypomanic episodes and periods of dysthymia that are not severe enough to qualify as major depressive episodes.

Mnemonic

Symptoms of a manic episode: **DIG FAST**
- **D**istractible
- **I**nsomnia (decreased sleep)
- **G**randiosity
- **F**light of ideas (racing thoughts)
- **A**gitation
- **S**peech (pressured)
- **T**houghtlessness (risky behavior)

Many causes have been proposed for mood disorders, ranging from genetics to socio-cultural factors. The most common explanation revolves around the neurotransmitters norepinephrine and serotonin. These two are often linked together into what is called the **monoamine** or **catecholamine theory of depression**. This theory holds that too much norepinephrine and serotonin in the synapse leads to mania, while too little leads to depression. Although more recent research has shown that it is not that simple, you should be aware of this theory for the MCAT.

ANXIETY DISORDERS

There are more than ten disorders listed in the anxiety disorders portion of the DSM-5. This type of disorder is the most common psychiatric disorder in women of all ages. For men, in contrast, substance use disorder is the most common psychiatric disorder.

Generalized Anxiety Disorder

Generalized anxiety disorder is common in the population and is defined as a disproportionate and persistent worry about many different things—making mortgage payments, doing a good job at work, returning emails, political issues, and so on—for at least six months. These individuals often have physical symptoms like fatigue, muscle tension, and sleep problems that accompany the worry.

Specific Phobias

The most common type of anxiety disorder is a phobia. A phobia is an irrational fear of something that results in a compelling desire to avoid it. Most of the phobias that you are probably familiar with are what the DSM-5 calls specific phobias. A **specific phobia** is one in which anxiety is produced by a specific object or situation. For example, *claustrophobia* is an irrational fear of closed places, *acrophobia* is an irrational fear of heights, and *arachnophobia* is an irrational fear of spiders, as shown in Figure 7.2.

Figure 7.2. Specific Phobia
Arachnophobia, the fear of spiders, is a common example of a specific phobia.

Bridge

Notice that a large number of the symptoms of panic disorder are caused by excess activation of the sympathetic nervous system (autonomic overdrive). These include trembling, sweating, hyperventilation, shortness of breath, a racing heart rate, and palpitations. The autonomic nervous system is discussed in Chapter 1 of *MCAT Behavioral Sciences Review* and Chapter 4 of *MCAT Biology Review*.

Social Anxiety Disorder

Social anxiety disorder is characterized by anxiety that is due to social situations. Individuals with social anxiety disorder have persistent fear when exposed to social or performance situations that may result in embarrassment; for example, delivering a speech, socializing at a party, or using a public restroom.

Agoraphobia

Agoraphobia is an anxiety disorder characterized by a fear of being in places or in situations where it might be hard for an individual to escape. These individuals tend to be uncomfortable leaving their homes for fear of a panic attack or exacerbation of another mental illness.

Panic Disorder

Another type of anxiety disorder to know for the MCAT is **panic disorder**. This disorder consists of repeated panic attacks. Symptoms of a **panic attack** include fear and apprehension, trembling, sweating, hyperventilation, and a sense of unreality. The severity of a panic attack should not be underestimated: these individuals are suddenly struck with what is often described as a *sense of impending doom* and may be convinced they are about to lose their mind. Even after treatment for panic disorder, symptoms are common, so patients are treated for a long period of time. Panic disorder is frequently accompanied by agoraphobia because of the pervasive fear of having a panic attack in a public location.

OBSESSIVE–COMPULSIVE AND RELATED DISORDERS

Formerly classified under anxiety and somatic symptom disorders, the illnesses in this group were relabeled as obsessive–compulsive and related disorders in the DSM-5.

Obsessive–Compulsive Disorder

Obsessive–compulsive disorder (OCD) is characterized by **obsessions** (persistent, intrusive thoughts and impulses), which produce tension, and **compulsions** (repetitive tasks) that relieve tension but cause significant impairment in a person's life. The relationship between the two is key: obsessions raise the individual's stress level, and the compulsions relieve this stress. For instance, a person might obsess about dirt and compulsively wash his hands to neutralize the anxiety produced by the obsession.

Body Dysmorphic Disorder

In **body dysmorphic disorder**, a person has an unrealistic negative evaluation of his or her personal appearance and attractiveness, usually directed toward a certain body part. This person sees her nose, skin, or stomach as ugly or even horrific when it is actually normal in appearance. This body preoccupation also disrupts day-to-day life, and the sufferer may seek multiple plastic surgeries or other extreme interventions.

TRAUMA- AND STRESSOR-RELATED DISORDERS

By far, the most notable disorder in this category is **posttraumatic stress disorder** (**PTSD**). PTSD occurs after experiencing or witnessing a traumatic event, such as war, a home invasion, rape, or a natural disaster, and consists of intrusion symptoms, avoidance symptoms, negative cognitive symptoms, and arousal symptoms. **Intrusion symptoms** include recurrent reliving of the event, flashbacks, nightmares, and prolonged distress. **Avoidance symptoms** include deliberate attempts to avoid the memories, people, places, activities, and objects associated with the trauma. **Negative cognitive symptoms** include an inability to recall key features of the event, negative mood or emotions, feeling distanced from others, and a persistent negative view of the world. Finally, **arousal symptoms** include an increased startle response, irritability, anxiety, self-destructive or reckless behavior, and sleep disturbances. To meet the criteria of PTSD, a particular number of these symptoms must be present for at least one month. If the same symptoms last for less than one month (but more than three days), it may be called **acute stress disorder**.

DISSOCIATIVE DISORDERS

In **dissociative disorders**, the person avoids stress by escaping from his identity. The person otherwise still has an intact sense of reality. Examples of dissociative disorders include dissociative amnesia, dissociative identity disorder (formerly multiple personality disorder), and depersonalization/derealization disorder.

Dissociative Amnesia

Dissociative amnesia is characterized by an inability to recall past experiences. The qualifier *dissociative* simply means that the amnesia is not due to a neurological disorder. This disorder is often linked to trauma. Some individuals with this disorder may also experience **dissociative fugue**: a sudden, unexpected move or purposeless wandering away from one's home or location of usual daily activities. Individuals in a fugue state are confused about their identity and can even assume a new identity. Significantly, they may actually believe that they are someone else, with a complete backstory.

Dissociative Identity Disorder

In **dissociative identity disorder** (**DID**, formerly multiple personality disorder), there are two or more personalities that recurrently take control of a person's behavior, as represented in Figure 7.3. This disorder results when the components of identity fail to integrate. In most cases, the patients have suffered severe physical or sexual abuse as young children. After much therapy, the personalities can sometimes be integrated into one. The existence of dissociative identity disorder is justifiably debated within the medical community, but its characteristics are still important to recognize on Test Day.

Real World

One of the first and most famous cases of dissociative identity disorder in the media is Shirley Ardell Mason, also known as "Sybil," who had at least 13 separate personalities. Mason underwent years of therapy in an attempt to combine her personalities into a single one. Two separate TV movies, both called *Sybil,* have been produced to tell the story of Sybil's struggle with this disorder.

Figure 7.3. Dissociative Identity Disorder (DID)
One artist's interpretation of many personalities seen in DID.

Depersonalization/Derealization Disorder

In **depersonalization/derealization disorder**, individuals feel detached from their own mind and body (**depersonalization**), or from their surroundings (**derealization**). This often presents as a feeling of automation, and can have findings like a failure to recognize one's reflection. An out-of-body experience is an example of depersonalization. Derealization is often described as giving the world a dreamlike or insubstantial quality. They may also experience depersonalization and derealization simultaneously. These feelings cause significant impairment of regular activities. However, even during these times, the person does not display psychotic symptoms like delusions or hallucinations.

SOMATIC SYMPTOM AND RELATED DISORDERS

Diagnoses in this category are marked by somatic (bodily) symptoms that cause significant stress or impairment.

Somatic Symptom Disorder

Individuals with **somatic symptom disorder** have at least one somatic symptom, which may or may not be linked to an underlying medical condition, and that is accompanied by disproportionate concerns about its seriousness, devotion of an excessive amount of time and energy to it, or elevated levels of anxiety.

Illness Anxiety Disorder

Illness anxiety disorder is characterized by being consumed with thoughts about having or developing a serious medical condition. Individuals with this disorder are quick to become alarmed about their health, and either excessively check themselves for signs of illness or avoid medical appointments altogether. Most patients classified under hypochondriasis in the DSM-IV-TR now fit into somatic symptom disorder if somatic symptoms are present or illness anxiety disorder if they are not.

Conversion Disorder

A **conversion disorder** is characterized by unexplained symptoms affecting voluntary motor or sensory functions. The symptoms generally begin soon after the individual experiences high levels of stress or a traumatic event, but may not develop until some time has passed after the initiating experience. Examples include paralysis or blindness without evidence of neurological damage. The person may be surprisingly unconcerned by the symptom—what is called *la belle indifférence*. Conversion disorder was historically called *hysteria*. The symptoms seen in conversion disorder may sometimes be connected with the inciting event in a literal or poetic way; for example, a woman going blind shortly after watching her son die tragically.

PERSONALITY DISORDERS

A **personality disorder** is a pattern of behavior that is inflexible and maladaptive, causing distress or impaired functioning in at least two of the following: cognition, emotions, interpersonal functioning, or impulse control. Personality disorders are considered **ego-syntonic**, meaning that the individual perceives her behavior as correct, normal, or in harmony with her goals. This is in contrast to the other disorders covered in this chapter that are **ego-dystonic**, meaning that the individual sees the illness as something thrust upon her that is intrusive and bothersome. In addition to **general personality disorder**, there are ten personality disorders grouped into three **clusters**: cluster A (paranoid, schizotypal, and schizoid), cluster B (antisocial, borderline, histrionic, and narcissistic), and cluster C (avoidant, dependent, and obsessive–compulsive). Personality disorder criteria will continue changing over time; the DSM-5 includes a section specifically devoted to research models for redefining personality disorders.

Cluster A (Paranoid, Schizotypal, and Schizoid Personality Disorders)

The cluster A personality disorders are all marked by behavior that is labeled as odd or eccentric by others. Its three examples include paranoid, schizotypal, and schizoid personality disorders.

Paranoid personality disorder is marked by a pervasive distrust of others and suspicion regarding their motives. In some cases, these patients may actually be in the prodromal phase of schizophrenia and are termed premorbid.

Mnemonic

The three **W**s of personality disorders:
Cluster A—"**W**eird"
Cluster B—"**W**ild"
Cluster C—"**W**orried"

Schizotypal personality disorder refers to a pattern of odd or eccentric thinking. These individuals may have **ideas of reference** (similar to delusions of reference, but not as extreme in intensity) as well as **magical thinking**, such as superstitiousness or a belief in clairvoyance.

Finally, **schizoid personality disorder** is a pervasive pattern of detachment from social relationships and a restricted range of emotional expression. People with this disorder show little desire for social interactions; have few, if any, close friends; and have poor social skills. It should be noted that neither schizotypal nor schizoid personality disorder are the same as schizophrenia.

Cluster B (Antisocial, Borderline, Histrionic, and Narcissistic Personality Disorders)

The cluster B personality disorders are all marked by behavior that is labeled as dramatic, emotional, or erratic by others. Its four examples include antisocial, borderline, histrionic, and narcissistic personality disorders.

Antisocial personality disorder is three times more common in males than in females. The essential feature of the disorder is a pattern of disregard for and violations of the rights of others. This is evidenced by repeated illegal acts, deceitfulness, aggressiveness, or a lack of remorse for said actions. Many serial killers and career criminals who show no guilt for their actions have this disorder. Additionally, people with this disorder comprise about 20 to 40 percent of prison populations.

Borderline personality disorder is two times more common in females than in males. In this disorder, there is pervasive instability in interpersonal behavior, mood, and self-image. Interpersonal relationships are often intense and unstable. There may be profound identity disturbance with uncertainty about self-image, sexual identity, long-term goals, or values. There is often intense fear of abandonment. Individuals with borderline personality disorder may use **splitting** as a defense mechanism, in which they view others as either all good or all bad (an *angel vs. devil* mentality). Suicide attempts and self-mutilation (cutting or burning) are common.

Histrionic personality disorder is characterized by constant attention-seeking behavior. These individuals often wear colorful clothing, are dramatic, and are exceptionally extroverted. They may also use seductive behavior to gain attention.

In **narcissistic personality disorder**, one has a grandiose sense of self-importance or uniqueness, preoccupation with fantasies of success, a need for constant admiration and attention, and characteristic disturbances in interpersonal relationships such as feelings of entitlement. As used in everyday language, narcissism refers to those who like themselves too much. However, people with narcissistic personality disorder have very fragile self-esteem and are constantly concerned with how others view them. There may be marked feelings of rage, inferiority, shame, humiliation, or emptiness when these individuals are not viewed favorably by others.

Cluster C (Avoidant, Dependent, and Obsessive–Compulsive Personality Disorders)

The cluster C personality disorders are all marked by behavior that is labeled as anxious or fearful by others. Its three examples include avoidant, dependent, and obsessive–compulsive personality disorders.

In **avoidant personality disorder**, the affected individual has extreme shyness and fear of rejection. The individual will see herself as socially inept and is often socially isolated, despite an intense desire for social affection and acceptance. These individuals tend to stay in the same jobs, life situations, and relationships despite wanting to change.

Dependent personality disorder is characterized by a continuous need for reassurance. Individuals with dependent personality disorder tend to remain dependent on one specific person, such as a parent or significant other, to take actions and make decisions.

In **obsessive–compulsive personality disorder (OCPD)**, the individual is perfectionistic and inflexible, tending to like rules and order. Other characteristics may include an inability to discard worn-out objects, lack of desire to change, excessive stubbornness, lack of a sense of humor, and maintenance of careful routines. Note that obsessive–compulsive personality disorder is not the same as obsessive–compulsive disorder. Whereas OCD has obsessions and compulsions that are focal and acquired, OCPD is lifelong. OCD is also ego-dystonic (*I can't stop washing my hands because of the germs!*), whereas OCPD is ego-syntonic (*I just like rules and order!*).

> ## Key Concept
>
> Obsessive–compulsive disorder (OCD) and obsessive–compulsive personality disorder (OCPD) are not synonymous. OCD is marked by obsessions (intrusive thoughts causing tension) and compulsions (repetitive tasks that relieve this tension but cause significant impairment). OCPD is a personality disorder in which individuals are perfectionistic and inflexible.

MCAT Concept Check 7.2:

Before you move on, assess your understanding of the material with these questions.

1. What are the major positive symptoms of schizophrenia? What are the major negative symptoms?

   - Positive symptoms:

     _____

   - Negative symptoms:

     _____

2. What are the features of a major depressive episode? Of a manic episode?

   • Major depressive episode:

   _____

   _____

   • Manic episode:

   _____

   _____

3. For each of the following disorders, briefly describe their makeup with respect to depressive episodes, manic episodes, and other mood disturbances:

   • Major depressive disorder:

   _____

   • Bipolar I disorder:

   _____

   • Bipolar II disorder:

   _____

   • Cyclothymic disorder:

   _____

4. What are obsessions and compulsions? How are they related in obsessive–compulsive disorder?

   • Obsessions:

   _____

   • Compulsions:

   _____

   • Relationship:

   _____

5. What features describe each cluster of personality disorders? Which personality disorders fall into each cluster?

Cluster	Features	Personality Disorders
A		
B		
C		

7.3 Biological Basis of Nervous System Disorders

LEARNING GOALS

After Chapter 7.3, you will be able to:

- Describe the impact of depression on hormone and neurotransmitter levels
- Recall the general features and risk factors for Alzheimer's disease
- Explain the role of dopamine in schizophrenia and Parkinson's disease

In addition to knowing the psychological and sociological components of these diagnoses, the MCAT also expects you to know the biological basis of a few mental disorders. These disorders include schizophrenia, depression, Alzheimer's disease, and Parkinson's disease. Research into how to stop the progression of the biological component of these diseases is widespread and will also be something to stay apprised of as a medical student and a physician.

SCHIZOPHRENIA

Schizophrenia is an area of active research, though some biological factors have been isolated. Most potential causes are genetic, but trauma at birth, especially hypoxemia (low oxygen concentrations in the blood), is also considered to be a risk factor. Other exposures may also play a role; excessive marijuana use in adolescence is associated with increased risk. There is significant data to indicate that schizophrenia is partially inherited. If a person has this disorder, the risk that his or her first-degree relatives will also have the disorder is ten times that of an unrelated person in the general population; this measurement controls for environmental effects.

Schizophrenia may be associated with structural changes in the brain, but more research is needed to determine their significance and prevalence within the affected population. Schizophrenia is highly associated with an excess of dopamine in the brain; many medications used to treat schizophrenia, such as **neuroleptics**, block dopamine receptors. The term neuroleptic (also referred to as **antipsychotic**) arises from the side effects of these medications, which tend to include sedation.

DEPRESSIVE AND BIPOLAR DISORDERS

There are a host of markers associated with depression:

- Abnormally high glucose metabolism in the amygdala

- Hippocampal atrophy after a long duration of illness

- Abnormally high levels of glucocorticoids (cortisol)

- Decreased norepinephrine, serotonin, and dopamine (monoamine theory of depression)

It has been found that both these neurotransmitters and their metabolites are decreased, meaning that their actual production is decreased (rather than production staying the same and their degradation increasing).

For bipolar disorders, there exists a different set of biological factors and genetic corollaries that contribute to the disease:

- Increased norepinephrine and serotonin (monoamine theory)

- Higher risk if parent has bipolar disorder

- Higher risk for persons with multiple sclerosis

ALZHEIMER'S DISEASE

Alzheimer's disease is a type of dementia characterized by gradual memory loss, disorientation to time and place, problems with abstract thought, and a tendency to misplace things. Later stages of the disease are associated with changes in mood or behavior, changes in personality, difficulty with procedural memory, poor judgment, and loss of initiative. Now, each of these symptoms alone doesn't necessarily point to Alzheimer's; however, when all or almost all of these symptoms are seen in one person, and especially when the symptoms end up inhibiting normal daily function, this points to Alzheimer's disease. This disease is most common in patients older than 65, and women are at greater risk than men. Family history is a significant risk factor and, interestingly, there is a lower risk of developing disease with higher levels of education.

There is a genetic component to Alzheimer's disease. Research shows that mutations in the *presenilin* genes on chromosomes 1 and 14 contribute to having the disease, and mutations in the *apolipoprotein E* gene on chromosome 19 can also alter the likelihood of acquiring the disease. Finally, the *β-amyloid precursor protein* gene on chromosome 21 is known to contribute to Alzheimer's disease, explaining the much higher risk of Alzheimer's in individuals with Down syndrome.

While the precise biological cause of Alzheimer's disease is unknown, there are many biological markers that are found in patients with the disease. Don't worry about understanding each of these markers in depth, but rather be able to recognize these factors if you see them on the MCAT:

- Diffuse atrophy of the brain on CT or MRI
- Flattened sulci in the cerebral cortex
- Enlarged cerebral ventricles, shown in Figure 7.4a
- Deficient blood flow in parietal lobes, which is correlated with cognitive decline
- Reduction in levels of acetylcholine
- Reduction in *choline acetyltransferase* (ChAT), the enzyme that produces acetylcholine
- Reduced metabolism in temporal and parietal lobes
- Senile plaques of **β-amyloid** (a misfolded protein in β-pleated sheet form), shown in Figure 7.4b
- Neurofibrillary tangles of hyperphosphorylated tau protein, shown in Figure 7.4c

Figure 7.4(a). Findings of Alzheimer's Disease
Enlarged cerebral ventricles (left) *vs.* normal cerebral ventricles (right).

Figure 7.4(b). Findings of Alzheimer's Disease
Formation of senile plaques of β-amyloid.

Figure 7.4(c). Findings of Alzheimer's Disease
Neurofibrillary tangles of hyperphosphorylated tau protein (magenta).

PARKINSON'S DISEASE

Parkinson's disease, demonstrated in Figure 7.5, is characterized by **bradykinesia** (slowness in movement), **resting tremor** (a tremor that appears when muscles are not being used), **pill-rolling tremor** (flexing and extending the fingers while moving the thumb back and forth, as if rolling something in the fingers), **masklike facies** (a facial expression consisting of static and expressionless facial features, staring eyes, and a partially open mouth), **cogwheel rigidity** (muscle tension that intermittently halts movement as an examiner attempts to manipulate a limb), and a **shuffling gait** with stooped posture. A common but not characteristic symptom is depression. Dementia is also common in Parkinson's disease.

Figure 7.5. Findings of Parkinson's Disease
Note the masklike facies, shuffling gait, and stooped posture.

The biological basis of this disease is decreased dopamine production in the **substantia nigra**, a layer of cells in the brain that functions to produce dopamine to permit proper functioning of the **basal ganglia**, as shown in Figure 7.6. The basal ganglia are critical for initiating and terminating movements, as well as sustaining repetitive motor tasks and smoothening motions; thus, the symptoms of Parkinson's disease flow logically from its underlying cause. This condition can be partially managed, therefore, with **L-DOPA**, a precursor that is converted to dopamine once in the brain, replacing that which is lost due to Parkinson's disease. There have also been attempts to regenerate dopaminergic neurons in the substantia nigra using stem cells placed into the central nervous system. Similar stem cell-based therapies have been used in other contexts, such as after a spinal cord injury or stroke to attempt to regenerate function in the central nervous system, with limited results.

Figure 7.6. The Basal Ganglia
The substantia nigra in the midbrain (black) releases dopamine to activate the other regions of the basal ganglia (blue, red, and yellow).

Real World

Note the connection between schizophrenia and psychosis (caused by an excess of dopamine) and Parkinson's disease (caused by a deficit of dopamine). Antipsychotic medications often lead to "parkinsonian" side effects, like muscle rigidity and flattened affect. Medications used in Parkinson's disease often lead to psychotic side effects, such as hallucinations and delusions.

MCAT Concept Check 7.3:

Before you move on, assess your understanding of the material with these questions.

1. Which hormone and neurotransmitter concentrations are elevated in depression? Which ones are reduced?

   - Elevated:

     _____

   - Reduced:

     _____

2. Provide an example of a genetic factor that appears to increase risk of Alzheimer's disease.

   _____

3. How are dopamine levels related in schizophrenia and Parkinson's disease?

   _____

Conclusion

The content covered in this chapter will allow you to score more points on the MCAT—and to prepare for your clinical clerkships in psychiatry. This chapter is unique in that it covers not how the mind normally works, as we see in the other chapters in this book, but rather how the mind works when it is functioning abnormally. The MCAT tests critical thinking; one common way to do this is to ask what happens when a system—like the mind—is not functioning normally. Thus, this chapter covered very high-yield information that is very likely to appear on the MCAT because it connects all three subjects of the *Psychological, Social, and Biological Foundations of Behavior* section. In the next chapter, we move away from the individual as we begin to explore social psychology; from there, we'll continue expanding outward as we move into sociology.

CONCEPT SUMMARY

Understanding Psychological Disorders

- The **biomedical approach** to psychological disorders takes into account only the physical and medical causes of a psychological disorder. Thus, treatments in this approach are of a biomedical nature.

- The **biopsychosocial approach** considers the relative contributions of biological, psychological, and social components to an individual's disorder. Treatments also fall into these three areas.

- The *Diagnostic and Statistical Manual of Mental Disorders* is used to diagnose psychological disorders. Its current version is DSM-5 (published May 2013). It categorizes mental disorders based on symptom patterns.

- Psychological disorders, especially anxiety, depressive, and substance use disorders, are very common in the population.

Types of Psychological Disorders

- **Schizophrenia** is the prototypical disorder with psychosis as a feature. It contains positive and negative symptoms.
  - o **Positive symptoms** add something to behavior, cognition, or affect and include delusions, hallucinations, disorganized speech, and disorganized behavior.
  - o **Negative symptoms** are the loss of something from behavior, cognition, or affect and include disturbance of affect and avolition.

- **Depressive disorders** include major depressive disorder and seasonal affective disorder.
  - o **Major depressive disorder** contains at least one major depressive episode.
  - o **Persistent depressive disorder** is **dysthymia** for at least two years that does not meet criteria for major depressive disorder.
  - o **Seasonal affective disorder** is the colloquial name for major depressive disorder with seasonal onset, with depression occurring during winter months.

- **Bipolar and related disorders** have manic or hypomanic episodes.
  - o **Bipolar I disorder** contains at least one manic episode.
  - o **Bipolar II disorder** contains at least one hypomanic episode and at least one major depressive episode.
  - o **Cyclothymic disorder** contains hypomanic episodes with dysthymia.

- **Anxiety disorders** include generalized anxiety disorder, specific phobias, social anxiety disorder, agoraphobia, and panic disorder.
  - o **Generalized anxiety disorder** is a disproportionate and persistent worry about many different things for at least six months.
  - o **Specific phobias** are irrational fears of specific objects or situations.

- ○ **Social anxiety disorder** is anxiety due to social or performance situations.

- ○ **Agoraphobia** is a fear of places or situations where it is hard for an individual to escape.

- ○ **Panic disorder** is marked by recurrent panic attacks: intense, overwhelming fear and sympathetic nervous system activity with no clear stimulus. It may lead to agoraphobia.

- **Obsessive–compulsive disorder** is characterized by **obsessions** (persistent, intrusive thoughts and impulses) and **compulsions** (repetitive tasks that relieve tension but cause significant impairment in a person's life).

- **Body dysmorphic disorder** is characterized by an unrealistic negative evaluation of one's appearance or a specific body part. The individual often takes extreme measures to correct the perceived imperfection.

- **Posttraumatic stress disorder** (**PTSD**) is characterized by intrusion symptoms (reliving the event, flashbacks, nightmares), avoidance symptoms (avoidance of people, places, objects associated with trauma), negative cognitive symptoms (amnesia, negative mood and emotions), and arousal symptoms (increased startle response, irritability, anxiety).

- **Dissociative disorders** include dissociative amnesia, dissociative identity disorder, and depersonalization/derealization disorder.

  - ○ **Dissociative amnesia** is an inability to recall past experience without an underlying neurological disorder. In severe forms, it may involve **dissociative fugue**, a sudden change in location that may involve the assumption of a new identity.

  - ○ **Dissociative identity disorder** is the occurrence of two or more personalities that take control of a person's behavior.

  - ○ **Depersonalization/derealization disorder** involves feelings of detachment from the mind and body or from the environment.

- **Somatic symptom and related disorders** involve significant bodily symptoms.

  - ○ **Somatic symptom disorder** involves at least one somatic symptom, which may or may not be linked to an underlying medical condition, that causes disproportionate concern.

  - ○ **Illness anxiety disorder** is a preoccupation with thoughts about having, or coming down with, a serious medical condition.

  - ○ **Conversion disorder** involves unexplained symptoms affecting motor or sensory function and is associated with prior trauma.

- **Personality disorders** (**PD**) are patterns of inflexible, maladaptive behavior that cause distress or impaired functioning in at least two of the following: cognition, emotions, interpersonal functioning, or impulse control. They occur in three **clusters**: **A** (odd, eccentric, "weird"), **B** (dramatic, emotional, erratic, "wild"), and **C** (anxious, fearful, "worried").

- o Cluster A includes paranoid, schizotypal, and schizoid PDs. Cluster B includes antisocial, borderline, histrionic, and narcissistic PDs. Cluster C includes avoidant, dependent, and obsessive–compulsive PDs.
- o **Paranoid PD** involves a pervasive distrust and suspicion of others.
- o **Schizotypal PD** involves ideas of reference, magical thinking, and eccentricity.
- o **Schizoid PD** involves detachment from social relationships and limited emotion.
- o **Antisocial PD** involves a disregard for the rights of others.
- o **Borderline PD** involves instability in relationships, mood, and self-image. **Splitting** is characteristic, as are recurrent suicide attempts.
- o **Histrionic PD** involves constant attention-seeking behavior.
- o **Narcissistic PD** involves a grandiose sense of self-importance and need for admiration.
- o **Avoidant PD** involves extreme shyness and fear of rejection.
- o **Dependent PD** involves a continuous need for reassurance.
- o **Obsessive–compulsive PD** involves perfectionism, inflexibility, and pre-occupation with rules.

Biological Basis of Nervous System Disorders

- Schizophrenia may be associated with genetic factors, birth trauma, adolescent marijuana use, and family history. There are high levels of dopaminergic transmission.

- Depression is accompanied by high levels of glucocorticoids and low levels of norepinephrine, serotonin, and dopamine.

- Bipolar disorders are accompanied by high levels of norepinephrine and serotonin. They are also highly heritable.

- Alzheimer's disease is associated with genetic factors, brain atrophy, decreases in acetylcholine, senile plaques of β-**amyloid**, and **neurofibrillary tangles** of hyperphosphorylated tau protein.

- **Parkinson's disease** is associated with **bradykinesia**, **resting tremor**, **pill-rolling tremor**, **masklike facies**, **cogwheel rigidity**, and a **shuffling gait**. There is decreased production of dopamine by cells in the **substantia nigra**.

ANSWERS TO CONCEPT CHECKS

7.1

1. Whereas the biomedical model considers only the physical, pathological mechanisms that underlie mental illness, the biopsychosocial model considers the contributions of these biological factors along with psychology (thoughts, emotions, or behaviors) and social situation (environment, social class, discrimination, or stigmatization).

2. The following disorders occur in greater than 2 percent of the United States population per year: specific phobia, social anxiety disorder, major depressive disorder, alcohol use disorder, posttraumatic stress disorder, generalized anxiety disorder, panic disorder, and bipolar disorder

7.2

1. Positive symptoms of schizophrenia include delusions, hallucinations (usually auditory), disorganized thought, and disorganized behavior. Negative symptoms include disturbance of affect and avolition.

2. Major depressive episodes include a two-week duration of at least five of the following symptoms: depressed mood, loss of interest (anhedonia), sleep disturbance, feelings of guilt, lack of energy, difficulty concentrating, changes in appetite, psychomotor symptoms, and suicidal thoughts. At least one of the symptoms must be depressed mood or anhedonia. Manic episodes include a one-week duration of at least three of the following symptoms: elevated or expansive mood, distractibility, decreased need for sleep, grandiosity, flight of ideas or racing thoughts, agitation, pressured speech, and engagement in risky behavior.

3. Major depressive disorder contains at least one major depressive episode with no manic episodes. Bipolar I disorder has at least one manic episode with or without depressive episodes. Bipolar II disorder has at least one hypomanic episode with at least one major depressive episode. Cyclothymic disorder has hypomanic episodes and dysthymia that is not severe enough to be a major depressive episode.

4. Obsessions are persistent, intrusive thoughts and impulses that produce tension. Compulsions are repetitive tasks that relieve tension but cause significant impairment in a person's life. Obsessions raise tension while compulsions relieve that tension.

5.

Cluster	Features	Personality Disorders
A	Odd or eccentric ("weird")	Paranoid, schizotypal, schizoid
B	Dramatic, emotional, or erratic ("wild")	Antisocial, borderline, histrionic, narcissistic
C	Anxious or fearful ("worried")	Avoidant, dependent, obsessive–compulsive

7.3

1. In depression, levels of cortisol are increased. Many neurotransmitter levels are reduced, including norepinephrine, serotonin, and dopamine.

2. Mutations in the presenilin genes (chromosomes 1 and 14) and β-amyloid precursor protein gene (chromosome 21) are associated with increased risk for Alzheimer's disease.

3. Dopamine levels are elevated in schizophrenia and reduced in Parkinson's disease. Thus, treatments for one disorder may cause symptoms similar to those of the other.

SHARED CONCEPTS

Behavioral Sciences Chapter 1
Biology and Behavior

Behavioral Sciences Chapter 3
Learning and Memory

Behavioral Sciences Chapter 12
Social Stratification

Biology Chapter 4
The Nervous System

Biology Chapter 5
The Endocrine System

Biology Chapter 12
Genetics and Evolution

Discrete Practice Questions

Consult your online resources for Full-Length Exams and Passage-Based Questions (for certain chapters).

1. Which of the following is an example of a negative symptom seen in schizophrenia?

    A. Auditory hallucinations
    B. Disorganized behavior
    C. Disturbance of affect
    D. Delusions

2. During an interview with a schizophrenic patient, a psychiatrist notices that the patient keeps repeating what the psychiatrist says. This phenomenon is known as:

    A. echolalia.
    B. echopraxia.
    C. loosening of associations.
    D. neologisms.

3. A 42-year-old woman has always been extremely neat and tidy. She works as a secretary and stays long after normal working hours to check the punctuation and spelling of letters she prepared during the day. Her boss referred her for counseling after she repeatedly got into fights with her coworkers. "They don't take the job to heart," she says. "They just joke around all day." The most likely preliminary diagnosis for this patient is:

    A. obsessive–compulsive personality disorder.
    B. antisocial personality disorder.
    C. narcissistic personality disorder.
    D. borderline personality disorder.

4. Which of the following is true with regard to a major depressive episode?

    A. It may last less than two weeks.
    B. It must involve thoughts of suicide or a suicide attempt.
    C. It may involve a decrease in sleep.
    D. It must involve feelings of sadness.

5. A 36-year-old who works from home is referred for evaluation. He is reluctant to venture out to meet with other people and rarely has people in to visit. When selected for a company-wide award, he refused to have his picture taken for the company newsletter. During an assessment, he averts his face and asks the examiner to "stop looking at me." Although he is average in appearance, he is convinced that his face is ugly and misshapen. The most likely diagnosis for this man would be:

    A. schizophrenia.
    B. obsessive–compulsive disorder.
    C. body dysmorphic disorder.
    D. schizoid personality disorder.

6. A young woman of unknown age is brought by the Philadelphia police to the local emergency department for evaluation after they found her wandering in a park. She carries no purse or identification. She is unable to state her name or any details about her life, except that the name Phoenix seems familiar. The police in Arizona are contacted and find a missing persons report matching the patient's description. Based on this information, the most likely diagnosis for this patient is:

    A. depersonalization/derealization disorder.
    B. dissociative identity disorder.
    C. somatic symptom disorder.
    D. dissociative amnesia with dissociative fugue.

7. In addition to being a freestanding diagnosis, agoraphobia is most often seen in association with which other psychiatric diagnosis?

    A. Obsessive–compulsive disorder
    B. Avoidant personality disorder
    C. Generalized anxiety disorder
    D. Panic disorder

8. A 28-year-old male comes to a clinic concerned that he has pancreatic cancer. Review of his medical records shows that this is the fourth time in the past year that the patient has appeared for medical attention. No identifiable medical problem is found. When confronted with this history, he confesses that he feels relieved after being told that all of the tests are negative, but soon becomes worried again that he has cancer. Based on the information, the most likely diagnosis for this patient would be:

   A. major depressive disorder.
   B. illness anxiety disorder.
   C. conversion disorder.
   D. narcissistic personality disorder.

Questions 9–10 refer to the scenario described below.

A physician is attempting to diagnose a patient's mental disorder based on a set of symptoms. The confirmed symptoms currently include appetite disturbance, substantial weight change, decreased energy, a feeling of worthlessness, and excessive guilt.

9. What two disorders could these symptoms indicate?

   A. Major depressive and bipolar disorders
   B. Dissociative amnesia and depersonalization/derealization disorder
   C. Alzheimer's disease and Parkinson's disease
   D. Specific phobia and panic disorder

10. What should the physician ask about to distinguish between the two possible disorders affecting that patient?

   A. Whether the patient has amnesia
   B. Whether the patient has also had manic episodes
   C. Whether the patient is irrationally afraid of anything
   D. Whether the patient has experienced difficulty performing familiar tasks

11. A mother notices that her teenage son seems to have a phobia for snakes. In the past week, on several occasions, the teenager has had more severe fear symptoms than usual, without seeing or even thinking about a snake. Which mental disorder could cause this reaction?

   A. Schizophrenia
   B. Antisocial personality disorder
   C. Obsessive–compulsive disorder
   D. Panic disorder

12. Splitting is a defense mechanism commonly seen with which personality disorder?

   A. Antisocial personality disorder
   B. Borderline personality disorder
   C. Histrionic personality disorder
   D. Narcissistic personality disorder

13. A woman comes to the doctor with a two-week history of complete paralysis of her left arm. She has had no injury to the extremity, and full neurological workup fails to demonstrate any underlying cause. She seems surprisingly unconcerned about the paralysis, and seems more worried about an argument she had one month ago in which she hit her daughter. Based on this information, the woman's most likely diagnosis is:

   A. conversion disorder.
   B. generalized anxiety disorder.
   C. illness anxiety disorder.
   D. histrionic personality disorder.

14. A woman notices that her father has started to move his fingers in such a way that it looks like he is rolling something, despite nothing actually being there. She also notes slowed movement and a shuffling gait. Which neurotransmitter is likely to be present in decreased levels in her father's brain?

   A. Epinephrine
   B. Histamine
   C. Dopamine
   D. Serotonin

15. Which of the following is/are true regarding bipolar disorders?

   I. They have little, if any, genetic heritability.
   II. They are associated with increased levels of serotonin in the brain.
   III. They all require at least one depressive episode for diagnosis.

   A. I only
   B. II only
   C. I and III only
   D. II and III only

Explanations to Discrete Practice Questions

1. C

Negative symptoms are the absence of normal or desired behavior, which include disturbance of affect and avolition. Positive symptoms are the addition of abnormal behavior, including hallucinations, **choice (A)**, disorganized behavior, **choice (B)**, and delusions, **choice (D)**.

2. A

Echolalia is an involuntary repetition of others' words and utterances and may be seen in schizophrenia. Echopraxia, **choice (B)**, is imitation of others' actions. Loosening of associations, **choice (C)**, is a type of disordered thought in which the patient moves between remotely related ideas. Neologisms, **choice (D)**, are newly invented words.

3. A

Focusing on details, loving routine, having a sense that there is only one right way to do things, and lack of humor suggests an obsessive–compulsive personality disorder.

4. C

Depression is marked by a period of at least two weeks in which the patient has five of nine cardinal symptoms, one of which must be depressed mood or lack of interest (anhedonia). While decreased need for sleep is commonly seen in manic episodes, it may also appear in depression as sleep disturbance is one of the nine cardinal symptoms. Not all depressed individuals are suicidal, as in **choice (B)**. In older men, depression may often manifest as anhedonia without feelings of sadness, invalidating **choice (D)**.

5. C

The central issue is the negative appraisal of his own appearance, indicating body dysmorphic disorder. Thus, it is likely that all other symptoms this patient is experiencing arise from this disorder. The other disorders listed in the answer choices cannot explain all the symptoms.

6. D

Dissociative fugue is characterized by sudden travel or change in normal day-to-day activities and occurs in some cases of dissociative amnesia. Symptoms include an inability to recall one's past or confusion about one's identity.

7. D

Agoraphobia, or a fear of places or situations in which it would be difficult to escape, is commonly seen in panic disorder. Concern about having a panic attack in public may make these individuals fearful of leaving their home.

8. B

In illness anxiety disorder, the person is preoccupied with fears that he has—or will come down with—a serious disease, and these fears continue even after medical exams and tests have returned negative results.

9. A

The symptoms listed indicate a major depressive episode. However, depressive episodes can be a part of bipolar disorders, which also contain manic episodes. Thus, if manic episodes have not yet been asked about, one cannot choose depression or bipolar disorder as the correct diagnosis yet.

10. B

To determine if this patient has major depressive disorder or a bipolar disorder, the presence of manic (or hypomanic) episodes should be confirmed. Bipolar disorders contain manic (or hypomanic) episodes, while major depressive disorder does not.

11. D

Exhibiting signs of panic and irrational fear without any instigating object present indicates panic disorder. The teenager may have diagnoses of both specific phobia (for snakes) and panic disorder.

12. B

Splitting, the consideration of others as either "all good" or "all bad," is characteristic of borderline personality disorder.

13. A

Conversion disorder is marked by a motor or sensory symptom in the absence of an underlying physical or neurological cause. It is associated with an inciting event that, in this case, may have been the argument with her daughter. Her lack of concern over the deficit is referred to as *la belle indifférence*.

14. C

The symptoms indicate that the woman's father likely has Parkinson's disease. This disease is caused by decreased dopamine production in the substantia nigra.

15. B

Bipolar disorders have been shown to be highly heritable and are associated with increased levels of norepinephrine and serotonin in the brain. Bipolar I disorder can be diagnosed with a single manic episode and does not require a major depressive episode. Bipolar II disorder requires at least one hypomanic episode and one major depressive episode. Cyclothymic disorder contains at least one hypomanic episode and dysthymia.

8

Social Processes, Attitudes, and Behavior

In This Chapter

Chapter Profile

The content in this chapter should be relevant to about 8% of all questions about the Behavioral Sciences on the MCAT.

This chapter covers material from the following AAMC content categories:

7A: Individual influences on behavior

7B: Social processes that influence human behavior

7C: Attitude and behavior change

Introduction

The renowned Italian painter and sculptor Michelangelo Buonarroti stated that a sculptor simply releases and uncovers the ideal figures that are hidden within stone. This idea has led psychologists and sociologists to describe what is known as the **Michelangelo phenomenon**. The concept of self is made up of both the intrapersonal self, the ideas an individual has regarding his or her own abilities, traits, and beliefs, and the interpersonal self, the manner in which others influence creation of the ideal self. Analogous to what Michelangelo believed, the ideal self can thus be "sculpted" with help from others.

In this chapter, you will learn about the social processes and interactions that develop this self. The behavior and attitudes of individuals are highly influenced by the people with whom they interact, the society in which they live, and the culture in which they are immersed. Humans, being naturally social creatures, learn how to behave and react based on their relationships and experiences. The following pages will give us an in-depth look at the patterns in which behavior is affected by the presence of others, group processes, culture, and socialization, as well as how attitudes are formed and how they impact behavior.

8.1 Group Psychology

LEARNING GOALS

After Chapter 8.1, you will be able to:

- Describe social facilitation, deindividuation, the bystander effect, social loafing, and peer pressure
- Compare and contrast group polarization and groupthink
- Distinguish between assimilation and multiculturalism

Understanding social processes and interaction has long been a goal of sociologists, notably Max Weber, who was one of the first sociologists to study this interaction. Weber attempted to understand and describe **social action**, which he defined as actions and behaviors that individuals are conscious of and performing because others are around. The idea is that humans will behave in different ways based on their social environment and how their behavior will affect those around them. If individuals predict a negative reaction from those around them, they will often modify their behavior.

SOCIAL ACTION

Social action should be contrasted with social interaction. Social action considers just the individual that is surrounded by others. When examining social interaction, we will look at the behavior and actions of two or more individuals who take one another into account.

Social Facilitation

It has been observed that people tend to perform better on simple tasks when in the presence of others. This tendency is known as **social facilitation**, and it supports the idea that people naturally exhibit a performance response when they know they are being watched. Although being in the presence of others does not necessarily constitute an evaluation, the theory suggests that performance sparks a perceived evaluation in the individual performing. According to the **Yerkes–Dodson law of social facilitation**, being in the presence of others will significantly raise arousal, which enhances the ability to perform tasks one is already good at (or **simple tasks**), and hinders the performance of less familiar tasks (or **complex tasks**). For example, an expert pianist may perform better in concert than when alone in practice sessions. However, someone with very limited knowledge of music would perform worse in a social setting than when alone. This is demonstrated in Figure 8.1.

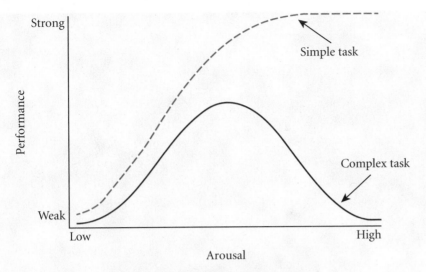

Figure 8.1.   Yerkes–Dodson Law

Note the difference between Figure 5.2 and Figure 8.1. Whereas Figure 5.2 focuses solely on new or less-familiar tasks, Figure 8.1 also includes simple tasks, which are not adversely affected by heightened arousal. Social facilitation reflects the idea that performance is not solely influenced by individual ability, but also by social environment and awareness of that environment.

Deindividuation

Deindividuation is another social phenomenon that occurs when individuals are in group settings. Individual behavior can be dramatically different in social environments. This is thought to be due to the presence of a large group that provides anonymity and causes a loss of individual identity. Deindividuation can also lead to **antinormative behavior**, or behavior against the norm. This aspect of deindividuation attempts to provide an explanation for violent behavior seen in crowds and riots: In group settings, the individual loses his sense of individuality and becomes an anonymous part of a group. With anonymity, he is more likely to act in a manner that is inconsistent with his normal self. This is further enhanced when the group is in uniform or masked, disguising the individual within the group and increasing anonymity, as shown in Figure 8.2.

Bridge

The Yerkes–Dodson law is also used to describe the relationship between stress or sympathetic arousal and performance. Just as social facilitation can enhance the ability to perform tasks, so can moderate levels of arousal. Arousal can also be an effect of being surrounded by others and feeling pressure to perform: if there's too much pressure, performance drops. Motivation and stress are discussed in Chapter 5 of *MCAT Behavioral Sciences Review*.

Figure 8.2. Deindividuation
Being masked or in uniform facilitates anonymity in a crowd.

Bystander Effect

The **bystander effect** is another observed phenomenon that occurs in social groups wherein individuals do not intervene to help victims when others are present. It has been shown that the likelihood and timeliness of response is inversely related to the number of bystanders. In other words, the more people standing by, the less likely any one of those people is to help. There are several factors at play in the bystander effect. First, when in groups, people are less likely to notice danger or anything out of the ordinary. This is thought to be due in part to social etiquette, in that it can be considered rude to watch others and their surroundings. Additionally, when in groups, humans take cues from others. If other people are not responding to a situation, an individual is less likely to perceive the situation as a threat or emergency. The degree of emergency or the danger to the victim plays a role in response. In low-danger scenarios, bystanders are less likely to provide aid; in high-danger scenarios, bystanders are more likely to intervene. Another factor is the degree of responsibility felt by the bystander. This is determined by the competency of the bystander, his or her relationship to the victim, and whether he or she considers the victim to be deserving of aid. Finally, cohesiveness of the group has been shown to influence the responsiveness of the bystanders. In groups made up of strangers, the likelihood of response and speed of response is much slower than a group of well-acquainted individuals.

Social Loafing

Social loafing refers to the tendency of individuals to put in less effort when in a group setting than individually. This may apply in many contexts: physical effort, such as carrying a heavy object; mental effort, such as working on a group project; or initiative, such as coming up with the solution to a problem.

Peer Pressure

Peer pressure refers to the social influence placed on an individual by a group of people or another individual. From a sociology perspective, **peers** are considered individuals who are equals within a social group. In adolescence, peers play an extremely important role in determining lifestyle, appearance, and social activities. While parents and other adults provide the foundation for development of beliefs and values, peers become very important as teenagers become independent from their parental figures. The pressure exerted by peers can cause changes in behavior, attitudes, or beliefs to conform to the norms of the group. Still, peer pressure exists at all ages. This pressure can come in many forms, including religious ideals, appearance, values, drug use, and sexual behavior. It can be positive or negative; certain types of peer pressure can benefit the individual experiencing the influence. In children, social acceptance is associated with being most like the social norm of the group, regardless of positive or negative connotations.

The mechanism behind peer pressure has been explained by the **identity shift effect**. When an individual's state of harmony is disrupted by a threat of social rejection, the individual will often conform to the norms of the group. Upon doing so, however, the individual will begin to experience internal conflict because the behavior is outside the normal character of the individual. To eliminate the sense of internal conflict, the individual experiences an identify shift wherein the individual adopts the standards of the group as her own. The identity shift effect also highlights a larger theme in psychology: **cognitive dissonance**, the simultaneous presence of two opposing thoughts or opinions. This generally leads to an internal state of discomfort, which may manifest as anxiety, fear, anger, or confusion. Individuals will try to reduce this discomfort by changing, adding to, or minimizing one of these dissonant thoughts.

Solomon Asch's conformity experiment showed that individuals will often conform to an opinion held by the group. In this experiment, male college students participated in simple tasks of perception. The study was set up to have one individual who made observations in the presence of confederates, or actors who were pretending to be a part of the experiment. The point of the study was to examine if the behavior of the individual was influenced by the confederates. The participants were shown two cards like the ones in Figure 8.3. They were then asked to say aloud which line on the second card, labeled A, B, or C, matched the length of the line on the first card. Prior to the experiment, the confederates were secretly told to unanimously respond correctly or incorrectly to the question. When the confederates answered correctly, the error rate for the real participants was less than 1 percent. However, when the confederates answered incorrectly, it was seen that the real participants answered incorrectly up to one-third of the time. Thus, Asch concluded, individuals will sometimes provide answers they know to be untrue if it avoids going against the group: the urge toward conformity could outweigh the desire to provide the correct answer.

MCAT Expertise

The MCAT is unlikely to ask you about psychological experiments by name; however, you should be familiar with some of the landmark experiments in social psychology. For example, rather than directly referring to the Asch conformity experiment, the MCAT would likely include an experiment with similar features and ask you to draw conclusions from it.

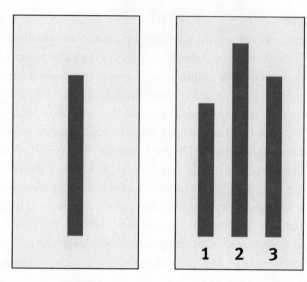

Figure 8.3. Example of Cards Used in the Asch Conformity Experiment

GROUP PROCESSES

In contrast to social action, **social interaction** explores the ways in which two or more individuals can both shape each other's behavior. These include group processes and establishment of culture.

Group Polarization

Group polarization describes the tendency for groups to make decisions that are more extreme than the individual ideas and inclinations of the members within the group. Thus, polarization can lead to riskier or more cautious decisions based on the initial tendencies of the group members toward risk or caution. This phenomenon has shown that individuals in group situations will form opinions that are more extreme than they would if making the same decision alone. The hypothesis underlying polarization is that initial ideas tend not to be extreme, but that through discussion within the group, these ideas tend to become more and more extreme. This concept was originally termed **risky shift** because it was noted that groups tended to make riskier decisions than individuals. However, when psychologists began to realize that groups could also shift toward caution, the term became **choice shift**. Choice shift and polarization refer to the same idea; however, polarization is used to describe behavior at the individual level, while choice shift describes the behavior change of the group as a whole.

Group polarization explains many real-life scenarios, including policy making, violence, and terrorism. For example, members of the same political party may espouse the same ideals and opinions in the group setting, but may waver slightly on issues when alone. This kind of polarization is also seen in jury deliberation. In the case of punitive damages (monetary penalties for a certain behavior), jurors that initially favor a high punishment may deliberate and decide upon an even higher punishment after discussion. As social media has exploded in recent decades, research has shown that the group does not necessarily need to be together physically in order for polarization to occur. Simply reading others' ideas on social media sites can result in more extreme ideas from individuals.

Groupthink

Groupthink refers to a social phenomenon in which desire for harmony or conformity results in a group of people coming to an incorrect or poor decision. In an attempt to eliminate or minimize conflict among the group members, consensus decisions are reached without alternative ideas being assessed. In these cases, the desire to agree with the group causes a loss of independent critical thinking. The group also begins to isolate and ignore external viewpoints, seeing their own ideas as correct without question.

Groupthink can have a large impact on group decision-making and is influenced by a variety of factors, including group cohesiveness, group structure, leadership, and situational context. Irving Janis conducted the first research on the theory in the 1970s. Janis studied the effect of extreme stress on group cohesiveness and its resulting effect on groupthink. Janis further investigated the decision-making of groups that had led to disastrous American foreign policy decisions, including the Bay of Pigs invasion. Janis specifically examined eight factors that are indicative of groupthink:

- **Illusion of invulnerability:** the creation of optimism and encouragement of risk-taking
- **Collective rationalization:** ignoring warnings against the ideas of the group
- **Illusion of morality:** the belief that the group's decisions are morally correct
- **Excessive stereotyping:** the construction of stereotypes against outside opinions
- **Pressure for conformity:** the pressure put on anyone in the group who expresses opinions against the group, viewing the opposition as disloyal
- **Self-censorship:** the withholding of opposing views
- **Illusion of unanimity:** the false sense of agreement within the group
- **Mindguards:** the appointment of members to the role of protecting against opposing views

Many of these factors, including illusion of morality, excessive stereotyping, pressure for conformity, and mindguards can be seen in Figure 8.4, a poster from the United States during the McCarthy era, which argues against public health measures (water fluoridation and polio vaccines) and equates anti-Semitism with lunacy for fear of Communist influence.

Figure 8.4. Groupthink as Seen in McCarthy-Era Propaganda

Similar patterns of thinking, in which a group arrives at a common (but often extreme) consensus also underlie many cultural phenomena, including riots, fads, and mass hysteria. Antinormative behavior in riots was described previously in the section on deindividuation. Still, like groupthink, a shared political or social motivation may urge groups to engage in potentially violent and destructive behavior. A **fad** is a behavior that is transiently viewed as popular and desirable by a large community. Fads can include owning certain objects (such as pet rocks in the 1970s, Rubik's cubes in the 1980s, and pogs in the 1990s) or engaging in certain behaviors (using catchphrases, altering clothing in some way, or engaging in particular types of media such as viral videos). Finally, **mass hysteria** refers to a shared, intense concern about the threats to society. In mass hysteria, many features of groupthink—collective rationalization, illusion of morality, excessive stereotyping, and pressure for conformity, in particular—lead to a shared delusion that is augmented by distrust, rumors, propaganda, and fear mongering. Perhaps the most notable historical case of mass hysteria was the Salem witch trials in colonial Massachusetts, which led to the execution of twenty individuals for fears of witchcraft.

CULTURE

Culture can be defined as the beliefs, behaviors, actions, and characteristics of a group or society of people. Culture is learned by living within a society, observing behaviors and traits, and adopting them. Culture is also passed down from generation to generation. While a "cultured" individual is often thought of as someone who has knowledge of the arts and expensive taste, sociology considers all people to be cultured by living within a society and participating in its culture. Culture is universal throughout humanity; while many animals exhibit purely instinctual behavior, humans show variable behaviors based on the cultures in which they reside. For example, while all wolf mothers care for their pups in the same manner, human mothers show vast differences in their caretaking. In some cultures, children are breastfed for years, while in others, infants are breastfed for mere months or not at all. Some groups have multiple caregivers who are not the mother, while others allow only the mother to care for the child. Even within "American" culture, beliefs about the correct way to respond to infant crying varies dramatically: some groups instantly comfort a crying child, and others let them "cry it out." The beliefs held by an individual are typically based on learned behavior, expectations, and pressure from the group one is in. Cultural differences include everything from typical jobs, common dwellings, and diet to what time of day one eats and where one travels on vacation, if at all. When traveling outside of one's own society, these cultural differences can seem quite dramatic and are often referred to as **culture shock**.

Assimilation and Multiculturalism

Cultural **assimilation** is the process by which an individual's or group's behavior and culture begin to resemble that of another group. This can also mean that groups with different cultures begin to merge into one. Assimilation integrates

Real World

The Bay of Pigs Invasion and Cuban Missile Crisis were used by Janis as case studies. When JFK took over the White House, the administration inherited a CIA Cuban invasion plan, and it was accepted without critique. When Senator Fulbright and Secretary Schlesinger expressed objections, they were ignored by the Kennedy team. Over time, Fulbright and Schlesinger started to perform self-censorship. After the invasion, it was revealed that there were many inaccuracies in the CIA plan, including underestimation of the Cuban air force and the assumption that Castro would not have the ability to quell uprisings.

new aspects of a society and culture with old ones, transforming the culture itself. While one society melds into another, it is typically not an even blend. One group will generally have more power and influence than the other, resulting in more traits of that culture being displayed after transformation. In terms of immigrant assimilation, there are four primary factors that can be used to assess the completeness of assimilation: socioeconomic status, geographic distribution, language attainment, and intermarriage.

Assimilation can be slowed by the creation of **ethnic enclaves**, which are locations (usually neighborhoods) with a high concentration of one specific ethnicity, as shown in Figure 8.5. These are most common in urban areas and often have names like Chinatown or Little Italy.

Figure 8.5. An Ethnic Enclave
Entrance to Chinatown, Sydney Australia

Key Concept

- Assimilation—(usually uneven) merging of cultures; a melting pot
- Multiculturalism—celebration of coexisting cultures; a cultural mosaic

Multiculturalism refers to communities or societies containing multiple cultures. From a sociology perspective, multiculturalism encourages, respects, and celebrates cultural differences, as shown in Figure 8.6. This view can enhance cultural diversity and acceptance within society, which contrasts with the concept of assimilation. While multiculturalism is often described as a creating a *cultural mosaic*, or mixture of cultures and ethnic groups that coexist in society, assimilationism is described as creating a *melting pot*, or melting together of different elements of culture into one homogenous culture.

Figure 8.6. Multiculturalism
Multiculturalism may be celebrated through holidays and festivals, such as Harmony Day in Australia, shown here.

Subcultures

Subcultures refer to groups of people within a culture that distinguish themselves from the primary culture to which they belong. When studying subcultures, symbolic attachment to things such as clothing or music can differentiate the group from the majority. Subcultures can be formed based on race, gender, ethnicity, sexuality, and other differentiating factors from the whole of society.

Subcultures can be perceived as negative when they subvert the majority culture's definitions of normalcy. In the case of **counterculture**, the subculture group gravitates toward an identity that is at odds with the majority culture and deliberately opposes the prevailing social mores.

MCAT Concept Check 8.1:

Before you move on, assess your understanding of the material with these questions.

1. Provide a brief definition for the following social phenomena:

    *   Social facilitation:

        _____

    *   Deindividuation:

        _____

    *   Bystander effect:

        _____

    *   Social loafing:

        _____

    *   Peer pressure:

        _____

2. What are the similarities and differences between group polarization and groupthink?

    _____

3. What are the differences between assimilation and multiculturalism?

    _____

8.2 Socialization

High-Yield

LEARNING GOALS

After Chapter 8.2, you will be able to:

*   Distinguish between conformity, compliance, and obedience
*   Compare and contrast primary and secondary socialization
*   Describe compliance techniques, such as foot-in-the-door, door-in-the-face, lowball, and that's-not-all

More than any other animal, humans use social experiences to learn acceptable behavior in the society in which they live. Sociologists and psychologists use the term **socialization** when discussing the process of developing, inheriting, and spreading norms, customs, and beliefs. Individuals gain the knowledge, skills, habits, and behaviors that are necessary for inclusion in society. The views of society become the accepted viewpoints and are generally adopted by the individuals within it. The manner in which a society socializes its members is termed **cultural transmission** or **cultural learning**, and the spread of norms, customs, and beliefs (especially new ones) throughout the culture is called **cultural diffusion**.

Socialization can be further categorized. **Primary socialization** occurs during childhood when we initially learn acceptable actions and attitudes in our society, primarily through observation of our parents and other adults in close proximity. In children, this sets the stage for future socialization and provides the foundation for creating personal opinions. **Secondary socialization** is the process of learning appropriate behavior within smaller sections of the larger society. This type of socialization occurs outside of the home and is based on learning the rules of specific social environments. For example, the behavior necessary to thrive in school is different from that in the home setting, and also from that which is acceptable on a sports field or in a church. Secondary socialization is typically associated with adolescents and adults and includes smaller changes and refinements to behavior that were established in primary socialization. Secondary socialization can also occur when moving to a new region or changing schools or professions. **Anticipatory socialization** is the process by which a person prepares for future changes in occupations, living situations, or relationships. A couple living together in preparation for married life is an example of anticipatory socialization. **Resocialization** is another process by which one discards old behaviors in favor of new ones to make a life change, and can have positive or negative connotations. The method by which members of the armed forces are trained to obey orders and commands without hesitation is a prime example of resocialization, but so is attracting and indoctrinating members into a cult.

NORMS

Sociologists define **norms** as societal rules that define the boundaries of acceptable behavior. **Mores** are widely observed social norms. While norms are not laws, they do provide a mechanism for regulating the behavior of individuals and groups and thereby serve as a means of **social control**. Penalties for misconduct or rewards for appropriate behavior, called **sanctions**, can also be used to maintain social control. Negative sanctions often include fines or incarceration; in some societies, corporal punishment (infliction of pain or bodily injury) and capital punishment (execution) may also be used. Sanctions can be either formal (enforced by social institutions) or informal (enforced by social behaviors).

Norms provide us with a sense of what is appropriate, what we should do, and what is considered **taboo**—socially unacceptable, disgusting, or reprehensible. Norms exist for behavior, speech, dress, home life, and more and can differ between groups within a society, and also between different cultures. For example, Americans tend to be extraverted and talkative, even among strangers, while Japanese culture teaches

Real World

Cults that have become a mainstay in media today are often "Doomsday cults." This term refers both to groups that prophesy catastrophe and apocalypse, and to those who attempt to bring it about. In December of 2012, nearly 1000 members of the Chinese cult Church of Almighty God were arrested for broadcasting fears of apocalypse and encouraging the overthrow of the Communist Party.

that showing too much of oneself in a public setting is a sign of weakness. Thus, a very quiet person that does not make eye contact could seem odd in America, while she may fit in perfectly in Japan. **Folkways** are norms that refer to behavior that is considered polite in particular social interactions, such as shaking hands after a sports match, as seen in Figure 8.7.

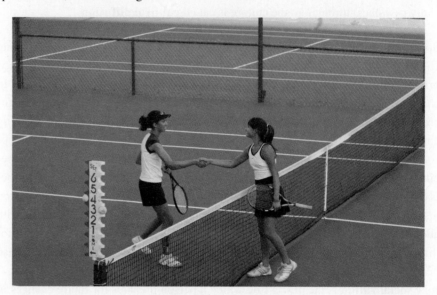

Figure 8.7. Folkways
An act as simple as shaking hands after a sporting match is an example of a folkway.

AGENTS OF SOCIALIZATION

There are many agents of socialization. For children, the primary agents of socialization are parents or family members. For adolescents, this can expand to social circles, including friends, peers, and teachers. For adults, colleagues and bosses can also facilitate socialization. Aside from personal relationships, the environment can also aid socialization. For example, when entering college, teenagers experience a complete lifestyle change and are in nearly constant interaction with people of their own age. This creates a shift in acceptable behavior that can include late nights out with friends, all-night study sessions, and significant time away from family. When entering the workforce, another change in environment leads to socialization within the organization. Ethnic background, religion, and government also play a role in learned behavior. Geography at the national, regional, and neighborhood levels also dictates norms of behavior: acceptable behavior in downtown Manhattan is not identical to acceptable behavior in rural Montana.

Furthermore, the media play a large role in what is accepted within a particular society. The media impact beliefs and can determine what is considered important in a particular society. Mass media is most commonly accessed through television, radio, newspapers, and the Internet. It delivers impersonalized communication to a vast audience, and can thereby establish trends in American or international **pop culture**. Many of the agents of socialization are summarized in Figure 8.8.

Real World

A study published in 2002 examined the link between television and violence. In the study, the researchers followed 707 subjects for 17 years. Study subjects who watched more than one hour of TV per day were approximately four times more likely to act aggressively toward others later in life than those who watched less than one hour of TV. Of those who watched more than three hours of TV per day, nearly 30% were involved in assaults, robberies, or other aggressive behaviors. While this is an interesting link, remember that it shows correlation—not causation!

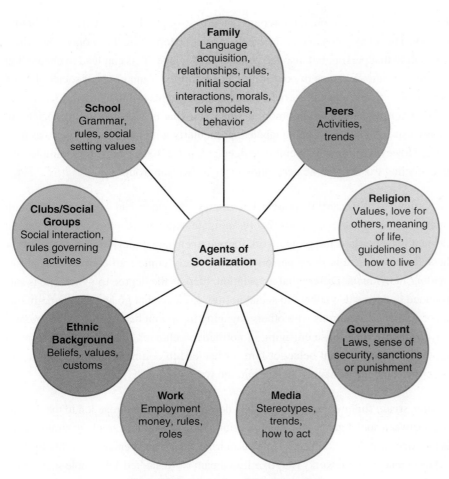

Figure 8.8. Agents of Socialization

DEVIANCE AND STIGMA

Deviance refers to any violation of norms, rules, or expectations within a society. It is important to note that using the term *deviant* is often associated with strongly negative connotations; however, in the sociological context, it simply refers to any act that goes against societal norms. Deviance can vary in severity, from something as simple as jaywalking to something as serious as committing murder. Deviance also includes any act that meets with disapproval from the larger society, such as promiscuous sexual behavior.

Social **stigma** is the extreme disapproval or dislike of a person or group based on perceived differences from the rest of society. These deviations from the norm can include differences in beliefs, abilities, behaviors, and appearance. Certain medical conditions such as HIV, achondroplasia (dwarfism), and obesity can also be stigmatized. Stigma can also spread to affect others who are associated with a particular individual. For example, family members of an alleged or convicted murderer or rapist can be stigmatized. Stigma also evolves over time: whereas divorce was stigmatized in the early twentieth century, it no longer has such strong negative connotations.

Bridge

Mental illness has long been stigmatized in American society. While this is slowly changing, the potential stigma associated with a mental health diagnosis continues to be a hurdle to many patients seeking out or receiving care. Many common psychological disorders are discussed in Chapter 7 of *MCAT Behavioral Sciences Review*.

Deviance, stigmatization, and reputation are strongly linked with the **labeling theory**. This theory posits that the labels given to people affect not only how others respond to that person, but also the person's self-image. This can lead to channeling of behavior into deviance or conformity. For example, if members of society label a woman as promiscuous, this could either lead to further promiscuity or to a change in behavior toward something more in line with what is accepted in that society. In many instances, we resist being labeled, particularly with labels we perceive as negative. However, groups may embrace deviant labels. Biker gangs, for example, utilize labeling to enhance the perception of their own subgroup.

According to **differential association theory**, deviance can be learned through interactions with others. In this theory, intimate exposure to others who engage in deviant behavior lays the groundwork for one to engage in deviant behavior him- or herself. However, this same person will also likely come into contact with norm-abiding individuals. Differential association, then, is the degree to which one is surrounded by ideals that adhere to social norms *vs.* ideals that go against them. In this theory, when associations with others engaging in deviant behavior are more numerous or intense than those engaging in normative behavior, the individual begins to gravitate toward deviant behavior him- or herself. In common language, we might describe someone as having "fallen into the wrong group."

Finally, **strain theory** attempts to explain deviance as a natural reaction to the disconnect between social goals and social structure. One common example in strain theory is the American dream, which refers to acquiring wealth and personal stability through achievement and hard work. The American dream is considered a desirable social goal, but the structure of society is unable to guarantee the education and opportunity needed to achieve this goal to all citizens. Therefore, deviant behavior such as theft may arise as an attempt to achieve the social goal *outside* of the limiting social structure.

While deviance is often associated with negative behavior such as crime, functional theorists argue that it is necessary for social order. These theorists argue that deviance provides a clear perception of social norms and acceptable boundaries, encourages unity within society, and can even promote social change.

CONFORMITY, COMPLIANCE, AND OBEDIENCE

While deviance is defined as going against societal norms, conformity, compliance, and obedience are manners of adhering to social expectations or others' requests.

Conformity

Conformity is matching one's attitudes, beliefs, and behaviors to societal norms. The pressure to conform can be real or imagined: an actual pressure from others, or a perceived pressure or expectation. Conformity is also known as **majority influence**. The Asch experiments, described earlier, showed the strength of social influence on **normative conformity**, the desire to fit into a group because of fear of rejection.

Key Concept

Internalization and identification both deal with accepting others' ideas, but whereas internalization also reflects a change in internal thoughts to agree with the idea, identification is acceptance of the idea on the surface level without internalizing it.

There are distinct types of conformity, including internalization and identification. **Internalization** involves changing one's behavior to fit with a group while also privately agreeing with the ideas of the group. **Identification** refers to the outward acceptance of others' ideas without personally taking on these ideas.

A classic experiment looking at internalization was Philip Zimbardo's Stanford Prison Experiment. Zimbardo advertised for a role-playing experiment in which he recruited 21 male college students. The study participants were randomly assigned the role of prisoner or guard. The prisoners were arrested in their homes and taken to a "prison" created in the Stanford University psychology building. Guards were issued uniforms, including whistles, handcuffs, and dark glasses to prevent eye contact. The prisoners and guards quickly fell into their roles and displayed related behaviors almost immediately. Guards began to taunt and harass prisoners, appearing to enjoy their role. Prisoners also adopted their new role, taking the prison rules very seriously, and becoming more and more dependent on the guards. As the guards became more aggressive, the prisoners became more submissive, although they also attempted to mount a revolt. The study had to be ended after six days because the guards had begun to physically abuse the prisoners so severely that ethical concerns were raised. After the study ended, Zimbardo interviewed each participant. The guards and prisoners, who had internalized their roles, were both shocked by their behavior during the experiment.

The likelihood of conformity differs among cultures. For instance, Western cultures tend to value independent thought and unique ideas and are thus less likely to conform; in Eastern cultures, group mentality often supersedes the individual. This type of collectivist society tends toward conformity.

Compliance

Compliance is a change in behavior based on a direct request. The person or group that asks the individual to make the change typically has no actual power or authority to command the individual, yet will ask him to change his behavior. There are several notable techniques used to gain compliance of others, particularly within the marketing arena. The first technique is known as the **foot-in-the-door technique**, in which a small request is made, and after gaining compliance, a larger request is made. An example of this scenario could be a fellow classmate asking to borrow your notes because he had to miss class. You agree and offer to share the notes at the next class session. Later in the day, you see the student again, and he asks you if you would be willing to make copies of your notes because he does not have access to a copier. Many people will still agree at this point, as the first request opened the door to continued compliance.

The next technique is called the **door-in-the-face technique**. This is the opposite of the foot-in-the-door technique, wherein a large request is made at first and, if refused, a second, smaller request is made. Often, this smaller request is the actual goal of the requester. Using this technique, a fellow student might ask you to make a copy of your notes from class and bring them to the next class. If you deny the request, the student might follow up with a smaller request, asking to borrow your notes so he can make copies for himself. The second, more reasonable request may be granted.

Another common method of achieving compliance is the **lowball technique**. In this technique, the requestor will get an initial commitment from an individual, and then raise the cost of the commitment. It is important to note that cost need not only include money, but can also include effort and time. An example of this technique is a scenario in which you are asked by your boss to head a committee with a time commitment of five hours per month of meetings. You agree to head the committee, but discover afterwards that the commitment also includes written reports from each meeting and a quarterly presentation.

Yet another technique used to gain compliance is the **that's-not-all technique**. In this method, an individual is made an offer, but before making a decision, is told the deal is even better than she expected. This method is frequently seen in infomercials: *For the low price of $19.99, you will receive two bottles of salon-grade shampoo. But, if you call in the next thirty minutes, you will receive not only those two bottles, but also a bottle of conditioner!*

Obedience

While compliance deals with requests made by people without actual authority over an individual, **obedience** is changing one's behavior in response to a direct order from an authority figure. While a classmate has no authority to demand notes from you, an authority figure has social power over other individuals. For instance, if a teacher demands that you provide your notes from class to him, you would be obeying rather than complying. People are far more likely to obey than comply due to the real or perceived social power of the individual.

The most notable obedience experiment was conducted by Stanley Milgram. In this classic study, Milgram claimed to be recruiting participants for a study to test the effects of punishment on learning behavior. Participants were told they would be randomly assigned to be the "teacher" or "learner"; however, the "learner" was actually a paid actor (confederate). The teachers were told that they would be controlling an electrical panel that would administer shocks to the learners if they made mistakes. Prior to giving the first shock, the teachers were given a sample 45 V shock to make them aware of what they would be doing to the learners. The teachers were then told that they would need to increase the voltage by 15 V each time an incorrect response was given. The learners, who received no actual shock, were provided with scripts telling them to show pain, ask to stop the experiment, scream, and even feign passing out. As the learners acted more and more uncomfortable, the teachers became less willing to increase the shock voltage. However, by using increasingly demanding language (from *Please continue* to *You have no other choice, you must go on*), the researchers were able to get 65 percent of the participants to administer shocks to the maximum of 450 V, even if they showed discomfort in doing so. Milgram and other researchers were surprised at the level of obedience the participants showed during the experiment. This type of experiment has been repeated many times and has consistently shown that more than 60 percent of people will obey even if they do not wish to continue.

MCAT Concept Check 8.2:

Before you move on, assess your understanding of the material with these questions.

1. What is the difference between primary and secondary socialization?

   _____

2. What are conformity, compliance, and obedience?

   - Conformity:

     _____

   - Compliance:

     _____

   - Obedience:

     _____

3. For each of the compliance techniques listed below, provide a brief description:

   - Foot-in-the-door:

     _____

   - Door-in-the-face:

     _____

   - Lowball:

     _____

   - That's-not-all:

     _____

8.3 Attitudes and Behavior High-Yield

> ## LEARNING GOALS
>
> After Chapter 8.3, you will be able to:
>
> - Recall the three components of attitude
> - Describe the four functional areas of the functional attitude theory
> - Identify the roles of central route and peripheral route processing in the elaboration likelihood model
> - Recall the three interactive factors of Bandura's triadic reciprocal causation

Social cognition focuses on the ways in which people think about others and how these ideas impact behavior. Our attitudes—the ways in which we perceive others—impact the ways we behave toward them.

COMPONENTS OF ATTITUDES

An **attitude** is the expression of positive or negative feelings toward a person, place, thing, or scenario. Attitudes develop from experiences with others who affect our opinions and behaviors. Even prior to meeting someone, past experiences and information from others can influence your attitude toward a person.

There are three primary components of attitude: affective, behavioral, and cognitive. The **affective** component of attitude refers to the way a person feels toward something, and is the emotional component of attitude. *Snakes scare me* and *I love my family* are both affective expressions of attitude. The **behavioral** component of attitude is the way a person acts with respect to something. For example, avoiding snakes and spending time with one's family would reflect the behavioral component of the attitudes described earlier. Finally, the **cognitive** component of attitude is the way an individual thinks about something, which is usually the justification for the other two components. In the snake example above, knowing that snakes can be dangerous (and sometimes poisonous) provides a reason to be afraid of snakes and to avoid them.

THEORIES OF ATTITUDES

The **functional attitudes theory** states that attitudes serve four functions: knowledge, ego expression, adaptation, and ego defense. The **knowledge** function is important in that it provides consistency and stability: attitudes help provide organization to thoughts and experiences, and knowing the attitudes of others helps to predict their behavior. For example, one would predict that an individual who

---

Mnemonic

Components of Attitude: **ABC**
- **A**ffective
- **B**ehavioral
- **C**ognitive

---

cares about political action would vote in an upcoming election. Attitudes can also be **ego-expressive**, allowing us to communicate and solidify our self-identity. For instance, if a person strongly identifies with a sports team, she may wear a hat that helps identify her as a fan of that team. **Adaptive** attitude is the idea that one will be accepted if socially acceptable attitudes are expressed. Lastly, attitudes are **ego-defensive** if they protect our self-esteem or justify actions that we know are wrong. For example, a child who has difficulty doing math may develop a negative attitude toward the subject.

Learning theory posits that attitudes are developed through different forms of learning. Direct contact with the object can influence attitudes. For example, children form a positive attitude toward sweets almost immediately after tasting them. Direct instruction from others can also influence attitudes. For instance, a child who is taught by her parents not to use curse words can form a negative attitude toward curse words and, indirectly, a negative attitude toward those who use curse words. Our attitudes can also be influenced by others' attitudes. For example, a teenager may begin to have a positive attitude toward smoking if his friends all smoke. Finally, attitudes may be formed through classical conditioning, operant conditioning, or observational learning, all of which are discussed in Chapter 3 of *MCAT Behavioral Sciences Review*.

The **elaboration likelihood model** separates individuals on a continuum based on their processing of persuasive information. At one extreme are those who elaborate extensively; that is, those who think deeply about information, scrutinize its meaning and purpose, and draw conclusions or make decisions based on this thought. This deep thinking is referred to as **central route processing**. At the other extreme are those who do not elaborate, focusing on superficial details: the appearance of the person delivering the argument, catchphrases and slogans, and credibility. This is known as **peripheral route processing**. Consider two voters watching a political campaign: while one may be swayed by the cogent arguments made by one candidate (high elaboration, central route processing), the other may be swayed by the perception that the other candidate is more personable (low elaboration, peripheral route processing). Most individuals fall in the middle of this continuum, and the degree to which we elaborate on information can vary depending on the specific situation.

Social cognitive theory postulates that people learn how to behave and shape attitudes by observing the behaviors of others. According to this idea, behavior is not learned by trial-and-error, but develops through direct observation and replication of the actions of others, and in tandem with the influence of personal factors (such as thoughts about the behavior) and the environment in which we observe the behavior. These three factors—behavior, personal factors, and environment—are not independent concepts, but influence each other, as shown in Bandura's triadic reciprocal causation in Figure 8.9. For example, the work ethic of employees in a company (behavior) is affected by how hard their colleagues work, their previous

Key Concept

- Central route processing (high elaboration)—scrutinizing and analyzing the content of persuasive information
- Peripheral route processing (low elaboration)—focusing on superficial details of persuasive information, such as appearances, catchphrases and slogans, and credibility

attitudes toward hard work (personal), and the systems and infrastructure of the company (environment). Reciprocally, this behavior may create a change in the employee's attitude toward work (personal) and the systems within the company (environment).

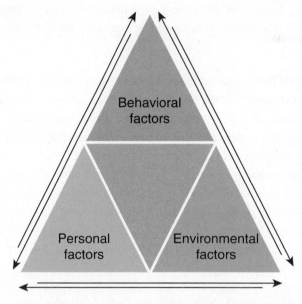

Figure 8.9. Bandura's Triadic Reciprocal Causation

MCAT Concept Check 8.3:

Before you move on, assess your understanding of the material with these questions.

1. What are the three components of attitude?

   • _____

   • _____

   • _____

2. What are the four functional areas of the functional attitudes theory?

   • _____

   • _____

   • _____

   • _____

3. What are the routes of processing used to explain the elaboration likelihood model? Which is associated with high elaboration?

- _____

- _____

4. What are the three interactive factors of Bandura's triadic reciprocal causation?

- _____

- _____

- _____

Conclusion

Human behavior is learned and influenced by those around us. Simply being around others leads to changes in behavior from how we act when alone. Pressure from others can also lead to changes in behavior as we crave acceptance: inclusion in a group can lead to changes in thought processes and decision-making. Social norms, which are learned through experience and observation, can be rejected by individuals, leading to deviance and stigmatization. However, the need to fit in can lead to conformity, compliance, and obedience. Attitudes are also developed through observations, experiences, and interactions with others, and there are multiple theories explaining their specific methods of formation.

This chapter focused primarily on how groups influence an individual's behavior. In the next chapter, we'll look at the structure of these groups and how we present ourselves to the larger society. We'll explore methods of communication between individuals—both verbal and nonverbal—and consider how we encourage others to gain certain impressions about us.

CONCEPT SUMMARY

Group Psychology

- **Social facilitation** describes the tendency of people to perform at a different level based on the fact that others are around.

- **Deindividuation** is a loss of self-awareness in large groups, which can lead to drastic changes in behavior.

- The **bystander effect** describes the observation that when in a group, individuals are less likely to respond to a person in need.

- **Peer pressure** refers to the social influence placed on individuals by others they consider equals.

- Group decision-making may differ from individual decision-making.

  o Group **polarization** is the tendency toward making decisions in a group that are more extreme then the thoughts of the individual group members.

  o **Groupthink** is the tendency for groups to make decisions based on ideas and solutions that arise within the group without considering outside ideas. Ethics may be disturbed as pressure is created to conform and remain loyal to the group.

- **Culture** describes the beliefs, ideas, behaviors, actions, and characteristics of a group or society of people.

  o **Assimilation** is the process by which a group or individual's culture begins to melt into another culture.

  o **Multiculturalism** refers to the encouragement of multiple cultures within a community to enhance diversity.

  o **Subcultures** refer to a group of people within a culture that distinguish themselves from the primary culture to which they belong.

Socialization

- **Socialization** is the process of developing and spreading norms, customs, and beliefs.

- **Norms** are what determine the boundaries of acceptable behavior within society.

- Agents of socialization include family, peers, school, religious affiliation, and other groups that promote socialization.

- **Stigma** is the extreme disapproval or dislike of a person or group based on perceived differences from the rest of society.

- **Deviance** refers to any violation of norms, rules, or expectations within a society.

- **Conformity** is changing beliefs or behaviors in order to fit into a group or society.

- **Compliance** occurs when individuals change their behavior based on the requests of others. Methods of gaining compliance include the foot-in-the-door technique, door-in-the-face technique, lowball technique, and that's-not-all technique, among others.

- **Obedience** is a change in behavior based on a command from someone seen as an authority figure.

Attitudes and Behavior

- **Attitudes** are tendencies toward expression of positive or negative feelings or evaluations of something.

- There are affective, behavioral, and cognitive components to attitudes.

- The **functional attitudes theory** states that there are four functional areas of attitudes that serve individuals in life: knowledge, ego expression, adaptability, and ego defense.

- The **learning theory** states that attitudes are developed through forms of learning: direct contact, direct interaction, direct instruction, and conditioning.

- The **elaboration likelihood model** states that attitudes are formed and changed through different routes of information processing based on the degree of elaboration (**central route processing, peripheral route processing**).

- The **social cognitive theory** states that attitudes are formed through observation of behavior, personal factors, and environment.

ANSWERS TO CONCEPT CHECKS

8.1

1. Social facilitation describes the tendency of people to perform at a different level based on the fact that others are around. Deindividuation is the idea that people will lose a sense of self-awareness and can act dramatically different because of the influence of a group. The bystander effect describes the observation that individuals are less likely to respond to a person in need when in a group. Social loafing refers to a decrease in effort seen when individuals are in a group. Peer pressure refers to the social influence placed on individuals by others they consider their equals.

2. Group polarization and groupthink are both social processes that occur when groups make decisions. Group polarization is the tendency toward extreme decisions in a group. Groupthink is the tendency for groups to make decisions based on ideas and solutions that arise within the group without considering outside ideas, given the pressure to conform and remain loyal to the group.

3. Societies that contain multiple cultures can exhibit multiculturalism or assimilation. Assimilation is the process by which multiple cultures begin to merge into one, typically with an unequal blending of ideas and beliefs. Multiculturalism refers to the idea that multiple cultures should be encouraged and respected without one culture becoming dominant overall.

8.2

1. Primary socialization refers to the initial learning of acceptable behaviors and societal norms during childhood, which is facilitated mostly by parents and other trusted adults. Secondary socialization refers to learning the norms of specific subgroups or situations during adolescence and adulthood.

2. Conformity is changing beliefs or behaviors in order to fit into a group or society. Compliance occurs when individuals change their behavior based on the request of others who do not wield authority over the individual. Obedience is a change in behavior because of a request from an authority figure.

3. The foot-in-the-door technique refers to asking for favors that increase in size with each subsequent request. The door-in-the-face technique refers to making a large request and then, if refused, making a smaller request. The lowball technique refers to gaining compliance without revealing the full cost (money, effort, or time) of the favor. The that's-not-all technique refers to increasing the reward for a request before an individual has the chance to make a decision.

8.3

1. The three components of attitude are affective, behavioral, and cognitive.

2. The four functional areas of the functional attitudes theory are knowledge, ego expression, adaptation, and ego defense.

3. The routes of processing used to explain the elaboration likelihood model are central route processing and peripheral route processing. Central route processing is associated with high elaboration.

4. The three interactive factors of Bandura's triadic reciprocal causation are behavior, personal factors, and environment.

SHARED CONCEPTS

Discrete Practice Questions

Consult your online resources for Full-Length Exams and Passage-Based Questions (for certain chapters).

1. The behavior of the individuals in the Stanford prison experiment is best explained by which of the following terms?

   I. Bystander effect

   II. Deindividuation

   III. Internalization

   IV. Social loafing

   A. I only
   B. III only
   C. II and III only
   D. II and IV only

2. A jury member who initially feels that a strict penalty should be placed on the defendant votes for an even stricter penalty after deliberation with the other jury members. This behavior is best described by which social phenomenon?

   A. Social facilitation
   B. Group polarization
   C. Assimilation
   D. Socialization

3. Which of the following would decrease the likelihood of a bystander lending aid to a victim?

   A. Increasing the number of people in the room
   B. Increasing the degree of danger experienced by the victim
   C. Making the victim an acquaintance instead of a stranger
   D. Being alone in the room with the victim

4. During groupthink, members of the group do all of the following EXCEPT:

   A. stereotype members outside of the group.
   B. withhold opposing views.
   C. ignore warnings against the ideas of the group.
   D. create a sense of negativity against risk-taking.

5. Adult prison systems may attempt to change the behavior of inmates through all of the following mechanisms of socialization EXCEPT:

   A. primary socialization.
   B. secondary socialization.
   C. anticipatory socialization.
   D. resocialization.

6. Your neighbor asks you to check her mail while she is out of town and you agree. Later that day, she asks you to water her plants as well. What technique for compliance is she using in this scenario?

   A. Lowball technique
   B. That's-not-all technique
   C. Foot-in-the-door technique
   D. Door-in-the-face technique

7. Which of the following statements represents the affective component of an attitude?

   A. "I love action movies."
   B. "I'm going to see a new action movie at the theater."
   C. "Action movies are much better than comedies."
   D. "Tomorrow, I'm going to rent an action movie."

K

8. After sitting in a lecture, determining that a professor is a bad teacher based on his unprofessional attire and monotone speech is an example of which type of processing?

    A. Knowledge route processing
    B. Adaptive route processing
    C. Central route processing
    D. Peripheral route processing

9. In the Milgram shock experiment, many subjects were willing to give the maximal voltage shock because they were influenced by which psychological principal?

    A. Deviance
    B. Obedience
    C. Conformity
    D. Compliance

10. Each individual in a group of teenagers is asked to estimate the height of a tree. One individual estimates the height to be 25 feet, but after discussing with the group is convinced that the height is likely closer to 40 feet. Which type of conformity is seen here?

    A. Normative
    B. Identification
    C. Internalization
    D. Compliance

11. Which of the following is NOT a component of the functional attitudes theory?

    A. Knowledge
    B. Acceptance
    C. Ego defense
    D. Ego expression

12. The swimming times for all members of a swim team are tracked over a six-month period in team-only practices and at public meets. For 14 of the 16 members, top times were clocked at the meets. What social phenomenon does this evidence support?

    A. Social facilitation
    B. Peer pressure
    C. Identification
    D. Group polarization

13. A 18-year-old male is completing his final months of high school and begins to wake up early each day to run five miles in preparation for joining the Army. What type of socialization is this young man experiencing?

    A. Normative socialization
    B. Informative socialization
    C. Resocialization
    D. Anticipatory socialization

14. Which of the following best reflects the difference between social action and social interaction?

    A. Social action refers to positive changes one makes in their society; social interaction refers to the route by which these changes occur.
    B. Social action refers to the effects of a group on an individual's behavior; social interaction refers to the effects that multiple individuals all have on each other.
    C. Social action refers to changes in behavior caused by internal factors; social interaction refers to changes in behavior caused by external factors.
    D. Social action refers to changes in behaviors that benefit only the individual; social interaction refers to changes in behavior that benefit others.

15. In the group setting, the mentality of "If you aren't with us, you're against us" is most representative of which factor of groupthink?

    A. Illusion of invulnerability
    B. Illusion of morality
    C. Pressure for conformity
    D. Self-censorship

Explanations to
Discrete Practice Questions

1. C

When fulfilling particular roles, an individual's behavior can be very out of character. The changing of one's behavior (and internal ideas) to match a group is called internalization conformity. This was a key part of the experiment. The experiment also involved deindividuation, the loss of self-identity in the group setting that can lead to antinormative or violent behavior.

2. B

The fact that individual opinions became more extreme during group discussion is explained by group polarization. The jury member initially felt that a strict penalty should be given, but this opinion became more extreme after conversation with the rest of the group.

3. A

It has been observed that increasing the number of bystanders decreases the likelihood that any of them will aid a victim. Increasing the degree of danger experienced by the victim, **choice (B)**, making the victim an acquaintance instead of a stranger, **choice (C)**, and being alone in the room with the victim, **choice (D)**, would increase the likelihood that the bystander would help the victim.

4. D

With groupthink, a member would perform all of the actions described by the answer choices except create a sense of negativity against risk-taking; in fact, there is optimism and encouragement toward risk-taking in groupthink.

5. A

Primary socialization is the teaching of acceptable actions and attitudes during childhood, which would occur too early to be part of the adult prison system. Resocialization, **choice (D)**, is the process by which one changes behaviors by discarding old routines and patterns and transitions to new behaviors necessary for a life change. The prison environment is designed to change bad behavior into desired behavior, making this an incorrect choice. When entering prison, an inmate must also undergo secondary socialization, **choice (B)**, learning the rules of the specific social environment of the prison. Finally, if the inmate is not incarcerated for life, attempts at anticipatory socialization, **choice (C)**, must be made before releasing the inmate in preparation for life outside of the prison.

6. C

This is a prime example of the foot-in-the-door technique. The neighbor first asks for a small favor and, after receiving commitment, asks for a larger favor.

7. A

The affective component of attitude consists of feelings and emotions toward something.

8. D

Peripheral route processing deals with processing information that is not based on content, but instead on superficial parameters such as boring speech patterns or appearance of the speaker. Central route processing, **choice (C)**, is the processing of information through analysis of its content.

9. B

The Milgram shock experiment showed that individuals would obey orders from authority figures even if they were not comfortable with the task at hand. Conformity and compliance, **choices (C)** and **(D)**, also deal with changes in individual behavior, but are not based on the requests of an authority figure.

10. C

Internalization refers to the type of conformity in which an individual changes his or her outward opinion to match the group and also personally agrees with those ideas.

11. B

The four functional areas of the functional attitudes theory are knowledge, adaptability, ego expression, and ego defense. Acceptance into a group may influence attitudes or opinions; however, this is not a part of the functional attitudes theory.

12. A

For 14 out of the 16 members, the record times were obtained during public meets. The fact that the team members performed better when in front of a crowd supports the notion of social facilitation.

13. D

This young man is preparing for life in the Army, a new social setting that he will be joining. The process of preparing for future changes in environment is considered anticipatory socialization.

14. B

Social action is best described as the effects that a group has on individual behavior, including social facilitation, deindividuation, the bystander effect, social loafing, and peer pressure. Social interaction describes how two or more individuals influence each other's behavior, including group polarization and groupthink.

15. C

Placing spoken or unspoken expectations on individuals to agree with the ideas of the group is best described as pressure for conformity.

Social Interaction

In This Chapter

Chapter Profile

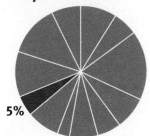

5%

The content in this chapter should be relevant to about 5% of all questions about the Behavioral Sciences on the MCAT.

This chapter covers material from the following AAMC content categories:

7B: Social processes that influence human behavior

8C: Social interactions

Introduction

Every day, you present yourself to others and interact with society. You use a number of means to interact with others, from cultural norms to emotional expression to verbal communication. You also interact with nonhuman animals on a day-to-day basis. This interaction can be just as complex and meaningful to your emotional state and life experiences. What shapes and molds your interactions? How do you know the appropriate way to connect with other members of society?

9.1 Elements of Social Interaction

High-Yield

> ## LEARNING GOALS
>
> After Chapter 9.1, you will be able to:
>
> - Identify the meaning of social interaction terms such as status, role, group, network, and organization
> - List the three types of status and provide an example of each

Society has developed out of necessity for human beings to survive and develop. Social interaction is the basis of social life and helps humans reach their full potential. Social interaction is facilitated by preexisting commonalities between individuals and shared understanding or experiences, such as a shared language. Through our social interactions, we develop culture.

STATUSES

In most human societies, people do not view every individual as an equal. Instead, we create a hierarchical structure with inequalities of material goods, social opportunities, social acceptance, and skills. Some are rich, and some are poor; some are talented in sports, while others are not. Some are admired by others, most are liked, and some are disliked or even stigmatized. **Statuses** are positions in society that are used to classify individuals. Being a premed student, for example, is considered a status. Most statuses exist in relation to other statuses: being a premed student does not have meaning unless there are other statuses with which to compare it, such as *medical student* or *resident*. It is important to note that not all personal characteristics are considered a social status. For example, being left-handed is not considered a status.

There are three key types of statuses: ascribed, achieved, and master statuses. An **ascribed status** is one that is given involuntarily, due to such factors as race, ethnicity, gender, and family background. An **achieved status** is a status that is gained as a result of one's efforts or choices, such as being a doctor. A **master status** is the status by which a person is most identified. This status is typically the most important status the individual holds and affects all aspects of that person's life. It is also generally how people view themselves and often holds a symbolic value. Master statuses can also cause pigeonholing: we may view an individual only through the lens of his or her master status, without regard to any other personal characteristics (such as with a president or other major political figure).

ROLES

Each status has a **role**, or a set of beliefs, values, attitudes, and norms that define expectations for those who hold the status. **Role performance** is the carrying out of behaviors associated with a given role. Individuals can vary in how successful they are at performing a role. For example, part of a doctor's role is to translate medical information into language their patients can understand; however, some doctors are far better at this skill than others. Role performance can also change depending on the social situation and context of the interaction. When doctors interact with each other, the pertinent parts of their role are quite different than when interacting with patients. Behaviors and expectations thus change as a result of the **role partner**—the person with whom one is interacting. Doctors have many role partners: patients, nurses, patients' relatives, other doctors, residents, and hospital administration. The various roles associated with a status are referred to as a **role set**.

Through our lives, we each take on numerous statuses, each of which may contain a variety of roles. Additionally, we are often playing several roles at one time. Due to the complex nature of statuses and role sets, it is not surprising that conflict, challenges, uncertainty, and ambivalence arise as we try to navigate the many expectations of day-to-day life. **Role conflict** is difficulty in satisfying the requirements or expectations of multiple roles, whereas **role strain** is difficulty in satisfying multiple requirements of the same role. **Role exit** is the dropping of one identity for another.

Key Concept

Types of statuses:
- Ascribed—given involuntarily, based on race, ethnicity, gender, family background, and so on
- Achieved—gained as a result of one's efforts or choices
- Master—status by which one is most identified; is pervasive in that person's life

---

Real World

A great example of role conflict is a single parent who also works a full-time job. Both of these roles carry a very large set of expectations, which are often at odds with each other.

GROUPS

Another major component of social interaction involves groups. A **group** (also known as a **social group**) consists of two or more people who share similar characteristics and a sense of unity. The simplest of social groups is called a **dyad** (two people), followed by a **triad** (three people). As group size increases, the group trades intimacy for stability. Social groups are more complex than a group of individuals who happen to be in the same physical space. For example, people waiting to cross the street at a crosswalk do not constitute a social group. Common characteristics shared by social groups include values, interests, ethnicity, social background, family ties, and political representation. Many sociologists see social interaction as the most important characteristic that strengthens a social group.

We center most of our lives around social groups, from the camaraderie of teammates to the complexity of governments. Social groups also meet many of the needs we have; they provide an opportunity to belong and be accepted, and offer protection, safety, and support. We also learn, earn a living, and practice religion in groups. Groups can also be a source of conflict, including discrimination, persecution, oppression, and war. These sprout from the relationships within and between groups.

There are several types of groups. A **peer group** is one that is defined by association of self-selected equals around similar interests, ages, and statuses. Peer groups provide an opportunity for friendship and feelings of belonging. A **family group**, by contrast, is not self-selected but determined by birth, adoption, and marriage. It joins members of various ages, sexes, and generations through emotional ties. The family group can be filled with conflict at times; this is often true in adolescence when peer groups begin to compete with family groups for time and loyalty. Family groups may also struggle with cultural gaps and social differences between generations, such as speaking in different languages. **In-groups** are groups to which an individual belongs and can be contrasted with **out-groups**, with which an individual competes or is in opposition. Finally, **reference groups** are groups that establish the terms by which individuals evaluate themselves: to determine how strong of a medical school applicant you are, you may consider yourself in relation to the reference group of all medical school applicants.

Primary and Secondary Groups

Groups can also be categorized into primary and secondary groups. In a **primary group**, the interactions are direct, with close bonds providing warm, personal, and intimate relationships to members. These groups often last a long period of time and may include a core circle of friends, a tightly knit family, or members of a team. In a **secondary group**, the interactions are superficial, with few emotional bonds. Secondary groups typically last for a short period of time, and they form and dissolve without any special significance, such as students working together on a group project.

Community and Society

The German sociologist Ferdinand Tönnies distinguished two major types of groups. His theory is known as *Gemeinschaft und Gesellschaft*, which translates to *community and society*. *Gemeinschaft* (community) refers to groups unified by feelings of togetherness due to shared beliefs, ancestry, or geography. Families and neighborhoods are examples of *Gemeinschaften*. *Gesellschaft* (society) refers to groups that are formed because of mutual self-interests working together toward the same goal. Companies and countries are examples of *Gesellschaften*.

Observing and Analyzing Groups

Group size may vary; the smallest size a group can be is two people. Smaller group sizes, like dyads or triads, allow individuals to present more of themselves to the group. **Interaction process analysis** is a technique for observing, classifying, and measuring the interactions within small groups. In the 1970s, it was revised to the **system for multiple level observation of groups** (**SYMLOG**), which is based on the belief that there are three fundamental dimensions of interaction: dominance *vs.* submission, friendliness *vs.* unfriendliness, and instrumentally controlled *vs.* emotionally expressive.

Through extensive research on groups, we have learned that a group holds power over its members, creating group pressure that ultimately shapes members' behaviors. This is called **group conformity**; individuals are compliant with the group's goals, even when the group's goals may be in direct contrast to the individual's goal. Individuals conform in an attempt to fit in and be accepted by the group. Individuals will often participate in behaviors they normally would not.

Groupthink is related to group conformity, and occurs when members begin to focus solely on ideas generated within the group, while ignoring outside ideas. This can lead to groups not exploring all sides of an issue and may limit the group's options or views; further, group members may self-censor by not expressing their beliefs. A more extensive discussion of the effects of groups on individual behavior (social action) and group dynamics is explored in Chapter 8 of *MCAT Behavioral Sciences Review*.

NETWORKS

The term **network** is used to describe the observable pattern of social relationships among individuals or groups. Patterns of relationship can be determined by mapping the interactions between individual units, the nature of which can be highly variable. For example, a sociologist may look at the patterns in the interactions between friends, family members, or societal institutions. Researchers often display networks with maps containing a series of points, with each point representing a unit in the network. They connect the points with lines to display the interactions between units, as shown in Figure 9.1. Not all contact points within a network are necessarily unique. If there are overlapping connections with the same individual, it is referred to as **network redundancy**. Network analysis can be used to gain understanding of the actions of individuals and groups and to study the broader social structure.

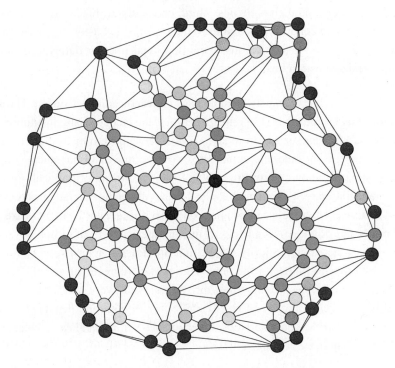

Figure 9.1. Example of a Social Network Diagram

Individuals in networks face the demands and expectations of other members, constraining what they are able to do. They also may have access to resources through the network. An example of a network is a university's alumni association: the members are held to certain standards and commitments, but also may reap the benefits of the network when searching for a job. **Immediate networks** are dense with strong ties, whereas **distant networks** are looser and contain weaker ties; immediate networks may be composed of friends, whereas distant networks may include acquaintances. The combination of immediate and distant networks provide the most benefit to individuals, which is augmented if the networks work complementarily to provide different resources.

Bridge

A genetic pedigree can be thought of as a specific type of network map, in which geneticists can track genetic patterns. The lines in genetic pedigrees represent mating patterns, parent–child relationships, and other familial structures. While pedigree analysis does not appear on the MCAT, the related topic of genetics is discussed in Chapter 12 of *MCAT Biology Review*.

ORGANIZATIONS

In sociology, **organizations** are entities that are set up to achieve specific goals and are characterized by having a structure and a culture. We have all been members of multiple organizations, such as schools, companies, music groups, sports teams, fraternities and sororities, political organizations, community action committees, and so on. The study of organizations is at the heart of sociology because of the importance that organizations have throughout a person's life.

Formal organizations are different from groups in many ways. First, organizations continue despite the departure of an individual member. This means that the organization can have a history before and after an individual member. Second, organizations have expressed goals. These are generally recorded in a written format and guide the members and their activities. Third, organizations have enforcement procedures that seek to control the activities of their members. Lastly, organizations are characterized by the hierarchical allotment of formal roles or duties to members. Formal organizations can be quite large.

The basic organization of society is found in its **characteristic institution**. Throughout history this has changed. In prehistoric times, the characteristic institution was primarily the kin, clan, or sib. In modern times, as we have transformed our cities into urban centers of trade and commerce, we have moved to bureaucracy as the characteristic institution. A **bureaucracy** is a rational system of political organization, administration, discipline, and control. Generally, a bureaucracy has these six characteristics: paid, nonelected officials on a fixed salary; officials who are provided rights and privileges as a result of making their career out of holding office; regular salary increases, seniority rights, and promotions upon passing exams or milestones; officials who enter the organization by holding an advanced degree or training; responsibilities, obligations, privileges, and work procedures rigidly defined by the organization; and responsibility for meeting the demands of one's position. Due to these characteristics, bureaucracies are often slow to change and less efficient than other organizations.

Bureaucracies have been criticized over time. The **iron law of oligarchy** states that democratic or bureaucratic systems naturally shift to being ruled by an elite group. This shift is due to a number of factors, including the necessity of a core body of individuals to carry out the day-to-day activities of the organization, increased need for specialization, and leadership characteristics of certain members of the group. Thus, even a group established with democratic principles and complete egalitarianism will ultimately centralize, placing power in the hands of a few key leaders.

McDonaldization is commonly used to refer to a shift in focus toward efficiency, predictability, calculability, and control in societies. While the original model for McDonaldization was, of course, the fast-food restaurant, examples of these same characteristics can be seen in many other institutions. For example, the establishment of 24-hour news channels, which feature a running footer of the latest news stories as "bite-size" headlines, demonstrate an efficient and predictable source of information. Corporations may mine "big data" to make business decisions using controlled, standardized methods, allowing the business to focus on the calculable outcomes of a choice such as profit and loss analysis and market share.

MCAT Concept Check 9.1:

Before you move on, assess your understanding of the material with these questions.

1. List the three types of statuses and provide an example of each:

Status	Example

2. For each of the sociological terms below, provide a brief definition:

- Status: _____

- Role: _____

- Group: _____

- Network: _____

- Organization: _____

9.2 Self-Presentation and Interacting with Others

High-Yield

LEARNING GOALS

After Chapter 9.2, you will be able to:

- Classify forms of communication as verbal or nonverbal
- Distinguish between front stage self and back stage self
- Identify examples of body language, facial expression, visual display, scent, and vocalization in communication

Self-presentation is the process of displaying oneself to society through culturally accepted behaviors. The implication of self-presentation is that people use specific strategies to shape what others will think of them. The term self-presentation is often used interchangeably with **impression management**.

EXPRESSING AND DETECTING EMOTIONS

Expressed emotions include both verbal and nonverbal behaviors that communicate internal states. We can express emotions with or without conscious awareness.

Bridge

Paul Ekman's work with universal emotions, as detailed in Chapter 5 of *MCAT Behavioral Sciences Review*, was a key development in the basic model of emotional expression. Individuals knowledgeable about Ekman's work are capable of detecting very subtle and transient facial expressions that may indicate that an individual is trying to be deceptive about the emotions being conveyed.

The **basic model of emotional expression** was first established by Charles Darwin. Darwin stated that emotional expression involves a number of components: facial expressions, behaviors, postures, vocal changes, and physiological changes. Darwin claimed that expression is consistent with his theories on evolution and should be similar across cultures. Darwin also stated that primates and animals exhibit rudimentary muscle actions that are similar to those used by humans for facial expressions. Since Darwin, many researchers have found that a number of basic human emotions are universally experienced and that their corresponding facial expressions are universally recognized. The **appraisal model** is closely related, and accepts that there are biologically predetermined expressions once an emotion is experienced, but that there is a cognitive antecedent to emotional expression.

Three of the primary models that describe individual emotion (James–Lange, Cannon–Bard, and Schachter–Singer) were discussed in Chapter 5 of *MCAT Behavioral Sciences Review*. In this chapter, we will look at how emotions are shaped by social context and culture.

The **social construction model** assumes that there is no biological basis for emotions. Instead, emotions are based on experiences and the situational context alone. It also suggests that certain emotions can only exist within social encounters and that emotions are expressed differently—and thus play different roles—across cultures. In this model, one must be familiar with social norms for a certain emotion to perform the corresponding emotional behaviors in a given social situation.

Culture provides the foundation to understand and interpret behaviors. Studies have suggested that cultural differences can lead to very different social consequences when emotions are expressed. Cultural expectations of emotions are often referred to as **display rules**. For example, in Utkuhikhalik Inuit society, anger is rarely expressed; individuals who demonstrate anger are considered social pariahs. Display rules govern which emotions can be expressed and to what degree. They may differ as a function of the culture, gender, or family background of an individual. Emotional expressions can be managed in several different ways: by simulating feelings one does not actually feel; by qualifying, amplifying, or deamplifying feelings; by masking an emotion with another emotion; or by neutralizing any emotional expression whatsoever.

A **cultural syndrome** is a shared set of beliefs, attitudes, norms, values, and behaviors among members of the same culture that are organized around a central theme. Cultural syndromes influence the rules for expressing or suppressing emotions, and can even influence the ways emotions are experienced. For example, happiness is generally considered a positive emotion across cultures. However, in countries with more individualistic cultural syndromes, like the United States, happiness is viewed as infinite, attainable, and internally experienced. In contrast, in countries with a more collectivist cultural syndrome, such as Japan, happiness is a very rational emotion and generally applied to collective experiences more than to individual successes or experiences. This difference is illustrated in the contrast between the phrases *I am happy* and *I am sharing happiness with others*.

Gender also plays an important role in emotional expression. Research on the expression of emotion in the United States has shown that women are expected to express anger in public less often than men, while men are expected to repress the expression of sadness. Research also supports the conclusion that women are better at detecting subtle differences in emotional expression than men.

IMPRESSION MANAGEMENT

Impression management refers to our attempts to influence how others perceive us. This is done through the regulation or controlling of information in social interactions. Impression management is often used synonymously with self-presentation. When describing impression management, theorists describe three "selves": the authentic self, the ideal self, and the tactical self. The **authentic self** describes who the person actually is, including both positive and negative attributes. The **ideal self**, as described in Chapter 6 of *MCAT Behavioral Sciences Review*, refers to who we would like to be under optimal circumstances. The **tactical self** refers to who we market ourselves to be when we adhere to others' expectations of us. This is similar to the ought self described in Chapter 6 of *MCAT Behavioral Sciences Review*.

People use a number of impression management strategies when in the presence of others. Some common strategies are summarized in Table 9.1, with examples of each.

Strategy	Definition	Example(s)
Self-disclosure	Giving information about oneself to establish an identity	Disclosing that you are a premedical student
Managing appearances	Using props, appearance, emotional expression, or associations with others to create a positive image	Wearing a white coat, keeping calm while dealing with a difficult patient, mentioning associations with important researchers during an interview
Ingratiation	Using flattery or conforming to expectations to win someone over	Blindly agreeing to someone else's opinion, complimenting a friend before asking for a favor
Aligning actions	Making questionable behavior acceptable through excuses	Justifications for missing deadlines, blaming a bad grade on too little sleep
Alter-casting	Imposing an identity onto another person	Any example in this course that says *As a good MCAT student, you should...* in which Kaplan is assigning *you* the role of *good MCAT student*

Table 9.1. Impression Management Strategies

Erving Goffman described impression management through the **dramaturgical approach**, using the metaphor of a theatrical performance to describe how individuals create images of themselves in various situations. In this analogy, Goffman

MCAT Expertise

Many of the sociological theories tested on the MCAT are far more extensive than the knowledge base the AAMC expects of test takers. The dramaturgical approach, for example, describes over twenty sociological concepts in theatrical terms; however, the MCAT only expects you to know front stage *vs.* back stage self. Likewise, the "I" and the "me" would be tested conceptually.

Bridge

Strong communication skills are tested everywhere on the MCAT, but are particularly important in the *Critical Analysis and Reasoning Skills* section. See Chapter 2 of *MCAT Critical Analysis and Reasoning Skills Review* for a discussion of analyzing rhetoric.

likens a person's status to that person's part in the performance and role in the script. While Goffman stretched this analogy to its very limits, the MCAT will only expect you to be familiar with the concepts of front stage and back stage self. The **front stage** is where the actor is in front of the audience, and performs according to the setting, role, and script in order to conform to the image he wants others to see. In contrast, the **back stage** is where the actor is not being observed by an audience and is free to act in ways that may not be congruent with his desired public image without having to worry about ruining his performance.

Another theory of self that is dependent on social interaction was described by George Mead, who built on previous work by James, outlining the two parts of the self as the "I" and the "me." "Me" is the part of self that is a response to the environment, whereas "I" is the creative expression of the individual. For example, going to school and studying hard would be a part of "me" since this is a societal expectation, whereas deciding that studying may not be the only path toward a goal, and choosing to find alternative approaches would be a part of "I".

VERBAL AND NONVERBAL COMMUNICATION

Communication is the ability to convey information by speech, writing, signals, or behavior. It is the foundation of social interaction and is often used to elicit changes, generate action, create understanding, share a point of view, or inform. Effective communication occurs when the desired message is received by the recipient.

Verbal communication is the transmission of information via the use of words, whether spoken, written, or signed. It is tied to nonverbal communication and is often dependent on nonverbal cues for the receiver to understand the sender's full meaning. While face-to-face conversations are rich with nonverbal communication, even phone conversations include nonverbal means of communication, such as pauses and changes in tone.

Nonverbal communication refers to how people communicate, intentionally or unintentionally, without words. Some examples of nonverbal communication are facial expressions, tone of voice, gestures, body position and movement, touches, and eye positioning. Nonverbal cues serve a number of functions in communication, including expression of emotions, as shown in Figure 9.2, conveyance of attitudes and personality traits, and facilitation of verbal communication. Nonverbal communication is often dictated by culture. For example, in US culture, people can be suspicious of someone who does not make eye contact, as this is widely considered to be a sign of lying. However, in many Asian cultures, direct eye contact is used far less often than in the United States. For example, children in Thailand are taught not to make eye contact with teachers and adults in order to show respect. Some types of verbal and nonverbal communication are listed in Table 9.2.

Figure 9.2. Human Body Language
Sadness is associated with drooping upper eyelids, staring into the distance, frowning, and slumping of shoulders, the last of which is seen here.

Verbal	Nonverbal
Spoken language	Facial expressions
Written language (print and electronic)	Body language (posture)
Sign languages (American Sign Language)	Gestures
Tactile languages (Braille alphabet)	Tone of voice (prosody)
	Eye contact
	Amount of personal space

Table 9.2. Verbal and Nonverbal Communication

ANIMAL SIGNALS AND COMMUNICATION

We not only communicate with other people, but also with other living creatures. **Animal communication** is defined as any behavior of one animal that affects the behavior of another.

Nonhuman animals communicate with one another in order to convey information such as emotions, intent, status, health, and the location of resources. They communicate with one another through a variety of nonverbal means, including body language, rudimentary facial expressions, visual displays, scents, and vocalizations.

The use of body language is common across a number of species. Body language can indicate that an animal is frightened, as shown in Figure 9.3, aggressive, relaxed, or even embarrassed; dogs often tuck their tails between their legs when scolded or fearful. Body language can also have significance for reproduction, as many animals will get into certain positions to signify readiness to mate.

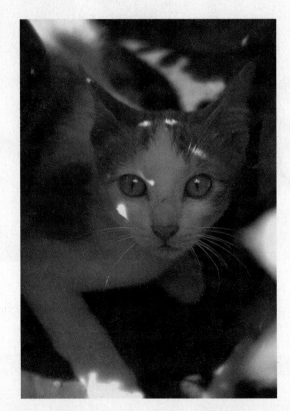

Figure 9.3. Animal Body Language
When surprised or scared, cats will recoil, crouch,
and remain relatively motionless.

While humans possess far finer motor control of the muscles of facial expression, many animals (especially mammals) use facial expressions to indicate similar emotions to body language. It is noteworthy, however, that facial expressions appear to be more highly conserved between species than body language. For example, baring teeth and lunging forward as shown in Figure 9.4, are perceived almost universally as signs of aggression or readiness to attack.

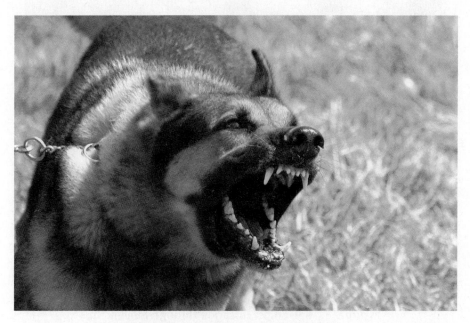

Figure 9.4. Animal Facial Expressions
Baring teeth and lunging forward are recognized by many animals
as signs that an attack is imminent.

Animals may also use visual displays for communication. This is common for sex discrimination in birds; females are often less colorful than males because it permits them a greater degree of camouflage and protection when caring for their young. However, this also serves as communication between birds, as sex is readily apparent from the bird's appearance. Other visual displays include bioluminescence (the production of light), colorful plumage (as in peacocks), and dancing. Bees are well-known for communicating through dancing, as shown in Figure 9.5.

Figure 9.5. Bee Communication through Movement
The "waggle dance," illustrated here, indicates the location of
food relative to the hive.

Bridge

It is debatable if pheromones actually
have an effect on humans because we
lack many of the genes necessary for
function of the vomeronasal organ, an
accessory olfactory organ seen in other
animals. Olfaction and scent detection
is discussed in Chapter 2 of *MCAT
Behavioral Sciences Review*.

Many animals use scents to communicate both intraspecifically (between members
of the same specifies) and interspecifically (between members of different species).
Pheromones are a common example and are given off by members of a species to
attract a mate. Scents can be used to mark an animal's territory or as a method of
defense, such as in skunks.

Finally, animals also communicate through vocalizations with various levels of
sophistication. For example, research has shown that prairie dogs have different
"words" for specific predators, and can even create new words for novel objects.
Bird calls are species specific and are used to attract a mate or warn of a threat.

In addition to interacting in the wild, humans use both verbal and nonverbal communication when interacting with domesticated animals, as is often seen between
owners and their pets. Dog owners may use vocal commands to tell their pets to
come, stay, or sit. Additionally, just as tone of voice can express joy or anger to a
person, it can communicate the same information to a pet. Pets can be scolded with
a look or a gesture. Communication works in the opposite direction as well, as a
pet's body language and expressions convey information to its owner.

Communication between humans and animals is not confined strictly to pets. One of the most famous examples of animal communication is Koko, a gorilla who is able to communicate with humans through the use of American Sign Language. Koko's vocabulary includes over one thousand words.

MCAT Concept Check 9.2:

Before you move on, assess your understanding of the material with these questions.

1. Classify the following forms of communication as verbal or nonverbal:

• American Sign Language:	Verbal	Nonverbal
• Turning your body away from another person:	Verbal	Nonverbal
• Text messages:	Verbal	Nonverbal
• Giving a "high-five":	Verbal	Nonverbal
• Frowning:	Verbal	Nonverbal

2. What is the front stage self? The back stage self?

   • Front stage self:

   _____

   • Back stage self:

   _____

   _____

3. For each of the methods of animal communication below, provide one example:

Method of Communication	Example
Body language	
Facial expressions	
Visual displays	
Scents	
Vocalizations	

Conclusion

Skunks are unique in how they communicate with other animals they perceive as threats. Their anal glands are capable of producing high concentrations of thiol-containing compounds, which create a distinctive malodorous scent. But it is noteworthy that skunks only carry five or six sprays' worth of material at a time—thus, they tend to use other forms of animal communication, such as body language, hissing, and foot stamping before resorting to spraying. The spray, however, is an ultimate defense: intense, caustic, and very sticky. Animals who are sprayed quickly learn that the skunk is not an animal to mess with.

Humans also use many methods of communication. While they may certainly not follow the same patterns as skunks, humans use combinations of vocalization, body language, facial expressions, and gestures to interact with each other socially. The whole field of sociology flows from these interactions as we create groups, networks, and organizations; organize our society into hierarchies with statuses; and fulfill the roles dictated by our statuses. We put much of our energy into controlling how we communicate with others, trying to create the optimal image of ourselves through impression management.

The content of this chapter plays a large role in your day-to-day life. Every day you interact with other people, and how you interact is largely determined by the culture and society in which you live. In the next chapter, we begin to analyze specific types of interactions, like attraction and altruism, and then examine the dark side of human society: bias, prejudice, discrimination, and stereotypes.

CONCEPT SUMMARY

Elements of Social Interaction

- A **status** is a position in society used to classify individuals.
  - An **ascribed status** is involuntarily assigned to an individual based on race, ethnicity, gender, family background, and so on.
  - An **achieved status** is voluntarily earned by an individual.
  - A **master status** is the status by which an individual is primarily identified.
- A **role** is a set of beliefs, values, and norms that define the expectations of a certain status in a social situation.
  - **Role performance** refers to carrying out the behaviors of a given role.
  - A **role partner** is another individual who helps define a specific role within the relationship.
  - A **role set** contains all of the different roles associated with a status.
  - **Role conflict** occurs when one has difficulty in satisfying the requirements of multiple roles simultaneously; **role strain** occurs when one has difficulty satisfying multiple requirements of the same role simultaneously.
- **Groups** are made up of two or more individuals with similar characteristics that share a sense of unity.
  - A **peer group** is a self-selected group formed around similar interests, ages, and statuses.
  - A **family group** is the group into which an individual is born, adopted, or married.
  - An **in-group** is one with which an individual identifies.
  - An **out-group** is one that an individual competes with or opposes.
  - A **reference group** is a group to which an individual compares him- or herself.
  - **Primary groups** are those that contain strong, emotional bonds.
  - **Secondary groups** are often temporary and contain fewer emotional bonds and weaker bonds overall.
  - *Gemeinschaft* (**community**) is a group unified by feelings of togetherness due to shared beliefs, ancestry, or geography.
  - *Gesellschaft* (**society**) is a group unified by mutual self-interests in achieving a goal.
  - **Groupthink** occurs when members begin to conform to one another's views and ignore outside perspectives.
- A **network** is an observable pattern of social relationships between individuals or groups.

- **Organizations** are bodies of people with a structure and culture designed to achieve specific goals. They exist outside of each individual's membership within the organization.

Self-Presentation and Interacting with Others

- Various models have been proposed for how we express emotion in social situations.
  - The **basic model** states that there are universal emotions, along with corresponding expressions that can be understood across cultures.
  - The **social construction model** states that emotions are solely based on the situational context of social interactions.
- **Display rules** are unspoken rules that govern the expression of emotion.
- A **cultural syndrome** is a shared set of beliefs, norms, values, and behaviors organized around a central theme, as is found among people sharing the same language and geography.
- **Impression management** refers to the maintenance of a public image, which is accomplished through various strategies.
  - **Self-disclosure** is sharing factual information.
  - **Managing appearances** refers to using props, appearance, emotional expression, or associations to create a positive image.
  - **Ingratiation** is using flattery or conformity to win over someone else.
  - **Aligning actions** is the use of excuses to account for questionable behavior.
  - **Alter-casting** is imposing an identity onto another person.
- The **dramaturgical approach** says that individuals create images of themselves in the same way that actors perform a role in front of an audience.
  - The **front stage** is where the individual is seen by the audience and strives to preserve his desired image.
  - The **back stage** is where the individual is not in front of an audience and is free to act outside of his desired image.
- Communication includes both verbal and nonverbal elements.
  - **Verbal communication** is the conveyance of information through spoken, written, or signed words.
  - **Nonverbal communication** is the conveyance of information by means other than the use of words, such as body language, prosody, facial expressions, and gestures.
  - **Animal communication** takes place not only between nonhuman animals, but between humans and other animals as well. Animals use body language, rudimentary facial expressions, visual displays, scents, and vocalizations to communicate.

ANSWERS TO CONCEPT CHECKS

9.1

1.

Status	Example
Ascribed	Any status given involuntarily, due to factors such as race, ethnicity, gender, and family background
Achieved	Any status that is gained as a result of one's efforts or choices
Master	Any status by which a person would be most readily identified and that pervades all aspects of an individual's life

2. Statuses are positions in society used to classify individuals. Roles are the behaviors and expectations associated with a status in a particular context. A group is a collection of at least two individuals. A network is a more formal illustration of the relationships between individuals, usually through graphic representation. An organization is a body with a specific set of goals, a structure, and a culture; organizations are made up of members and may exist before and after an individual member's association with the organization.

9.2

1. Verbal: American Sign Language, text messages
   Nonverbal: turning your body away (body language), giving a "high-five" (gesture), frowning (facial expression)
2. The front stage self refers to when we are on stage and performing. This requires us to live up to the roles and expectations assumed by our status. The back stage self is when we are away from others and may include behaviors that would not be appropriate or consistent with the front stage self.
3. Examples may vary.

Method of Communication	Example
Body language	Dogs: tail between the legs
Facial expressions	Various animals: baring teeth
Visual displays	Peacocks: colorful plumage
Scents	Insects (and others): pheromones
Vocalizations	Birds: birdcalls

SHARED CONCEPTS

Discrete Practice Questions

1. Which of the following best describes the sociological definition of a status?

   A. The emotional state of a social interaction
   B. Expectations that are associated with a specific title in society
   C. A position in society used to classify an individual
   D. A means to describe one's peers

2. Becoming a college graduate requires hard work and diligence in academics. As such, being a college graduate could be considered a(n):

   A. ascribed status.
   B. achieved status.
   C. master status.
   D. cardinal status.

3. A bureaucracy is a specific example of a(n):

   A. immediate network.
   B. primary group.
   C. organization.
   D. reference group.

4. Which of the following is NOT characteristic of a bureaucracy?

   A. Rigidly defined work procedures
   B. Requirement for officials to hold an advanced degree
   C. Regular salary increases
   D. Election by constituents

5. Which of the following is a form of verbal communication?

   A. Facial expressions
   B. Hand gestures
   C. Written text
   D. Body movements

6. Which of the following best describes the impression management strategy of aligning actions?

   A. Adhering to the behaviors that are expected for a given role in society
   B. Relieving tension brought about by holding conflicting views in one's head
   C. Providing socially acceptable reasons to explain unexpected behavior
   D. Dictating that members of a group should follow similar practices to one another

7. While on the phone, a friend says: "A good friend would let me borrow the bike." This friend is using which impression management strategy?

   A. Managing appearances
   B. Alter-casting
   C. Ingratiation
   D. Self-disclosure

8. Which of the following is an example of a *Gesellschaft*?

   A. A large corporation
   B. A small rural neighborhood
   C. Members of the same family
   D. An ethnic enclave in a large city

9. In some cultures, it is considered taboo for one to show too much sadness at a funeral. In other cultures, wailing and crying loudly is expected. These cultures differ in their:

   A. characteristic institutions.
   B. display rules.
   C. authentic selves.
   D. peer groups.

10. Which of the following is NOT a dimension of the system for multiple level observation of groups (SYMLOG)?

    A. Friendliness *vs.* unfriendliness
    B. Dominance *vs.* submission
    C. Conformity *vs.* contrast
    D. Instrumentally controlled *vs.* emotionally expressive

11. Political campaign ads often focus on "exposing" an opposing candidate's negative characteristics. In the dramaturgical approach, one would describe this as:

    A. bringing the front stage self to the back stage.
    B. bringing the back stage self to the front stage.
    C. removing the front stage self.
    D. removing the back stage self.

12. In the context of impression management, which of the following selves is most similar to the ought self?

    A. The ideal self
    B. The tactical self
    C. The authentic self
    D. The presented self

13. The evolutionary role of emotions has been used as support for which model(s) of emotional expression?

    A. The basic model only
    B. The social construction model only
    C. Both the basic model and social construction model
    D. Neither the basic model nor the social construction model

14. Which of the following is an example of intraspecific animal communication?

    A. A dog who barks when a stranger enters the house
    B. An anglerfish that uses a bioluminescent appendage to attract prey
    C. Bats using echolocation to detect the surrounding environment
    D. A cat who uses scent glands to mark his territory for other cats

15. Primary groups differ from secondary groups in that:

    A. primary groups are shorter-lived than secondary groups.
    B. primary groups are larger than secondary groups.
    C. primary groups are formed of stronger bonds than secondary groups.
    D. primary groups are assigned while secondary groups are chosen.

Explanations to Discrete Practice Questions

1. C

A status is a position in society used to classify a person and exists in relation to other statuses. The specific behaviors associated with this status, **choice (B)**, best describe a role.

2. B

An achieved status is one that is acquired through personal efforts. This is in contrast to an ascribed status, **choice (A)**, in which the status is involuntarily given based on race, ethnicity, gender, family background, and so on. A master status, **choice (C)**, is one that influences all aspects of an individual's life. While being a college graduate is an important aspect of day-to-day life, it does not usually pervade every part of our lives.

3. C

A bureaucracy is an example of an organization, specifically one with the goal of performing complex tasks as efficiently as possible. Immediate networks and primary groups, **choices (A)** and **(B)**, are characterized by strong, intimate bonds, which are not commonly seen in bureaucracies. Reference groups, **choice (D)**, are those groups to which we compare ourselves for various characteristics.

4. D

Generally, bureaucracies are marked by six characteristics: paid officials on a fixed salary; nonelected officials who are provided rights and privileges as a result of making their career out of holding office; regular salary increases, seniority rights, and promotions upon passing exams or milestones, **choice (C)**; officials who enter the organization by holding an advanced degree or training, **choice (B)**; responsibilities, obligations, privileges, and work procedures rigidly defined by the organization, **choice (A)**; and responsibility for meeting the obligations of the office one holds.

5. C

Verbal communication uses words (whether spoken, written, or signed). Nonverbal communication uses other means of signaling emotions or ideas, such as gestures, body language, facial expressions, prosody, eye contact, and personal space.

6. C

Aligning actions is an impression management technique in which one provides socially acceptable reasons for unexpected behavior. This may manifest as providing an excuse for poor performance or laughing off an inappropriate comment as a joke. Tension created from having conflicting thoughts or opinions, as mentioned in **choice (B)**, refers to cognitive dissonance.

7. B

Imposing a role on another person (in this case, "good friend") is the hallmark of alter-casting. This example is also the opposite of ingratiation, **choice (C)**, because the implication behind the statement is that one is a "bad friend" if he or she does not lend the bike; ingratiation is the use of flattery or conformity to win over someone else.

8. A

A *Gesellschaft* (society) is one in which individuals are working toward the same goal, such as a company or country. *Gemeinschaften* (communities), on the other hand, are those that are bonded together by beliefs, ancestry, or geography.

9. B

Display rules are those that dictate cultural expectations of emotion. In some cultures, sadness is considered personal and internal; in others, sadness is shared externally with the community.

10. C

SYMLOG is a method for analyzing group dynamics and considers groups along three dimensions: dominant *vs.* submissive, friendliness *vs.* unfriendliness, and instrumentally controlled *vs.* emotionally expressive.

11. B

If a candidate is "exposed," then personal characteristics that are usually shielded from public view have been brought in front of the public. This would be pulling aspects of the back stage self to the front stage. It would not be considered removing the front stage self, **choice (C)**, because the candidate still has a public image, even if it has been tarnished.

12. B

The ought self is who others think we should be: the expectations imposed by others on us. This is most similar to the tactical self, which is the self we present to others when we adhere to their expectations. The presented self, **choice (D)**, is a combination of the authentic, ideal, and tactical selves.

13. A

The basic model of emotion, as proposed by Charles Darwin, states that emotions serve an evolutionary purpose, and thus are similar across cultures. The seven universal emotions have also been used as support for this theory. The social construction model states that emotions are always a product of the current social situation and does not posit any biological basis for emotions, implying a lack of a role for emotions in evolution.

14. D

Intraspecific communication refers to communication between members of the same species. Interspecific communication, on the other hand, refers to communication between members of different species. Echolocation is not an example of intraspecific communication because the sender of the signal and the recipient are the same organism; this would be considered autocommunication.

15. C

Primary groups have direct and close bonds between members, providing warm, personal, and intimate relationships to its members. Secondary groups, in contrast, form superficial bonds and tend to last for a shorter period of time.

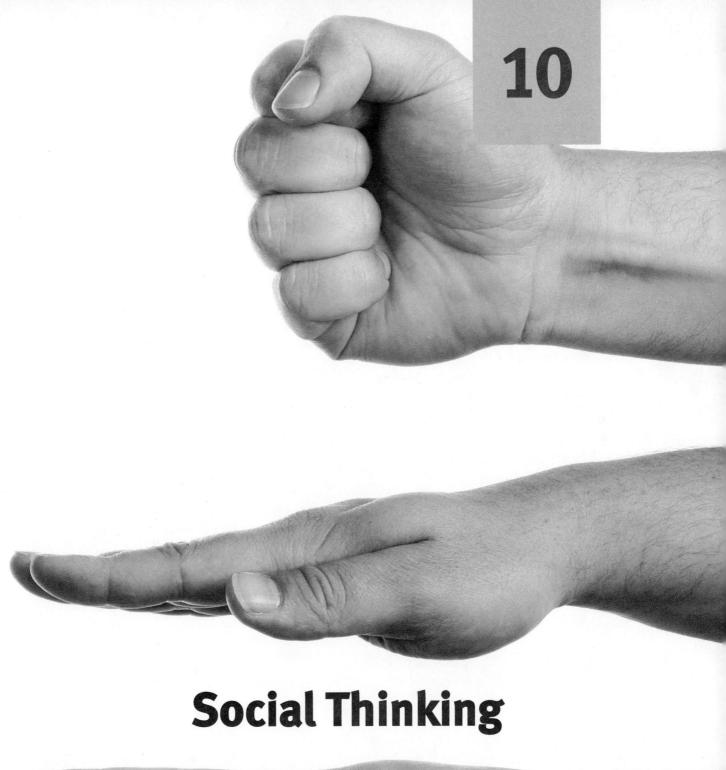

Social Thinking

In This Chapter

Chapter Profile

11%

The content in this chapter should be relevant to about 11% of all questions about the Behavioral Sciences on the MCAT.

This chapter covers material from the following AAMC content categories:

8B: Social thinking

8C: Social interactions

Introduction

Social psychology is concerned with social behavior, including the ways people influence each other's attitudes and behavior, the impact that individuals have on one another, the impact that social groups have on individual group members, the impact that individual group members have upon the social group, and the impact that social groups have on other social groups. In this chapter, we will continue our discussion of social psychology. We will continue to highlight its close relationship to sociology and the other fields within psychology, theoretical perspectives on human behavior within the social environment, and key concepts and classical studies in the field of social psychology. But whereas the last two chapters focused on how individuals are affected by groups and how individuals interact within groups, we will turn our attention in this chapter to specific behaviors seen across human beings, including attraction, aggression, attachment, and the need for social support. We'll also take a look at the dark side of social psychology as we look at patterns of blame in attribution theory and the misappropriation of social structure for prejudice and discrimination. This will be highly relevant for you as a physician, as many patients face prejudice based on their diagnoses, or are discriminated against because of personal characteristics, including age, sex, race, ethnicity, socioeconomic status, sexual orientation, gender identity, and more.

10.1 Social Behavior

> ## LEARNING GOALS
>
> After Chapter 10.1, you will be able to:
>
> - Describe interpersonal attraction, including the factors that influence interpersonal attraction
> - Recall the meaning of the term aggression, including examples of aggressive behaviors
> - List the four types of attachment and how they affect childhood behavior
> - Identify the common types of social support
> - Explain the relationship between altruism and inclusive fitness

Social behaviors allow us to interact with others. These may flow from positive feelings, such as attraction or attachment, or they may flow from negative feelings, such as aggression.

ATTRACTION

Have you ever wondered what makes some people friends and others enemies? How second graders choose their best friends? Why you keep eyeing that cute person in your physics class? Social psychologists call this phenomenon of individuals liking each other **interpersonal attraction**. Researchers have found several factors that affect attraction, including similarity, self-disclosure, reciprocity, and proximity. Outward appearance also plays a role; the more symmetric someone's face is, the more physically attractive we find him or her to be. Humans are also attracted to individuals with certain body proportions approximating the **golden ratio** (1.618:1).

We tend to be attracted to people who are similar to us in attitudes, intelligence, education, height, age, religion, appearance, and socioeconomic status. One reason for this may be convenience: it's easier to spend time together if you both want to go on a bike ride or if you both enjoy Thai food. Also, people are drawn to having their values and choices validated by another person. So why is there a cliché about opposites attracting? Social psychologists find that attraction also occurs if opposing qualities match up with each other; for example, a nurturer is attracted to someone who craves being nurtured. Notably, successful complementary relationships still have fundamental similarities in some attitudes that make the complementary aspects of the relationship work.

Another component of attraction lies in the opportunity for **self-disclosure**, or sharing one's fears, thoughts, and goals with another person and being met with nonjudgmental empathy. Engaging in this behavior deepens attraction and friendship.

Key Concept

Interpersonal attraction is influenced by many factors, including physical characteristics, similarity, self-disclosure, reciprocity, and proximity.

This must be a reciprocal behavior, however. Revealing one's innermost secrets creates a sense of vulnerability that, if not met by the other person, can be interpreted as being taken advantage of. Reciprocity is important in other aspects of interpersonal attraction as well. **Reciprocal liking** is the phenomenon whereby people like others better when they believe the other person likes them. Researchers have shown that even if we disagree with someone on important issues, we will have increased interest in them if we have indications that they like us.

Finally, **proximity**, or just being physically close to someone, plays a factor in our attraction to him or her. Studies have shown that we are more likely to form friendships with people in the same dorm as us or with the people who sit closest to us in class. Part of this is convenience; it's easier to have conversations and make plans with people in the same area. Another explanation is the **mere exposure effect** or **familiarity effect**, which says that people prefer stimuli that they have been exposed to more frequently. You may have observed this in your everyday life: Have you disliked a song the first time you heard it, only to find yourself singing along and saying, *I like this song!* after hearing it many more times? This principle is also used in marketing: the more people hear the name of a product, the more likely they are to be attracted to and purchase that product.

AGGRESSION

Aggression is defined as a behavior that intends to cause harm or increase social dominance. Aggression can take the form of physical actions as well as verbal or nonverbal communication. Ethologists study aggression in terms of the interactions between animals in natural settings. Aggression in these settings can include bodily contact, as seen in Figure 10.1, but most displays of aggression are settled by threat and withdrawal without actual bodily harm. Threat displays are common in both animals and humans. Before a fight, a man might puff up his chest or pull back his fist to threaten another person. This display may or may not result in physical harm or violence. Other examples of aggression include a bully hurling insults at another child, or a teenage gang member making threatening gestures to a member of another gang.

What is the purpose of aggressive behavior if it causes so much destruction? Evolutionarily, aggression offers protection against perceived and real threats. Aggression helped our ancestors fight off predators. It also helps organisms gain access to resources such as food, additional territory, or mates. In cases of limited resources, aggression could be the deciding factor that allows one to pass on genes.

Figure 10.1. Aggression Following Threat Displays of Elephant Seals
While threat displays may lead to violence as seen here, threat displays commonly lead to withdrawal to prevent fights.

Bridge

The prefrontal cortex is critically important to managing the limbic system, which is important in managing emotion and stress. These roles of the prefrontal cortex are discussed in Chapter 5 of *MCAT Behavioral Sciences Review*.

Real World

Alcohol has been shown to increase aggressive behavior. Alcohol impairs judgment and limits one's ability to control aggressive reactions. It also makes one feel less inhibited by social mores that would normally restrict aggressive behavior.

From a biological perspective, multiple parts of the brain contribute to violent behavior. The **amygdala** is the part of the brain responsible for associating stimuli and their corresponding rewards or punishments. In short, it is responsible for telling us whether or not something is a threat. If the amygdala is activated, this increases aggression. However, higher-order brain structures, such as the prefrontal cortex, can place brakes on a revved-up amygdala, reducing emotional reactivity and impulsiveness. Reduced activity in the prefrontal cortex has been linked to increased aggressive behavior.

Aggression is also under hormonal control. Higher levels of testosterone have been linked to more aggressive behavior in both males and females. The higher levels of testosterone in men compared to women may explain the fact that men are generally more aggressive than women across cultures, and that men commit a disproportionate majority of violent crimes.

Beyond the biological contributions to aggressive behavior, studies have found many psychological and situational predictors of aggression. Do you find yourself snapping at people more when you're in pain? Have you ever gotten annoyed with a waiter when you were extremely hungry? Our responses are accounted for by the **cognitive neoassociation model**, which states that we are more likely to respond to others aggressively whenever we are feeling negative emotions, such as being tired, sick, frustrated, or in pain. This can also be seen on a large scale: riots are more likely to happen on hot days than cool ones; drivers without air conditioning are more likely to honk at other drivers than those with air conditioning.

Another factor that contributes to aggressive behavior is exposure to violent behavior. The effects on children of media portrayals of violence continue to be a hot topic. Research findings are mixed but tend to show that viewing violent behavior indeed

K

correlates to an increase in aggressive behavior. The contribution of modeling to violence in children was also explored in Albert Bandura's Bobo doll experiment, described in Chapter 3 of *MCAT Behavioral Sciences Review*.

ATTACHMENT

Attachment is an emotional bond between a caregiver and a child. Development of attachment begins during infancy. While parental figures are most common, emotional bonds can occur with any caregiver who is sensitive and responsive during social interaction. After World War II, psychiatrist John Bowlby noticed the negative effects of isolation on social and emotional development in orphaned children and started the study of attachment. In the 1970s, psychologist Mary Ainsworth expounded on this theory, saying that infants need a secure base in the form of a consistent caregiver during the first six months to two years of life from which to explore the world and develop appropriately. Four main types of attachment styles have been described: secure, avoidant, ambivalent, and disorganized.

Secure Attachment

Secure attachment is seen when a child has a consistent caregiver and is able to go out and explore, knowing that he or she has a secure base to return to. The child will be upset at the departure of the caregiver and will be comforted by the return of the caregiver. The child trusts that the caregiver will be there for comfort, and while the child can be comforted by a stranger, he or she will clearly prefer the caregiver. Having a secure attachment pattern is thought to be a vital aspect of a child's social development. Children with avoidant, ambivalent, or disorganized attachment can have deficits in social skills.

Avoidant Attachment

Avoidant attachment results when the caregiver has little or no response to a distressed child. Given the choice, these children will show no preference between a stranger and the caregiver. They show little or no distress when the caregiver leaves and little or no relief when the caregiver returns.

Ambivalent Attachment

Ambivalent attachment occurs when a caregiver has an inconsistent response to a child's distress, sometimes responding appropriately, sometimes neglectfully. As such, the child is unable to form a secure base as he or she cannot consistently rely on the caregiver's response. The child will be very distressed on separation from the caregiver but has a mixed response when the caregiver returns, often displaying ambivalence. This is sometimes referred to as **anxious–ambivalent attachment** because the child is always anxious about the reliability of the caregiver.

> **Key Concept**
>
> In attachment, a secure base is a caregiver who is consistent, available, comforting, and responsive.

> **Real World**
>
> As a physician, you will be a mandated reporter. This means that you are required by law to report suspected cases of child abuse. Remember: It is better to report and be incorrect than to miss a potentially fatal scenario.

Disorganized Attachment

Children with **disorganized attachment** show no clear pattern of behavior in response to the caregiver's absence or presence, but instead can show a mix of different behaviors. These can include avoidance or resistance; seeming dazed, frozen, or confused; or repetitive behaviors like rocking. Disorganized attachment is often associated with erratic behavior and social withdrawal by the caregiver. It may also be a red flag for abuse.

SOCIAL SUPPORT

In psychology, **social support** is the perception or reality that one is cared for by a social network. Social support can be divided into many different categories: emotional, esteem, material, informational, and network support. While social support is present at all times, it is often most pronounced—and necessary—when someone suffers a personal or family tragedy.

Emotional support is listening, affirming, and empathizing with someone's feelings. It's the *I'm sorry for your loss* condolence card or a trip to the hospital to visit a sick relative. Many people equate social support with emotional support, but other forms of support exist as well.

Esteem support is similar, but touches more directly on affirming the qualities and skills of a person. Reminding someone of the skills they possess to tackle a problem can bolster their confidence. For example, consider a friend who has missed a significant amount of school due to illness. Telling her that she should have no problem making up the work because she is smart and an efficient worker would be providing esteem support.

Material support, also called **tangible support**, is any type of financial or material contribution to another person. It can come in the form of making a meal for a friend after they have lost a loved one or donating money to a person in need.

Informational support refers to providing information that will help someone. You will spend much of your career providing informational support to patients as you explain their diagnoses, potential treatment options, and risks and benefits of those treatment options.

Network support is the type of social support that gives a person a sense of belonging. This can be shown physically, as demonstrated in Figure 10.2, or can be accomplished through gestures, group activities, and shared experiences.

Figure 10.2. Network Support
A group hug creates a sense of belonging.

No matter the form, all of these social supports offer many different types of health benefits. Social support helps reduce psychological distress such as anxiety and depression. People with low social support show higher levels of major mental disorders, alcohol and drug use, and suicidal ideation. Beyond these intuitive improvements in mental health, there are also improvements to our physical health. Studies have found that people with low social support have a higher mortality risk from many different diseases, including diabetes, cardiovascular disease, and cancer. Strong social support appears to correlate with immunological health, too: those with higher social support are less likely to get colds and recover faster when they do.

SOCIAL BEHAVIORS AND EVOLUTIONARY FITNESS

Many behaviors have neurological corollaries. Here, we will look at some specific behaviors and the brain regions that are implicated in causing them.

Foraging

The behavior of **foraging**, or seeking out and eating food, is driven by biological, psychological, and social influences. Biologically, hunger is driven by a complex pathway involving both neurotransmitters and hormones. The sensation of hunger is controlled by the **hypothalamus**. Specifically, the lateral hypothalamus promotes hunger, while the ventromedial hypothalamus responds to cues that we are full and promotes satiety. Thus, damage to the lateral hypothalamus will cause a person to lose all interest in eating; meanwhile, damage to the ventromedial hypothalamus will result in obesity because the individual never feels satiated.

Foraging is also impacted by genetics. Certain genes play a role in the onset of foraging behavior and the division of tasks between members of the same group. Some species forage together while others engage in solitary foraging.

Cognitive skills play a role in the success of both solitary and group foraging. These skills include spatial awareness, memory, and decision-making. In species that forage as a group, foraging is primarily a learned behavior. Young individuals learn through observation how to find and consume food and determine what is safe to eat, as shown in Figure 10.3. Animals also learn how to hunt by watching others. Some animals, such as wolves, hunt in packs that have strict rules regarding the order in which individuals are allowed to eat after a successful hunt.

Figure 10.3. Foraging Is Learned through Observational Learning

Mating and Mate Choice

A **mating system** describes the organization of a group's sexual behavior. Mating systems seen among animals include monogamy, polygamy, and promiscuity. **Monogamy** refers to an exclusive mating relationship. **Polygamy** involves a male having exclusive relationships with multiple females (**polygyny**) or a female having exclusive relationships with multiple males (**polyandry**). **Promiscuity** refers to a member of one sex mating with any member of the opposite sex, without exclusivity. In most animal species, there is one dominant mating system; however, humans exhibit more flexibility. In humans, mating behavior is highly influenced by both biological and social factors. Humans also differ from animals by having formal relationships to correspond with mate choice. Mating may or may not be associated with these social relationships, such as marriage or dating.

Mate choice, or **intersexual selection**, is the selection of a mate based on attraction. **Mate bias** refers to how choosy members of the species are while choosing a mate. This bias is an evolutionary mechanism aimed at increasing the fitness of the species. It may carry **direct benefits** by providing material advantages, protection, or emotional support, or **indirect benefits** by promoting better survival in offspring. There are five recognized mechanisms of mate choice:

Key Concept

Direct benefits provide advantages to the mate. Indirect benefits provide advantages to offspring.

- **Phenotypic benefits:** observable traits that make a potential mate more attractive to the opposite sex. Usually, these traits indicate increased production and survival of offspring. For example, males that appear more nurturing are more likely to care for, and promote the survival of, their offspring.
- **Sensory bias:** development of a trait to match a preexisting preference that exists in the population. For example, fiddler crabs are naturally attracted to structures that break up the level horizon because they may indicate a food source; male crabs take advantage of this fact by building pillars around their territory to attract mates.
- **Fisherian** or **runaway selection:** a positive feedback mechanism in which a particular trait that has no effect or a negative effect on survival becomes more and more exaggerated over time. In this model, a trait is deemed sexually desirable and thus is more likely to be passed on. This increases the attractiveness of the trait, which in turn increases the likelihood that it continues to be passed on. The bright plumage of the peacock, shown in Figure 10.4, is the prototypical example of Fisherian selection.

Figure 10.4. Fisherian Selection
The exaggerated plumage of the peacock is the prototypical example of Fisherian selection, in which the attractiveness of a trait that imparts a survival disadvantage leads to its continuation and exaggeration within the species.

- **Indicator traits:** traits that signify overall good health and well-being of an organism, increasing its attractiveness to mates. Notably, these traits may or may not be genetic in origin. For example, female cats are more attracted to male cats with clean and shiny coats; a dirty and dull coat may be related to an underlying genetic problem, or to malnutrition or infection.

- **Genetic compatibility:** the creation of mate pairs that, when combined, have complementary genetics. This theory provides a mechanism for the reduced frequency of recessive genetic disorders in the population: attraction to others who have starkly different genetic makeups reduces the probability of offspring being homozygotic for a disease-carrying allele.

Altruism

Altruism is a form of helping behavior in which the person's intent is to benefit someone else at some cost to him- or herself. Helping behavior can be motivated by selflessness, but can also be motivated by egoism or ulterior motives, such as public recognition. **Empathy** is the ability to vicariously experience the emotions of another, and it is thought by some social psychologists to be a strong influence on helping behavior. The **empathy–altruism hypothesis** is one explanation for the relationship between empathy and helping behavior. According to this theory, one individual helps another person when he or she feels empathy for the other person, regardless of the cost. This theory has been heavily debated, and more recent conceptions of altruism posit that an individual will help another person only when the benefits outweigh the costs for the individual.

Game Theory

Game theory attempts to explain decision-making behavior. The theory was originally used in economics and mathematics to predict interaction based on game characteristics, including strategy, winning and losing, rewards and punishments, and profits and cost. A game is defined by its players, the information and actions available to each player at decision points, and the payoffs associated with each outcome.

In the context of biology, game payoffs refer to fitness. Game theorists studying sex ratios in various species developed the concept of the **evolutionary stable strategy** (**ESS**). When an ESS is adopted by a given population in a specific environment, natural selection will prevent alternative strategies from arising. The strategies are thus inherited traits passed along with the population, with the object of the game being becoming more fit than competitors.

One of the classic evolutionary games is the Hawk–Dove game. The game focuses on access to shared food resources. In each round, a player chooses one of two strategies: hawk or dove. The hawk exhibits a fighter strategy, displaying aggression and fighting until he wins or is injured. The dove exhibits a fight avoidance strategy, displaying aggression at first but retreating if the fight escalates. If the dove is not faced with a fight, he will attempt to share the food resources. There are three potential outcomes. If two hawks compete, one will win and one will lose. If a hawk and a dove compete, the hawk will invariably win. If two doves compete, they will share the food resources. The payoff in this case is based on both the value of the reward and the cost of fighting: If the reward is significantly larger than the cost of fighting, then hawks have an advantage. If the cost of fighting is significantly larger, doves have an advantage. There thus exists an equilibrium point where, based on the magnitude of the reward and the cost of fighting, the hawk and dove strategies can coexist as evolutionary stable strategies.

The Hawk–Dove game represents pure competition between individuals. However, social influences apply in nature and can result in four possible alternatives for competitors when dealing with strategic interactions. The four alternatives are shown in Figure 10.5 and are:

- **Altruism:** the donor provides a benefit to the recipient at a cost to him- or herself
- **Cooperation:** both the donor and recipient benefit by cooperating
- **Spite:** both the donor and recipient are negatively impacted
- **Selfishness:** the donor benefits while the recipient is negatively impacted

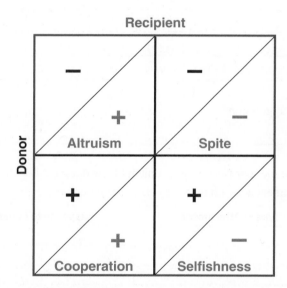

Figure 10.5. Strategic Alternatives for Socially Influenced Competitors

Other common strategy games, like rock–paper–scissors and chicken, can also be explained by game theory.

Inclusive Fitness

In evolutionary psychology, **inclusive fitness** is a measure of an organism's success in the population. This is based on the number of offspring, success in supporting offspring, and the ability of the offspring to then support others. Early descriptions of evolutionary success were based solely on the number of viable offspring of an organism. However, contemporary theories take into account the benefits of certain behaviors on the population at large. For example, the existence of altruism could be supported by the observation that close relatives of an individual will share many of the same genes; thus, promoting the reproduction

Real World

Altruism creates a bit of a problem for the traditional Darwinist model of evolution. Why would an organism sacrifice its own fitness for the fitness of another? Evolutionary biologists still wrestle with this question, but inclusive fitness offers at least one potential solution.

and survival of related or similar individuals can also lead to genetic success. Other species show examples of inclusive fitness by protecting the offspring of the group at large. By sacrificing themselves to protect the young, these organisms ensure the passing of genes to future generations. Inclusive fitness therefore promotes the idea that altruistic behavior can improve the fitness and success of a species as a whole.

MCAT Concept Check 10.1:

Before you move on, assess your understanding of the material with these questions.

1. What is interpersonal attraction, and what are three factors that influence this attraction?

   _____

   • _____

   • _____

   • _____

2. What is aggression?

   _____

3. What are the four types of attachment? How does a child with each form of attachment act with regard to his or her caregiver?

Type of Attachment	Response to Caregiver

4. What is social support? List three of the common types of social support.

   _____

   _____

   • _____

   • _____

   • _____

5. What is altruism?

   _____

   _____

10.2 Social Perception and Behavior

Social perception is the name social psychologists give to how we form impressions about the characteristics of individuals and groups of people. We form impressions of others through observation of their behavior, past experiences, and personal beliefs and attitudes. We also feel the need to be able to explain and understand the behavior of others, a process we perform through attribution.

SOCIAL PERCEPTION

Social perception is also referred to as **social cognition**, and provides the tools to make judgments and impressions regarding other people.

Components of Social Perception

There are three primary components of social perception: the perceiver, the target, and the situation. The **perceiver** is influenced by experience, motives, and emotional state. Past experiences affect our attitudes toward current and future experiences and can lead to particular expectations of events. Our motives influence what information we deem important and what we choose to ignore. Finally, emotional state can flavor our interpretation of an event. The **target** refers to the person about which the perception is made. Knowledge of the target can include past experiences or specific information that affect perception. When little information is available, there is a need for greater observation and interpretation by the perceiver. Finally, the **situation** is also very important in developing perception. A given social context can determine what information is available to the perceiver.

Impression Bias

One model of social perception focuses on our selection of cues to form interpretations of others that are consistent over time. When a perceiver comes into contact with an unfamiliar target, they take in all cues from the target and environment,

Bridge

Social perception is highly linked to attitudes; social perception focuses on how we form attitudes about specific characteristics of individuals and groups. Attitudes are discussed in detail in Chapter 8 of *MCAT Behavioral Sciences Review*.

unfiltered. As the perceiver becomes more familiar with a given target, they use these cues to categorize the target: friend *vs.* enemy, caring *vs.* standoffish, open-minded *vs.* bigoted, and so on. Additional time spent with the target in the situational context will lead the perceiver to confirm his or her categorization. After this point, the perception of additional cues becomes selective in order to paint a picture of the target that is consistent with the perceptions the perceiver has already made. This theory supports the **primacy effect**, which is the idea that first impressions are often more important than subsequent impressions. Sometimes, however, it is actually the most recent information we have about an individual that is the most important in forming our impressions; this is called the **recency effect**.

Individuals tend to organize the perception of others based on traits and personal characteristics of the target that are most relevant to the perceiver. This idea is referred to as the **reliance on central traits**. People may also project their own beliefs, opinions, ideas, and actions onto others. The categories we place others in during impression formation is based on **implicit personality theory**. This theory states that there are sets of assumptions people make about how different types of people, their traits, and their behavior are related. Making assumptions about people based on the category in which they are placed is known as **stereotyping**, and will be discussed in detail in the next section.

Halo Effect

The **halo effect** is a cognitive bias in which judgments about a specific aspect of an individual can be affected by one's overall impression of the individual. It is the tendency to allow a general impression about a person (*I like Judy*) to influence other, more specific evaluations about a person (*Judy is a good mother, Judy is trustworthy, Judy can do no wrong*). The halo effect explains why people are often inaccurate when evaluating people that they either believe to be generally good, or those that they believe to be generally bad. An individual's attractiveness has also been seen to produce the halo effect. As described earlier, attractiveness can be determined by a variety of traits, and the perception of these traits can impact the view of an individual's personality. It has been shown that people who are perceived as attractive are also more likely to be perceived as trustworthy and friendly.

Just-World Hypothesis

Another cognitive bias during impression formation is the **just-world hypothesis**. In a so-called just world, good things happen to good people, and bad things happen to bad people; noble actions are rewarded, and evil actions are punished. Consequences may be attributed to a universal restoring force; in Hinduism, this force is referred to as *karma*. A strong belief in a just world increases the likelihood of "blaming the victim" or stating that a victim is *getting what he or she deserves* because such a worldview denies the possibility of innocent victims.

Self-Serving Bias

Self-identity and perception can be skewed through **self-serving bias**, also known as **self-serving attributional bias**. This bias refers to the fact that individuals will view their own success based on internal factors, while viewing failures based on external factors. The notion that all good things that happen are based on our good traits and behaviors and that all bad things are based on situational factors beyond our control is used to protect our self-esteem. For example, a student who earns a good grade on a test may attribute her success to her intelligence or to how intensely she studied. However, if she received a bad grade, she might attribute it to poor teaching by the professor, unfair questions, or too long a test for the allotted time. These types of attributions have been found to occur in many settings including the workplace, school, interpersonal relationships, and athletics. Both motivational processes, such as self-enhancement, and cognitive processes, such as **locus of control**, influence self-serving bias. **Self-enhancement** focuses on the need to maintain self-worth and can be done through internal attribution of successes and external attribution of failures, as described here. Emotion is also a factor in self-serving bias because it can impact self-esteem, which influences the need to protect one's self-identity. Individuals with higher self-esteem are more likely to protect this image and thus more likely to exhibit self-serving bias. Relationships to others also determine the likelihood of the bias: individuals who have close relationships are less likely to attribute failures to one another, and instead will make joint attributions. On the other hand, strangers are much more likely to self-serve by placing blame for a failure on each other.

ATTRIBUTION THEORY

Another aspect of social cognition is explaining the behavior of others. It is human nature to observe and try to understand why others act the way they do. **Attribution theory** focuses on the tendency for individuals to infer the causes of other people's behavior.

Dispositional and Situational Causes

Fritz Heider, one of the founding fathers of attribution theory, divided the causes for attribution into two main categories: dispositional (internal) and situational (external). This distinction is very important. **Dispositional (internal)** attributions are those that relate to the person whose behavior is being considered, including his or her beliefs, attitudes, and personality characteristics. **Situational (external)** attributions are those that relate to features of the surroundings, such as threats, money, social norms, and peer pressure. For instance, suppose you hear that a friend has been nominated for an academic award. Believing that the friend has been nominated because of hard work and personal effort would be a dispositional attribution. Contrarily, chalking up the nomination to luck would be a situational attribution. Situational attributions, therefore, consider the characteristics of the social context rather than the characteristics of the individual as the primary cause.

Real World

People with depression often have a reversed attributional bias, viewing their successes as caused by external factors (*I got lucky this time*) and failures as caused by internal factors (*It was all my fault*).

Key Concept

- Consistency cues—has consistent behavior over time
- Consensus cues—matches others' behavior
- Distinctiveness cues—uses similar behavior in similar situations

MCAT Expertise

Actor-observer asymmetry (or **bias**) results from the self-serving bias (by the actor) and the fundamental attribution error (by the observer). Actor-observer bias holds that, due to our unique knowledge about our own actions, we are more likely to make situational attributions for the self as compared to others. Were you to be the one who failed to complete an assignment, for example, you would be far more likely to consider the situational factors involved in your behavior because you are intimately aware of them. This effect is most commonly seen with negative behaviors.

Cues

In order to understand the behavior of others, a variety of cues are used. These include consistency cues, consensus cues, and distinctiveness cues. **Consistency cues** refer to the consistent behavior of a person over time. The more regular the behavior, the more we associate that behavior with the motives of the person. **Consensus cues** relate to the extent to which a person's behavior differs from others. If a person deviates from socially expected behavior, we are likely to form a dispositional attribution about the person's behavior. **Distinctiveness cues** refer to the extent to which a person engages in similar behavior across a series of scenarios. If a person's behavior varies in different scenarios, we are more likely to form a situational attribution to explain it.

The **correspondent inference theory** takes this concept one step further by focusing on the intentionality of others' behavior. When an individual unexpectedly performs a behavior that helps or hurts us, we tend to explain the behavior by dispositional attribution. Thus, we may correlate these unexpected actions with the person's personality.

Fundamental Attribution Error

The **fundamental attribution error** posits that we are generally biased toward making dispositional attributions rather than situational attributions, especially in negative contexts. For example, suppose that you were working on a team project and another team member was unable to complete his assignment. Our immediate response may be to assume that this team member is lazy, unreliable, or even stupid—all of which are dispositional attributions. We may ignore the possibility that the team member got ill, has too many concurrent assignments, or suffered a personal tragedy—all of which are situational attributions.

Attribute Substitution

Attribute substitution occurs when individuals must make judgments that are complex, but instead they substitute a simpler solution or apply a heuristic. When making automatic or intuitive judgments on difficult questions or scenarios, an individual may address a different question or scenario without even realizing a substitution has been made. In one study, individuals were asked to envision a sphere that could just fit inside a cube. They were then asked what percentage of the volume of the cube would be taken up by the sphere. This is challenging to envision, so most individuals likely simplified the problem in their minds to imagine a circle inside a square. The answers given in this study averaged around 74 percent, which is approximately the area of a square taken up by a circumscribed circle (79%), but significantly higher than the volume of a cube taken up by a circumscribed sphere (52%).

Attribute substitution can take place in far simpler setups as well. A classic example used in many psychology classes is the following question: *A pencil and an eraser cost $1.10 together. If the pencil costs one dollar more than the eraser,* *how much does the eraser cost?* Most individuals respond instinctively with the answer ten cents. It is easy to recognize that the pencil costs more, and to integrate the information given in the question stem (*$1.10* and *one dollar*) incorrectly.

This process is also common when dealing with size and color in optical illusions. For instance, when judging the size of figures in an image with perspective, the apparent sizes shown in the image can be distorted by three-dimensional context, as shown in Figure 10.6. The expected three-dimensional size of the figure, based on perspective cues, substitutes for the actual two-dimensional size of the birds within the image. It is interesting to note that painters and photographers with experience in two-dimensional images are less likely to substitute due to the fact that two-dimensional size is more understandable to their perception.

Figure 10.6. Attribute Substitution for Size in Optical Illusions
The birds are of identical size, but three-dimensional cues affect our interpretation of the image.

Shadows, patterns, the position of the sun, and other visual cues can also cause attribute substitution for color, as shown in Figure 10.7.

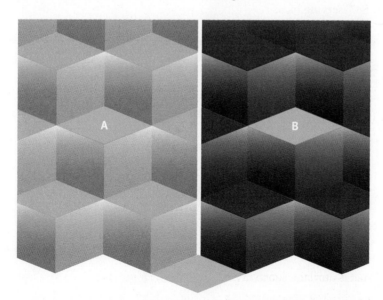

Figure 10.7. Attribute Substitution for Color in Optical Illusions
The central boxes labeled A and B are of identical color, but shadow cues affect our interpretation of the image.

Cultural Attribution

Another important factor in attribution is culture. The type of culture an individual is a part of plays a major role in the types of attributions the individual makes. Individualist cultures, including Anglo-American and Anglo-Saxon European cultures, put high value on the individual, personal goals, and independence. Collectivist cultures, including many Asian and African societies, view individuals as members of a group and place high value on conformity and interdependence. Individualists tend to make more fundamental attribution errors than those in collectivist cultures. Individualists are also more likely to attribute behavior to dispositional factors, whereas collectivists are more likely to attribute behavior to situational factors.

MCAT Concept Check 10.2:

Before you move on, assess your understanding of the material with these questions.

1. For each of the social cognitive biases below, provide a brief description:

   • Primacy effect:

   _____

   • Recency effect:

   _____

   • Halo effect:

   _____

   • Just-world hypothesis:

   _____

   • Self-serving bias:

   _____

2. What is attribution theory? What are the two types of attribution?

   _____

   _____

   • _____

   • _____

3. What is the fundamental attribution error?

   _____

   _____

4. What is attribute substitution?

   _____

   _____

10.3 Stereotypes, Prejudice, and Discrimination

LEARNING GOALS

After Chapter 10.3, you will be able to:

- Distinguish between stereotypes, prejudice, and discrimination
- List the types of social inequality that can influence prejudice
- Compare and contrast ethnocentrism and cultural relativism

While stereotypes, prejudice, and discrimination are terms that are related and often used together, they are very different concepts. Stereotypes are viewed as cognitive, prejudice as affective, and discrimination as behavioral. Stereotypes refer to the expectations, impressions, and opinions about the characteristics of members of a group. Prejudice reflects the overall attitude and emotional response to a group. Discrimination refers to differences in actions toward different groups.

Note: Kaplan Test Prep does not endorse or encourage any of the stereotypes mentioned in this chapter; they are included only as examples.

Key Concept

- Stereotypes are cognitive
- Prejudices are affective
- Discrimination is behavioral

STEREOTYPES

Despite their negative connotations, stereotypes are fundamentally necessary to everyday life. In a psychological sense, the purpose of a stereotype is to make sense of a complex world by categorizing and systematizing information in order to better identify items, predict their behavior, and react. In the context of stereotyping what different items of furniture look like, how different types of stores operate, or how different cuisines taste, stereotypes are extremely useful in defining categories and determining what does or does not fit into that category. However, when stereotypes are used to develop prejudices toward others and to discriminate, they are being appropriated for negative uses.

In the context of sociology, **stereotypes** occur when attitudes and impressions are based on limited and superficial information about a person or a group of individuals. The content of stereotypes are the attributes that people believe define and characterize a group. The **stereotype content model** attempts to classify stereotypes with respect to a hypothetical in-group using two dimensions: warmth and competence. Warm groups are those that are not in direct competition with the in-group for resources; competent groups are those that have high status within society. The four possible combinations of warmth and competence are shown in Figure 10.8 and are associated with distinct emotions.

		Competence	
		low	high
Warmth	high	**Paternalistic stereotype** low status, not competitive (housewives, elderly people, disabled people)	**Admiration stereotype** high status, not competitive (in-group, close allies)
	low	**Contemptuous stereotype** low status, competitive (welfare recipients, poor people)	**Envious stereotype** high status, competitive (Asians, Jews, rich people, feminists)

Figure 10.8. Classifications of Stereotypes in the Stereotype Content Model
Adapted from Fiske *et al.* (2002)

Paternalistic stereotypes are those in which the group is looked down upon as inferior, dismissed, or ignored. **Contemptuous** stereotypes are those in which the group is viewed with resentment, annoyance, or anger. **Envious** stereotypes are those in which the group is viewed with jealousy, bitterness, or distrust. **Admiration** stereotypes are those in which the group is viewed with pride and other positive feelings.

Self-Fulfilling Prophecy

Stereotypes can lead to expectations of certain groups of individuals. This expectation can create conditions that lead to confirmation of those expectations, a process referred to as **self-fulfilling prophecy**. You may experience a self-fulfilling prophecy during your first days of surgery clerkship in medical school. During their first year in the wards, medical students are stereotyped as being unable to quickly and efficiently throw knots during a surgery. With this knowledge in mind, many medical students are nervous to suture for the first time and may struggle with every step of the knot-tying process. This validates the stereotype and thus completes the self-fulfilling prophecy.

Stereotype Threat

Stereotype threat refers to the concept of people being concerned or anxious about confirming a negative stereotype about one's social group. Stereotype threat can cause reduced performance, encourage self-handicapping strategies, and lower one's personal investment in an activity. Some examples of stereotype threat include white males in sports, women driving, and homosexual couples providing childcare. Due to the awareness of stereotypes, individuals may perform worse or avoid performance altogether. The vulnerability of an individual to stereotype threat is in part based on how highly he or she identifies with the stereotyped group. However, stereotype threat can occur simply based on the presence of others. It has been shown that women taking a math exam with other women present scored higher than when taking a math exam when only men were present. Gender was not mentioned or emphasized, but it is possible that self-identification with a group and awareness of a stereotype resulted in reduced performance.

PREJUDICE

From a social psychology approach, **prejudice** is defined as an irrational positive or negative attitude toward a person, group, or thing, prior to an actual experience with that entity. The process of socialization results in the formation of attitudes regarding our own groups and a sense of identity as an individual and a group member. Prejudice can form in response to dissimilarities among groups, races, ethnicities, or even environments. While racial and ethnic prejudices against individuals are at the forefront of most people's minds, prejudices exist against objects and places as well. For instance, people have attitudes toward different regions of the country based on culture, weather, and history; which car manufacturers are the most reliable; what types of food are considered unhealthy; and even what types of animals make good pets. Prejudicial attitudes can run the gamut from hate to love, contempt to admiration, and indifference to loyalty.

Prejudices may be kept internally or shared with the larger community. **Propaganda** is a common way by which large organizations and political groups attempt to create prejudices in others. Propaganda posters often invoke messages of fear, and depictions of the target group are often exaggerated to an absurd degree.

Power, Prestige, and Class

There are a variety of social factors that influence prejudice. Three of the most important are power, prestige, and class. **Power** refers to the ability of people or groups to achieve their goals despite any obstacles, and their ability to control resources. **Prestige** is the level of respect shown to a person by others. **Class** refers to socioeconomic status. Social inequality, or the unequal distribution of power, resources, money, or prestige, can result in the grouping of *haves* and *have-nots*. *Have-nots* may develop a negative attitude toward *haves* based on jealousy. *Haves* may develop a negative attitude toward *have-nots* as a defense mechanism to justify the fact that they have more.

ETHNOCENTRISM

Ethnocentrism refers to the practice of making judgments about other cultures based on the values and beliefs of one's own culture, especially when it comes to language, customs, and religion. Ethnocentrism can manifest in many ways, from innocent displays of ethnic pride to violent supremacy groups.

Key Concept

Stereotype threat is concern or anxiety about confirming a negative stereotype about one's group. This may hinder performance, which may actually create a self-fulfilling prophecy.

In-Group and Out-Group

Two concepts related to ethnocentrism are in-groups and out-groups. An **in-group** is a social group with which a person experiences a sense of belonging or identifies as a member. An **out-group**, on the other hand, refers to a social group with which an individual does not identify. An in-group can form based on a variety of identifying characteristics, including but not limited to race, culture, gender, religion, profession, or education. Notably, negative feelings toward an out-group are not based on a sense of dislike toward the characteristics of the out-group; rather, they are based on favoritism for the in-group and the absence of favoritism for the out-group.

Cultural Relativism

In order to avoid ethnocentrism, the concept of cultural relativism has been employed by sociologists to compare and understand other cultures. **Cultural relativism** is the perception of another culture as different from one's own, but with the recognition that the cultural values, mores, and rules of a culture fit into that culture itself. In other words, while one group may follow a given set of rules (say, the dietary rules of *kashrut* or *halal*), that group does not perceive those rules as superior to those of other cultures—just different.

DISCRIMINATION

Discrimination occurs when prejudicial attitudes cause individuals of a particular group to be treated differently from others. While prejudice is an attitude, discrimination is a behavior. As prejudice is typically a negative attitude, discrimination is typically a negative behavior. It is also important to note that prejudice does not always result in discrimination. For instance, a person might have strong feelings against a particular race (prejudice), but may not express those feelings or act on them. As social inequality influences prejudice, the same idea applies to discrimination. The unequal distribution of power, prestige, and class influence discrimination.

Individual *vs.* Institutional Discrimination

Discrimination can be either individual or institutional. **Individual discrimination** refers to one person discriminating against a particular person or group, whereas **institutional discrimination** refers to the discrimination against a particular person or group by an entire institution. Individual discrimination is considered to be conscious and obvious. This type of discrimination can be eliminated by removing the person who is displaying the behavior. Sociologists have begun to stress the need to focus on institutional discrimination, as it is discrimination built into the structure of society. It is far more covert and harder to extricate. Because it is part of society, it is perpetuated by simply maintaining the status quo.

The United States has a long history of institutional discrimination against myriad groups. Perhaps the most overt example was that of racial segregation that existed in the early to mid-twentieth century. Even today, there are still concerns of institutional discrimination against women, racial and ethnic minorities, sexual minorities, and certain religions.

MCAT Concept Check 10.3:

Before you move on, assess your understanding of the material with these questions.

1. What are the distinctions between stereotypes, prejudice, and discrimination?

   - Stereotypes:

     _____

   - Prejudice:

     _____

   - Discrimination:

     _____

2. List three types of social inequality that can influence prejudice:

   - _____

   - _____

   - _____

3. What is the difference between ethnocentrism and cultural relativism?

   _____

Conclusion

Social psychology focuses on social behavior and the attitudes, perceptions, and influences of others that impact behavior. In this chapter, we first looked at social behaviors, including attraction, aggression, attachment, and social support. We also looked at the biological explanations of specific social behaviors, including foraging, mate choice, altruism, game theory, and inclusive fitness. We further defined the components of social perception and impression biases. The way we view ourselves also influences the way we view others and how we attribute behavior to others. Finally, we took a look at stereotypes, prejudice, and discrimination.

These last few topics demonstrate a negative side of classifying individuals. We can use classification to create hierarchies, inequities in opportunity and finances, as well as to silence or suppress communities. But classification can also serve a positive purpose. In social science, we often classify populations to study interactions between groups, changes in population makeup over time, and to track migration patterns. These classifications are considered in the field of demographics, which we will explore in the next chapter.

CONCEPT SUMMARY

Social Behavior

- **Interpersonal attraction** is what makes people like each other and is influenced by multiple factors:
  - Physical attractiveness, which is increased with symmetry and proportions close to the **golden ratio**.
  - Similarity of attitudes, intelligence, education, height, age, religion, appearance, and socioeconomic status.
  - **Self-disclosure**, which includes sharing fears, thoughts, and goals with another person and being met with empathy and nonjudgment.
  - **Reciprocity**, in which we like people who we think like us.
  - **Proximity**, or being physically close to someone.
- **Aggression** is a physical, verbal, or nonverbal behavior with the intention to cause harm or increase social dominance.
- **Attachment** is an emotional bond to another person, and usually refers to the bond between a child and a caregiver. There are four types of attachment:
  - **Secure attachment** requires a consistent caregiver so the child is able to go out and explore, knowing he or she has a secure base to return to; the child will show strong preference for the caregiver.
  - **Avoidant attachment** occurs when a caregiver has little or no response to a distressed, crying child; the child shows no preference for the caregiver compared to strangers.
  - **Ambivalent attachment** occurs when a caregiver has an inconsistent response to a child's distress, sometimes responding appropriately, sometimes neglectful; the child will become distressed when caregiver leaves and is ambivalent when he or she returns.
  - **Disorganized attachment** occurs when a caregiver is erratic or abusive; the child shows no clear pattern of behavior in response to the caregiver's absence or presence and may show repetitive behaviors.
- **Social support** is the perception or reality that one is cared for by a social network.
  - **Emotional support** includes listening to, affirming, and empathizing with someone's feelings.
  - **Esteem support** affirms the qualities and skills of the person.
  - **Material support** is providing physical or monetary resources to aid a person.
  - **Informational support** is providing useful information to a person.
  - **Network support** is providing a sense of belonging to a person.

- **Foraging** is searching for and exploiting food resources.
- A **mating system** describes the way in which a group is organized in terms of sexual behavior.
  - **Monogamy** consists of exclusive mating relationships.
  - **Polygamy** consists of one member of a sex having multiple exclusive relationships with members of the opposite sex, including **polygyny** (a male with multiple females) and **polyandry** (a female with multiple males).
  - **Promiscuity** allows a member of one sex to mate with any member of the opposite sex without exclusivity.
- **Mate choice**, or **intersexual selection**, is the selection of a mate based on attraction and traits.
- **Altruism** is a form of helping behavior in which the person's intent is to benefit someone else at some cost to him- or herself.
- **Game theory** attempts to explain decision-making between individuals as if they are participating in a game.
- **Inclusive fitness** is a measure of an organism's success in the population. This is based on the number of offspring, success in supporting offspring, and the ability of the offspring to then support others.

Social Perception and Behavior
- **Social perception** or **social cognition** is the way by which we generate impressions about people in our social environment. It contains a **perceiver**, his or her **target**, and the **situation** or social context of the scenario.
- **Implicit personality theory** states that people make assumptions about how different types of people, their traits, and their behavior are related.
- Certain cognitive biases impact our perceptions of others.
  - The **primacy effect** refers to when first impressions are more important than subsequent impressions.
  - The **recency effect** is when the most recent information we have about an individual is most important in forming our impressions.
  - A **reliance on central traits** is the tendency to organize the perception of others based on traits and personal characteristics that matter to the perceiver.
  - The **halo effect** is when judgments of an individual's character can be affected by the overall impression of the individual.
  - The **just-world hypothesis** is the tendency of individuals to believe that good things happen to good people and bad things happen to bad people.
  - **Self-serving bias** refers to the fact that individuals will view their own successes as being based on internal factors, while viewing failures as being based on external factors.

- **Attribution theory** focuses on the tendency for individuals to infer the causes of other people's behavior.

  - **Dispositional** (**internal**) causes are those that relate to the features of the person whose behavior is being considered.

  - **Situational** (**external**) causes are related to features of the surroundings or social context.

- **Correspondent inference theory** is used to describe attributions made by observing the intentional (especially unexpected) behaviors performed by another person.

- **Fundamental attribution error** is the bias toward making dispositional attributions rather than situational attributions in regard to the actions of others.

- **Attribute substitution** occurs when individuals must make judgments that are complex but instead substitute a simpler solution or heuristic.

- Attributions are highly influenced by the culture in which one resides.

Stereotypes, Prejudice, and Discrimination

- **Stereotypes** occur when attitudes and impressions are made based on limited and superficial information about a person or a group of individuals.

- Stereotypes can lead to expectations of certain groups, which can create conditions that lead to confirmation of the stereotype, a process referred to as **self-fulfilling prophecy**.

- **Stereotype threat** is concern or anxiety about confirming a negative stereotype about one's social group.

- **Prejudice** is defined as an irrational positive or negative attitude toward a person, group, or thing prior to an actual experience.

- **Ethnocentrism** refers to the practice of making judgments about other cultures based on the values and beliefs of one's own culture.

  - An **in-group** is a social group with which a person experiences a sense of belonging.

  - An **out-group** refers to a social group with which an individual does not identify.

- **Cultural relativism** refers to the recognition that social groups and cultures should be studied on their own terms.

- **Discrimination** is when prejudicial attitudes cause individuals of a particular group to be treated differently from others.

  - **Individual discrimination** refers to one person discriminating against a particular person or group.

  - **Institutional discrimination** refers to the discrimination against a particular person or group by an entire institution.

ANSWERS TO CONCEPT CHECKS

10.1

1. Interpersonal attraction is what makes people like each other and is influenced by at least five factors discussed in the chapter: physical attractiveness, similarity, self-disclosure, reciprocity, and proximity.

2. Aggression is a behavior with the intention to cause harm or increase relative social dominance. It can be physical, verbal, or nonverbal.

3.

Type of Attachment	Response to Caregiver
Secure	Upset at departure of caregiver, comforted by return; trusts caregiver, who is viewed as a secure base
Avoidant	Shows no preference for a stranger or caregiver; shows little distress at departure and little relief by return of caregiver
Ambivalent	Distressed by departure of caregiver with mixed reactions at return
Disorganized	No clear pattern of behavior; sometimes exhibits repetitive behaviors or seems dazed, frozen, or confused

4. Social support is the perception or reality that one is cared for by a social network. There are five types discussed in this chapter: emotional support, esteem support, material support, informational support, and network support.

5. Altruism is a form of helping behavior in which the person's intent is to benefit someone else at some cost to him- or herself.

10.2

1. The primacy effect is the power of first impressions over later impressions of an individual. The recency effect is weighing the most recent information of a person as the most important. The halo effect occurs when one applies general feelings about a person (usually, "good" or "bad") to specific characteristics of that person. The just-world hypothesis is the belief that good things happen to good people and bad things happen to bad people. Self-serving bias is the tendency to attribute our successes to internal factors and our failures to external factors.

2. Attribution theory focuses on the tendency of individuals to infer the causes of other people's behavior. Attributions are divided into two types: dispositional (internal) causes, which relate to the features of the target, and situational (external) causes, which relate to features of the surroundings or context.

3. Fundamental attribution error is the general bias toward making dispositional attributions rather than situational attributions about the behavior of others, especially in negative contexts.

4. Attribute substitution occurs when individuals must make judgments that are complex but instead substitute a simpler solution or heuristic.

10.3

1. Stereotypes occur when attitudes and impressions are made based on limited and superficial information about a person or a group of individuals and are cognitive. Prejudice is defined as an irrational negative, or occasionally positive, attitude toward a person, group, or thing, which is formed prior to an actual experience and is affective. Discrimination is when prejudicial attitudes cause individuals of a particular group to be treated differently than others and is behavioral.

2. Power, prestige, and class all influence prejudice through unequal distribution of wealth, influence, and resources.

3. Ethnocentrism refers to the practice of making judgments about other cultures based on the values and beliefs of one's own culture. Cultural relativism refers to the recognition that social groups and cultures must be studied on their own terms. In both cases, an individual perceives another group to which he or she does not belong; however, it is the reaction to that other group that determines which paradigm is being used.

SHARED CONCEPTS

Discrete Practice Questions

Consult your online resources for Full-Length Exams and Passage-Based Questions (for certain chapters).

1. The tendency to become close friends with neighbors rather than people in other neighborhoods is most strongly related to which of the following factors?

   A. Proximity
   B. Reciprocity
   C. Self-disclosure
   D. Similarity

2. Which of the following would be associated with high levels of aggression?

   I. Increased amygdala activity
   II. Decreased amygdala activity
   III. Increased prefrontal cortex activity
   IV. Decreased prefrontal cortex activity

   A. I and III only
   B. I and IV only
   C. II and III only
   D. II and IV only

3. A child who cries when his mother departs and smiles and runs to his mother when she returns is displaying which type of attachment pattern?

   A. Avoidant attachment
   B. Ambivalent attachment
   C. Disorganized attachment
   D. Secure attachment

4. Elephant seal males mate with multiple females each mating season, while females only have one mate each. What type of mating system is this?

   A. Polyandry
   B. Polygyny
   C. Monogamy
   D. Promiscuity

5. A person with a ventromedial hypothalamus injury will likely show which behavior?

   A. Increased empathy
   B. Decreased empathy
   C. Increased food intake
   D. Decreased food intake

6. Female great reed warblers are attracted to males with larger song repertoires because they tend to produce offspring with higher viability. This is an example of which of the following?

   A. Runaway selection
   B. Sensory bias
   C. Direct phenotypic benefits
   D. Indirect phenotypic benefits

7. In several species of shrimp, the larger adults will sacrifice themselves to protect the younger, smaller shrimp. How is this behavior best explained?

   A. Inclusive fitness
   B. Direct benefit
   C. Sensory bias
   D. Foraging

8. Which of the following is NOT a component of social perception?

   A. The target
   B. The situation
   C. The perceiver
   D. The process

9. When you first meet Dustin, he is very rude to you. You run into him twice more and he is very friendly, but you still dislike him because of your first meeting. What impression bias does this describe?

   A. Primacy effect
   B. Recency effect
   C. Reliance on central traits
   D. Proximity

10. Glen brings cookies to work. Although you have not yet tasted them, you say to another coworker, "Glen is such a great guy; I'm sure these cookies are fantastic!" What type of bias is this?

    A. Reliance on central traits
    B. Direct benefits
    C. Halo effect
    D. Similarity

11. A friend wins a tennis game and says, "I trained so hard—that was a great win!" When she loses a subsequent match, she says, "My baby brother kept me up all night crying; I was tired for the match." These statements reflect which of the following principles?

    A. Fundamental attribution bias
    B. Fundamental attribution error
    C. Self-serving bias
    D. Esteem bias

12. Carl is always happy and smiling. Today, you notice he seems down and think something must have happened to upset him. What types of attribution are you making?

    I. Internal
    II. External
    III. Situational
    IV. Dispositional

    A. I and III only
    B. I and IV only
    C. II and III only
    D. II and IV only

13. A group of men and women are going to be rated on their driving abilities. The role of gender is emphasized in the experiment and the women perform worse than the men. In another experiment, the role of gender is not mentioned and the ratings are comparable between the two groups. Which principle do these results support?

    A. Institutional discrimination
    B. Stereotype threat
    C. Prejudice
    D. The just-world hypothesis

14. The behavior that accompanies the negative attitudes a person has toward a group or individual is referred to as:

    A. stereotyping.
    B. cultural relativism.
    C. prejudice.
    D. discrimination.

15. Game theory is designed to study:

    A. reliance on central traits.
    B. behavior attribution.
    C. decision-making behavior.
    D. self-enhancement.

Explanations to Discrete Practice Questions

1. A

Each of the answer choices influences social attraction; however, proximity deals with the tendency to be attracted to those who are physically close by.

2. B

Aggression is influenced both by the amygdala and prefrontal cortex activity. Activity of the amygdala increases aggression. The prefrontal cortex should control aggression; decreased activity in the prefrontal cortex, therefore, is associated with increased aggression.

3. D

This attachment pattern is representative of secure attachment. Secure attachment is seen when a child has a consistent caregiver and is able to go out and explore, knowing he or she has a secure base to return to. The child will be upset at the departure of the caregiver and will be comforted and resume exploring upon the return of the caregiver.

4. B

Polygamy involves a male having exclusive relationships with several females (polygyny) or a female having exclusive relationships with several males (polyandry), **choice (A)**. Monogamy, **choice (C)**, consists of exclusive mating relationships. Promiscuity, **choice (D)**, refers to a member of one sex mating with any member of the opposite sex.

5. C

A person with a ventromedial hypothalamus injury will never feel satiated when eating and will therefore never feel the sensation to stop eating. A person with a lateral hypothalamus injury will never feel hunger and will have decreased food intake, **choice (D)**.

6. D

Phenotypic benefits refer to observed traits in an individual that make them more attractive to the opposite sex. Benefits associated with increased fitness through direct material advantages are direct benefits, **choice (C)**, while indirect benefits involve increased genetic fitness for offspring.

7. A

In evolutionary psychology, inclusive fitness is a measure of the number of offspring an individual has, how they support their offspring, and how their offspring can support others. Inclusive fitness promotes the idea that altruistic behavior can improve the fitness and success of a species; the behavior in this scenario can be described as altruism: benefiting another at one's own expense.

8. D

There are three primary components of perception: the perceiver, the target, and the situation.

9. A

The impressions we form when meeting others are influenced by a number of perceptual biases. The primacy effect refers to those occasions when first impressions are more important than subsequent impressions.

10. C

The halo effect is a cognitive bias in which judgments of an individual's character can be affected by the overall impression of the individual.

11. C

Self-serving bias refers to the fact that individuals will view their own successes as being based on internal factors, while viewing failures as being based on external factors.

12. C

Types of attribution fall into two main categories: dispositional (internal) and situational (external). Dispositional (internal) causes are related to the features of the person whose behavior is being considered. Situational (external) causes are related to features of the surroundings.

13. B

Stereotype threat refers to the concept of people being concerned or anxious about confirming a negative stereotype of their social group. Stereotype threat can hinder performance, creating a self-fulfilling prophecy.

14. D

Discrimination is when prejudicial attitudes cause individuals of a particular group to be treated differently than others. While prejudice is an attitude, discrimination is a behavior.

15. C

Game theory was originally designed to study decision-making behavior in economics and mathematics; it has since been used to describe decision-making in politics, biology, philosophy, and other fields.

Social Structure and Demographics

In This Chapter

Chapter Profile

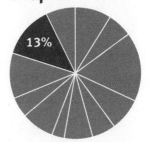

The content in this chapter should be relevant to about 13% of all questions about the Behavioral Sciences on the MCAT.

This chapter covers material from the following AAMC content categories:

7B: Social processes that influence human behavior

9A: Understanding social structure

9B: Demographic characteristics and processes

Introduction

A frail, elderly Chinese man is admitted to the Intensive Care Unit at a local hospital. He is gaunt, weighing just over one hundred pounds, in severe respiratory distress, and nearing circulatory collapse. The intensive care team works to stabilize the patient by starting intravenous lines and pumping fluids. The patient screams incomprehensible statements in Mandarin and is eventually sedated so the team can intubate and ventilate him. They begin to run tests and discover that the man has widespread metastatic lung cancer that is unlikely to be cured or even controlled through chemotherapy or radiation. The patient's wife and children visit the next morning and are told of the bad news. After crying for some time, they turn to the intensive care team and ask them not to inform the patient of this grave diagnosis. In their culture, family members are supposed to make healthcare decisions for the ill to avoid burdening them with such matters. The members of the medical team, however, feel that they must adhere to the tenets of American medical ethics—and American law—and allow the patient to make his own healthcare decisions. As the head of the hospital ethics committee, you get a call from the team to help them make this decision. What would you do?

Ethicists and sociologists alike wrestle with medical dilemmas like these. As a clinician in an ever-diversifying society, you will certainly run into difficult decisions like these, which try to balance a patient's cultural beliefs with one's own beliefs. In this chapter, we'll explore some of the sociological topics on the MCAT, focusing on theoretical models and the key institutions on which you are likely to be tested. We'll then explore culture itself. Finally, we'll describe demographics, the mathematical and statistical modeling of sociological concepts.

11.1 Sociology: Theories and Institutions

> **LEARNING GOALS**
>
> After Chapter 11.1, you will be able to:
>
> - Recall the primary theses of major sociological theories, including functionalism, conflict theory, symbolic interactionism, social constructionism, rational choice theory, and feminist theory
> - Contrast manifest and latent functions of given elements of a sociological system
> - List the four key tenets of American medical ethics

Sociology is the study of society: how we create society, how we interact within it, how we define what is normal and abnormal in society, and how we institutionalize these ideas. The underpinnings of sociology thus flow from these explanatory theories and the institutions that make up society as a whole. **Macrosociology** focuses on large groups and social structure, whereas **microsociology** focuses on small groups and the individual.

THEORETICAL APPROACHES

In building a theory, a sociologist asks two key questions: *What societal issues should we study?* and *How do we connect the facts?* These theoretical approaches provide frameworks for what we observe within a **social structure**; that is, a system of people within a society organized by a characteristic pattern of relationships. While sociological theories may converge on certain key issues, they remind us that a single unified sociological perspective of social reality does not exist. Thus, sociologists have utilized various theoretical approaches to embrace competing perspectives or paradigms, to advance research in the field, and to gain understanding within facts and figures.

Functionalism

Functionalism or **functional analysis** is the study of the structure and function of each part of society. Early functionalists viewed society as a living organism. Like an organism, if society is to function smoothly, its parts and systems must work together in harmony. When all the parts of society fulfill their functions, society is in a normal state. If they do not fulfill their functions, society is in an abnormal or pathologic state. Later theorists used the term **function** to refer to the beneficial consequences of people's actions. According to these theorists, functions help keep society in balance. In contrast, **dysfunctions** are harmful consequences of people's actions as they undermine a social system's equilibrium.

Functions can either be manifest or latent. If an action is intended to help some part of a system, it is a **manifest function**. However, manifest functions can also have unintended positive consequences on other parts of society; these are called **latent functions**. Latent functions may flow logically from manifest functions, but are unstated or unrecognized. For example, annual meetings of medical societies have the manifest function of educating a group of physicians, sharing research findings, and setting goals for the next year. Latently, they create stronger interpersonal bonds between physicians and provide a sense of identity for the group.

Relating the theory of functionalism to health and illness, some theorists have identified illness as a social phenomenon rather than a purely physical condition. In this model, a sick individual is unable to be a productive member of society and therefore is deviant from society. Remember that deviance does not necessarily imply judgment; it merely refers to an act or a behavior that goes against social norms. The manifestation of deviance in healthcare and medicine is that the individual who has fallen ill is not only physically sick, but now adheres to the specifically patterned social role of being sick that disrupts the normal social order of society.

Conflict Theory

In a sociological context, **power** refers to a form of influence over other people. **Conflict theory**, which is based on the works of Karl Marx, focuses on how power differentials are created and how these differentials contribute to the maintenance of social order. Further, power differentials can lead to the dominance of a particular group if it successfully outcompetes other groups for economic, political, and social resources.

Symbolic Interactionism

During the first half of the twentieth century, many American cities witnessed a significant influx of immigration. While some of these immigrant populations sought to assimilate into American culture as quickly as possible, others formed ethnic enclaves in urban areas. In response, a group of sociologists at the University of Chicago began to study the interactions of race, ethnicity, and immigration. These sociologists popularized the study of **symbolic interactionism**, which is the study of the ways individuals interact through a shared understanding of words, gestures, and other symbols. The central idea of symbolic interactionism is that **symbols**—that is, things to which we attach meaning—are the key to understanding how we view the world and communicate with one another. These symbols include everything from how we codify concepts in language to hand gestures and body language to the role of certain behaviors. These symbols do not always match across cultures, as shown in Figure 11.1; thus, part of acculturation is learning the appropriate symbols and their use in a given culture.

Bridge

Deviance is defined as an act or behavior that goes against social norms. In some cases, deviance can lead to stigmatization. These topics are discussed in Chapter 8 of *MCAT Behavioral Sciences Review*.

Real World

Conflict theory can be applied to healthcare and medicine. Conflict theorists would not deny that modern healthcare can help people maintain or restore their health; however, they may ask who holds the power in the healthcare system. Is it the patient? The doctor? Hospitals? Pharmaceutical companies? Insurance companies? The government? This is an issue the United States continues to grapple with.

Figure 11.1. Symbolic Interactionism
Hand gestures do not always carry the same meaning across cultures.
The *thumbs-up* is a sign of approval in American culture; in some Middle
Eastern cultures, it is an offensive gesture.

Key Concept

Symbolic interactionism reflects on how we use symbols to interact with each other. Social constructionism reflects on how we, as a society, construct concepts and principles. While the names of these theories sound like jargon, they're actually perfect descriptions.

Social Constructionism

Social constructionism focuses on how individuals put together their social reality. Social constructs arise from humans communicating and working together to agree on the significance of a concept or principle. Social constructionism can be applied to intangible concepts; how a society defines *honor* and *justice* is dependent on the interactions and decisions of the individuals within that society. Notably, because these concepts depend on the society itself, they are subject to change as social norms and opinions develop over time. Social constructionism can also be applied to physical objects, such as money. Paper money and coinage do not inherently have significant value; it is only because we, as a society, imbue them with value that they can be used to trade for goods and services. Other examples of social constructs include work ethic, acceptable dress, and gender roles.

Rational Choice and Exchange Theory

Rational choice theory focuses on decision-making in an individual and attempts to reduce this process to a careful consideration of benefits and harms to the individual. Every outcome in a given social interaction can be associated with particular rewards (such as money, accolades, honor, prestige, and social approval) and with particular punishments (such as embarrassment, humiliation, sanctions, and stigmatization). In this theory, an individual carefully considers all of the possible rewards and punishments of each social action and chooses the option that has the highest benefit-to-harm ratio. Thus, this theory can be likened to a mental *pros and cons* list, and the course of action an individual takes is that which maximizes personal benefit. This theory is problematized by concepts like altruism, in which an individual benefits another at some cost to him- or herself.

Exchange theory is an extension of rational choice theory. Whereas rational choice theory can be applied to an individual independently of social interactions (such as choosing *What do I want to eat for dinner tonight?*), exchange theory focuses on interactions in groups. Exchange theory posits that an individual will carry out certain behaviors because of anticipated rewards and will avoid certain behaviors because of anticipated punishments. Similar to operant conditioning, described in Chapter 3 of *MCAT Behavioral Sciences Review*, exchange theory assumes that a behavior that is met with approval by others will reinforce that behavior and encourage its continuation. On the other hand, behavior that is met with disapproval by others is punished, discouraging its continuation.

Feminist Theory

Feminist theory attempts to explain social inequalities that exist on the basis of gender. This theory focuses on the subordination of women through social structures and institutional discrimination. This subordination takes many forms, including expected gender roles, sexuality, financial opportunity, and social mobility. **Gender roles** refer to the behaviors expected of a given gender; in the United States, the Industrial Revolution begat a doctrine of "separate spheres," in which men served as breadwinners and protectors of the family's finances and safety whereas women served as caretakers of the children and home. While the feminist movement of the mid- to late twentieth century helped diversify these gender roles, biases may still exist against individuals who step out of traditional roles. Sexual inequality includes differential expectations of behavior between men and women; for example, men may be rewarded for promiscuity (being seen as a *womanizer* or *player*) whereas women may be stigmatized for carrying out the same behavior. Women are also more frequently **objectified** than men—being viewed as a sexual object rather than as a person.

Institutional discrimination also creates limits on women, sometimes marginalizing or devaluing their contributions to society. Financial inequality is extremely common in the workforce, as women are frequently paid less for equal work. Women are also less frequently promoted in the workplace and may have more difficulty attaining top-level administrative positions within a company, a phenomenon often referred to as the **glass ceiling**.

SOCIAL INSTITUTIONS

Social institutions are well-established social structures that dictate certain patterns of behavior or relationships and are accepted as a fundamental part of culture. Social institutions regulate the behavior of individuals in core areas of society. For example, family is a social institution that encourages learning of acceptable behavior, socialization, and bonding. A summary of six of the major social institutions is provided in Table 11.1 at the end of this section.

Family

Family is influenced by a number of different factors including culture, value systems, beliefs, practices, gender, age, race, ethnicity, and others. Family does not have a fixed definition across cultures or through time; what is accepted as a family in the current day does not necessarily match expectations from even a few generations ago. In fact, even terms for different family members (such as *sister*, *father*, *cousin*, and so on) are not conserved across time and culture; different **patterns of kinship** may be reflected by these terms. For example, it is common in Hawaiian culture to refer to all family members as *cousins*, while this term would not be used by many other Americans to describe one's mother's brother (the term *uncle* being preferred). Different patterns of kinship between societies have bearing on responsibility for child-rearing, familial loyalty, and even the boundaries of what is considered incest.

Sociologists studying family relationships may examine the stages of coupling (courtship, cohabitation, engagement, and marriage), changes in relationships between spouses through time, as well as parenting. Parenting is a complex topic that involves socialization of children; varied definitions of the role of father, mother, and child; and single parenting, same-sex parenting, adoption, and foster parenting. Not all families are composed of a mother, a father, and children. Alternative forms exist, including single-parent families; families that cohabitate with other family members beyond the nuclear family, such as grandparents, aunts, uncles, cousins, godparents, and surrogate kin; and families with marital disunions (divorce). A number of different family structures are illustrated in Figure 11.2.

Figure 11.2. Various Family Structures

Divorce rates in the United States rose significantly in the second half of the twentieth century; over the last two decades, however, these rates have started to drop.

While the family can be a source of joy and support, it can also be a source of violence. Spousal abuse (**domestic violence**) is seen across all social classes and can include not only physical violence, but sexual abuse, emotional abuse, and financial abuse. Domestic violence is the #1 cause of injury to American women, and is most common in families with drug abuse, especially alcoholism. Victims of domestic violence may find it challenging to leave the abusive relationship for a variety of reasons, including lack of a safe haven to escape to, financial restrictions, and psychological disorders (consider the connection to learned helplessness, described in Chapter 6 of *MCAT Behavioral Sciences Review*). **Elder abuse** is also seen across all socioeconomic classes, and most commonly manifests as neglect of an older relative—although physical, psychological, and financial abuse may occur as well. The caretaker of the individual is most commonly the source of abuse. Finally, **child abuse** also most commonly manifests as neglect, although physical, sexual, and psychological abuse are also common. During medical school, you will be trained to recognize certain signs suggestive of nonaccidental trauma, such as a broken femur in a child who is too young to have begun walking or burn marks on the buttocks from placing a child in scalding water. As a physician, you will be considered a **mandated reporter**, which means that you are legally required to report suspected cases of elder or child abuse. Domestic abuse does not fall under mandated reporting laws, but counseling and information about shelters for victims of intimate partner violence should be provided.

Education

Education systems aim to arm the population with information. This information may be in the form of facts, figures, and mental processes, but the education system also emphasizes the social role of education, creates statuses within society, and stimulates learners to add to their knowledge base. Education, therefore, includes not only the information and cognitive skills students learn but also the **hidden curriculum** of transmitting social norms, attitudes, and beliefs to students. Sociological investigations into education may focus on the ethics, morals, practices, political influence, finances, and values of an education system. Sociologists also explore educational trends, including grade inflation and deflation, adult education, online education, and accessibility of education.

Performance in the education system depends not only on a student's intrinsic abilities, but also on the education system itself. **Teacher expectancy** refers to the idea that teachers tend to get what they expect from students. Thus, a teacher who places high demands on students—but who also believes that her students can rise to the challenge—will more often see students succeed than a teacher who places the same demands but doubts that the students can achieve them.

MCAT Expertise

The MCAT will not expect you to know any specific demographic numbers for the exam, but you should be familiar with some of the recent trends seen in the United States population.

This is an example of a self-fulfilling prophecy, discussed in Chapter 10 of *MCAT Behavioral Sciences Review*, and may be due to differences in how teachers motivate, interact, and offer feedback to their students.

Education is also susceptible to inequalities across socioeconomic class. Lower socioeconomic status is associated with decreased accessibility and quality of education. This is not an easy trend to reverse. Low funding, deprioritization of education, and poor historical performance can make it challenging for a failing school district to acquire resources and improve education to its students.

It is often the case that institutions are intentionally or unintentionally connected. For example, there is a well-known, persistent association between education and medicine. Health disparities between more and less educated individuals are significant, and lack of education may be a hurdle to accessing or trusting healthcare providers.

Religion

From a sociological point of view, **religion** is considered to be a pattern of social activities organized around a set of beliefs and practices that seek to address the meaning of existence. As an organization, religion persists over time and has a structure into which members are resocialized. **Religiosity** refers to how religious one considers him- or herself to be, and includes strength of religious beliefs, engagement in religious practices, and attitudes about religion itself. When studying religion from a sociological perspective, it is not important to agree with the belief system. Rather, it is important to examine religion objectively within its social and cultural context.

Religious groups can be organized in multiple ways. Large umbrella religions, such as Christianity, Judaism, and Islam can be divided into multiple **denominations** or **sects** that may share certain beliefs and practices but not others. These words have slightly different connotations. A **church** is a large, universal religious group that can be divided into multiple coexisting denominations. Whereas the word *sect* was historically a pejorative term, it now refers more properly to a religious group that has chosen to break off from the parent religion. In rare cases, a religious sect may take on extreme or deviant philosophies and transform into a **cult**.

As the twenty-first century continues, religious groups—many of which have existed in more or less the same form for thousands of years—grapple with finding a place in contemporary society. For many religious groups, this is reflected by a shift toward modernization within the religion and relaxing historical practices. For others, there is a shift away from religion as society **secularizes**, or moves from a world dominated by religion toward rationality and scientific thinking. For other groups, maintenance of strict adherence to religious code, or **fundamentalism**, predominates.

While spirituality and religion are not equivalent terms, they are often linked to each other because they both seek to understand the meaning of existence and to identify what is sacred. Spirituality and religion may play a role in a patient's understanding of disease, may impact healthcare decisions, and can be an essential component of the patient's coping mechanisms.

Government and Economy

As institutions, the **government** and **economy** can be defined as systematic arrangements of political and capital relationships, activities, and social structures that affect rule making, representation of the individual in society, rights and privileges, division of labor, and production of goods and services. Notably, political and economic institutions impact all other institutions to some extent. That is, the government may sanction or define specific family structures, may finance and regulate education, may recognize some religions but not others, and may play a key role in funding and certifying healthcare and medicine. The effects of the economy on institutions can also be viewed from the individual level. For example, when the economy takes a downturn, large swaths of the population may have trouble supporting their families and paying for health insurance. Note that this institutional influence is bidirectional: because of the economic downturn and changes in family, education, or health, an individual may choose to vote a new political candidate into office, or to support or oppose a particular piece of legislation.

While an in-depth exploration of the American (or any other) government is outside the scope of the MCAT, it should be noted that different governments may work in different ways. A **democracy** allows every citizen a political voice, usually through electing representatives to office (representative democracy). **Monarchies** include a royal ruler (a king or queen), although the ruler's powers may be significantly limited by the presence of a constitution and parliamentary system. A **dictatorship** is a system where a single person holds power, and usually includes mechanisms to quell threats to this power. A **theocracy** is a system where power is held by religious leaders. Many of these systems of leadership are based around a **charismatic authority** (a leader with a compelling personality).

In comparative economics, the largest division is between capitalist and socialist economies. **Capitalist** economies focus on free market trade and laissez-faire policies, where success or failure in business is primarily driven by consumerism with as little intervention from central governing bodies as possible. In capitalism, a private owner or corporation maintains and profits from the success of the business. Capitalist societies encourage **division of labor**, where specific components of a larger task (say, developing, manufacturing, quality testing, and marketing goods) are separated and assigned to skilled and trained individuals. This promotes specialization and efficiency. **Socialist** economies, on the other hand, treats large industries as collective, shared businesses, and compensation is provided based on the work contribution of each individual into the system. Profit, then, is distributed equally to the workforce. There are many other forms of government and economy, as well, but these will be defined and explained if necessary on Test Day.

Healthcare and Medicine

The institutions of **healthcare** and **medicine** are aimed at maintaining or improving the health status of the individual, family, community, and society as a whole. Healthcare is an ever-changing field, but some of the key goals in American healthcare over the past few decades include:

- Increased access to care

- Decreased costs of healthcare

- Prevention of disease before it occurs

- Association of patients with a primary care physician or a patient-centered medical home

- Increased education for the public with public health outreach

- Decreased paternalism (*doctor knows best* mentality)

- Reduced economic conflicts of interest for physicians

- **Life course approach to health** (maintaining and considering a comprehensive view of the patient's history beyond the immediate presenting symptoms)

There has also been a shift in the role of the patient in the medical system. In the mid-twentieth century, a patient was expected to carry out the **sick role**, in which he or she was not responsible for the illness and is exempt from normal social roles. Further, the patient had the obligation to want to become well and seek out competent help. While this paradigm still exists, patients are now expected to take more ownership of their health through diet, exercise, seeking help before it is needed (through annual primary care visits and screenings), and so on.

Even our understanding of disease has shifted over time. While some entities formerly defined as illnesses are now considered a normal part of the human condition, such as homosexuality and transgenderism, other entities have become **medicalized**, or defined and treated as medical conditions. This shift can be seen in the addition of a number of diagnostic entities to the DSM-5, such as hoarding disorder and binge eating disorder.

In addition, many sociologists investigate medical ethics. In the United States, physicians are expected to adhere to four key tenets of medical ethics:

- **Beneficence:** the physician has a responsibility to act in the patient's best interest.

- **Nonmaleficence:** *do no harm*; the physician has a responsibility to avoid treatments or interventions in which the potential for harm outweighs the potential for benefit.

- **Respect for patient autonomy:** the physician has a responsibility to respect patients' decisions and choices about their own healthcare. While there are exceptions to this rule (significant psychiatric illness interfering with decision-making capacity, children, public health threats), patients do have the right to refuse life-saving therapies.

- **Justice:** the physician has a responsibility to treat similar patients with similar care, and to distribute healthcare resources fairly.

Social Institution	Needs Met by Institution	Statuses	Values	Norms
Education	Transmit knowledge and skills across generations	Teacher, student, dean, principal	Academic honesty, good grades	Doing homework, preparing for lectures, being kind to other students
Family	Regulate reproduction, socialize and protect children	Father, mother, son, daughter, brother, sister, uncle, aunt, grandparent	Sexual fidelity, providing for children, keeping a clean home, respect for parents	Having as many children as one desires, being faithful to one's spouse
Religion	Concerns about life and death, the meaning of suffering and loss, desire to connect with a creator	Priest, pastor, rabbi, imam, worshipper, teacher, disciple, missionary, prophet, convert	God and holy texts (Bible, Torah, Qur'an, and others) should be honored	Going to services, following teachings of the religion, applying beliefs outside of worship
Government	Maintain social order, enforce laws	President, senator, lobbyist, voter, candidate	Transparency, accountability, professionalism	Acting in the best interest of constituents, debating political issues
Economy	Organize money, goods, and services	Worker, boss, buyer, seller, creditor, debtor, advertiser	Making money, paying bills on time, producing efficiently	Maximizing profits, *the customer is always right*, working hard
Medicine	Heal the sick and injured, care for the dying	Doctor, nurse, pharmacist, insurer, patient	Hippocratic oath, staying in good health, following care providers' recommendations	Beneficence, nonmaleficence, respect for autonomy, justice

Table 11.1. Social Institutions

MCAT Concept Check 11.1:

Before you move on, assess your understanding of the material with these questions.

1. What are manifest and latent functions?

   • Manifest functions:

   _____

   • Latent functions:

   _____

2. For each of the theoretical approaches listed below, what is the primary thesis or idea of the theory?

Theoretical Approach	Primary Thesis or Idea
Functionalism	
Conflict theory	
Symbolic interactionism	
Social constructionism	
Rational choice theory	
Feminist theory	

3. What are the four key tenets of American medical ethics? Provide a short description of each.

Ethical Principle	Description

11.2 Culture

LEARNING GOALS

After Chapter 11.2, you will be able to:

- Distinguish between material and symbolic culture
- Recall the definitions of, and the differences between, the values, beliefs, norms, and rituals of a culture

The study of culture is likely the most diverse and complex dimension within sociology. **Culture** can be defined as encompassing the entire lifestyle for a given group. It binds our nation-states, political institutions, marketplaces, religions, and ideologies. Culture flavors our interpretations of the world, and is generally passed through familial lines. In short, culture is what makes human societies unique from one another.

MATERIAL AND SYMBOLIC CULTURE

Sociologists view culture according to two different categories: material culture and symbolic culture.

Material Culture

One can discern a lot about people by looking at their **artifacts**: material items that they make, possess, and value. This examination drives the concept of **material culture**, in which sociologists explore the meaning of objects of a given society. Material culture includes the physical items one associates with a given group, such as artwork, emblems, clothing, jewelry, foods, buildings, and tools.

An example of material culture in the United States is the American flag. This item is used to reinforce a sense of belonging via shared American citizenship. Other symbols considered traditionally American include barbecue, baseball, apple pie, and rock and roll.

MCAT Expertise

Ethnography is the study of cultures and customs, and **ethnographic methods** are experimental methods used to study the ethnicity or culture of a group.

Bridge

Symbols are also discussed in Chapter 6 of *MCAT Behavioral Sciences Review*

Material culture is often most visible during ceremonies, such as birthdays, weddings, and funerals. Some artifacts of traditional Indian material culture are shown in Figure 11.3.

Figure 11.3. Material Culture
Material culture includes objects important to a group, including clothing, jewelry, cuisine, ceremonial objects, and so on.

Symbolic Culture

Symbolic culture, also called **nonmaterial culture**, focuses on the ideas that represent a group of people. These may be encoded in mottos, songs, or catchphrases, or may simply be themes that are pervasive in the culture. Phrases like *free enterprise* and *life, liberty, and the pursuit of happiness* are examples of American symbolic culture. Material culture is often the tangible embodiment of the underlying ideas of symbolic culture.

For any social group to remain connected over time, there must be a culture that binds its members together. In times of war and crisis, governments often draw upon symbolic culture to rally people to action, using songs, parades, discussion of heroes past, and so on, as shown in Figure 11.4. It is not a coincidence that most high schools have a school mascot, school colors, and a school song. Such cultural artifacts are in place to help create a shared sense of identity, loyalty, and belonging. Symbolic culture includes both cognitive and behavioral components; that is, it informs cultural values and belief, as well as cultural norms and communication styles.

Key Concept

Material culture is associated with artifacts (objects). Symbolic culture is associated with ideas.

Figure 11.4. Symbolic Culture
Symbolic culture includes ideas that identify a culture; it may be drawn upon to encourage loyalty or patriotism, as shown here.

Symbolic culture is usually slower to change than material culture, which can lead to the phenomenon of **culture lag**. The expansion of devices and technology in contemporary times are prototypical examples of culture lag: whereas American culture still prizes individuality and privacy, the development of smartphones and social media push toward a more community-oriented and less private world. Still, there is evidence that symbolic culture is beginning to change in response to these technological (material) innovations: younger generations appear to have less concern about what personal information is publicly accessible than older generations.

LANGUAGE

Language is the most highly developed and complex symbol system used by most cultures. Language consists of spoken, written, or signed symbols, which are regulated according to certain rules of grammar and syntax. Language enables us to share our ideas, thoughts, experiences, discoveries, fears, plans, and desires with others. Written language extends our capacity to communicate across both spatial and temporal boundaries. Without language, it would be difficult to transmit culture. Understanding a group's language is critical to understanding its culture.

Bridge

Language is critically important in the transmission of culture. It requires a complex interplay of multiple brain circuits, which are discussed in Chapter 4 of *MCAT Behavioral Sciences Review*.

VALUES, BELIEFS, NORMS, AND RITUALS

Values are what a person deems important in life, which dictates one's ethical principals and standards of behavior. A **belief** is something that an individual accepts to be truth. Every culture has its own beliefs and value systems. This will be important to your practice of medicine because patients tend to carry their beliefs into the healthcare system—and these beliefs may conflict with yours. For example, as described in the chapter introduction, some Asian cultures believe that healthcare decisions should be the responsibility of a patient's family, which avoids burdening the patient (who is already ill) with having to make such a decision. This is in direct contrast to the American belief that patient autonomy should be prized and that healthcare decisions should be made by a patient whenever possible. These conflicts can prove challenging to healthcare professionals, and there is not always one correct answer to such a dilemma. Such situations—when a cultural difference impedes interaction with others—are called **cultural barriers**.

As described in Chapter 8 of *MCAT Behavioral Sciences Review*, **norms** are societal rules that define the boundaries of acceptable behavior. While norms are not laws, they do govern the behavior of society and provide a sense of social control. Norms are what provide us with a sense of what is appropriate, what we should do, and what we should not do. Norms exist for behavior, speech, dress, home life, and more.

A **ritual** is a formalized ceremony that usually involves specific material objects, symbolism, and additional mandates on acceptable behavior. Rituals tend to have a prescribed order of events or routine. These rituals can be associated with specific milestones, such as a baby-naming, graduation ceremony, wedding, or funeral; with holidays, such as a Thanksgiving dinner, trick-or-treating on Halloween, or a Passover seder, shown in Figure 11.5; or with regular activities, such as a Catholic mass, a pregame pep rally, or even just getting ready in the morning (showering, brushing teeth, eating breakfast, and so on).

> ### Real World
>
> Many health systems have an ethics board to deal with conflicts that may arise from differences in belief systems between patient and practitioner, among other ethical issues. These committees tend to facilitate discussion, rather than simply issuing a decision.

Figure 11.5. A Passover Seder Is an Example of a Ritual
Seder means "order" in Hebrew; most rituals have a specific order of events.

EVOLUTION AND HUMAN CULTURE

Evolution both influences and is influenced by culture. In some ways, it makes sense that culture would have been evolutionarily beneficial for early human populations. Culture serves as a method of passing down information from generation to generation; in prehistoric times, culture likely served as a conduit for teaching future generations how to create tools, hunt, domesticate animals, and grow crops. Culture also creates a sense of loyalty and allegiance, which, as described in Chapter 10 of *MCAT Behavioral Sciences Review*, may help explain altruistic behavior. Finally, culture creates a sense of *us vs. them*, which presumably served a role in the dispersion of populations across the globe in different environmental niches.

Culture may also have effects on evolution. There is evidence that some genetic traits may have been favored because of cultural values and beliefs. For example, human beings—at least those who are not lactose intolerant—are the only animals that are able to digest milk after adolescence; they are also the only animals that ingest another animal's milk. This may have arisen out of Northern European cultures, which relied heavily on cattle farming for sustenance. A mutation permitting digestion of milk into adulthood presumably imparted a nutritional and survival advantage to certain individuals, and would thus be retained within the population.

MCAT Concept Check 11.2:

Before you move on, assess your understanding of the material with these questions.

1. What are material and symbolic culture?

   - Material culture:

     _____

   - Symbolic culture:

     _____

2. What is the difference between a value and a belief?

   _____

11.3 Demographics

LEARNING GOALS

After Chapter 11.3, you will be able to:

- Distinguish between race and ethnicity
- Describe symbolic ethnicity
- Describe fertility rate, birth rate, and mortality rate, and how they shift during a demographic transition
- Recall examples of proactive and reactive social movements, and how the two types of movements differ

---

Demographics refer to the statistics of populations and are the mathematical applications of sociology. Demographics can be gathered informally, such as a professor asking how many freshmen, sophomores, juniors, and seniors are in a given course, or may be gathered formally. For example, the United States Census Bureau gathers full demographic data about every individual in the country every ten years.

COMMON DEMOGRAPHIC CATEGORIES

Demographers can classify individuals based on hundreds of different criteria. The MCAT will not expect you to know advanced topics within demographics, but familiarity with some of the common demographic categories is important. In this section, we'll explore age, gender, race and ethnicity, sexual orientation, and immigration status.

Age

Many sociologists document a "graying of America" as the Baby Boomer generation ages. Over 70 million Americans will be 65 or older by 2030, representing nearly 20 percent of the population. The fastest-growing **age cohort** in the United States is the 85-or-older group. This has profound effects on healthcare: more than 40 percent of adult patients in acute care hospital beds are 65 or older.

Ageism is prejudice or discrimination on the basis of a person's age. This can be seen at all ages. For example, young professionals entering the workplace are often viewed as being inexperienced, and their opinions and ideas may therefore be ignored or downplayed. Older individuals may be perceived as frail, vulnerable, or less intelligent, and may thus be treated with less respect.

Gender

Gender is a social construct that corresponds to the behavioral, cultural, or psychological traits typically associated with a biological sex. Gender differences tend to emphasize the distinct roles and behaviors of men and women in a given culture, which is influenced by cultural norms and values. Differences between genders do not necessarily imply inequity, although it occurs in many cultures. **Gender inequality**, however, is the intentional or unintentional empowerment of one gender to the detriment of the other. **Gender segregation**, on the other hand, is the separation of individuals based on perceived gender. This includes division into male, female, and gender-neutral bathrooms; separating male and female sports teams; and establishment of single-sex schools.

Note that sex and gender are not synonymous terms. Sex is biologically determined; an XY genotype corresponds to male sex, and an XX genotype corresponds to female sex. Gender relates to a set of behavioral, cultural, or psychological traits. In most cultures, there are two genders: male and female. However, some cultures consider more than two genders, and some individuals' gender identities do not match their biological sex.

Race and Ethnicity

Race is a social construct based on phenotypic differences between groups of people. These may be either real or perceived differences. It is notable that race is not strictly defined by genetics, and rather classifies individuals based on superficial traits such as skin color. **Racialization** refers to the definition or establishment of a group as a particular race; for example, while Judaism was historically viewed only as a religion, the concept of a Jewish race has become more prevalent over the last century. Even then, the definition features of a given race are not static. **Racial formation theory** posits that racial identity is fluid and dependent on concurrent political, economic, and social factors.

Ethnicity is also a social construct, which sorts people by cultural factors, including language, nationality, religion, and other factors. The distinction between race and ethnicity can be important because one can choose whether or not to display ethnic identity, while racial identities are always on display. For example, a person could be considered black due to physical characteristics; however, this same person's ethnicity could be Latino, African, African American, or a number of other ethnic identities.

Symbolic ethnicity describes a specific connection to one's ethnicity in which ethnic symbols and identity remain important, even when ethnic identity does not play a significant role in everyday life. For example, many Irish-Americans in the United States celebrate "Irishness" only one day per year: St. Patrick's Day. In all other facets of life, these individuals' Irish-American ethnicity does not play a significant role. Other examples include attending folk festivals, visiting specific cultural locales for holidays, or participating in an ethnic pride rally.

Real World

Certain racial and ethnic groups have a higher incidence of specific health problems. For example, the Chinese population accounts for a disproportionate number of chronic hepatitis B infections and liver cancer. Mediterranean and African populations have a significantly higher rate of hemoglobinopathies (diseases related to hemoglobin). Ashkenazi Jews have a higher rate of autoimmune diseases. Certain Native American populations are associated with gallbladder and biliary tree diseases. Being of a particular race or ethnicity is not necessary for the development of any disease, but may certainly be associated with increased risk.

It is important to consider how race and ethnicity may affect one's ability to receive proper health care. The Agency for Healthcare Research and Quality (AHRQ), a government agency, reports that race and ethnicity influence a patient's chance of receiving many specific procedures and treatments. Whether due to conscious or unconscious bias, there is evidence that different races are not always offered the same level of care escalation in a medical emergency.

On the other hand, there are a number of public health outreach projects that target at-risk racial or ethnic populations through education, screening, and treatment. These specific strategies are geared to close gaps in health disparities. Many large university health systems run free clinics in local neighborhoods and may target specific populations; for example, some of these clinics will staff Spanish-speaking doctors and medical students to cater to the Hispanic immigrant population.

Sexual Orientation

Sexual orientation can be defined as the direction of one's sexual interest toward members of the same, opposite, or both sexes. It is generally divided into three categories:

- **Heterosexual:** attraction to individuals of the opposite sex
- **Bisexual:** attraction to members of both sexes
- **Homosexual:** attraction to individuals of the same sex

Sexual orientation involves a person's sexual feelings and may or may not be a significant contributor to that person's sense of identity. It may or may not be evident in the person's appearance or behavior. Disclosure of minority sexual orientations, sometimes called *coming out of the closet*, is a major milestone in the absorption of sexuality into one's identity. This has also been shown to have therapeutic effects: coming out is associated with decreases in depressive and anxious symptoms that can even be measured physiologically as cortisol levels drop during this time.

Human sexuality continues to be an important area of research for psychologists, sociologists, and biologists alike, but evidence shows that sexuality is likely more fluid than previously believed. Alfred Kinsey was a pioneer in this area, and—in addition to a number of other models and publications—described sexuality on a zero to six scale, with zero representing exclusive heterosexuality and six representing exclusive homosexuality. When ranked on this **Kinsey scale**, few people actually fell into the categories of zero and six, with a significant proportion of the population falling somewhere between the two.

Bridge

Many public health outreach efforts are aimed at closing the gap in health disparities between populations. Health and healthcare disparities are discussed in Chapter 12 of *MCAT Behavioral Sciences Review*.

Sexual and gender identity minorities are often grouped together under the umbrella term **LGBT** (lesbian, gay, bisexual, and transgender). In some cases, this acronym has been expanded to include other self-definitions of sexuality and sexual identity, including Q (queer or questioning), I (intersex), or A (asexual).

Several health disparities have been recognized within the LGBT community. The most significant historical disparity is HIV, which disproportionately affected gay men in urban environments during the early 1980s. While the prevalence of HIV is still slightly higher in men who have sex with men (MSM), it exists in all populations. Efforts to encourage safe sex and increase screening have helped slow the epidemic of HIV, as has increased awareness of those with HIV/AIDS with projects like the AIDS Memorial Quilt, shown in Figure 11.6. Within the healthcare system, lesbians receive less screening for cervical cancer and may not be screened for other sexually transmitted infections. Transgender individuals have multiple areas of increased risk, including use of "street hormones" without proper counseling on their side effects.

Figure 11.6. The AIDS Memorial Quilt

Mental health disparities are also common in the LGBT community. LGBT youth are at significantly higher risk for bullying, victimization, and violence, and have higher rates of suicide. In adults, the LGBT population has a higher prevalence of depression and anxiety than their heterosexual counterparts; gay men have an increased rate of eating disorders. A host of campaigns and outreach efforts have begun to target these disparities.

Immigration Status

According to the Census Bureau, the nation's total immigrant population is growing rapidly; it was quantified at 40.4 million in 2011 and is expected to increase by roughly 20 million in the next two decades. This tells us that immigrants, whether documented or undocumented, are interwoven into every social structure and institution in the United States and make up a significant demographic bloc. The nativity of immigrant populations changes over time; in the most recent census, the largest proportions of immigrants had emigrated from Mexico, the Caribbean, and India.

Considering the number of immigrants, there are often barriers that affect interactions with social structures and institutions. The complex organization of the United States healthcare system is starkly different from those of most other nations, and this may present a barrier to understanding for immigrants. Language barriers may also make it difficult for immigrants to access healthcare or to take control of their healthcare decisions; telephone translation services have been created to help facilitate the conversation between clinician and patient. Racial and ethnic identity may be more pronounced in first-generation immigrants, and the same biases and prejudices against certain racial and ethnic minorities might be compounded by the individual's immigrant status; this interplay between multiple demographic factors—especially when it leads to discrimination or oppression—is termed **intersectionality**. Finally, undocumented status presents a major barrier for many immigrants to access healthcare for fear of reporting and deportation.

DEMOGRAPHIC SHIFTS AND SOCIAL CHANGE

Since 1950, the United States population has roughly doubled. In addition to increasing in size, the makeup of the American population has changed significantly. The average age in the United States has increased, and the population is continuing to become more racially and ethnically diverse. These are examples of **demographic shifts**: changes in the makeup of a population over time.

Population projections attempt to predict changes in population size over time, and can be assisted by historical measures of growth, understanding of changes in social structure, and analysis of other demographic information. In this last category, **population pyramids** provide a histogram of the population size of various age cohorts, as shown in Figure 11.7.

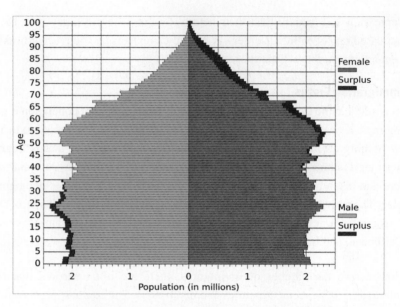

Figure 11.7. U.S. Population Pyramid, 2014
Surplus occurs when one sex has a larger population than the other.

Fertility, Mortality, and Migration

The increased population of the United States is due to a number of factors that center around fertility, mortality, and migration. **Fertility rate** refers to the average number of children born to a woman during her lifetime in a population. In many parts of the world, fertility rate is the primary driver of population expansion; for example, in many parts of Africa, the average fertility rate is between four and eight children per woman, as seen in Figure 11.8. In the United States, fertility rates have trended downward over time; however, the rate is still above two, indicating that fertility rates are still contributing to population growth.

Key Concept

Demographic statistics:
- Fertility rate = children per woman per lifetime
- Birth rate = children per 1000 people per year
- Mortality rate = deaths per 1000 people per year
- Migration rate = immigration rate minus emigration rate

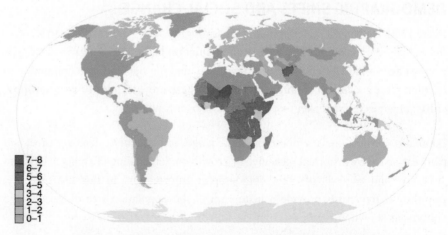

Figure 11.8. Fertility Rates around the World, 2013
Based on data from the CIA World Factbook; measured in children born per woman in the population

Mortality rates refer to the number of deaths in a population per unit time. Usually, this is measured in deaths per 1000 people per year. With advancements in healthcare and access, the mortality rate in the United States has dropped significantly over the past century. However, mortality rates are a significant brake on population growth in many parts of the world, as demonstrated in Figure 11.9. The decreased mortality rate in the United States is one contributor to the increase in average age of the population, as is a decreased fertility rate. In addition, the aging of the baby boomer generation, one of the largest generations in United States history, increases this average age. Both birth and mortality rates can be reported in multiple forms: the total rate for a population, the **crude rate** (adjusted to a certain population size over a specific period of time and multiplied by a constant to give a whole number), or age-specific rates.

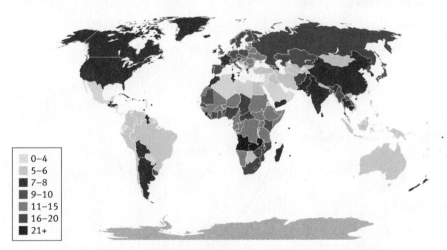

Figure 11.9. Mortality Rates around the World, 2009
Based on data from the CIA World Factbook; measured in deaths per 1000 individuals per year.

Finally, **migration** is a contributor to population growth. **Immigration** is defined as movement into a new geographic space, whereas **emigration** is movement away from a geographic space. As described earlier, the United States continues to have larger net immigration than emigration, driving an increase in the population size. This also increases the racial and ethnic diversity of the United States, as do increased mobility within the country and increases in intermarriage between different races and ethnicities. Migration can be motivated by both **pull factors**, which are positive attributes of the new location that attract the immigrant, and **push factors**, which are negative attributes of the old location that encourage the immigrant to leave.

Demographic Transition

While demographic shift is a general term referring to changes in population makeup over time, **demographic transition** is a specific example of demographic shift referring to changes in birth and death rates in a country as it develops from

Key Concept

The United States population is getting bigger, older (average age has increased), and more diverse (through immigration, mobility, and intermarriage).

a preindustrial to industrial economic system. This transition has been seen in the United States since the Industrial Revolution. Demographic transition can be divided into four stages:

- **Stage 1:** preindustrial society; birth and death rates are both high
- **Stage 2:** improvements in healthcare, nutrition, sanitation, and wages cause death rates to drop
- **Stage 3:** improvements in contraception, women's rights, and a shift from an agricultural to an industrial economy cause **birth rates** (births per 1000 individuals per year) to drop. Further, with an industrializing society, children must go to school for many years to be productive in society and may need to be supported by parents for a longer period of time than was formerly the case; families thus have fewer children
- **Stage 4:** an industrialized society; birth and death rates are both low

A model of demographic transition can be seen in Figure 11.10.

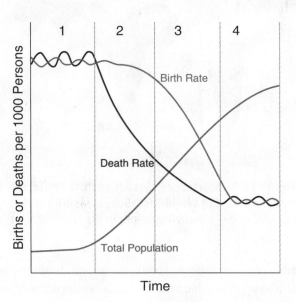

Figure 11.10. Demographic Transition

Key Concept

During demographic transition, mortality rate drops before birth rate. Therefore, the population grows at first while mortality rate is dropping, and then plateaus as the birth rate decreases as well.

Malthusian theory focuses on how the exponential growth of a population can outpace growth of the food supply and lead to social degradation and disorder. A Malthusian catastrophe, then, is the prediction that as third-world nations industrialize and undergo demographic transition, the pace at which the world population will grow is much faster than the ability to generate food and mass starvation will occur. This is similar to the death phase of bacterial growth, when resources in the environment have been depleted, as described in Chapter 1 of *MCAT Biology Review*.

Social Movements

Social movements are organized either to promote or to resist social change. These movements are often motivated by perceived **relative deprivation**, or a decrease in resources, representation, or agency relative to the past or to the whole of society. Social movements that promote social change are termed **proactive**; those that resist social change are **reactive**. Members of social movements work to correct what they perceive as social injustices. Some examples of proactive movements include the civil rights movement, women's rights movement, gay rights movement, animal rights movement, and environmentalism movement. Some examples of reactive movements include the white supremacist movement, counterculture movement, antiglobalization movement, and anti-immigration movement. To further their goals, social movements may establish coordinated organizations. For example, some organizations associated with the proactive movements above include the National Association for the Advancement of Colored People (NAACP), American Civil Liberties Union (ACLU), Human Rights Campaign (HRC), The Humane Society, and Greenpeace. Social movements may also seek to share their message through the media and demonstrations. Political involvement is also common through lobbying and carefully directed donations.

Globalization

Globalization is the process of integrating the global economy with free trade and the tapping of foreign markets. This is a relatively recent phenomenon spurred on by improvements in global communication technology and economic interdependence. Globalization leads to a decrease in the geographical constraints on social and cultural exchanges and can lead to both positive and negative effects. For example, the availability of foods (especially produce) from around the world during the entire calendar year can only be accomplished through trade with an extremely large number of world markets. However, significant worldwide unemployment, rising prices, increased pollution, civil unrest (particularly in unindustrialized or undemocratic nations), and global terrorism are negative effects of globalization.

Traditionally, the health sector has been organized at the national, state, or local level, but this is beginning to change. Groups such as the World Health Organization (WHO), the American Red Cross, and Doctors Without Borders supply aid to populations in need around the globe. Many medical schools are also increasing opportunities for medical students to complete rotations in other countries.

Urbanization

Urbanization refers to dense areas of population creating a pull for migration. In other words, cities are formed as individuals move into and establish residency in these new urban centers. Urbanization is not a new phenomenon; ancient populations established cities in Jerusalem, Athens, Timbuktu, and other locations. The economic opportunities offered in cities and creation of a large number of "world cities" has fueled an increase in urbanization during the last few decades. Currently, more than half of the world's populations live in what are considered urban areas. Sociologists and other professionals have found links between urban societies and health challenges related to water sanitation, air quality, environmental hazards, violence and injuries, infectious diseases, unhealthy diets, and physical inactivity.

Cities are rarely homogenous with respect to their population makeup. Most cities have areas that are more socioeconomically well-off and others that are more impoverished. **Ghettoes** are defined as areas where specific racial, ethnic, or religious minorities are concentrated, usually due to social or economic inequities. In the most extreme cases, slums may be formed. A **slum,** as shown in Figure 11.11, is an extremely densely populated area of a city with low-quality, often informal housing and poor sanitation.

Figure 11.11. Slum in Jakarta, Indonesia

MCAT Concept Check 11.3:

Before you move on, assess your understanding of the material with these questions.

1. What is the difference between race and ethnicity?

    _____

2. What is symbolic ethnicity?

    _____

3. Define the following demographic statistics:
- Fertility rate:

_____

- Birth rate:

_____

- Mortality rate:

_____

4. During demographic transition, what happens to the mortality rate? To the birth rate?

_____

- Mortality rate:

_____

- Birth rate:

_____

5. What are the two types of social movements? How do they differ?

- _____

- _____

Conclusion

There are three major trends that are changing our nation's healthcare needs and our patient population. First, the increased diversity in the American population as a whole (from immigration, increased social and academic mobility, and interconnectedness through technology) puts us in front of patients whose thoughts and beliefs about health and well-being may be starkly different from our own. Second, increased access to healthcare through reform legislation has allowed millions of Americans to reach providers for the first time. Finally, our successes in medicine and public health have increased survival rates of many formerly fatal conditions and have enabled us to live longer. This leaves us with an aging population, in which individuals may be coping with multiple illnesses simultaneously.

To arm physicians of the future with the skills needed to take care of this population, many medical schools are increasing their coursework in interpersonal skills (*Doctor–Patient Relationship*; *Doctoring*; or *Physician, Patient, and Society* are such courses at various schools), as well as **cultural sensitivity**, the recognition and respect of differences between cultures, and research ethics. This is part of the biopsychosocial model of medicine described in Chapter 7 of *MCAT Behavioral Sciences Review*. Knowledge of the structure of society and how it shifts over time, as explained in this chapter, will enhance your ability to counsel patients. Unlike the old model of *doctor knows best* (often referred to as the paternalistic approach to medicine), today's doctors must work together with patients to find solutions to their health problems. By working with patients on their own terms, you will be able to help maintain and improve their health status, and begin to correct the health inequities that exist in today's population. In the next chapter—the last of *MCAT Behavioral Sciences Review*—we will explore these inequities in resources, health status, and healthcare.

CONCEPT SUMMARY

Sociology: Theories and Institutions

- Theoretical approaches provide frameworks for the interactions we observe within society.

  o **Functionalism** focuses on the function of each component of society and how those components fit together. **Manifest functions** are deliberate actions that serve to help a given system; **latent functions** are unexpected, unintended, or unrecognized positive consequences of manifest functions.

  o **Conflict theory** focuses on how power differentials are created and how these differentials contribute to the maintenance of social order.

  o **Symbolic interactionism** is the study of the ways individuals interact through a shared understanding of words, gestures, and other symbols.

  o **Social constructionism** explores the ways in which individuals and groups make decisions to agree upon a given social reality.

  o **Rational choice theory** states that individuals will make decisions that maximize potential benefit and minimize potential harm; **exchange theory** applies rational choice theory within social groups.

  o **Feminist theory** explores the ways in which one gender can be subordinated, minimized, or devalued compared to the other.

- **Social institutions** are well-established social structures that dictate certain patterns of behavior or relationships and are accepted as a fundamental part of culture. Common social institutions include the family, education, religion, government and the economy, and health and medicine.

- There are four key ethical tenets of American medicine.

  o **Beneficence** refers to acting in the patient's best interest.

  o **Nonmaleficence** refers to avoiding treatments for which risk is larger than benefit.

  o **Respect for autonomy** refers to respecting patients' rights to make decisions about their own healthcare.

  o **Justice** refers to treating similar patients similarly and distributing healthcare resources fairly.

Culture

- **Culture** encompasses the lifestyle of a group of people and includes both material and symbolic elements.

  o **Material culture** includes the physical items one associates with a given group, such as artwork, emblems, clothing, jewelry, foods, buildings, and tools.

  o **Symbolic culture** includes the ideas associated with a cultural group.

- **Cultural lag** refers to the idea that material culture changes more quickly than symbolic culture.

- A **cultural barrier** is a social difference that impedes interaction.

- **Language** consists of spoken or written symbols combined into a system and governed by rules.

- A **value** is what a person deems important in life.

- A **belief** is something a person considers to be true.

- A **ritual** is a formalized ceremonial behavior in which members of a group or community regularly engage. It is governed by specific rules, including appropriate behavior and a predetermined order of events.

- **Norms** are societal rules that define the boundaries of acceptable behavior.

- There is evidence that culture flows from evolutionary principles, and that culture can also influence evolution.

Demographics

- **Demographics** refer to the statistics of populations and are the mathematical applications of sociology. One can analyze hundreds of demographic variables; some of the most common are age, gender, race and ethnicity, sexual orientation, and immigration status.

  - **Ageism** is prejudice or discrimination on the basis of a person's age.

  - **Gender** is the set of behavioral, cultural, or psychological traits typically associated with a biological sex. **Gender inequality** is the intentional or unintentional empowerment of one gender to the detriment of the other.

  - **Race** is a social construct based on phenotypic differences between groups of people; these may be either real or perceived differences.

  - **Ethnicity** is also a social construct that sorts people by cultural factors, including language, nationality, religion, and other factors. **Symbolic ethnicity** is recognition of an ethnic identity that is only relevant on special occasions or in specific circumstances and does not specifically impact everyday life.

  - **Sexual orientation** can be defined by one's sexual interest toward members of the same, opposite, or both sexes.

  - **Immigration** is the movement into a new geographic area. **Emigration** is the movement away from a geographic area.

- A **fertility rate** is the average number of children born to a woman during her lifetime in a population. A **birth rate** is relative to a population size over time, usually measured as the number of births per 1000 people per year.

- A **mortality rate** is the average number of deaths per population size over time, usually measured as the number of deaths per 1000 people per year.

- **Migration** refers to the movement of people from one geographic location to another.

- **Demographic transition** is a model used to represent drops in birth and death rates as a result of industrialization.

- **Social movements** are organized to either promote (**proactive**) or resist (**reactive**) social change.

- **Globalization** is the process of integrating a global economy with free trade and tapping of foreign labor markets.

- **Urbanization** refers to the process of dense areas of population creating a pull for migration; in other words, creating cities.

ANSWERS TO CONCEPT CHECKS

11.1

1. Manifest functions are actions that are intended to help some part of a system. Latent functions are unintended, unstated, or unrecognized positive consequences of these actions on society.

2.

Theoretical Approach	Primary Thesis or Idea
Functionalism	Each part of society serves a function; when these functions work together correctly, society overall can function normally
Conflict theory	Power differentials are created when groups compete for economic, social, and political resources; these differentials contribute to the maintenance of social order
Symbolic interactionism	Humans communicate through words, gestures, and other symbols to which we attach meaning
Social constructionism	Individuals and groups make decisions to agree upon a given social reality
Rational choice theory	Individuals will make decisions that maximize potential benefit and minimize potential harm
Feminist theory	Explores the ways in which one gender can be subordinated, minimized, or devalued compared to the other

3.

Ethical Principle	Description
Beneficence	Act in the patient's best interest
Nonmaleficence	*Do no harm*; avoid interventions where the potential for harm outweighs the potential for benefit
Respect for autonomy	Respect patients' decisions and choices about their own healthcare
Justice	Treat similar patients with similar care; distribute healthcare resources fairly

11.2

1. Material culture focuses on the artifacts associated with a group: the physical objects, such as artwork, emblems, clothing, jewelry, foods, buildings, and tools. Symbolic culture focuses on the ideas and principles that belong to a particular group.

2. A value is what a person deems to be important; a belief is what a person deems to be true. While these terms are often used interchangeably in everyday life, they have specific definitions in the social sciences.

11.3

1. Race is based on phenotypic differences between groups of people. Ethnicity is based on common language, religion, nationality, or other cultural factors.

2. Symbolic ethnicity is recognition of an ethnic identity on special occasions or in specific circumstances, but not during everyday life.

3. Fertility rate is the average number of children a woman has during her lifetime in a population. Birth rate is the number of births in a population per unit time, usually measured as births per 1000 people per year. Mortality rate is the number of deaths in a population per unit time, usually measured as deaths per 1000 people per year.

4. During demographic transition, both the mortality and birth rate decrease.

5. Proactive social movements are in favor of a specific social change. Reactive social movements run against a specific social change.

SHARED CONCEPTS

Behavioral Sciences Chapter 6
Identity and Personality

Behavioral Sciences Chapter 8
Social Processes, Attitudes, and Behavior

Behavioral Sciences Chapter 9
Social Interaction

Behavioral Sciences Chapter 10
Social Thinking

Behavioral Sciences Chapter 12
Social Stratification

Biology Chapter 12
Genetics and Evolution

Discrete Practice Questions

Consult your online resources for Full-Length Exams and Passage-Based Questions (for certain chapters)

1. Which of the following best describes a manifest function?

    A. An intended positive effect on a system
    B. An intended negative effect on a system
    C. An unintended positive effect on a system
    D. An unintended negative effect on a system

2. Studying why a nod means "yes" in many cultures is most representative of which of the following sociological concepts?

    A. Demographic transition
    B. Expectancy theory
    C. Symbolic interactionism
    D. Demographic shift

3. Which of the following ethical principles states that physicians should avoid using treatments with greater potential for harm than benefit?

    A. Autonomy
    B. Beneficence
    C. Justice
    D. Nonmaleficence

4. A Cuban-American man living in the United States has the dominant physical features of a black man. He speaks Spanish, prefers Latin foods, and listens to Latin music. His preferences are best defined through which of the following attributes?

    I. Race
    II. Ethnicity
    III. Culture

    A. I only
    B. II only
    C. II and III only
    D. I, II, and III

5. A patient who resides in the United States says, "I love you," and hugs his doctor after every routine visit. This behavior violates:

    A. personal beliefs.
    B. patient autonomy.
    C. social values.
    D. social norms.

6. Which of the following demographics can be measured in events per 1000 people per year?

    I. Birth rate
    II. Fertility rate
    III. Mortality rate

    A. I only
    B. I and III only
    C. II and III only
    D. I, II, and III

7. Because there are more than 500 Native American tribes, there are several different healing practices among them. Some tribes may have ceremonies that include chanting, singing, body-painting, dancing, and even use of mind-altering substances to persuade the spirits to heal the sick person. These ceremonies are examples of:

    A. latent functions.
    B. rituals.
    C. cultural barriers.
    D. social movements.

8. Over the last few decades, the United States population has become:

    A. bigger, older, and more diverse.
    B. bigger, younger, and more diverse.
    C. smaller, older, and less diverse.
    D. smaller, older, and more diverse.

9. Which of the following is NOT an example of material culture?

   A. Traditional African clothing
   B. Japanese cuisine
   C. American values
   D. Native American sand paintings

10. During which stage of demographic transition are both birth rates and mortality rates low?

   A. Stage 1
   B. Stage 2
   C. Stage 3
   D. Stage 4

11. Shortly after a state legalizes gambling in casinos, a formal coalition forms to oppose the building of any casinos in the major cities of the state. This scenario includes:

   I. conflict theory.
   II. social institutions.
   III. a social movement.

   A. I only
   B. I and III only
   C. II and III only
   D. I, II, and III

12. A young adult male claims to have had sexual relationships mostly with other men, although he has been attracted to women at times. What would be his most likely score on the Kinsey scale?

   A. 0
   B. 1
   C. 5
   D. 6

13. Which of the following demographic variables is known to be biologically determined?

   A. Gender
   B. Sex
   C. Ethnicity
   D. Sexual orientation

14. Which of the following would contribute to increasing population growth over time?

   A. A fertility rate less than 2
   B. An immigration rate larger than emigration rate
   C. An increase in mortality rate
   D. A decrease in birth rate

15. Urbanization can cause all of the following negative effects EXCEPT:

   A. decreased opportunity for social interaction.
   B. increased transmission of infectious disease.
   C. decreased air quality and sanitation.
   D. increased rates of violent crime.

Explanations to
Discrete Practice Questions

1. A

A manifest function is an intended positive effect on a system. A latent function is an unintended positive effect on a system, **choice (C)**. A negative effect on a system, **choices (B) and (D)**, is termed a dysfunction.

2. C

Symbolic interactionism studies how individuals interact through a shared understanding of words, gestures, and other symbols. A nod is thus a symbol in many cultures that signifies "yes."

3. D

The principle of nonmaleficence states that physicians must not only act in their patient's best interest (beneficence, **choice (B)**), but must also avoid treatments where the potential for harm outweighs the potential for benefit.

4. C

Although one's dominant physical features are associated with race, this man's preferences are those of Latino ethnicity and culture. Ethnicity is a social construct that considers language, religion, nationality, and cultural factors. Culture relates to a group's way of life; the preferences listed in the question are examples of material and symbolic culture.

5. D

In the United States, it is not a common practice to say, "I love you," and hug one's physician after each routine checkup; therefore, this behavior could be considered deviant, going against the social norm. Values, **choice (C)**, are what an individual deems to be important.

6. B

Both birth rate and mortality rate can be measured per 1000 people per year. Fertility rate is measured in number of children per woman during her lifetime.

7. B

Rituals are formalized ceremonial behaviors in which members of a group or community regularly engage. Therefore, these activities are examples of rituals performed for healing.

8. A

With a decrease in mortality rate and a higher immigration rate than emigration rate, the United States population continues to grow, with an increasing average age and increasing racial and ethnic diversity.

9. C

Material culture includes any cultural artifact—objects to which we assign meaning. Values are ideas, which are associated with symbolic culture.

10. D

During demographic transition, both birth rates and mortality rates are high in stage 1, **choice (A)**. Mortality rates drop during stage 2, **choice (B)**, and then birth rates drop during stage 3, **choice (C)**. In stage 4, both birth rates and mortality rates are low.

11. D

In this scenario, a group is fighting for social power, which is an aspect of conflict theory. Further, this group is an example of a reactive social movement because it is running counter to social change. The fact that gambling had been legalized implies the involvement of the government, a social institution.

12. C

This man is describing his sexuality as mostly homosexual, although he has also had some heterosexual attractions. The Kinsey scale scores a 6, **choice (D)**, as exclusively homosexual. A score of 3 would equate to bisexuality. Thus, this man would likely score a 4 or 5.

13. B

Sex is determined by one's genotype, and therefore is biologically determined. Gender, **choice (A)**, may or may not match biological sex and therefore is not biologically determined. Ethnicity, **choice (C)**, is a social construct that sorts people by cultural factors, and therefore is not biologically determined. Sexual orientation, **choice (D)**, may have some biological component, but the relative role of biology and environment is not yet known.

14. B

If the immigration rate in a geographic area is larger than the emigration rate, then there is a larger influx than efflux of people. This will increase the population of that area.

15. A

Urbanization is the migration of people into urban centers to create cities. The increased population density should provide additional opportunities for social interaction, not decreased opportunities.

12

Social Stratification

In This Chapter

Chapter Profile

The content in this chapter should be relevant to about 7% of all questions about the Behavioral Sciences on the MCAT.

This chapter covers material from the following AAMC content categories:

8B: Social thinking

8C: Social interactions

10A: Social inequality

Introduction

The wonderfully witty Oscar Wilde once said, *Work is the curse of the drinking classes.* While this quote is intended to be humorous, it does speak to the stereotypical characteristics associated with socioeconomic class differences. Americans often think that class and social stratification are nonissues in our society. Unlike earlier feudal societies, most Americans are not royals or gentry, possessing inherited titles, land, or palaces; we're often considered to be a much more equality-orientated society, in keeping with our Constitutional ideals. Yet, how do we explain such lavish displays of wealth, power, and privilege as a Manhattan lawyer driving a shiny Porsche past a homeless person rooting through a trashcan? Such exhibitions make it hard to ignore the uneven distributions of material wealth and the overall social inequality in the United States.

To understand social inequalities in America and how such disparities impact health and healthcare services, we will examine several aspects of social stratification in terms of class, status, and social capital, and how these intersect with race, gender, and age. We will also focus on patterns of social mobility and how poverty and spatial disparities play a major role in health and illness. Later, we will connect how race, gender, and socioeconomic inequalities impact one's health profile and access to quality healthcare.

12.1 Social Class

> **LEARNING GOALS**
>
> After Chapter 12.1, you will be able to:
>
> - Explain how socioeconomic status of an individual or a community is determined
> - Define social capital and social cohesion
> - Identify groups that suffer disproportionate social inequality
> - Describe the relationship between social mobility and merit

Social class is defined as a category of people who share a similar socioeconomic position in society. This can be identified by looking at the economic opportunities, job positions, lifestyles, attitudes, and behaviors of a given slice of society.

ASPECTS OF SOCIAL STRATIFICATION

Social stratification focuses on social inequalities and studies the basic question of who gets what and why. Social stratification is thus related to one's **socioeconomic status (SES)**, which may depend on ascribed or achieved status. **Ascribed status** derives from clearly identifiable characteristics, such as age, gender, and skin color; **achieved status** is acquired via direct, individual efforts. In other words, ascribed status is involuntary, while achieved status is obtained through hard work or merit. Caste and estate systems stratify by ascribed SES, while class systems stratify by achieved SES. After breaking free from British colonial rule, the United States moved toward a class-based system of social stratification.

Class, Status, and Power

There are three major classes—upper, middle, and lower—although these vary to different degrees in different locations. The upper class consists of those who have great wealth, along with recognized reputations and lifestyles, and have a larger influence on society's political and economic systems. In other words, the upper class has a high concentration of prestige and power. The middle class can be further divided into three levels: upper, middle, and lower. The middle class includes successful business and professional people (upper-middle), those who have been unable to achieve the upper-middle lifestyle because of educational and economic shortcomings (middle-middle), and those who are skilled and semiskilled workers with fewer luxuries (lower-middle). The lower class is at the poorer end of the economic spectrum, with a greatly reduced amount of sociopolitical power.

Key Concept

It's important to keep in mind that socioeconomic status is not only determined by merit (achieved status), but also external characteristics or outward appearances like skin color and gender (ascribed status).

Bridge

There are three major types of status: ascribed, achieved, and master status. While ascribed and achieved statuses are described here, remember that a master status is one that pervades all aspects of an individual's life. The role of statuses in social interaction is discussed in Chapter 9 of *MCAT Behavioral Sciences Review*.

Prestige refers to the amount of positive regard society has for a given person or idea. Certain occupations, such as physicians, are broadly viewed with high levels of respect and importance. Particular educational institutions, organizations, awards, and accolades may also be considered prestigious.

Power can be described as the ability to affect others' behavior through real or perceived rewards and punishments, and is based on the unequal distribution of valued resources. At its core, power defines the relationship between individuals, groups, and social institutions. Power relationships function to maintain order, organize economic systems, conduct warfare, and rule over and exploit people. As a result, power creates worldwide social inequalities as people tend to fall somewhere between the *haves* and the *have-nots*.

Marxist theory proposes that the *have-nots*, called the **proletariat**, could overthrow the *haves*, called the **bourgeoisie**, as well as the entire capitalist economy by developing class consciousness. **Class consciousness** refers to the organization of the working class around shared goals and recognition of a need for collective political action. By working together as one unit, the proletariat could revolt and take control of the political and economic system, laying the groundwork for a socialist state. The one major barrier to class consciousness, however, was **false consciousness**, a misperception of one's actual position within society. Members of the proletariat either could not see just how bad conditions were, could not recognize the commonalities between their own experiences and others, or otherwise were too clouded to assemble into the revolutionaries Marx envisioned.

In the modern, globalized world, capitalist economics has led to an increase in social inequality, a reduction in social cohesion, and a waning of social capital. Early sociologists explained that social inequality is further accelerated by what is called *anomie*. **Anomie** refers to a lack of social norms, or the breakdown of social bonds between an individual and society. **Strain theory** focuses on how anomic conditions can lead to deviance. Anomic conditions include excessive individualism, social inequality, and isolation; these all erode social solidarity. Other sociologists have focused on the importance of social trust in the proper functioning of civil society. Social trust comes from two primary sources: social norms of reciprocity (*I'll scratch your back if you scratch mine*) and social networks. In the past several decades, as society has become more urbanized, self-oriented, and materialistic, associational ties have diminished and consequently have led to a decline in social capital. What is the relationship between social stratification, social capital, and power?

Social Capital

Essentially, **social capital** can be considered the investments people make in their society in return for economic or collective rewards; the greater the investment, the higher the level of **social integration** (peaceful movement into mainstream society) and inclusion. One of the main forms of social capital is the social network. Social networks can create two types of social inequality: situational

Key Concept

Anomic conditions in postindustrial modern life have accelerated the decline of social inclusion and, as a result, have further obstructed opportunities to acquire social capital.

Real World

Those with mental health problems are one of the largest disadvantaged groups to lack both strong and weak ties. People without multiple weak ties may find it extremely difficult to contribute to and access social capital. Due to repercussions of social exclusion, mental health sufferers may find that social capital is out of their reach. Consequently, this group is personally and socially disempowered, further propelling a cycle of exclusion. Social exclusion has huge financial repercussions on healthcare, with greater morbidity rates.

(socioeconomic advantage) and positional (based on how connected one is within a network, and one's centrality within that network). It is claimed that inequality in networks creates and reinforces **privilege**, or inequality in opportunity. Moreover, low social capital leads to greater social inequality. If social capital refers to the benefits one receives from group association, **cultural capital** refers to the benefits one receives from knowledge, abilities, and skills.

Communities are joined together through what are called strong and weak ties. **Strong ties** refer to peer group and kinship contacts, which are quantitatively small but qualitatively powerful. **Weak ties** refer to social connections that are personally superficial, such as associates, but that are large in number and provide connections to a wide range of other individuals. Social networking websites—especially those focusing on professional relationships—are examples of groups of weak ties. People without multiple weak ties, such as disadvantaged groups, may find it extremely difficult to contribute to and access social capital.

Intersections with Race, Gender, and Age

Social stratification or, more properly, social inequality, remains higher among certain disadvantaged groups than others, including racial and ethnic minorities (specifically Hispanics and African Americans), female-headed families, and the elderly. Think about who you know who may fall into these underprivileged or underserved groups. Your friends? Your relatives? Yourself? Socioeconomic inequalities remain high in America, despite the numerous policies created to encourage equality in the law. As described in Chapter 11 of *MCAT Behavioral Sciences Review*, this is partially due to **intersectionality**—the compounding of disadvantage seen in individuals who belong to more than one oppressed group. Some consider this to be the result of the oversimplification of racial categories or over-reliance on the **five ethnicities model** used by the United States Census Bureau and the National Institutes of Health (NIH): white, black, Asian, Latino, and Native American. Some argue that racial and ethnic boundaries are more ambiguous and fluid in our increasingly diverse population. This argument promotes a model that recognizes this state of hyperdiversity, which reimagines our dynamic population as a complex, multicultural, mosaic-like mix of national origin, ethnicity, race, and immigration status. These sociodemographic characteristics, in conjunction with social policies, can either enhance or obstruct social mobility.

PATTERNS OF SOCIAL MOBILITY

Unlike a caste-based or estate-based system of social stratification, we in America have the ability to move up or down from one class to another. In a class system, **social mobility** is typically the result of an economic and occupational structure that allows one to acquire higher-level employment opportunities given proper credentials and experience requirements. In the United States, our class system encourages this type of ambition through dedication and hard work. This is often captured in the phrase *The American Dream*.

> **Key Concept**
>
> Social inequality is more pronounced in racial and ethnic minorities, such as Hispanics and African Americans, female-headed families, and the elderly.

Intergenerational and Intragenerational Mobility

Social mobility can either occur within a generation or across generations. **Intragenerational** changes in social status happen within a person's lifetime, while **intergenerational** changes are from parents to children. Many people consider America to be *the land of opportunity*, where intragenerational and intergenerational mobility can easily occur. However, others argue that this is no longer the case as the gap between the upper class and the middle and lower classes continues to widen. As a result, America's social inequality is at its highest point in over a century. Therefore, it may no longer be the case that social mobility primarily occurs in a positive, upward direction.

Meritocracy

One of the largest factors driving American social mobility has been meritocratic competition or a merit-based system of social mobility. **Meritocracy** is based on intellectual talent and achievement, and is a means for a person to advance up the social ladder. Given the rising levels of social inequality and concentration of wealth in the United States, some argue that motivation, a strong work ethic, a conscientious drive, and mastery of skills no longer offer opportunities for advancement. Some fear that America's meritocratic system is quickly becoming a **plutocracy**, or a rule by the upper classes. Nonetheless, while merit still plays a key role in many segments of society, such as academia, it does not always guarantee positive social mobility.

Upward and Downward Mobility

Social mobility usually occurs one of two directions: up or down. Upward mobility is considered to be a positive change in a person's status, resulting in a higher position. Downward mobility is the opposite: a negative change in a person's status, wherein they fall to a lower position. Social mobility is not directly correlated with education, although education can certainly help with achieving upward mobility. Some of the best examples of upward mobility are seen with professional athletes and professional musicians. In addition to education, athletics and music may offer opportunities for disadvantaged individuals to move to a higher social status.

Horizontal Mobility

Upward and downward mobility both refer to patterns of **vertical mobility**, or movement from one social class to another. **Horizontal mobility**, on the other hand, is a change in occupation or lifestyle that remains within the same social class. For example, a construction worker who switches jobs to work in custodial services or mechanical maintenance has made a shift in occupation but remains in the lower-middle class.

POVERTY

Poverty is defined by low socioeconomic status and a lack of possessions or financial resources. Poverty can be handed down from generation to generation, and can be defined on its own terms or in comparison to the rest of the population.

Social Reproduction

Social inequality, especially poverty, can be reproduced or passed on from one generation to the next. This idea is referred to as **social reproduction**. Some consider this to be a culture-of-poverty explanation for social inequality. In other words, the lifestyle of poverty, powerlessness, isolation, and even apathy is handed down from one generation to another as a feature of the society. However, there are many other factors that contribute to poverty, including where one lives and an emphasis on present-orientation, in which people do not plan for the future. One theory, that of **structural poverty,** is based in the concept of "holes" in the structure of society rather than poverty due to the actions of the individual. Proponents of structural poverty argue that the same individuals do not by necessity occupy these "holes" from year to year, but the percentage of a society that falls under the poverty line stays relatively constant due to their existence. To understand how poverty is reproduced, it may be helpful to examine what types of poverty exist.

Absolute and Relative

On an **absolute** level, poverty is a socioeconomic condition in which people do not have enough money or resources to maintain a quality of living that includes basic life necessities such as shelter, food, clothing, and water. This absolute poverty view applies across locations, countries, and cultures. Poverty can also be defined as **relative**, in which one is poor in comparison to the larger population in which they live. For example, if one survived on a low teaching salary while living in the Upper East Side of Manhattan, they may very well be considered poor relative to the other wealthy residents.

In the United States, the official definition of the **poverty line** is derived from the government's calculation of the minimum income requirements for families to acquire the minimum necessities of life. Poverty is highly related to geography, as can be seen in Figure 12.1. One of the main problems with the official poverty line is that it is not contextualized according to geographic location, and as a result, does not take into account the cost of living in different communities. For example, the price of renting an apartment in a major urban center is much higher than the cost of rent in a rural small town. Some define poverty as a form of powerlessness or a sociological and psychological condition of hopelessness, indifference, and distrust. In other words, poverty can be the result of the inability to control events that shape a person's life, often leading to a large degree of dependency on others.

Key Concept

In the United States, poverty is determined by the government's estimation of the minimum income requirements for families to acquire their minimum needs, such as shelter, food, water, and clothing. The problem with this official definition is that it fails to take into account geographical variables that impact the value of money in different locations. Certain areas are more costly to live in than others.

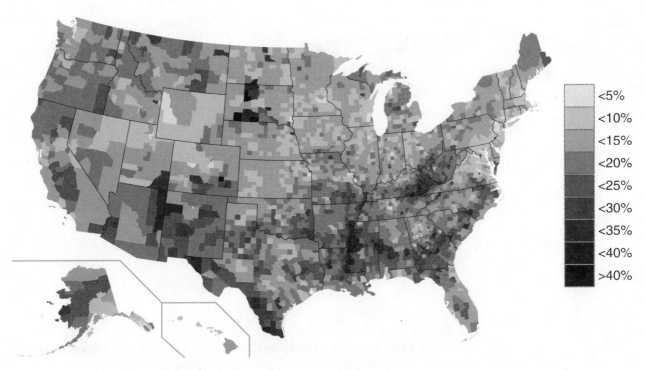

Figure 12.1. Percentage of Population Living Below the Poverty Line by County, 2009

Social Exclusion

Social exclusion can arise from this sense of powerlessness when poor individuals feel segregated and isolated from society. However, the problem is that this attitude can create further obstacles to achieving self-help, independence, and self-respect. Disadvantaged groups, such as racial and ethnic minorities, can experience magnified feelings of alienation and powerlessness when living in an affluent community. These are similar to anomic conditions, which tend to further accelerate social inequality. Another important factor influencing poverty is the spatial setting of social life.

SPATIAL INEQUALITY

Where one lives plays a major role in the distribution of valuable resources. Does a person living in an inner-city neighborhood in Mumbai have the same access to water and electricity as someone living in the posh neighborhood of London's West End? **Spatial inequality** focuses on social stratification across territories and their populations. Examining space helps to illuminate social inequalities because it attends to how geography influences social processes. Social categories such as gender, ethnicity and race, and class are distributed across spaces differently, as shown in Figure 12.2. In turn, these groups use spaces differently. For example, some cultures consider the home the center of family life, culture, and entertainment, while other cultures may view the home as merely a stop-off point for eating and sleeping while spending most of their time outside of the home.

Figure 12.2. White and Black Population Distribution in Milwaukee County, WI

Space also channels inequalities and can even amplify their effects, particularly poverty. This can lead to population segregation and the formation or expansion of ghettoes or slums. Space itself can also create social inequalities. In other words, social relationships between different agents, such as capitalists, laborers, the government, and citizens, result in spatially varied social structures, built environments, and unequal regional development. For example, poorer neighborhoods tend to have less political and social influence than more affluent neighborhoods; as a result, "undesirable" buildings, like water refineries, trash-smoldering plants, and chemical manufacturers tend to be placed in poorer areas, as shown in Figure 12.3. Citizens of these areas may lack the social resources to fight government and industry. To further understand spatial inequality, we must explore this idea on three levels: residential, environmental, and global.

Figure 12.3. Industrial Park in a Low Socioeconomic Area

Residential Segregation

Where one resides—an urban, suburban, or rural environment, and which neighborhood in that environment—has a substantial effect on how people interact, cooperate, and advance. The cultural diversity and anonymity of urban neighborhoods offer a person a greater range of opportunities than normally found in rural areas. For example, people are less likely to fall into their occupations and social positions because of familial ties in urban environments. In rural environments, this is more likely to occur: *My father was a farmer, my grandfather was a farmer, my great-grandfather was a farmer; therefore, I will take up the family business when it's handed down to me.* People in urban areas tend to have more career options to choose from and can more easily improve their SES through such avenues as education, career choice, and marriage. This exists, but is less universally available, in rural environments. Such opportunities also do not always extend across urban environments. The neighborhood in which one lives plays a major role; affluent neighborhoods tend to have more homeowners, professionals and managers, college graduates, and higher-quality schools. Low-income neighborhoods tend to have greater poverty, unemployment rates, lower-quality schools, and higher rates of homelessness. Low-income neighborhoods are also less safe, with higher rates of violent crime, organized crime, and gang activity. These key attributes stratify neighborhoods and create uneven chances for people who live in these communities. The overall greater concentration of poor individuals in urban centers helps to explain **suburbanization**, or the migration pattern of the middle classes to suburban communities, as shown in Figure 12.4. The suburbs have become more attractive as they are generally cleaner and less crowded, have lower crime rates, and often have better school systems. Unlike the middle or upper classes, members of the lower class are often less able to relocate to areas that might offer them better opportunities. Many disadvantaged groups therefore remain in urban centers under poor living conditions. To make matters worse, this type of environment can easily expose low-income groups to illness and disease. Suburbanization can also lead to **urban decay**, in which a previously functional portion of a city deteriorates and becomes decrepit over time. Interestingly, this process can spontaneously reverse in the process of **urban renewal**, in which city land is reclaimed and renovated for public or private use. Urban renewal is often fueled by **gentrification**, when upper- and middle-class populations begin to purchase and renovate neighborhoods in deteriorated areas, displacing the low-SES population.

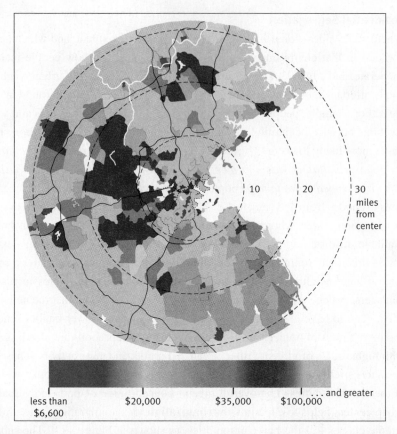

10   20   30
     miles
     from
     center

less than $20,000 $35,000 $100,000   . . . and greater
$6,600

Figure 12.4. The Boston "Doughnut" of Income and Socioeconomic Status
Urban centers tend to contain lower-SES communities, surrounded by a ring of middle- to upper-SES suburbs. Further out are lower-SES exurbs and rural areas.

Environmental Justice

Poor living conditions and dangerous environmental conditions can result in an increase in illness and disease. Many poor and minority groups tend to reside closer to sites of environmental pollution because these areas are usually cheaper housing markets. Environmental risks, such as hazardous waste–producing plants and toxic waste dumps, tend to be located in low-income areas with a high concentration of racial and ethnic minorities. It is no surprise that inadequate housing, heating, and sanitation, in concert with toxin exposure, can contribute to acute medical problems. Illnesses such as influenza, pneumonia, substance use disorders, tuberculosis, and whooping cough are much more common among people living in poor-quality conditions. As mentioned earlier, these low-income areas also may lack the social and political power to prevent environmental risks from encroaching on their communities.

Global Inequalities

Poverty and social inequalities are not limited to hierarchies within a country. The **world system theory** categorizes countries and emphasizes the inequalities of the division of labor at the global level. **Core nations** focus on higher skills, and higher paying productions, while exploiting **peripheral nations** for their lower-skilled productions. **Semi-peripheral nations** are midway between the two—these nations work toward becoming core nations, while having many characteristics of peripheral nations. Much of the world, especially within semi-peripheral and peripheral nations, lives on less than the equivalent of $1.25 per day. This is especially seen in parts of India, sub-Saharan Africa, and South Central Asia, as shown in Figure 12.5.

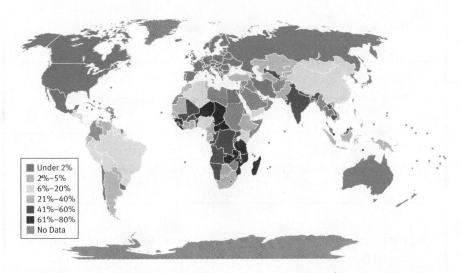

Figure 12.5. Percentage of Population Living on Less than $1.25 per Day, 2008

Largely due to the effects of globalization, massive restructuring of industry and trade patterns have had a major impact on local communities, specifically because of the production of cheap goods at suppressed rates for the global market. This reconfiguration obstructs or limits access to power and resources as the production of goods constantly shifts from location to location. Social inequalities have increased on a worldwide level as local communities become more and more subject to the ebb and flow of the global market. Since the advent of globalization, with the development of world cities, international communication chains, and global immigration, interaction between industrialized and developing nations has had more of an impact on peoples and regions within the state, and has thereby led to further inequalities in space, food and water, energy, housing, and education. Global inequality has been further exacerbated by an unprecedented large population spike, placing strain on the world's resources. The majority of the world also has limited access to healthcare. Consequently, many people around the globe suffer from malnutrition and parasitic and infectious diseases, and have higher rates of morbidity and mortality.

MCAT Concept Check 12.1:

Before you move on, assess your understanding of the material with these questions.

1. How is socioeconomic status (SES) determined?

_____

2. How does social capital affect social cohesion?

_____

3. What are some groups that suffer disproportionate social inequality?

_____

4. What is the relationship between merit and social mobility?

_____

5. With regard to health, which groups are most often affected by environmental hazards?

_____

12.2 Epidemiology and Disparities

LEARNING GOALS

After Chapter 12.2, you will be able to:

- Identify the causes of Waitzkin's "second sickness"
- Explain why women are more likely to have better health profiles than men
- Describe the links between class, ethnicity, and healthcare disparities

An old saying intones that *Your health is your wealth*. This same correlation certainly holds true in reverse: the wealthier tend to have better health and better access to healthcare. Wherever there is low social capital, high urban degradation, interpersonal violence, and low social trust, the social environment is poor, and there is less protection against disease. As a result, class gradients often increase. Poor health conditions and lower life expectancy, as shown in Figure 12.6, are some of the many consequences of social stratification. Low-income groups are significantly worse off than the middle or upper classes when it comes to health disparities, meaning they tend to be sicker than others.

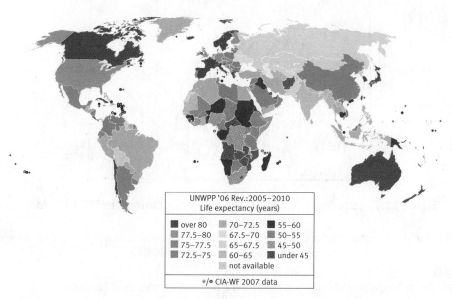

Figure 12.6. Life Expectancy at Birth, 2005–2010

To understand health statistics, it is important to define a few epidemiological terms. **Incidence** is defined as the number of new cases of an illness per population at risk in a given amount of time; for example, the number of new cases of lung cancer per 1000 at-risk people per year. **Prevalence** is a measure of the number of cases of an illness overall—whether new or chronic—per population in a given amount of time; for example, the number of people with new or chronic lung cancer per 1000 people per year. Health statistics are also given in terms of morbidity and mortality. **Morbidity** is the burden or degree of illness associated with a given disease, while **mortality** refers to deaths caused by a given disease.

INEQUITIES IN HEALTH

It has been clearly demonstrated that poor environmental and social factors negatively impact health. This was first demonstrated in the nineteenth century through public health efforts. One landmark example linking geography with disease was John Snow's investigation of a cholera outbreak in London in 1854. Snow tracked cases of cholera on a map, as shown in Figure 12.7, and was able to deduce that a water pump in the neighborhood was causing the spread of the infectious agent (a bacterium called *Vibrio cholerae*).

> **Key Concept**
>
> Epidemiology statistics:
> • Incidence = new cases / population at risk / time
> • Prevalence = total cases / total population / time
> Note that incidence is relative to the population at risk, not the total population; if you already have the illness, you are no longer at risk!

Figure 12.7. John Snow's Map of Disease Cases during the 1854 Cholera Outbreak in London
By tracing the geography of the disease, Snow deduced that a water pump was responsible for cholera transmission.

Health is dependent not only on geography, but also on social and economic factors. Over time, socioeconomic improvements lead to greater general health in the population, and the best health outcomes are generally seen in egalitarian societies. However, despite the ambitions of the modern welfare state, the Black Report of 1980 showed that class differences in health still exist, with professional groups having longer life expectancies than working-class people. Howard Waitzkin described this outcome as the **second sickness**, which is an exacerbation of health outcomes caused by social injustice. As the Centers for Disease Control and Prevention (CDC) have shown, low-income groups are more likely to have poorer health, be uninsured, and die younger than middle- or upper-class adults. Poverty, in combination with a culture of inequality, leads to worse health outcomes, and this effect runs across gender, age, and racial and ethnic boundaries. For example, low-income women are more likely to deliver babies with low birth weights, thereby placing them at risk for numerous physical and cognitive problems in life. Similarly, poor racial and ethnic minorities have lower life expectancies. Members of the lower class, overall, are four times more likely to view themselves in worse health compared with affluent groups. Low-income groups are much more likely to develop life-shortening diseases such as lung cancer, diabetes, heart disease, and other degenerative illnesses. They are also more likely to commit suicide and die from homicide in comparison to wealthier adults. The infant mortality rate among the poor is also much higher;

in some populations of the United States, the infant mortality rate can approximate that of developing countries. However, because of the correlation between poverty and racial and ethnic minorities, many of these characteristics apply to particular ethnic groups more than others.

When it comes to health and illness among racial and ethnic minorities, Asian Americans and Pacific Islanders have some of the best health profiles. Reports illustrate that, in comparison to white Americans, these groups have a lower rate of death associated with cancer, heart disease, diabetes, and infant mortality. African Americans appear to have a worse health profile in comparison to white Americans, showing higher rates of death linked to cancer, heart disease, diabetes, drug and alcohol use, infant mortality, and HIV/AIDS. African American infants have twice the infant mortality rate of white infants. Specifically, African American males have the lowest life expectancy of any racial or gender category. Latinos or Hispanic Americans have a mixed profile in comparison to white Americans, in that they have lower mortality rates attributable to cancer, heart disease, and infant mortality, but higher mortality rates attributable to diabetes, alcohol and drug use, and HIV/AIDS. Hispanics also have a high mortality rate from influenza, pneumonia, and accidents. Native Americans are also mixed in this regard, showing higher rates of death from diabetes, alcohol and drug use, and infant mortality, but lower mortality rates compared to white Americans from cancer, heart disease, and HIV/AIDS. Native Americans also show some of the highest rates of death by suicide in comparison to the general population. This group also has some of the highest mortality rates linked to diabetes compared to any racial category.

When it comes to gender-related health disparities, most statistical information shows that females have better health profiles than males. This is true throughout the world. Female life expectancy has been consistently higher than male life expectancy since records began. While the gap in life expectancy is beginning to narrow in the United States, most countries still have higher life expectancies for female citizens than male citizens, as shown in Figure 12.8.

MCAT Expertise

The MCAT will not expect you to be able to rattle off the relative rates of these illnesses across racial groups, but a sensitivity to these differences between groups may be important in sociology and public health–related passages.

Key Concept

Low-income groups, especially racial and ethnic minorities, have an overall worse health profile in terms of morbidity and mortality rates.

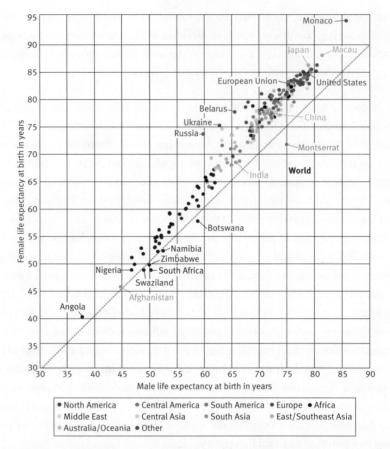

Figure 12.8. Male and Female Life Expectancies by Region and Country
Note that female life expectancies are almost universally higher than male life expectancies. Based on data from the CIA World Factbook.

Mortality rates from heart disease, cancer, chronic lower respiratory diseases, diabetes, and accidents are higher for males than females. Men are also three times more likely than women to die from accidents, suicide, and homicide. Males are far less likely to seek medical attention than females. Men, especially those raised to have hypermasculine behaviors, may try to "tough it out" rather than go to a doctor. When men do seek health care, they are less likely to comply with medical instructions or adhere to medical advice.

While women show better mortality rates, this is not the case when it comes to morbidity rates for certain acute and chronic diseases. More women than men suffer from infectious and parasitic diseases, digestive problems, respiratory conditions, high blood pressure (hypertension), arthritis, diabetes, and inflammatory bowel diseases (colitis). Women tend to suffer more from illnesses and disabilities than men, but their conditions are less often life threatening.

The reasons that men tend to have lower life expectancy rates are both sociological and biological. Sociologically, men are considered to be bigger risk-takers, and therefore more likely to expose themselves to accidents and unintentional injuries. This is especially true of young men. Men are also more likely to be employed in dangerous jobs, such as the police force, steel industry, and coal mining. Men also have higher rates of alcohol use, speeding, and participation in potentially violent sports. Biologically speaking, men are at a disadvantage from infancy onward. Throughout life, men are more likely to come down with diseases that are life threatening.

INEQUITIES IN HEALTHCARE

While the United States has one of the most advanced healthcare systems in the world, quality healthcare and services are not always extended to all. Like many institutions, quality healthcare favors those in higher social classes. Many people are frustrated by the way healthcare is delivered in the United States, especially with regard to health insurance. Further, the healthcare system of the United States is one of the few among industrialized nations that is not organized and planned by a central (governmental) system. Since the passing of the Affordable Care Act (ACA) in 2010, the United States has attempted to address this problem by increasing the coverage rate and affordability of insurance for all Americans, and also by reducing the overall costs of healthcare. However, disadvantaged groups, especially poor Americans, are still affected by disparities in healthcare both in terms of access and quality. Even those individuals who have Medicare or Medicaid may lack access, as many physicians will not accept such public insurance programs. **Medicare** covers patients over the age of 65, those with end-stage renal disease, and those with amyotrophic lateral sclerosis (ALS). **Medicaid** covers patients who are in significant financial need. Additionally, some doctors will not open up practices in low-income neighborhoods, making access even harder for low-SES populations. Consequently, individuals in the lower class are less likely to seek medical assistance at overcrowded clinics until they are seriously ill; by then, intervention may be too late.

Some of the primary reasons low-income groups have higher mortality rates include poor access to quality medical care, poor nutrition, and feeling less in control of life circumstances. The poor are more likely to smoke and be overweight or obese; they are less likely to engage in physical activity. In addition to socioeconomic status, race and ethnicity can create barriers to care. Sometimes, culture and non-native language are viewed as contributors to pathology because they can act as obstacles to diagnosis and treatment. Further, despite efforts to systemically address unequal treatment of minority populations by physicians, there are still inequalities and disparities in treatment relative to race and ethnicity over a wide range of medical specialties. In other words, minorities and low-income groups tend to face greater barriers to care, and poorer quality of care when they receive it. To be specific, it has been demonstrated that African Americans, Asian Americans, Native Americans, and Hispanics receive worse care than white Americans.

Quality of preventative care, acute treatment, and chronic disease management also differ regionally. States in New England and the Mid-Atlantic are shown to be in the top quartile of healthcare quality while states in the South are in the bottom quartile.

Key Concept

In comparison to females, males tend to have worse mortality rates. However, women have higher morbidity rates. Differences in male and female health profiles are both biologically and sociologically determined, the latter being the result of risk-taking behavior, hypermasculinity, and dangerous employment.

Key Concept

Medicare covers patients over 65, those with end-stage renal disease, and those with amyotrophic lateral sclerosis (ALS). Medicaid covers patients in significant financial need.

Outside of race and ethnicity, other identifiable characteristics may have a large impact on how patients are treated by their providers. One of the most common biases is discrimination against overweight and obese patients. This can apply to any overweight individual, regardless of socioeconomic status, gender, age, and racial and ethnic background, although there is a higher prevalence of obesity in low-income groups. Doctors are less likely to recommend effective weight loss programs to obese patients, sometimes based on the flawed assumption that obese patients lack the willpower to effectively lose weight. This, in turn, damages the trust necessary to form a strong doctor–patient relationship. As a result, overweight and obese patients are more likely than normal-weight patients to switch doctors repeatedly. When one does not have a consistent primary care doctor, continuity of care is nearly nonexistent. Additionally, overweight or obese patients are less likely to have quality preventative care and screenings, including screenings for breast and colon cancer.

In terms of gender, women tend to be favored by the healthcare system. As a whole, women tend to fare better when it comes to accessing healthcare, largely because women are more likely to be insured. Women tend to utilize healthcare services more than men, with more examinations, blood pressure checks, lab tests, drug prescriptions, and physician visits per year. Women also receive more services per visit than men do. Healthcare use is likely more common among women on account of higher morbidity rates among women for many illnesses, thereby facilitating the need to seek medical attention. On the other hand, women are more likely to be delayed or unable to obtain necessary medical care, dental care, and prescription medicines. Also, for LGBT men and women, discrimination and decreased access to healthcare are quite common, largely due to remaining prejudices and homophobia.

MCAT Concept Check 12.2:

Before you move on, assess your understanding of the material with these questions.

1. What is Waitzkin's second sickness?

_____

2. What is the relationship between class, ethnicity, and health?

_____

3. Why are women more likely to have better health profiles than men?

_____

4. What is the relationship between class and healthcare disparities?

_____

Conclusion

So what have learned? We do not live in a perfect world where valuable materials and resources are unlimited and evenly distributed. In the United States and on a worldwide level, social stratification is an unfortunate reality. In a class-based economic system, such as ours, status and power are inextricably linked, which can either facilitate or hinder access to social capital and its associated rewards. This is especially the case for certain disadvantaged groups based on categories of class, race, gender, and age. While not perfect, our class system does tend to allow for upward social mobility either in one's lifetime or across generations. At the heart of America's socioeconomic values is the principle of meritocracy, which means that through hard work, credentials, and dedication, one can move up in society. However, principles alone do not lead to success and many people remain impoverished. This produces greater social inequities and social exclusion, which makes it increasingly difficult for low-income groups to improve their socioeconomic condition. Some hold that social inequalities such as poverty remain because they are passed down from one generation to another. While there is some truth to the social reproduction of poverty, one's situational context also plays a role through spatial inequality. Where one lives in this world has an impact on one's position in life, especially in terms of accessing key resources and prosperous opportunities. Spatial inequality remains at the residential, environmental, and global level.

But how do such social inequalities influence health and healthcare disparities? Well, as is the case with many facets of life, wealth matters. Those with greater income typically have easier access to and better quality of healthcare. This is especially the case in the U.S. healthcare system because of uneven levels of coverage and high healthcare costs. Socioeconomic status or class greatly impacts one's ability to navigate the system and procure healthcare in the United States. Low-income racial and ethnic minorities tend to be worse off, having both poorer health and poorer access to healthcare. Women, despite being more prone to chronic and degenerative diseases, tend to fare better than men when it comes to overall health and accessing and utilizing healthcare resources.

While the U.S. healthcare system is undergoing a significant reorientation and taking on a more preventative approach, it is more important now than ever to place a greater emphasis on sociological issues to understand the relationship between social stratification and health and healthcare disparities. Illness and disease are a product of social as well as psychological and physiological issues. This is the last chapter in *MCAT Behavioral Sciences Review*; you have therefore covered all of the psychology and sociology content required for the MCAT. This is a fitting chapter to finish this discussion, and we leave you with a charge: as you prepare for the MCAT, medical school, and life as the physician you deserve to be, think about the changes that are needed in the U.S. healthcare system. Serve your local, national, and international community and improve the health status of those around you, while contributing to a future where everyone can access quality healthcare.

CONCEPT SUMMARY

Social Class

- Social stratification is based on **socioeconomic status** (**SES**). Socioeconomic status depends on ascribed status and achieved status.

  o **Ascribed status** is involuntary and derives from clearly identifiable characteristics, such as age, gender, and skin color.

  o **Achieved status** is acquired through direct, individual efforts.

- A **social class** is a category of people with shared socioeconomic characteristics. The three main social classes are upper, middle, and lower class. These groups also have similar lifestyles, job opportunities, attitudes, and behaviors.

- **Prestige** is the respect and importance tied to specific occupations or associations.

- **Power** is the capacity to influence people through real or perceived rewards and punishments. It often depends on the unequal distribution of valued resources. Power differentials create social inequality.

- *Anomie* is a state of normlessness. Anomic conditions erode social solidarity by means of excessive individualism, social inequality, and isolation.

- **Social capital** is the investment people make in their society in return for economic or collective rewards. Social networks, either situational or positional, are one of the most powerful forms of social capital and can be achieved through establishing strong and weak social ties.

- **Meritocracy** refers to a society in which advancement up the social ladder is based on intellectual talent and achievement.

- **Social mobility** allows one to acquire higher-level employment opportunities by achieving required credentials and experience. Social mobility can either occur in a positive upward direction or a negative downward direction depending on whether one is promoted or demoted in status.

- **Poverty** is a socioeconomic condition. In the United States, the poverty line is determined by the government's calculation of the minimum income requirements for families to acquire the minimum necessities of life.

- **Social reproduction** refers to the passing on of social inequality, especially poverty, from one generation to the next.

- Poverty can either be absolute or relative.

  o **Absolute poverty** is when people do not have enough resources to acquire basic life necessities, such as shelter, food, clothing, and water.

  o **Relative poverty** is when one is poor in comparison to a larger population.

- **Social exclusion** is a sense of powerlessness when individuals feel alienated from society.

- **Spatial inequality** is a form of social stratification across territories and their populations, and can occur along residential, environmental, and global lines.

  o Urban areas tend to have more diverse economic opportunities and more ability for social mobility than rural areas. Urban areas also tend to have more low-income racial and ethnic minority neighborhoods than rural areas.

  o Formation of higher-income suburbs is a common occurrence, and is due in part to the limited mobility of lower-income groups in urban centers.

  o **Environmental injustice** refers to an uneven distribution of environmental hazards in communities. Lower-income neighborhoods may lack the social and political power to prevent the placement of environmental hazards in their neighborhoods.

- **Globalization** has led to further inequalities in space, food and water, energy, housing, and education as the production of goods shifts to cheaper and cheaper labor markets. This has led to significant economic hardship in industrializing nations.

Epidemiology and Disparities

- **Incidence** is calculated as the number of new cases of a disease per population at risk in a given period of time: for example, new cases per 1000 at-risk people per year.

- **Prevalence** is calculated as the number of cases of a disease per population in a given period of time: for example, cases per 1000 people per year.

- **Morbidity** is the burden or degree of illness associated with a given disease.

- **Mortality** refers to deaths caused by a given disease.

- Health is dependent on geographic, social, and economic factors.

  o The **second sickness** refers to an exacerbation of health outcomes caused by social injustice.

  o Poverty is associated with worse health outcomes, including decreased life expectancy, higher rates of life-shortening diseases, higher rates of suicide and homicide, and higher infant mortality rates.

  o Certain racial and ethnic minorities have worse health profiles than others. African Americans are, on average, the worst off; white Americans, Native Americans, and Hispanic Americans are next; and Asian Americans and Pacific Islanders have the best health profiles.

  o Females have better health profiles than males, including higher life expectancy, lower rates of life-threatening illnesses, and higher rates of accessing and utilizing health resources. However, females have higher rates of chronic diseases and higher morbidity rates.

- Efforts to improve healthcare for underserved populations include the **Affordable Care Act** (**ACA**) and the **Medicare** and **Medicaid** programs.

- Healthcare access and quality differ across the population.
  - Low-income groups and racial and ethnic minorities (specifically, African Americans, Asian Americans, Native Americans, and Hispanic Americans) receive worse care than white Americans.
  - Biases against overweight or obese patients are associated with lower-quality treatment, including less preventative care and fewer screenings.
  - Women tend to have better access to healthcare and utilize more healthcare resources than men.
  - LGBT men and women may have barriers to care due to prejudices, discrimination, and homophobia.

ANSWERS TO CONCEPT CHECKS

12.1

1. SES is determined by two factors: it can be ascribed according to physical or external characteristics such as age, gender, or skin color, or acquired through direct efforts such as hard work or merit.

2. The less social capital a person has (reduced network equality and equality of opportunity), the more social inequality. This, in turn, decreases social cohesion.

3. Social inequality is highest among racial and ethnic minorities (especially African Americans and Hispanics), female-headed families, and the elderly. It is also most prevalent among those living in poverty.

4. Social mobility can be dependent on intellectual talent and achievement (meritocratic competition) but can also be obstructed by concentrated power as well as discrimination based on ethnicity, gender, age, or other identifiable characteristics.

5. Environmental hazards tend to be located in low-income areas with a higher population of racial and ethnic minorities. Poor living conditions can result in increased illness and disease among these groups of people.

12.2

1. The second sickness refers to the fact that health outcomes are exacerbated by social inequalities and social injustice. As a result, higher-income groups have longer life expectancies than lower-income groups.

2. Low-income racial and ethnic minorities have higher morbidity rates and overall worse health compared to the middle and upper classes. The lower class also has higher infant mortality rates, homicide rates, and suicide rates in comparison to wealthier classes.

3. Women typically have longer life expectancies and an overall better health profile in comparison to men. This can be attributed to both biological and sociological causes: women are less likely to have life-threatening conditions, although they do have higher morbidity rates. Women are also more likely to seek care and to utilize healthcare services than men.

4. Low-income groups have worse access to healthcare services and worse healthcare quality. Poor Americans are less likely to be insured and consequently are less likely to seek medical attention until conditions have become extremely serious, thereby limiting available interventions. As a result, morbidity and mortality rates are highest among low-income groups.

SHARED CONCEPTS

Discrete Practice Questions

Consult your online resources for Full-Length Exams and Passage-Based Questions (for certain chapters).

1. Which of the following best describes the component of socioeconomic status attributable to direct individual efforts?

    A. Ascribed status
    B. Meritocratic competition
    C. Anomic condition
    D. Achieved status

2. Which of the following displays a correct association?

    A. High social networking and low social capital
    B. High social mobility and low social capital
    C. Low social class and low social capital
    D. Low social networking and high social capital

3. Which of the following concepts are LEAST likely to coincide?

    A. Hazardous waste facilities and low-income neighborhoods
    B. Tuberculosis and poor living conditions
    C. Environmental pollution and high minority population
    D. Globalization and global equality

4. Which of the following trends is most likely FALSE?

    A. Mortality rates are increased in low-income racial and ethnic minorities.
    B. Life expectancy is decreased in high-income groups.
    C. Birth weights are decreased in children of low-income women.
    D. Rates of lung cancer are increased in low-income groups.

Questions 5–6 refer to the scenario described below.

A small town has 1000 residents, including 500 men and 500 women. In this town, 20 of the men have prostate cancer. During a calendar year, 10 more men are diagnosed with prostate cancer. Assume none of the men are cured or die during the year.

5. What is the prevalence of prostate cancer in this population at the end of the year?

    A. $10 \div 480$
    B. $10 \div 1000$
    C. $20 \div 500$
    D. $30 \div 1000$

6. What is the incidence of prostate cancer in this population during the year?

    A. $10 \div 480$
    B. $10 \div 1000$
    C. $20 \div 500$
    D. $30 \div 1000$

7. A low-income single mother works a part-time job and lives in a small apartment in the city. When her children grow up, they take similar jobs and live in similar housing. This is an example of:

    A. upward social mobility.
    B. downward social mobility.
    C. social exclusion.
    D. social reproduction.

8. Which of the following is true with regard to relative poverty?

   A. Individuals in relative poverty have incomes below the poverty line.

   B. Individuals in relative poverty exhibit downward social mobility.

   C. Individuals in relative poverty may be in the upper class.

   D. Individuals in relative poverty exhibit upward social mobility.

9. In comparison to urban centers, suburbs tend to have:

   A. larger racial and ethnic minority populations.

   B. higher rates of poverty.

   C. larger upper- and middle-class populations.

   D. higher rates of crime and homicide.

10. Which of the following terms refers to the burden or degree of disease associated with a given illness?

    A. Morbidity

    B. Mortality

    C. Second sickness

    D. Chronicity

11. Compared to white Americans, which of the following racial or ethnic groups tends to have a better overall health profile?

    A. African Americans

    B. Asian Americans

    C. Hispanic Americans

    D. Native Americans

12. Which of the following best describes the populations targeted by Medicare and Medicaid, respectively?

    A. Medicare: mostly patients without employer-guaranteed healthcare; Medicaid: mostly patients who have recently immigrated

    B. Medicare: mostly patients who have recently immigrated; Medicaid: mostly patients without employer-guaranteed healthcare

    C. Medicare: mostly patients in older age groups; Medicaid: mostly patients with low socioeconomic status

    D. Medicare: mostly patients with low socioeconomic status; Medicaid: mostly patients in older age groups

13. Morbidity is increased in low-income groups because of all of the following EXCEPT:

    A. higher rates of obesity.

    B. less access to healthcare.

    C. higher rates of homicide.

    D. lower rates of physical activity.

14. Hypertension (high blood pressure) can be diagnosed by having two or more blood pressure readings higher than 140/90 on two different occasions, separated by a week. Suppose that the criteria were changed to include anyone with a reading higher than 130/80 on at least one occasion. How would this change the prevalence of diagnosed hypertension in the population?

    A. The prevalence would increase.

    B. The prevalence would decrease.

    C. The prevalence would remain the same.

    D. There is not enough information to determine the change in prevalence.

15. Which of the following trends regarding healthcare disparities has NOT been documented?

    A. Females are more likely to be insured than males.

    B. Primary care use is more likely among males than females.

    C. Low-income individuals have more difficulty accessing care than high-income individuals.

    D. LGBT individuals have more barriers to health-care than heterosexuals.

Explanations to
Discrete Practice Questions

1. D

Social stratification based on direct efforts, such as merit, is a form of achieved socioeconomic status. Ascribed socioeconomic status, **choice (A)**, is based on identifiable external characteristics. Achieved status may be due to meritocratic competition, **choice (B)**, but other individual efforts can also be associated with achieved status. Anomic conditions, **choice (C)**, are those that cause a breakdown between the individual and society and erode social solidarity.

2. C

Low social class may lead to low social capital. Members of the lower class often have smaller numbers of weak ties in social networks, and therefore have less opportunity to invest in society and reap its benefits.

3. D

Globalization does not typically lead to global equality; rather, globalization tends to create further global inequalities. In regard to environmental justice, higher numbers of hazardous waste facilities tend to be found in low-income neighborhoods, **choice (A)**. Poor living conditions tend to be associated with greater health problems, including tuberculosis, **choice (B)**. Finally, environmental pollution is more prevalent in areas with minority populations, especially low-income minority populations, **choice (C)**.

4. B

High-income groups tend to have increased life expectancy rates, not decreased. Low-income racial and ethnic minorities have higher mortality rates than high-income groups, **choice (A)**. Low-income women tend to have children with lower birth weights, **choice (C)**. Finally, rates of various diseases, including lung cancer, are increased among low-income groups, **choice (D)**.

5. D

Prevalence is defined as the total number of cases divided by the total population during a period of time. Here, the period of time is defined as one point: the end of the year. At the end of the year, there are 30 total cases in a population of 1000 individuals, meaning the prevalence is $30 \div 1000$.

6. A

Incidence is defined as the total number of new cases divided by the at-risk population during a period of time. Here, the period of time is one year. There were 10 new cases in this year, and the at-risk population will be only the males who do not already have prostate cancer; the 20 men already diagnosed and the 500 women should not be included in the at-risk population. Therefore, the incidence in this population is $10 \div 480$.

7. D

In this scenario, the children remain in the same socioeconomic class as their mother, indicating a lack of social mobility, **choices (A)** and **(B)**. Rather, this is an example of social reproduction, in which social inequality, especially poverty, is passed from one generation to the next.

8. C

Relative poverty is a comparative term: it describes being poorer than those in the surrounding population. Members of the upper class can live in relative poverty compared to others in their neighborhood if they are not as well-off as their neighbors. Relative poverty is not directly associated with upward or downward social mobility, eliminating **choices (B)** and **(D)**; individuals living in relative poverty could exhibit mobility in either direction or no social mobility at all.

9. C

Suburbs tend to have larger upper- and middle-class populations than urban centers; urban centers tend to have larger low-socioeconomic status populations than suburbs. This is due, in part, to the increased mobility seen in upper- and middle-class populations, which permits their migration into the suburbs.

10. A

Morbidity refers to the burden of illness, or the severity or degree of illness. Mortality, **choice (B)**, refers to deaths caused by a given illness. Second sickness, **choice (C)**, is a term used to describe the exacerbation of health outcomes due to social injustice. Chronicity, **choice (D)**, refers to the duration of a disease, not its severity or significance for the patient.

11. B

In comparison to white Americans, Asian Americans tend to have better overall health profiles. African Americans, **choice (A)**, tend to have worse overall health profiles. Hispanic Americans and Native Americans, **choices (C)** and **(D)**, both have mixed health profiles in comparison to white Americans: they are better off in some categories and worse off in others. However, Hispanic and Native Americans do not have better overall health profiles than white Americans.

12. C

Medicare covers patients over the age of 65 (older age groups), those with end-stage renal disease, and those with amyotrophic lateral sclerosis (ALS). Medicaid covers patients below a certain socioeconomic level.

13. C

Morbidity refers to the burden or severity of disease. All of the factors listed are true with regard to low-socioeconomic status populations; however, high homicide rates cause increases in mortality, not morbidity.

14. A

If the threshold for hypertension (high blood pressure) were lowered, more individuals would be fit the criteria for the disease. If the number of individuals with the disease increases and the population stays the same overall, there will be an increased prevalence of the disease.

15. B

In comparison to females, males visit primary care doctors less frequently. All of the other trends listed here have been documented.

Glossary

Absolute poverty–Poverty wherein people do not have enough resources to acquire basic life necessities such as shelter, food, clothing, and water.

Absolute threshold–The minimum stimulus energy needed to activate a sensory system.

Accommodation–Process by which existing schemata are modified to encompass new information.

Acetylcholine–A neurotransmitter associated with voluntary muscle control.

Achieved status–A status gained as a result of direct, individual action.

Acquisition–In classical conditioning, the process of taking advantage of reflexive responses to turn a neutral stimulus into a conditioned stimulus.

Actor-observer bias–The tendency to make situational attributions about the self, but dispositional attributions about others, regarding similar behaviors.

Adaptation–In perception, a decrease in stimulus perception after a long duration of exposure; in learning, the process by which new information is processed; consists of assimilation and accommodation.

Adaptive value–The extent to which a trait benefits a species by influencing the evolutionary fitness of the species.

Affect–The experience and display of emotion.

Afferent neuron–Sensory neurons which transmit information to the brain from the body in response to sensory input.

Ageism–Prejudice or discrimination on the basis of a person's age.

Aggression–A behavior with the intention to cause harm or increase relative social dominance; can be physical or verbal.

Agnosia–The loss of the ability to recognize objects, people, or sounds, though typically just one of the three.

Alcohol myopia–The inability to think about consequences and possible outcomes of one's actions due to alcohol intoxication.

Alertness–State of consciousness in which one is aware, able to think, and able to respond to the environment; nearly synonymous with arousal.

Algorithm–A formula or procedure for solving a certain type of problem.

Aligning actions–An impression management strategy in which one makes questionable behavior acceptable through excuses.

Alter-casting–An impression management strategy in which one imposes an identity onto another person.

Altruism–A form of helping behavior in which the person's intent is to benefit someone else at a cost to him- or herself.

Alzheimer's disease–Degenerative brain disorder that is characterized by dementia and memory loss. Neurofibrillary tangles and β-amyloid plaques are phenomena found in the brains of Alzheimer's patients.

Amphetamine–A central nervous system stimulant that increases activity of both dopamine and norepinephrine in the brain.

Amygdala–A portion of the limbic system that is important for memory and emotion, especially fear.

Anomie–A state of normlessness; anomic conditions erode social solidarity by means of excessive individualism, social inequality, and isolation.

Anterograde amnesia–Form of memory loss in which new long-term memories cannot be established.

Anxiety disorders–Disorders that involve worry, unease, fear, and apprehension about future uncertainties based on real or imagined events that can impair physical and psychological health.

Aphasia–Deficit of language production or comprehension.

Appraisal model–A similar theory to the basic model, accepting that there are biologically predetermined expressions once an emotion is experienced; accepts that there is a cognitive antecedent to emotional expression.

Archetype–In Jungian psychoanalysis, a thought or image that has an emotional element and is a part of the collective unconsciousness.

Arcuate fasciculus–A bundle of axons that connects Wernicke's area (language comprehension) with Broca's area (motor function of speech).

Arousal–A psychological and physiological state of being awake or reactive to stimuli; nearly synonymous with alertness.

Arousal theory–A theory of motivation that states there is a particular level of arousal required in order to perform actions optimally; summarized by the Yerkes–Dodson law.

Ascribed status–A status that one is given at birth, such as race, ethnicity, or sex.

Assimilation–In psychology, the process by which new information is interpreted in terms of existing

schemata; in sociology, the process by which the behavior and culture of a group or an individual begins to merge with that of another group.

Associative learning–The process by which a connection is made between two stimuli or a stimulus and a response; examples include classical conditioning and operant conditioning.

Attachment–An emotional bond to another person, particularly a parent or caregiver. The four main attachment styles are: secure, avoidant, ambivalent, and disorganized.

Attitude–A tendency toward expression of positive or negative feelings or evaluations of a person, place, thing, or situation.

Attribute substitution–A phenomenon observed when individuals must make judgments that are complex but instead substitute a simpler solution or perception.

Attribution theory–A theory that focuses on the tendency for individuals to infer the causes of other people's behavior.

Auditory cortex–Region of the temporal lobe devoted to sound processing.

Auditory pathway–After entering the brain, sound is processed by several regions, including the MGN, auditory cortex, superior olive, and inferior colliculus.

Authentic self–Who someone actually is, including both positive and negative attributes.

Automatic processing–The brain process most closely resembling autopilot, enabling performance of multiple activities at the same time.

Autonomic nervous system–The involuntary branch of the peripheral nervous system that controls involuntary functions such as heart rate, bronchial dilation, temperature, and digestion.

Autonomy–The ethical tenet that the physician has the responsibility to respect patients' choices about their own healthcare.

Availability heuristic–A shortcut in decision-making that relies on the information that is most readily available, rather than the total body of information on a subject.

Avoidance learning–A form of negative reinforcement in which one avoids the unpleasantness of something that has yet to happen.

Babbling–Precursor to language known to spontaneously occur in children.

Back stage–In the dramaturgical approach, the setting where players are free from their role requirements and not in front of the audience; back stage behaviors may not be deemed appropriate or acceptable and are thus kept invisible from the audience.

Barbiturate–A drug that acts as a central nervous system depressant; often used for anxiety, insomnia, and as an antiseizure medication.

Basal ganglia–A portion of the forebrain that coordinates muscle movement and routes information from the cortex to the brain and spinal cord.

Base-rate fallacy–Using prototypical or stereotypical factors while ignoring actual numerical information when making a decision.

Basic model–First established by Charles Darwin, a theory that states that emotional expression involves a number of systems: facial expression as well as behavioral and physical responses; claims that emotions are universal and should be similar across cultures.

Behaviorism–B. F. Skinner's theory that all behaviors are conditioned. Behaviorism can be applied across many bodies of psychological thought, including theories of development, of identity, and of personality.

Belief–An acceptance that a statement is true or that something exists.

Belief perseverance–The inability to reject a particular belief despite clear evidence to the contrary.

Beneficence–The ethical tenet that the physician has a responsibility to act in the patient's best interest.

Benzodiazepine–A central nervous system depressant that is often used to reduce anxiety or promote sleep.

Biomedical approach–An approach to psychological disorders that considers only pathophysiological causes and offers pharmaceutical and medical solutions for symptom alleviation.

Biopsychosocial approach–An approach to psychological disorders that considers conditions and treatments to be dependent on biological, psychological, and social causes. Treatment under this approach includes both direct and indirect therapy.

Bipolar disorders–Class of mood disorders characterized by both depression and mania.

Birth rate–The number of births per population in a period of time; usually the number of births per 1000 people per year.

Bisexual–A sexual orientation wherein individuals are attracted to members of both sexes.

Bottom-up processing–Object recognition by parallel processing and feature detection in response to sensory stimuli.

Brainstem–The most primitive portion of the brain, which includes the midbrain and hindbrain; controls the autonomic nervous system and communication between the spinal cord, cranial nerves, and brain.

Broca's aphasia–Loss of the motor function of speech, resulting in intact understanding with an inability to correctly produce spoken language.

Broca's area–A brain region located in the inferior frontal gyrus of the frontal lobe (usually in the left hemisphere); largely responsible for the motor function of speech.

Bureaucracy–A formal organization with the goal of performing complex tasks as efficiently as possible by dividing work among a number of bureaus.

Bystander effect–The observation that, when in a group, individuals are less likely to respond to a person in need.

Cannon–Bard theory–A theory of emotion that states that a stimulus is first received and is then simultaneously processed physiologically and cognitively, allowing for the conscious emotion to be experienced.

Cataplexy–Loss of muscle control with intrusion of REM sleep during waking hours, usually caused by an emotional trigger.

Catatonia–Disorganized motor behavior characterized by various unusual physical movements or stillness.

Central nervous system (CNS)–The portion of the nervous system composed of the brain and spinal cord.

Cerebellum–A portion of the hindbrain that maintains posture and balance and coordinates body movements.

Cerebral cortex–The outermost layer of the cerebrum, responsible for complex perceptual, behavioral, and cognitive processes.

Cerebrospinal fluid (CSF)–An aqueous solution in which the brain and spinal cord rest; produced by cells lining the ventricles of the brain.

Cerebrum–A portion of the brain that contains the cerebral cortex, limbic system, and basal ganglia.

Characteristic institution–The social structure or institution about which societies are organized.

Chemoreceptors–Sensory neurons that respond to chemical stimuli.

Choice shift–This term is analogous to group polarization, but describes the behavior change of the group as a whole rather than the individual.

Circadian rhythm–The alignment of physiological processes with the 24-hour day, including sleep–wake cycles and some elements of the endocrine system.

Circular reaction–A repetitive action that achieves a desired response; seen during Piaget's sensorimotor stage.

Classical conditioning–A form of associative learning in which a neutral stimulus becomes associated with an unconditioned stimulus such that the neutral stimulus alone produces the same response as the unconditioned stimulus; the neutral stimulus thus becomes a conditioned stimulus.

Class consciousness–In Marxist theory, the organization of the working class around shared goals and recognition of a need for collective political action.

Cocaine–Drug that decreases reuptake of dopamine, norepinephrine, and serotonin, with effects similar to amphetamines.

Cognition–The process of acquiring knowledge and understanding through thought, experiences, and the senses: how we think and respond to the world.

Cognitive appraisal–The subjective evaluation of a situation that induces stress, consisting of both an initial primary appraisal, and a potential secondary appraisal if a threat is revealed during primary appraisal.

Cognitive development–The development of one's ability to think and solve problems across the lifespan.

Cognitive dissonance–The simultaneous presence of two opposing thoughts or opinions.

Cognitive reassociation model–A model of aggression which states that we are more likely to respond aggressively when experiencing negative emotions.

Collective unconscious–In Jungian psychoanalysis, the part of the unconscious mind that is shared among all humans and is a result of our common ancestry.

Colliculi–Two structures in the midbrain involved in sensorimotor reflexes; the superior colliculus receives visual sensory input, and the inferior colliculus receives auditory sensory input.

Compliance–A change of behavior of an individual at the request of another.

Concordance rates–In twin studies, the presence of a trait in both twins.

Conditioned response–In classical conditioning paradigms, the reflexive response caused by a conditioned stimulus.

Conditioned stimulus–In classical conditioning paradigms, this is an initially neutral stimulus that is paired with an unconditioned stimulus to train a behavioral response, rendering the previously neutral stimulus a conditioned stimulus.

Conduction aphasia–A speech disorder characterized by the inability to repeat words with intact spontaneous speech production and comprehension; usually due to injury to the arcuate fasciculus.

Confirmation bias–A cognitive bias in which one focuses on information that supports a given solution, belief, or hypothesis and ignores evidence against it.

Conflict theory–A theoretical framework that emphasizes the role of power differentials in producing social order.

Conformity–The changing of beliefs or behaviors in order to fit into a group or society.

Consciousness–Awareness of oneself; can be used to describe varying levels of awareness that occur with wakefulness, sleep, dreaming, and drug-induced states.

Conservation–Concept seen in quantitative analysis performed by a child; develops when a child is able to identify the difference between quantity by number and actual amount, especially when faced with identical quantities separated into varying pieces.

Constancy–In sensory perception, perceiving certain characteristics of object to remain the same despite differences in the environment.

Context effect–A retrieval cue by which memory is aided when a person is in the location where encoding took place.

Contralateral–On the opposite side of the body, relative to something else (usually a side of the brain).

Controlled (conscious) processing–Processing method used when a task requires complete attention.

Correspondent inference theory–A theory that states that people pay closer attention to intentional behavior than accidental behavior when making attributions, especially if the behavior is unexpected.

Cortical homunculus–A "map" which relates regions of the brain to the anatomical regions of the body.

Critical period–A time during development during which exposure to language is essential for eventual development of the effective use of language; occurs between two years of age and puberty.

Crystallized intelligence–Cognitive capacity to understand relationships or solve problems using information acquired during schooling and other experiences.

Cues–In understanding the behavior of others, indicators of the underlying cause of a behavior. This includes consistency cues, consensus cues, and difference cues.

Culture–The beliefs, behaviors, actions, and characteristics of a group or society of people.

Cultural capital–The benefits one receives from knowledge, abilities, and skills.

Cultural diffusion–The spread of norms, cultures, and beliefs throughout a culture.

Cultural relativism–The theory that social groups and cultures must be studied on their own terms to be understood.

Cultural sensitivity–Recognizing and respecting the differences between cultures.

Culture shock–Cultural differences that are seen as quite dramatic when travelling outside of one's own society.

Cultural syndrome–A shared set of beliefs, attitudes, norms, values, and behaviors organized around a central theme and found among people who speak the same language and share a geographic region.

Cultural transmission–The means by which a society socializes its members.

Deductive reasoning–A form of cognition that starts with general information and narrows down that information to create a conclusion.

Defense mechanism–In Freudian psychoanalysis, a technique used by the ego that denies, falsifies, or distorts reality in order to resolve anxiety caused by undesirable urges of the id and superego.

Deindividuation–The idea that people will lose a sense of self-awareness and can act dramatically differently based on the influence of a group.

Delirium–Rapid fluctuation in cognitive function that is reversible and has a nonpsychological cause.

Delusions–Fixed, false beliefs that are discordant with reality and not shared by one's culture, and are maintained in spite of strong evidence to the contrary.

Dementia–Intellectual decline starting with impaired memory and progressing to impaired judgment and confusion.

Demographics–The statistical arm of sociology, which attempts to characterize and explain populations by quantitative analysis.

Demographic shift–A change in the makeup of a population over time.

Demographic transition–The transition from high birth and mortality rates to lower birth and mortality rates, seen as a country develops from a preindustrial to an industrialized economic system.

Depressant–Any substance that reduces nervous system function.

Depressive disorder–Sadness meeting certain conditions of severity and duration such that a diagnosis of a mental health issue is warranted. Depressive disorders include, among others: major depression, dyshtymic disorder, and seasonal affective disorder.

Depressive episode–A period of at least two weeks in which there is a prominent and persistent depressed mood or lack of interest and at least four other depressive symptoms.

Deviance–The violation of norms, rules, or expectations within a society.

Diagnostic and Statistical Manual of Mental Disorders (DSM)–The guide by which most psychological disorders are characterized, described, and diagnosed; currently in its fifth edition (DSM-5, published May 2013).

Diencephalon–A portion of the prosencephalon that becomes the thalamus, hypothalamus, posterior pituitary gland, and pineal gland.

Differential association theory–Theory that deviance can be learned through interactions with others who engage in deviant behavior, provided those interactions outnumber interactions with those who conform to social norms in number and/or importance.

Disconfirmation principle–The idea that states that if evidence obtained during testing does not confirm a hypothesis, then the hypothesis is discarded or revised.

Discrimination–In classical conditioning, the process by which two similar but distinct conditioned stimuli produce different responses; in sociology, when individuals of a particular group are treated differently than others based on their group.

Discriminative stimulus–In behavioral conditioning, a stimulus whose presence indicates the opportunity for reward.

Dishabituation–A sudden increase in response to a stimulus, usually due to a change in the stimulus or addition of another stimulus; sometimes called resensitization.

Displacement–A defense mechanism by which undesired urges are transferred from one target to another, more acceptable one.

Display rules–Cultural expectations of how emotions can be expressed.

Dispositional (internal) attributions–Attributions that relate to the decisions or personality of the person whose behavior is being considered.

Dissociative disorders–Disorders that involve a perceived separation from identity or the environment.

Distal stimulus–Part of the outside world that serves as a source for stimuli that reach the sensory neurons.

Distant networks–Networks that are looser and composed of weaker ties.

Distress–The stress response to unpleasant stressors.

Divided attention–The ability to attend to multiple stimuli simultaneously and to perform multiple tasks at the same time.

Dizygotic twins–Fraternal twins who share approximately 50% of their genes, as with most siblings.

Dominant hemisphere–The side of the brain that provides analytic, language, logic, and math skills; in most individuals, the left hemisphere.

Dopamine–A neurotransmitter associated with smooth movements, steady posture, the reward pathway, and psychosis.

Dramaturgical approach–An impression management theory that represents the world as a stage and individuals as actors performing to an audience.

Dreaming–Phenomenon which mostly occurs during REM sleep. Theories proposed to explain this phenomenon include activation-synthesis theory, problem-solving dream theory, and cognitive process dream theory.

Drive reduction theory–A theory that explains motivation as being based on the goal of eliminating uncomfortable internal states.

Drives–Deficiencies that activate particular behaviors focused on a goal, which can be further subdivided into either primary (body-sustaining) or secondary (not biologically necessary) drives.

Dual-coding theory–A cognitive theory that states that both visual and verbal associations are used to encode and retrieve information.

Duplicity theory of vision–A theory which holds that the retina contains two types of specialized photoreceptors: rods specialized for light and dark perception and cones specialized for color perception.

Dyssomnia–A sleep disorder in which one has difficulty falling asleep, staying asleep, or avoiding sleep.

Ecstasy–Common name for MDMA (3,4-methylenedioxy-*N*-methylamphetamine); a central nervous system stimulant with effects similar to both amphetamines and hallucinogens.

Efferent neurons–Motor neurons that transmits information from the central nervous system to the periphery.

Ego–In Freudian psychoanalysis, the part of the unconscious mind that mediates the urges of the id and super-ego; operates under the reality principle.

Egocentrism–Self-centered view of the world in which one is not necessarily able to understand the experience of another person; seen in Piaget's preoperational stage.

Elaboration likelihood model– A theory in which attitudes are formed and changed through different routes of information processing based on the degree of deep thought given to persuasive information. There are two possible processing routes within this model; central route processing (deep thinking or elaborative) and peripheral route processing (non-elaborative).

Elaborative rehearsal–The association of information in short-term memory to information already stored in long-term memory; aids in long-term storage.

Electroencephalography (EEG)–A test used to study the electrical patterns of the brain under varying conditions; consists of multiple electrodes placed on the scalp. Characteristic EEG patterns include beta, alpha, theta, and delta waves, as well as patterns associated with REM sleep.

Emotion–A feeling and state of mind derived from circumstances, mood, or relationships.

Emotional support–Listening to, affirming, and empathizing with someone's feelings as part of social support.

Empathy–The ability to vicariously experience the emotions of another.

Encoding–The process of receiving information and preparing it for storage; can be automatic or effortful.

Empathy-altruism hypothesis– Theory that one individual helps another when they feel empathy for the other person.

Endorphins–Natural painkillers produced by the brain.

Epinephrine–A neurotransmitter associated with the fight-or-flight response.

Errors of growth–Misuse of grammar characterized by universal application of a rule, regardless of exceptions; seen in children during language development.

Escape learning–A form of negative reinforcement in which one reduces the unpleasantness of something that already exists.

Esteem support–Affirming qualities and skills of the person as part of social support.

Ethnic enclave–Locations with a high concentration of one specific ethnicity that can often slow assimilation

Ethnicity–A social construct that sorts people by cultural factors, including language, nationality, religion, and other factors.

Ethnocentrism–The practice of making judgments about other cultures based on the values and beliefs of one's own culture.

Eustress–The stress response to positive conditions.

Evolutionary stable strategy–A strategy that, once adopted, will use natural selective pressure to prevent alternate strategies from arising.

Exchange theory–In social structure, an extension of rational choice theory that focuses on interactions in groups. Exchange theory holds that behavior is engaged in based on expectancy of future rewards and/or punishments.

Expectancy-value theory–The amount of motivation needed to reach a goal is the result of both expectation of success in reaching the goal and degree to which reaching the goal is valued.

Explicit memory–Memory that requires conscious recall, divided into facts (semantic memory) and experiences (episodic memory); also known as declarative memory.

Extinction–In classical conditioning, the decrease in response resulting from repeated presentation of the conditioned stimulus without the presence of the unconditioned stimulus.

Extraversion–In trait theory, the degree to which an individual is able to tolerate social interaction and stimulation.

Extrapyramidal system–Part of the basal ganglia that modulates motor activity.

Extrinsic motivation–Motivation that is external, or outside the self, including rewards and punishments.

False consciousness–In Marxist theory, a misperception of one's actual position within society.

Family group–A group determined by birth, adoption, and marriage rather than self-selection (as in a peer group).

Fertility rate–The average number of children born to a woman during her lifetime in a population.

Fisherian selection–Also called runaway selection, this is a positive feedback mechanism in which a trait with no impact (or a negative impact) on survival becomes more and more exaggerated over time, especially if the trait is deemed sexually desirable.

Fixation–In Freudian psychoanalysis, the result of overindulgence or frustration during a psychosexual stage causing a neurotic pattern of personality based on that stage.

Flat affect–Behavior characterized by showing virtually no signs of emotion or affective expression.

Fluid intelligence–Ability to quickly identify relationships and connections, and then use those relationships and connections to make correct deductions.

Foraging–The act of searching for and exploiting food resources.

Forebrain–A portion of the brain that is associated with complex perceptual, cognitive, and behavioral processes such as emotion and memory.

Fornix–A long projection from the hippocampus that connects to other nuclei in the limbic system.

Front stage–In the dramaturgical approach, the setting where players are in front of an audience and perform roles that are in keeping with the image they hope to project about themselves.

Frontal lobe–A portion of the cerebral cortex that includes the prefrontal cortex and the motor cortex; it controls motor processing, executive function, and the integration of cognitive and behavioral processes.

Functional attitudes theory–Theory that attitudes serve four function: knowledge, ego expression, adaptation, and ego defense.

Functional fixedness–The inability to identify uses for an object beyond its usual purpose.

Functionalism–A theoretical framework that explains how parts of society fit together to create a cohesive whole, via both manifest (intended to help some part of the system) and latent (unintended positive) functions.

Fundamental attribution error–The general bias toward making dispositional attributions rather than situational attributions when analyzing another person's behavior.

Game theory–A model that explains social interaction and decision-making as a game, including strategies, incentives, and punishments.

γ-aminobutyric acid (GABA)–A neurotransmitter associated with stabilizing and quelling brain activity.

Ganglia–Collections of neuron cell bodies found outside the central nervous system.

Gemeinschaft und Gesellschaft–Theory that distinguishes between two major types of groups: communities (*Gemeinschaften*), which share beliefs, ancestry, or geography; and societies (*Gesellschaften*), which work together toward a common goal.

Gender–The set of behavioral, cultural, or psychological traits typically associated with a biological sex.

Gender inequality–The intentional or unintentional empowerment of one gender to the detriment of the other.

Gender segregation–The separation of individuals based on perceived gender.

General adaptation syndrome–Sequence of physiological responses developed by Selye in response to stress, initiating with alarm, followed by resistance, and finally exhaustion.

Generalization–In classical conditioning, the process by which two distinct but similar stimuli come to produce the same response.

Genotype–The genetic makeup of an individual.

Gentrification–The process of renewal of low income areas by upper-class populations, ultimately displacing the lower income residents.

Gestalt principles–Governed by the law of prägnanz, ways for the brain to infer missing parts of a picture when a picture is incomplete.

Ghetto–An area where a specific religious, racial, or ethnic minority is concentrated, usually due to social or economic inequality.

Globalization–The process of integrating the global economy with free trade and tapping of foreign labor markets.

Glutamate–An excitatory neurotransmitter in the central nervous system.

Glycine–An inhibitory neurotransmitter in the central nervous system.

Group–A social entity that involves at least two people, usually those sharing common characteristics.

Group conformity–Compliance with a group's goals, even when the group's goals may be in direct contrast to an individual's goals.

Group polarization–The tendency toward decisions that are more extreme than the individual inclinations of the group members.

Groupthink–The tendency for groups to make decisions based on ideas and solutions that arise within the group without considering outside ideas and ethics; based on pressure to conform and remain loyal to the group.

Gyrus–A ridge of the cerebral cortex.

Habituation–A decrease in response caused by repeated exposure to a stimulus.

Hallucinations–Perceptions that are not due to external stimuli but have a compelling sense of reality.

Hallucinogens–A group of drugs that cause distortions of reality in users, including lysergic acid diethylamide (LSD) and psilocybin-containing mushrooms.

Halo effect–A cognitive bias in which judgments of an individual's character can be affected by the overall impression of the individual.

Heterosexual–A sexual orientation wherein individuals are attracted to members of the opposite sex.

Heuristic–A rule of thumb or shortcut that is used to make decisions.

Hidden curriculum–In education, the transmission to students of social norms, attitudes, and beliefs.

Hierarchy of Salience–Theory of identity organization that posits that we let situations dictate which identity holds the most importance at any given moment.

Hindbrain–A portion of the brain that controls balance, motor coordination, breathing, digestion, and general arousal processes.

Hippocampus–A portion of the limbic system that is important for memory and learning.

Homosexual–A sexual orientation wherein individuals are attracted to members of the same sex.

Humanistic theory–The set of theories that hold that personality is the result of the conscious feelings we have for ourselves as we attempt to attain our needs and goals. The theories of Kelly, Maslow, Lewin, and others fall into this category.

Hypnagogic hallucinations–Hallucinations that occur when going to sleep; seen in narcolepsy.

Hypnopompic hallucinations–Hallucinations that occur when awakening from sleep; seen in narcolepsy.

Hypnosis–An altered state of consciousness in which a person appears to be awake but is, in fact, in a highly suggestible state in which another person or event may trigger action by the person.

Hypothalamus–A portion of the forebrain that controls homeostatic and endocrine functions by controlling the release of pituitary hormones.

Id–In Freudian psychoanalysis, the part of the unconscious resulting from basic, instinctual urges for sexuality and survival; operates under the pleasure principle and seeks instant gratification.

Ideal self–The person one would optimally like to be.

Identity–A piece of an individual's self-concept based on the groups to which that person belongs and his or her relationships to others.

Identity shift effect–When an individual's state of harmony is disrupted by a threat of social rejection, the individual will often conform to the norms of the group, followed by a corresponding identity shift to reduce cognitive dissonance.

Immediate networks–Networks that are dense with strong ties; generally overlap with distant networks.

Implicit memory–Memory that does not require conscious recall; consists of skills and conditioned behaviors.

Implicit personality theory–A theory that states that people tend to associate traits and behavior in others, and that people have the tendency to attribute their own beliefs, opinions, and ideas onto others.

Impression management–Behaviors that are intended to influence the perceptions of other people about a person, object, or event.

Incentive–A reward intended to motivate particular behaviors.

Incentive theory–Theory that behavior is motivated by the desire to pursue rewards and avoid punishments.

Incidence–The number of new cases of a disease per population at risk in a given period of time; usually, new cases per 1000 at-risk people per year.

Inclusive fitness–A measure of reproductive success; depends on the number of offspring an individual has, how well they support their offspring, and how well their offspring can support others.

Individual discrimination–One person discriminating against a particular person or group.

Inductive reasoning–A form of cognition that utilizes generalizations to develop a theory.

Inferior colliculus–Region of the midbrain that receives and integrates sensory input from the auditory system, and is involved in reflexive reactions to auditory input.

Informational support–Support given by providing information to help another person.

Information processing model–Model of human cognition containing four key components: information intake, information analysis, situational modification, and content/complexity of problem.

Ingratiation–An impression management strategy that uses flattery to increase social acceptance.

In-group–A social group to which a person experiences a sense of belonging or one in which he or she identifies as a member.

Innate behavior–A behavior that is genetically programmed or instinctive.

Insomnia–Sleep disorder characterized by either an inability to fall asleep or difficulty staying asleep.

Instinct–An innate behavioral response to stimuli.

Instinctive drift–The tendency of animals to resist learning when a conditioned behavior conflicts with the animal's instinctive behaviors.

Instinct theory–In motivation, the theory that people are driven to engage in behaviors based on evolutionarily preprogrammed instincts.

Institutional discrimination–Discrimination against a particular person or group by an entire institution.

Intelligence quotient–Numerical measurement of intelligence, usually accomplished by some form of standardized testing.

Interaction process analysis–A technique of observing and immediately classifying the activities of small groups.

Interference–A retrieval error caused by the learning of information; can be proactive (old information causes difficulty learning new information) or retroactive (new information interferes with older learning).

Internalization–Changing one's behavior to fit with a group while also privately agreeing with the ideas of the group.

Interneuron–A neuron found between sensory and motor neurons; involved in the reflex arc.

Interpersonal attraction–The force that makes people like each other.

Intersectionality–The interconnected nature of social categorizations as they apply to a given individual/group, especially when they lead to discrimination or oppression.

Intrinsic motivation–Motivation that is internal or that comes from within.

Intuition–Perceptions about a situation that may or may not be supported by available evidence, but are nonetheless perceived as information that may be used to make a decision.

Ipsilateral–On the same side of the body, relative to something else (usually a side of the brain).

Iron law of oligarchy–Democratic or bureaucratic systems naturally shift to being ruled by an elite group.

James–Lange theory–A theory of emotion that states that a stimulus results in physiological arousal, which then leads to a secondary response in which emotion is consciously experienced.

Justice–In medical ethics, the tenet that the physician has a responsibility to treat similar patients with similar care and to distribute healthcare resources fairly.

Just-noticeable difference (jnd)–The minimum difference in magnitude between two stimuli before one can perceive this difference; also called a difference threshold.

Just-world hypothesis–The cognitive bias that good things happen to good people, and bad things happen to bad people.

Labeling theory–Theory that labels given to people affect not only how others respond to that person, but also the person's self-image.

Language–Spoken or written symbols (verbal and nonverbal symbols), which are regulated according to certain rules of conduct or social norms and used for communication.

Language acquisition device (LAD)–An innate capacity for language acquisition that is triggered by exposure to language; part of the nativist (biological) perspective of language acquisition.

Latent learning–Learning that occurs without a reward but that is spontaneously demonstrated once a reward is introduced.

Learned helplessness–A state of hopelessness and resignation resulting from being unable to avoid repeated negative stimuli; often used as a model of depression.

Learning–In psychology, the way in which new behaviors are acquired.

Learning (behaviorist) theory–A theory that attitudes are developed through forms of learning (direct contact, direct interaction, direct instruction, and conditioning).

Libido–In Freudian psychoanalysis, the sex or life drive.

Life course approach to health–An analysis of health and probable outcomes that includes consideration of the patient's entire history.

Limbic system–A portion of the cerebrum that is associated with emotion and memory and includes the amygdala and hippocampus.

Linguistic relativity hypothesis–A hypothesis suggesting that one's perception of reality is largely determined by the content, form, and structure of language; also known as the Whorfian hypothesis.

Locus of control–The characterization of the source of influences on the events in one's life; can be internal or external.

Long-term memory–The relatively limitless form of memory reserved for information that is sufficiently rehearsed or of sufficient impact. There are both implicit and explicit forms of long-term memory.

Long-term potentiation–The strengthening of neural connections due to rehearsal or relearning; thought to be the neurophysiological basis of long-term memory.

Looking-glass self–Social psychological construct stating that the self is developed through interpersonal reactions, specifically through a person's understanding of the perception others have of them.

Magnocellular cells–In vision processing, cells that have high temporal resolution and detect motion.

Maintenance rehearsal–Repetition of a piece of information to either keep it within working memory or to store it.

Malthusian theory–Theory of demographic transition that focuses on how population growth can outpace food supply growth and lead to social degradation and disorder.

Managing appearances–An impression management strategy in which one uses props, appearance, emotional expression, or associations with others to create a positive image.

Manic episode–A period of at least one week with prominent and persistent elevated or expansive mood and at least two other manic symptoms.

Maslow's heirarchy of needs–
Abraham Maslow's theory that certain needs will yield a greater influence on motivation. Maslow's hierarchy consists of 5 'levels' of need.

Mass hysteria–A shared, intense concern about the threats to society.

Master status–A status with which a person is most identified.

Mate bias–A measure of how choosy members of a species are in choosing a mate, based upon both direct and indirect benefits of mate selection.

Mate choice–The intersexual selection of a mate based on attraction and traits.

Material culture–The physical items one associates with a given cultural group.

Material support–Providing economic or other physical resources to aid a person as part of social support.

Mating system–The way in which a group organizes its sexual behavior and sexual relationships.

Mcdonaldization–A shift in focus toward efficiency, predictability, calculability, and control in societies.

Meditation–A state of consciousness entered voluntarily, characterized by a decreased level of physiological arousal and a quieting of the mind.

Medulla oblongata–A portion of the brainstem that regulates vital functions, including breathing, heart rate, and blood pressure.

Melatonin–A serotonin derivative secreted by the pineal gland that is associated with sleepiness.

Meninges–A thick layer of connective tissue that covers and protects the brain; composed of the dura mater, arachnoid mater, and pia mater.

Mental set–A tendency to repeat solutions that have yielded positive results at some time in the past.

Mere exposure effect–An explanation of attraction, also called the familiarity effect, which holds that people prefer stimuli that they have been exposed to more frequently.

Meritocracy–A society in which advancement up the social ladder is based on intellectual talent and achievement.

Mesencephalon–The embryonic portion of the brain that becomes the midbrain.

Metencephalon–The embryonic portion of the brain that becomes the pons and cerebellum.

Mesolimbic reward pathway–Dopaminergic pathway in the brain including the nucleus accumbens, ventral tegmental area, and the medial forebrain bundle. This pathway is normally involved in motivation and emotional response, and is involved in drug addiction.

Midbrain–A portion of the brainstem that manages sensorimotor reflexes to visual and auditory stimuli and gives rise to some cranial nerves.

Migration–the movement of people from one population to another, including immigration and emigration.

Mirror neurons–Neurons located in the frontal and parietal lobes and which fire both when an individual performs an action and when an individual sees that action performed.

Misinformation effect–A phenomenon in which memories are altered by misleading information provided at the point of encoding or recall.

Mnemonic–A technique that aids in memory recall.

Monogamy–An exclusive mating relationship.

Monozygotic twins– Identical twins, sharing the same genetic material.

Mood disorder–A mental health diagnosis category containing disorders primarily characterized by disturbance in mood. This includes depressive disorders, substance-induced, and bipolar disorders.

Moral reasoning–Kohlberg's theory of personality evelopment, which is focused on the development of moral thinking through preconventional, conventional, and postconventional stages.

Morbidity–The burden or degree of illness associated with a given disease.

Morphology–The structure of words, including their building blocks (prefixes, suffixes, and so on).

Mortality rate–The number of deaths in a population per unit time.

Motivation–The process of psychological and physical requirements, goals, or desires causing behavior.

Motor neuron–A neuron that transmits motor information from the spinal cord and brain to the periphery.

Multiculturalism–The encouragement of multiple cultures in a society to enhance diversity.

Multiple intelligences–The idea that intelligence may exist in multiple areas, not just in the areas typically assessed by traditional intelligence quotient tests.

Myelencephalon–The embryonic portion of the brain that becomes the medulla oblongata.

Narcolepsy–A sleep disorder characterized by a lack of voluntary control over the onset of sleep; also involves cataplexy and hypnagogic and hypnopompic hallucinations.

Nativist theory (of language)–Theory credited to Noam Chomsky that posits the existence of an innate capacity for language, referred to as the language acquisition device.

Needs–Physiological and psychological requirements that motivate and influence behavior.

Negative symptoms–In mental illness, symptoms characterized by the absence of normal or desired behaviors.

Neologism–Coining a new word; seen in schizophrenia.

Network–A term used to describe the observable pattern of social relationships among individual units of analysis.

Network redundancy–Overlapping contact points within a social network.

Network support–Providing a sense of belonging as part of social support.

Neurocognitive models of dreaming–Models of dreaming that correlate subjective, cognitive experiences of dreaming with measurable physiological changes.

Neuroleptics (antipsychotics)–A class of drugs used to treat schizophrenia by blocking dopamine receptors

Neuroplasticity–Change in neural connections caused by learning or a response to injury.

Neuropsychology–The study of functions and behaviors associated with specific regions of the brain.

Neuromodulator– Peptides that act as signaling molecules in the central nervous system; they are slower to act and longer lasting than neurotransmitters.

Neurosis–In Freudian theory, a disorder that occurs in response to the anxiety of a fixation during childhood that impacts personality development.

Neuroticism–In trait theory, the degree to which an individual is prone to emotional arousal in stressful situations.

Neurotransmitter–A chemical that transmits signals from a neuron to a target cell across a synapse.

Neurulation–Stage in developmet in which the ectoderm furrows over the notochord, forming the neural crest and neural tube.

Night terror–An experience of intense anxiety during sleep, causing the sleeper to scream in terror with no recall of the event in the morning; occurs during slow-wave sleep.

Nondominant hemisphere–The side of the brain associated with sensitivity to the emotional tone of language, intuition, creativity, music, and spatial processing; in most individuals, the right hemisphere.

Nonmaleficence–The ethical tenet that the physician has a responsibility to avoid interventions in which the potential for harm outweighs the potential for benefit.

Non-rapid eye movement (NREM) sleep–Stages 1 through 4 of sleep; contains ever-slowing brain waves as one gets deeper into sleep.

Nonverbal communication–How people communicate, intentionally or unintentionally, without using words; examples include body language, gestures, and facial expressions.

Norepinephrine–A neurotransmitter associated with wakefulness and alertness.

Norms–Societal rules that define the boundaries of acceptable behavior.

Obedience–The changing of behavior of an individual based on a command from someone seen as an authority figure.

Object permanence–Knowledge that an object does not cease to exist even when the object cannot be seen; a milestone in cognitive development.

Observational learning–A form of learning in which behavior is modified as a result of watching others.

Obsessive-compulsive disorders–This category, which also includes related disorders, describes the set of disorders where people feel the need to check things repeatedly or have certain thoughts repeatedly, without the ability to control these thoughts or activities.

Occipital lobe–A portion of the cerebral cortex that controls visual processing.

Operant conditioning–A form of associative learning in which the frequency of a behavior is modified using reinforcement or punishment.

Opiates–A drug family consisting of naturally occurring, highly addictive, pain-reducing drugs used in both medical and recreational settings; opioids are synthetic versions of these drugs.

Opponent-process theory–A theory that states that the body will adapt to counteract repeated exposure to stimuli, such as seeing afterimages or ramping up the sympathetic nervous system in response to a depressant.

Organization–A specific type of group characterized by five traits: formality, hierarchy of ranked positions, large size, complex division of labor, and continuity beyond its members.

Ought self–The representation of the way others think one should be.

Out-group–A social group with which an individual does not identify.

Overconfidence–A tendency to interpret one's decisions, knowledge, or beliefs as infallible.

Parallel play–Play style in which children can play alongside each other without interfering in each other's behavior.

Parallel processing–The ability to simultaneously analyze and combine information regarding multiple aspects of a stimulus, such as color, shape, and motion.

Parasomnia–A sleep disorder characterized by abnormal movements or behaviors during sleep.

Parasympathetic nervous system–A branch of the autonomic nervous system that promotes resting and digesting; associated with relaxed states, reductions in heart and respiration rates, and promotion of digestion.

Parietal lobe–A portion of the cerebral cortex that controls somatosensory and spatial processing.

Parkinson's disease–A disease characterized by slowness in movement, resting tremor, pill-rolling tremor, masklike facies, cogwheel rigidity, and a shuffling gait; caused by destruction of dopaminergic neurons in the substantia nigra.

Parvocellular cells–In visual processing, cells which have very high spatial resolution and detect shape.

Peer group–A group of self-selected equals that forms around common interests, ideas, preferences, and beliefs.

Peer pressure–The social influence placed on an individual by other individuals who are considered equals.

Perception–Processing of incoming information to comprehend and respond to the current incoming stimuli.

Peripheral nervous system (PNS)–The portion of the nervous system composed of nerve tissue and fibers outside the central nervous system.

Personality–The set of thoughts, feelings, traits, and behaviors that are characteristic of an individual across time and different locations.

Personality disorders–Disorders that involve patterns of behavior that are inflexible and maladaptive, causing distress or impaired function in at least two of the following: cognition, emotion, interpersonal functioning, or impulse control.

Phenotype–The expressed traits of an individual based on their genotype.

Phoneme–Individual speech sound associated with a language.

Phonology–The set of sounds that compose a language.

Piaget's theory–Piaget's theory of cognitive development divided the lifespan into sensorimotor, preoperational, concrete operational, and formal operational stages.

Pineal gland–A brain structure located near the thalamus that secretes melatonin.

Pituitary gland–The "master gland" of the endocrine system that triggers hormone release in other endocrine glands.

Place theory–Theory of sound conduction in the ear that holds that vibration on particular areas of the basilar membrane determines perception of pitch, also referred to as tonotopical organization.

Polyandry–A mating system in which a female has exclusive relationships with several males.

Polygamy–A mating system in which one member of a sex has multiple exclusive opposite-sex relationships.

Polygyny–A mating system in which a male has exclusive relationships with several females.

Pons–A portion of the brainstem that relays information between the cortex and medulla, regulates sleep, and carries some motor and sensory information from the face and neck.

Positive symptoms–Behaviors, thoughts, or feelings added to normal behavior.

Poverty–A socioeconomic condition of low resource availability; in the United States, the poverty line is determined by the government's calculation of the minimum income requirements for families to acquire the minimum necessities of life.

Power–The capacity to influence people through the real or threatened use of rewards and punishments; often based on unequal distribution of valued resources.

Pragmatics–The ways in which use of language can be altered, depending on social context.

Prejudice–An irrational positive or negative attitude toward a person, group, or thing, formed prior to actual experience.

Prestige–In sociology, the amount of positive regard society has for a given person or idea.

Prevalence–The number of cases of a disease per population in a given period of time; usually, cases per 1000 people per year.

Primacy effect–The phenomenon of first impressions of a person being more important than subsequent impressions.

Primary group–A group wherein the interactions are direct, with close bonds, providing relationships to members that are very warm, personal, and intimate.

Primary stress appraisal–An initial evaluation of the environment to determine if there is an associated threat.

Priming–A retrieval cue by which recall is aided by a word or phrase that is semantically related to the desired memory.

Primitive reflexes–Reflexes present in infants that disappear with age.

Prodromal phase–A phase of poor adjustment that precedes the full onset of schizophrenia.

Projection–A defense mechanism by which individuals attribute their undesired feelings to others.

Projection area–A portion of the cerebral cortex that analyzes sensory input.

Promiscuity–A mating system in which a member of one sex mates with any member of the opposite sex.

Proprioception–The ability to tell where one's body is in space.

Prosencephalon–The embryonic portion of the brain that becomes the forebrain.

Prosody–The rhythm, cadence, and inflection of speech.

Prospective memory–Remembering to perform a task at some point in a future.

Proximal stimulus–A stimulus that directly interacts with and affects sensory receptors.

Proximity–An aspect of interpersonal attraction based on being physically close to someone.

Psychoanalytic theory–In personality theory, the set of theories based on the assumption that unconscious internal states motivate overt actions and determine personality. The theories of several psychologists, including both Freud and Jung, fall into this category.

Psychological disorder–A set of thoughts, feelings, or actions that are considered deviant by the culture at hand and that cause noticeable distress to the sufferer.

Psychophysics–The study of the relationship between the physical nature of stimuli and the sensations/perceptions they evoke.

Psychosocial development–Erikson's theory of personality development, which is based in the concept that personality is developed based on a series of crises deriving from conflicts between needs and social demands.

Psychoticism–In trait theory, the measure of nonconformity or social deviance of an individual.

Punishment–In operant conditioning, the use of an aversive stimulus designed to decrease the frequency of an undesired behavior.

Race–A social construct based on phenotypic differences between groups of people; these may be either real or perceived differences.

Racial formation theory–Theory that racial identity is fluid and dependent on political, economic, and social factors.

Racialization–The definition or establishment of a group as a particular race.

Rapid eye movement (REM) sleep–Sleep stage in which the eyes move rapidly back and forth and physiological arousal levels are more similar to wakefulness than sleep; dreaming occurs during this stage.

Rational choice theory–In social structure, the theory that an individual considers benefits and harms to themselves in any given social interaction and chooses the best possible action.

Rationalization–A defense mechanism by which individuals explain undesirable behaviors in a way that is self-justifying and socially acceptable.

Reaction formation–A defense mechanism by which individuals suppress urges by unconsciously converting them into their exact opposites.

Reappraisal–Process for ongoing monitoring of a continuing source of stress that cannot be dealt with via the normal 2-step appraisal method.

Recency effect–The phenomenon in which the most recent information we have about an individual is most important in forming our impressions.

Reciprocal determinism–In the social cognitive perspective, the notion that thoughts, feelings, behaviors, and environment interact to determine behavior in a given situation.

Reciprocal liking–The phenomenon whereby people like others better when they believe the other person likes them.

Reciprocity–An aspect of interpersonal attraction based on the idea that we like people who we think like us.

Recognition-primed decision model–A decision-making model in which experience and recognition of

similar situations one has already experienced play a large role in decision-making and actions; also one of the explanations for the experience of intuition.

Reference group–The group to which an individual compares him- or herself for a given identity.

Reflex–A behavior that occurs in response to a given stimulus without higher cognitive input.

Reflex arc–A neural pathway that controls reflex actions.

Regional cerebral blood flow (rCBF)–A technique used to record patterns of neural activity based on blood flow to different areas of the brain measured using detection of inhaled radioactive markers.

Regression–A defense mechanism by which an individual deals with stress by reverting to an earlier developmental state.

Reinforcement–In operant conditioning, the use of a stimulus designed to increase the frequency of a desired behavior.

Reinforcement schedule–The schedule by which reinforcement is administered for behavior in operant conditioning; reinforcmeent schedules can be fixed or variable, and can be based on a ratio or an interval between rewards.

Relative poverty–Poverty wherein one is poor in comparison to the larger population.

Reliance on central traits–The tendency to organize the perception of others based on traits and personal characteristics of the target that matter to the perceiver.

REM rebound–Phenomenon in which one spends an increased time in REM sleep following a period of sleep deprivation.

Representativeness heuristic–A shortcut in decision-making that relies on categorizing items on the basis of whether they fit the prototypical, stereotypical, or representative image of the category.

Repression–A defense mechanism by which the ego forces undesired thoughts and urges to the unconscious mind.

Response bias–The tendency of subjects to respond systematically to a stimulus in a particular way due to nonsensory factors.

Reticular formation–A structure in the brainstem that is responsible for alertness.

Retrieval–The process of demonstrating that information has been retained in memory; includes recall, recognition, and relearning.

Retrograde amnesia–A form of memory loss which impacts long-term memories of events prior to the time of injury.

Rhombencephalon–The embryonic portion of the brain that becomes the hindbrain.

Ritual–A formalized ceremony that usually involves specific material objects, symbolism, and additional mandates on acceptable behavior.

Role–A set of beliefs, values, attitudes, and norms that define expectations for behavior associated with a given status.

Role conflict–A difficulty in satisfying role requirements or expectations among various roles.

Role partner–The person with whom one interacts while playing a particular role; each role partner provides a different set of behavioral expectations.

Role performance–Carrying out the behaviors associated with a given role.

Role set–A group of role partners relative to a given status.

Role strain–Difficulty in satisfying multiple requirements of the same role.

Role-taking–Roleplaying, by which children come to understand the perspectives of others and the ways in which these perspectives may differ from their own.

Sanction–A societally enforced punishment or reward for behavior. Formal sanctions are those enforced by social institutions (laws), and informal sanctions are enforced by social behaviors (ostracization, etc.).

Schachter–Singer theory–A theory of emotion that states that both physiological arousal and cognitive appraisal must occur before an emotion is consciously experienced.

Schema–An organized pattern of thought and behavior; one of the central concepts of Piaget's stages of cognitive development.

Schizophrenia–A psychotic disorder characterized by gross distortions of reality and disturbances in the content and form of thought, perception, and behavior.

Secondary group–Groups wherein interactions are based on weaker, impersonal bonds.

Secondary stress appraisal–The interpretation of primary stress appraisal to determine emotional response to a given threat.

Second sickness–The concept proposed by Howard Waitzkin that poor health outcomes are exacerbated by social injustice.

Selective attention–The ability to focus on a single stimulus even while other stimuli are occurring simultaneously.

Self-concept–The sum of the thoughts and feelings about oneself; includes self-schemata and appraisal of one's past and future self.

Self-determination theory–Need based motivational theory that emphasizes the importance of autonomy, competence, and relatedness.

Self-disclosure–An aspect of interpersonal attraction or impression management in which one shares his or her fears, thoughts, and goals with another person in the hopes of being met with empathy and nonjudgment.

Self-discrepancy theory–Theory that each of us has three selves: the actual self, the ideal self, and the ought self.

Self-efficacy–The degree to which an individual sees him- or herself as being capable at a given skill or in a particular situation.

Self-enhancement–In self-serving bias, the need to maintain self worth through internal attribution of success and external attribution of failure.

Self-esteem–An individual's feelings of self-worth.

Self-fulfilling prophecy–The phenomenon of a stereotype creating an expectation of a particular group, which creates conditions that lead to confirmation of this stereotype.

Self-handicapping–An impression management strategy wherein one creates obstacles to avoid self-blame when he or she does not meet expectations.

Self-presentation–The process of displaying oneself to society through culturally accepted actions and behaviors.

Self-reference effect–The tendency for individuals to best recall information that they can relate to their own experiences.

Self-schema–A self-given label that carries with it a set of qualities.

Self-serving bias–The idea that individuals will view their own success as being based on internal factors, while viewing failures as being based on external factors.

Semantic network–Organization of information in the brain by linking concepts with similar characteristics and meaning.

Semantics–The association of meaning with a word.

Sensation–Transduction of physical stimuli into neurologic signals.

Sensitive period–A time during which environmental input has a maximal impact on the development of a particular ability.

Sensory memory–Visual (iconic) and auditory (echoic) stimuli briefly stored in memory; fades very quickly unless attention is paid to the information.

Sensory neuron–A neuron that transmits information from sensory receptors to the central nervous system.

Septal nuclei–Part of the limbic system and one of the pleasure centers of the brain.

Serial position effect–The tendency to better remember items presented at the beginning or end of a list; related to the primacy and recency effects.

Serotonin–A neurotransmitter associated with mood, sleep, eating, and dreaming.

Sexual orientation–The direction of one's sexual interest toward members of the same, opposite, or both sexes.

Shadowing–An experimental technique in which participants recite speech immediately after hearing it.

Shaping–In operant conditioning, the process of conditioning a complicated behavior by rewarding successive approximations of the behavior.

Short-term memory–Memory which fades quickly, over about 30 seconds without rehearsal, and which is limited in capacity by the 7 ± 2 rule.

Sick role–Theory that a person who is ill enters a role of 'sanctioned deviance', in which they are not responsible for the illness and are exempt from social norms.

Signal detection theory–A theory of perception in which internal (psychological) and external (environmental) context both play a role in the perception of stimuli.

Similarity–An aspect of interpersonal attraction based on being alike in attitudes, intelligence, education, height, age, religion, appearance, or socioeconomic status.

Situational (external) attributions–Attributions that relate to features of the surroundings, such as threats, money, social norms, and peer pressure, rather than to features of the individual.

Sleep apnea–Sleep disorder in which a person may cease to breathe while sleeping; may be due to obstruction or a central (neurological) cause.

Sleep cycle–A single complete progression through each stage of sleep.

Slow-wave sleep–Consists of NREM sleep stages 3 and 4; also called delta-wave sleep.

Social action–Actions and behaviors that individuals are conscious of and performing because others are around.

Social capital–The investment people make in their society in return for economic or collective rewards.

Social class–A category of people with a shared socioeconomic background that exhibit similar lifestyles, job opportunities, attitudes, and behaviors.

Social cognitive theory–A theory that attitudes are formed through observation of behavior, cognition, and the environment.

Social construction model–A theory of emotional expression that assumes there are no biologically wired emotions; rather, they are based on experiences and situational context alone.

Social constructionism–A theoretical approach that uncovers the ways in which individuals and groups participate in the formation of their perceived social reality.

Social control–Regulating the behavior of individuals and groups within a society.

Social exclusion–The sense of being separated from and powerless in society when impoverished.

Social facilitation–The tendency of people to perform at a different level based on the fact that others are around.

Social institutions–Well-established, structured patterns of behavior or relationships that are accepted as a fundamental part of a culture.

Social interaction–The ways in which two or more individuals can shape each other's behavior.

Social interactionist theory–In language development, the theory that language acquisition is driven by the desire to communicate. This theory includes both biological and social processes.

Social loafing–The tendency of individuals to put in less effort in group settings as compared to an individual setting.

Social mobility–The movement of individuals in the social hierarchy through changes in income, education, or occupation.

Social movements–Philosophies that drive large numbers of people to organize to promote or resist social change.

Social perception–Understanding the thoughts and motives of other people present in the social world; also referred to as social cognition.

Social reproduction–The concept that social inequality, especially poverty, can be reproduced and passed on from one generation to the next.

Social stratification–Organization of societies into a hierarchical system, usually based on socioeconomic status and social class.

Social structure–A system of people within a society organized by a characteristic pattern of relationships.

Social support–The perception or reality that one is cared for by a social network.

Socialization–The process of developing and spreading norms, customs, and beliefs.

Socioeconomic Status–Social standing or class of an individual or group, determined as a combination of education, income, and occupation.

Sociology–The study of society, including how it is created, interacted with, defined, and institutionalized.

Somatic nervous system–The voluntary branch of the peripheral nervous system, which consists of sensory and motor neurons used to control bodily movements.

Somatic symptom disorders–Mental health disorders marked by bodily symptoms that cause significant stress or impairment. This category of disorder also includes related disorders, such as illness anxiety and conversion disorders.

Somatosensation–The sense of touch, which contains multiple modalities: pressure, vibration, pain, and temperature.

Somatosensory cortex–Region of the parietal lobe located on the postcentral gyrus and involved in somatosensory information processing.

Somnambulism–Sleep disorder in which one carries out actions in his or her sleep; also called sleepwalking.

Source-monitoring error–A memory error by which a person remembers the details of an event but confuses the context by which the details were gained; often causes a person to remember events that happened to someone else as having happened to him- or herself.

Spacing effect–The phenomenon of retaining larger amounts of information when the amount of time between sessions of relearning is increased.

Spatial inequality–A form of social stratification across territories and their populations that can involve residential, environmental, or global components.

Spontaneous recovery–The reappearance of a conditioned response previously determined to be extinct.

Spreading activation–The unconscious activation of closely linked nodes of a semantic network.

State-dependent memory–A retrieval cue by which memory is aided when a person is in the same state of emotion or intoxication as when encoding took place.

Status–A position in society used to classify individuals.

Stereocilia–Structures on hair cells in the ear that sway with the movement of endolymph, causing receptor potential in the hair cells and ultimately leading to detection of incoming sound.

Stereotype content model–A model that classifies stereotypes using two dimensions: warmth and competence.

Stereotype threat–A feeling of anxiety about confirming a negative stereotype about one's social group.

Stereotypes–Attitudes and impressions that are made based on limited and superficial information about a person or a group of individuals.

Stigma–The extreme disapproval or dislike of a person or group based on perceived differences in social characteristics from the rest of society.

Stimulant–A drug that causes an increase in central nervous system arousal.

Stimulus–Any energy pattern that is sensed in some way by the body; includes visual, auditory, and physical sensations, among others.

Storage–The retention of encoded information; divided into sensory, short-term, and long-term memory.

Strain theory–Theory that explains deviance as a natural reaction to the disconnect between social goals and social structure.

Stress–The response to significant events, challenges, and decisions.

Stressors–Biological elements, external conditions, or events that lead to a stress response.

Structural poverty–Theory that poverty is due to inadequacies in societal and economic structure.

Subcultures–Groups of people within a culture that distinguish themselves from the primary culture to which they belong.

Sublimation–A defense mechanism by which unacceptable urges are transformed into socially acceptable behaviors.

Subliminal perception–Perception of a stimulus below a threshold (usually the threshold of conscious perception).

Substantia nigra–Part of the basal ganglia responsible for dopamine release that permits proper functioning of the rest of the basal ganglia.

Sulcus–A fold in the cerebral cortex.

Superego–In Freudian psychoanalysis, the part of the unconscious mind focused on idealism, perfectionism, and societal norms.

Superior colliculus–Structure in the midbrain that receives visual input and impacts eye movements and object oriented behaviors.

Symbolic culture–The nonmaterial culture that represents a group of people; expressed through ideas and concepts.

Symbolic ethnicity–An ethnic identity that is only relevant on special occasions or in specific circumstances and that does not impact everyday life.

Symbolic interactionism–A theoretical framework that studies the way individuals interact through a shared understanding of words, gestures, and other symbols.

Sympathetic nervous system–The branch of the autonomic nervous system that controls the fight-or-flight response; associated with stressful situations that increase heart and respiration rates and decrease digestion.

Synaptic pruning–Adjustment of neural connections throughout life, involving breaking of weak neural connections and bolstering of strong neural connections.

Syntax–The way in which words are organized to create meaning.

System for multiple level observation of groups (SYMLOG)–A method of studying group dynamics; focuses on three fundamental dimensions of interaction: dominance *vs.* submission, friendliness *vs.* unfriendliness, and instrumentally controlled *vs.* emotionally expressive.

Tactical self–In impression management, the person one markets him- or herself to be when adhering to others' expectations.

Telencephalon–A portion of the prosencephalon that becomes the cerebrum.

Temporal lobe–A portion of the cerebral cortex that controls auditory processing, memory processing, emotional control, and language.

Tetrahydrocannabinol (THC)–The main active ingredient in marijuana.

Thalamus–A portion of the forebrain that serves as a relay and sorting station for sensory information, and then transmits the information to the cerebral cortex.

Theory of mind–The ability to sense how another's mind works.

Threshold–Also called limina; the minimum amount of a stimulus that renders a difference in perception.

Tolerance–Decreased response to a drug after physiological adaptation.

Top-down processing–Object recognition driven by memories and expectations that allow the brain to first recognize the whole object, and then recognize components based on existing expectations.

Trait theory–Personality theory that is focused on describing individual personalities as the sum of characteristic behaviors.

Transduction–Conversion of physical, electromagnetic, auditory, and other stimuli to electrical signals in the nervous system.

Transformational grammar–A linguistic theory that focuses on how changes in word order affect meaning.

Two-point threshold–The minimum distance necessary between two points of stimulation on the skin such that the points will be felt as two distinct stimuli.

Type theory–Theorifes of personality that are focused on creating taxonomies, or finite lists, of personality types.

Unconditioned response–In classical conditioning paradigms, the innate response brought about by an unconditioned stimulus prior to any conditioning.

Unconditioned stimulus–In classical conditioning paradigms, a stimulus that brings about an innate response.

Universal emotions–Emotions that are recognized by all cultures; include happiness, sadness, contempt, surprise, fear, disgust, and anger.

Urbanization–The process whereby large numbers of people migrate to and establish residence in relatively dense areas of population.

Value–What one deems important in life.

Ventricle–An internal cavity within the brain; cells lining the ventricles produce cerebrospinal fluid.

Verbal communication–The use of spoken or signed language.

Vestibular sense–One of the functions of the ear, the detection of rotational and linear acceleration to maintain awareness of body rotation and movement.

Visual Cortex–Region of the occipital lobe devoted to processing visual information.

Visual pathways–Term which refers to both anatomical connections between eyes and brain and the flow of information from eyes to brain. The visual pathway contains several brain regions including the LGN, the visual cortex, and the superior colliculus.

Vygotsky theory–In cognitive development, the theory that the engine driving cognitive development is chilhood internalization of culture.

Weber's law–A theory of perception that states that there is a constant ratio between the change in stimulus magnitude needed to produce a just noticeable difference and the magnitude of the original stimulus.

Wernicke–Korsakoff Syndrome– A condition resulting from chronic thiamine (vitamin B_1) deficiency, which is common in alcoholics; characterized by severe memory impairment with changes in mental status and loss of coordination.

Wernicke's aphasia–Loss of language comprehension, resulting in fluid production of language without meaning.

Wernicke's area–A brain region located in the superior temporal gyrus of the temporal lobe (usually in the left hemisphere); largely responsible for language comprehension.

Working memory–Form of memory that allows limited amounts of information in short-term memory to be manipulated.

World system theory–World system theory argues there are global level inequalities in the division of labor between core, semi-peripheral, and peripheral nations.

Yerkes-Dodson law–A theory that there is a U shaped function relating arousal level and performance, dictating that performance is worst at the extreme high and low ends of arousal and optimal at intermediate arousal levels. This law is the basis of the Yerkes-Dodson law of social facilitation, a specific application of the Yerkes-Dodson law.

Zone of proximal development– Those skills which a child has not yet mastered but can accomplish with the help of a more knowledgeable other.

Index

Note: Material in figures or tables is indicated by italic *f* or *t* after the page number.

N

Narcissistic personality disorder, 272–273
Narcolepsy, 150
Nationality, 221
Nativist (biological) theory of language development, 164
Natural selection, 32
Nature *vs.* nurture, 32
Need-based theories, 188–189, 188*f*
Need for achievement (N-Ach), 244
Negative cognitive symptoms, 269
Negative feedback, 187, 187*f*
Negative punishment, 102
Negative reinforcement, 101–102
Negative symptoms, psychotic disorders, 263–265
Neocortex, 22
Neologisms, 264
Nervous system. *See also* Central, Peripheral nervous systems
  development of, 34–36, 35*f*
  organization of, 6–11, 6*f*
Nervous system disorders
  biological basis for, 275–279
  concept summary, 283
Network redundancy, 331
Networks, 330–331, 331*f*
Network support, 358, 359*f*
Neural crest, 34, 35*f*
Neural folds, 34, 35*f*
Neural groove, 34, 35*f*
Neural tube, 34, 35*f*
Neurobiology
  concept summary, 120, 122
  learning and memory, 118–119
Neurocognitive models of dreaming, 149
Neurofibrillary tangles, 114, 277, 277*f*
Neuroleptics, 275
Neuromodulators, 29–30
Neurons
  mirror neurons, 105–106, 106*f*
  motor (efferent), 6–7
  sensory (afferent), 6–7
Neuropeptides, 29–30
Neuroplasticity, 119
Neuropsychology
  brain mapping, 16–18
  concept summary, 41–43
  history, 4–5

Neurosis, 225
Neuroticism, 243
Neurotic needs, 240
Neurotransmitters, 28–30
  acetylcholine, 28
  dopamine, 29
  epinephrine, 28–29
  functions, 30*t*
  GABA, 29
  glutamate, 29
  glycine, 29
  norepinephrine, 28–29
  Parkinson's disease, 29
  peptides, 29–30
  serotonin, 29
Neurulation, 34, 35*f*
Neutral stimuli, 99
Night terrors, 150
Nociceptors, 77
Noise trials, 60
Nondeclarative memory, 111
Nondirective therapy, 242
Nondominant hemisphere, 26, 27*t*
Nonmaleficence, 398
Nonmaterial culture, 401–402, 402*f*
Non-rapid eye movement (NREM) sleep, 148
Nonverbal communication, 336, 337*f*, 337*t*
Norepinephrine, 28–29, 203
Normative conformity, 308–309
Norms, 305–306, 306*f*
  culture and, 403
Nucleus accumbens (NAc), 157, 158*f*
Nurture *vs.* nature, 32

O

Obedience, 229, 310–311
Objectification, 393
Object permanence, 135, 135*f*
Object recognition, 78–81
Object relations theory, 241
Observational learning, 105–106, 230
  foraging and, 360, 360*f*
Obsessions, 268
Obsessive-compulsive disorders (OCDs), 268, 273
Obsessive-compulsive personality disorder (OCPD), 273
Occipital lobe, 22*f*, 25, 67, 67*f*
Oedipal conflict, 226

Oedipal stage, 226
Olds, James, 21
Olfactory bulb, 76
Olfactory chemoreceptors (olfactory nerves), 75–76
Olfactory pathway, 76
Olfactory tract, 76
Operant conditioning, 101–105, 101*f*
  language acquisition and, 164
Opiates and opioids, 155
Opponent-process theory, 189–190
Optical illusions, 368–369, 369*f*
Optic disk, 65, 65*f*
Optic nerve, 65
Oral stage, 225
Organizations, 331–332
Organ of Corti, 72, 73*f*
Ossicles, 71, 71*f*
Otoliths, 73
Ought self, 223, 335
Out-groups, 329, 374
Oval window, 72*f*
Overconfidence, 142, 223
Oxytocin, 20

P

Pacinian corpuscles, 76–77
Pain, 76
*Paivio, 133
Panic attack, 268
Panic disorder, 268
Papillae, 76
Paradoxical sleep, 148
Parallel play, 38
Parallel processing, 67–68
Paranoid personality disorder, 271
Parasomnias, 150
Parasympathetic nervous system, 8, 9*f*
Parenting styles, cognition and, 137–138
Parietal lobe, 22*f*, 24, 24*f*, 25*f*
Parkinson's disease, 21, 29–30, 278–279, 278*f*, 279*f*
  schizophrenia and psychosis and, 279
Partial-report procedure, 110
Parvocellular cells, 68
Paternalistic stereotypes, 372, 372*f*
Patterns of kinship, 394
Pavlov, Ivan, 99
Peak experiences, 241
Peer groups, 329

U

Umbilical cord, 35
Unconditional positive regard, 242
Unconditioned response, 99, 100*f*
Unconditioned stimulus, 99, 100*f*
Unconscious, 233*f*, 234, 237–238
Undifferentiated identify, 221
Universal emotions, 192–193, 193*f*
Universal human ethics, 229
Upward mobility, 433
Urban decay, 437
Urbanization, 413–414
Urban renewal, 437
Utricle, 72*f*, 73

V

Values, culture and, 403
Variable-interval (VI) schedules, 103–104
Variable-ratio (VR) schedules, 103–104
Vascular dementia, 137
Vasopressin, 20
Ventral prefrontal cortex, 198
Ventral tegmental area (VTA), 157, 158*f*
Ventricles, 13, 13*f*
Ventromedial hypothalamus (VMH), 20
Ventromedial prefrontal cortex, 198, 199*f*

Verbal communication, 336, 337*t*
Vertical mobility, 433
Vestibular sense, 70–74
Vestibule, 71, 71*f*, 72*f*, 73
Violent video games, aggressive behavior and, 105
Viral infection, nervous system development and, 36
Vision, 62–68
    eye structure and function, 63–66, 63*f*, 64*f*, 65*f*, 66*f*
    parallel processing, 67–68
    visual pathways, 66–67, 67*f*
Visual cortex, 25, 67, 67*f*
Visual encoding, 109
Visual pathways, 66–67, 67*f*
Visuospatial sketchpad memory model, 111
Vitreous, 63*f*, 64
Vygotsky, Lev, 136, 230

W

Waitzkin, Howard, 442
Weak ties, 432
Weber, Max, 294
Weber's law, 59

Wernicke-Korsakoff syndrome, 154
Wernicke's (receptive) aphasia, 166, 264
Wernicke's area, 25, 165, 166*f*
Whole-report procedure, 110
Whorf, Benjamin, 165
Whorfian hypothesis, 165
Wilde, Oscar, 429
WISC exam, 144
Wish fulfillment, 233
Word salad, 264
Working memory, 111
World system theory, 438–439

Y

Yerkes-Dodson law of social facilitation, 186, 186*f*, 294, 295*f*

Z

Zimbardo, Philip, 309
Zone of proximal development, 230

Art Credits

Chapter 1 Cover—Image credited to nobeastsofierce. From Shutterstock.

Figure 1.2—Image credited to Alila Medical Media. From Shutterstock.

Figure 1.3—Image credited to Alila Medical Media. From Shutterstock.

Figure 1.4—Image credited to Carol Donner. From Scars that Won't Heal: The Neurobiology of Child Abuse by Martin Treicher. Copyright © 2002 by Scientific American, Inc. All rights reserved.

Figure 1.7—Image credited to User: _moep_. From Wikimedia Commons.

Figure 1.15—From Shutterstock.

Chapter 2 Cover—Image credited to Phatic Photography. From Shutterstock.

Chapter 3 Cover—Image credited to Fer Gregory. From Shutterstock.

Figure 3.4—Image credited to Public Library of Science. From Wikimedia Commons. Copyright © 2006. Used under license: CC-BY-2.5.

Chapter 4 Cover—Image credited to Igor Zh. From Shutterstock.

Figure 4.10—Image credited to User: Nitramas. From Wikimedia Commons.

Figure 4.13—Image credited to William Rafti. From Wikimedia Commons. Copyright © 2006. Used under license: CC-BY-2.5.

Figure 4.14—Image credited to User: Saxo. From Wikimedia Commons.

Chapter 5 Cover—Image credited to A.B.G. From Shutterstock.

Figure 5.6—Image credited to Roberto Osti. From The Emotion, Memory, and the Brain by Joseph E. LeDoux. Copyright © 1997 by Scientific American, Inc. All rights reserved.

Figure 5.11—Image credited to Bryan Christie Design. From Sick of Poverty by Robert Sapolsky. Copyright © 2005 by Scientific American, Inc. All rights reserved.

Chapter 6 Cover—Image credited to Kanea. From Shutterstock.

Figure 6.1a—Image credited to Maglara. From Shutterstock.

Chapter 7 Cover—Image credited to hikrcn. From Shutterstock.

Figure 7.3—Image credited to User: Stepan Kapl. From Shutterstock.

Figure 7.4c—Image credited to Jose Luis Calvo. From Shutterstock.

Chapter 8 Cover—Image credited to file404. From Shutterstock.

Notes

Notes

Notes

Notes

Notes

Notes

Notes